Creating and
Understanding
Drawings

STUDIO

AESTHETICS

CRITICISM

HISTORY

Creating and Understanding Drawings

GENE A. MITTLER
PROFESSOR OF ART
TEXAS TECH UNIVERSITY

JAMES D. HOWZE
PROFESSOR OF ART
TEXAS TECH UNIVERSITY

Chapter 13 by
HOLLE HUMPHRIES

GLENCOE
Macmillan/McGraw-Hill

New York, New York
Columbus, Ohio
Mission Hills, California
Peoria, Illinois

Send all inquiries to:
GLENCOE DIVISION
Macmillan/McGraw-Hill
15319 Chatsworth Street
P.O. Box 9609
Mission Hills, CA 91346-9609

ISBN 0-02-662273-4

Printed in the United States of America.

4 5 6 7 8 9 10   VHJ   99 98 97 96 95 94 93

ACKNOWLEDGMENTS

Consultants
Dr. Faye Becker
Elsik North High School
Alief, Texas

Frances Merrill
R. L. Turner High School
Carrollton, Texas

Design and production
Design Office, San Francisco

Contents

Preface

Of all the art skills, drawing has always been regarded as the most fundamental. The lively images of animals found on prehistoric cave walls and ceilings testify to its origins at the dawn of civilization. Since then, artists in every part of the world have continued to use drawing as a way of recording their ideas and feelings about every conceivable topic and experience. Drawing activities, however, are not restricted to artists alone. Children make marks that represent their thoughts long before they learn to express these thoughts in writing. This urge to draw continues into adulthood and is demonstrated in a variety of ways. For example, what adult, when talking on the telephone, fails to pick up a pencil and make drawings on any available surface—drawings that suggest figures, buildings, animals? Similar doodles are found on the notepads of executives and on the desk blotters of politicians. It seems as if the impulse to give visible form to ideas and feelings is irresistible.

This book is intended to achieve two important objectives pertaining to drawing: (1) to increase students' understanding and appreciation of drawings created by others and (2) to help students gain the knowledge, skill, and confidence needed to improve their own drawing efforts. Obviously, it was impossible to include everything we would have liked to see between the covers of this book. It had to be limited in length—but not in scope. Because of its importance, aesthetics, criticism, and history content was combined with studio experiences to produce a book that emphasizes a comprehensive approach to the study of drawing.

Our enthusiasm for this project was sustained by the encouragement and assistance of a great many people. It is proper that we acknowledge these people—being conscious, of course, of the possibility that we might overlook someone in the process.

Gratitude is first extended to the many students who contributed more than their work to the pages of this book. Without their enthusiasm and desire for learning it is unlikely that the authors would have initiated or sustained the effort required to produce this book. Certainly their teachers—like Linda Kennedy, M. J. Eissinger, Nancy Stewart, and Julie Storey—must be credited with instilling in students that enthusiasm and desire. We are indebted to Hugh J. Gibbons for contributing the highly successful performance piece ''Formal Drawing of Fragmented Objects'' in Chapter 8.

Our resident computer expert, Holle Humphries, gets total credit for the computer graphics chapter in Unit V. Without her, our book would have no claim to a place in the last quarter of the twentieth century.

This book could not have been written without the cooperation of the highly skilled personnel of museums and galleries across the country. We wish we could list each by name, but such a list is impossible given the limitations of time and space. Nevertheless, we would be remiss if we failed to thank the many museum administrators, curators, and especially the staff members of photographic services departments for their valued and valuable assistance.

Gratitude is also extended to our colleagues in the Art Department at Texas Tech University for their uncommon patience, encouragement, and assistance. To Terry Morrow, chairman of the department, our special thanks.

Katrina Callahan Dolcater and David Dolcater deserve recognition here for supplying all of the photographs in the studio chapters that are not otherwise credited. A similar acknowledgement goes to James Hanna and Nick Olson, who provided the photographs of works from the collection of the Texas Tech Museum.

Finally, our thanks to the editorial and production staffs at Glencoe Publishing, who recognized the need for a drawing text that touches on all aspects of making, knowing about, understanding, and appreciating this enduring form of visual expression.

Gene A. Mittler
James D. Howze

Introduction

As you read and use this book, *Creating and Understanding Drawings*, you will find that it differs from most books used by students in drawing classes. Why? Because it includes information on *aesthetics*, *art history*, and *art criticism*. What are these topics, and what do they have to do with learning to draw? Perhaps the following three stories will help you answer these questions.

When John was quite young, he liked to draw pictures. Of course other children his age also liked to draw, but John's pictures always seemed to be so much better than theirs.

John was especially skilled at drawing sailing ships. He never stopped to think when he started drawing them. He didn't know how he was able to reproduce so accurately those splendid vessels with the wind filling their sails.

John's teacher often told him that his sailing ships were beautiful. She pinned them up on the bulletin board where John's classmates marveled at them. His mother proudly taped his pictures to the refrigerator door. She confidently told anyone who would listen that there was an artist in the family.

Then one day John's teacher suggested that he draw something other than a sailing ship. John thought that this was a fine idea. So he took out his crayons and some paper. After a struggle, he managed to draw a house with a tree in front of it.

John showed his drawing to his teacher and she smiled, but he could see that it didn't have the same effect on her as his pictures of sailing ships. Later, he showed his picture to his mother, who said that it was a strange sailing ship indeed. John corrected her, and they had a good laugh, but he noticed that his new picture didn't join the others on the refrigerator door.

John never tried to draw another house and tree. And, after a while, he stopped drawing sailing ships. There were other things to do. Soon his mother was taping his perfect arithmetic papers to the refrigerator door and telling everyone who would listen that there was a mathematician in the family.

Artists rarely improve their drawing skills by experience alone.

The exhibition was a great success. Judy couldn't remember when she had been more thrilled. Everyone seemed to like her paintings—even the critic from the big city newspaper. He moved slowly from one canvas to the next, making careful notes on a small pad of paper. Three of Judy's paintings were sold within the first hour of the opening.

The critic from the big city newspaper finally finished looking through the gallery and promptly found the artist. He asked Judy several questions that she answered deliberately and thoughtfully. She certainly didn't want to be misquoted in the big city newspaper. Finally, the big city newspaper critic asked, ''What made you decide to become an artist?''

This time Judy answered immediately. ''While I was still in high school, I saw a painting by Claude Monet in a Chicago museum. It changed my life. I knew at once that I wanted to be an artist.''

When artists are asked why they began to create art, they almost always mention an emotional experience they had upon seeing a particular picture or the works of a certain artist.

''I tell you, it's a fake! The old man is trying to trick the entire art world! He claims that the paintings he discovered on the walls of that cave are the work of prehistoric artists. What nonsense!''

''But Professor, how can you be so certain that they aren't prehistoric paintings?''

''Because it's ridiculous to think that primitive artists, working with the crudest instruments and materials, could have painted those bison. I ask you, how could a prehistoric artist have learned to paint that well? Those paintings are too sophisticated, too sensitive, too lifelike . . .''

No matter how far back in time we travel, we always suspect that other art forms, even further back, must have provided inspiration for artists of any given period in history.

Obviously these three tales were presented to make several points. First, artists need much more than practice to learn how to improve their drawing skills. Second, they obtain inspiration from their contact with the achievements of other artists. And third, successful artists learn from the artists who preceded them and apply this knowledge to their own works.

As one of today's student artists, you must be given the opportunity to learn in the same way. You should have access to an array of artist teachers who include masters like Michelangelo, Raphael, Dürer, and Rubens. These masters can teach you through their art.

Before you can profit from your encounters with drawings, you need to understand how artists communicate with viewers—the visual vocabulary they use. After you can use this language to talk about drawings, you need to know what makes drawings successful. When you are considering definitions of successful art, you are using **aesthetics**—ideas about what separates art from everything else people make.

As you learn how to make informed, personal judgments about drawings and how to defend your judgments with good reasons, you will be practicing **art criticism**. With this background in aesthetics and art criticism, you will want to learn how different artistic styles developed and how other artists have responded to artistic problems. You can learn these things from studying **art history**. You can add what you learn from other artists' experiences in creating drawings to what you have learned from responding to the drawings themselves.

You may wonder why drawing is an important subject for you to study and practice. As you will see, drawing will sharpen your powers of observation. It will heighten your awareness of your environment. And drawing skills will allow you to express what you see—in the world around you and in your imagination. You will be able to effectively use the basic visual symbols and communicate emotions and ideas.

As you learn about drawing, you will be learning concepts that are important to understanding all forms of art. Being able to appreciate art made by others and to make art yourself enriches your life. Human beings respond to art because it is a source of beauty and meaning. We enjoy looking at drawings and other kinds of art because they appeal to our imagination and senses. They touch our hearts or make us think about important issues.

Besides the personal satisfaction that interacting with art provides, you can learn about other cultures and your own culture through drawings and other art forms. Art is one record of culture. By studying it you can learn about other people in other times and places. This knowledge will help you understand your own culture better.

Whether or not you want to become a professional artist, learning to understand and create drawings is important. As you study the qualities to look for in drawings, how other artists have created drawings, and how to use aesthetic qualities to produce your own drawings, we hope that you will become actively involved in the process of drawing.

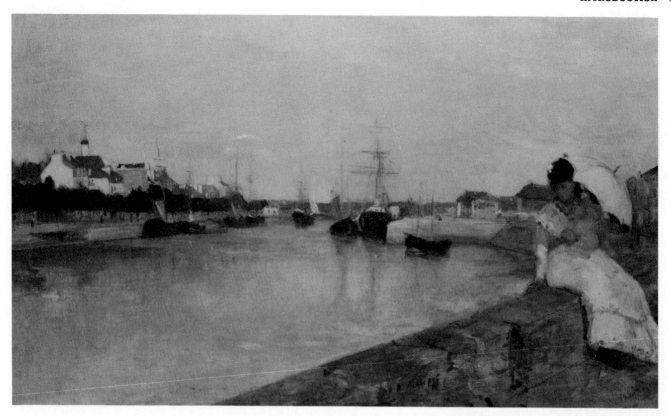

You may never create artworks as magnificent as this painting by Berthe Morisot. You can, however, learn to appreciate and understand more fully great works of art such as this one by Morisot. You can also learn to use your knowledge and understanding of art to develop your own artistic skills.

Berthe Morisot, *The Harbor at Lorient*, 1869. Oil on canvas, 17⅛ × 28¾″ (43.5 × 73 cm). National Gallery of Art, Washington, DC. Ailsa Mellon Bruce Collection.

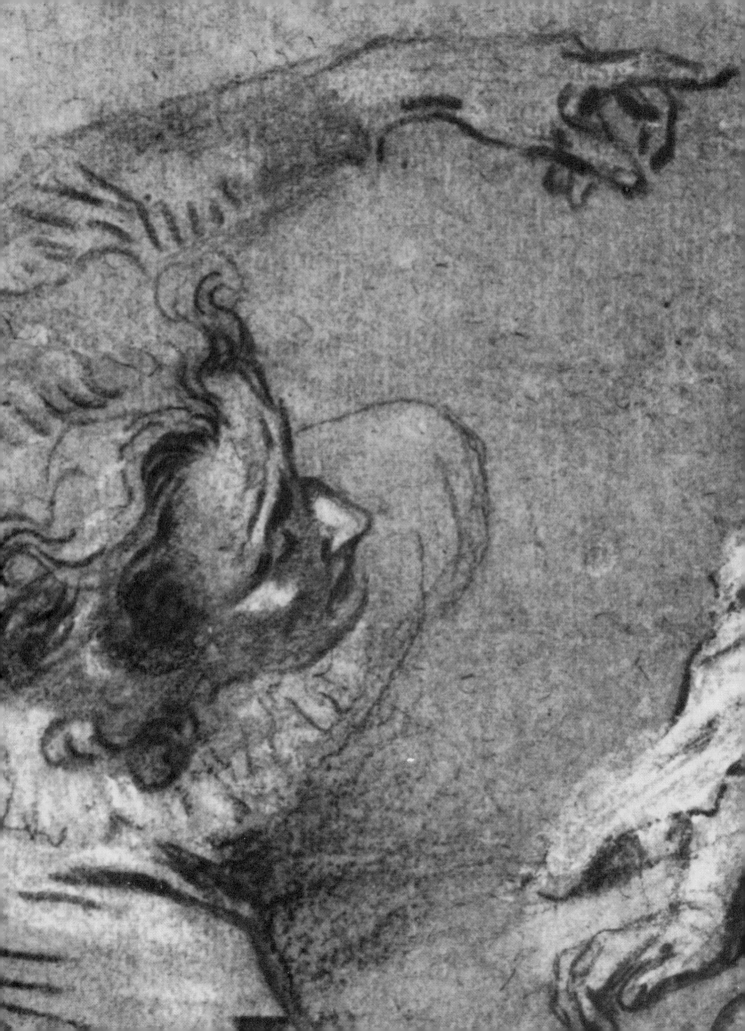

An Introduction to Drawing

All artists use the same basic components to communicate visually with viewers. These visual symbols are explained in Chapter 1, ''Drawing and the Visual Vocabulary.''

After you have learned the language necessary to talk about drawings, you need to know what makes drawings successful. Chapter 2, ''Aesthetics and Art Criticism,'' explains three theories of art. You will also learn an art criticism process that will help you find these aesthetic qualities in an artwork. This process is designed to help you make judgments about drawings for yourself.

Art criticism is concerned with information you can learn *from* an artwork itself. Art history, however, deals with information *about* a work of art— about the artist, the time and place in which the artist lived, and the artist's influence on other artists. Chapter 3, ''Drawings and the History of Art,'' provides a chronological outline with information about important developments in drawing for each period of history.

With this background in art criticism and art history, you will be prepared to begin the drawing process. Chapter 4, ''Entering the Studio,'' provides experience with the basic drawing materials and techniques.

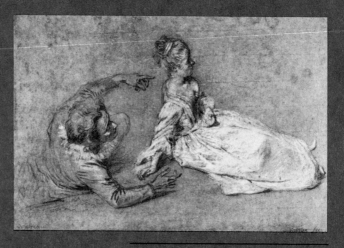

Antoine Watteau, *Couple Seated on a Bank*, c. 1716. Red, black, and white chalk on buff paper, 9½ × 13¾'' (24.1 × 34.9 cm). The Armand Hammer Collection, Los Angeles, CA (detail at left).

CHAPTER ONE

Drawing and the Visual Vocabulary

OBJECTIVES

After reading this chapter and doing the activities, you will be able to

■ explain the importance of knowing the *visual vocabulary*;

■ list the elements of art;

■ identify the elements of art in drawings;

■ list the principles of art;

■ describe the ways that artists use the principles and elements of art together to design their drawings; and

■ determine whether or not the elements and principles used have been blended to achieve an overall sense of unity.

Imagine that you are standing in a gallery with a friend, looking at the drawing in Figure 1.1. Several minutes go by before your friend asks, ''What do you think of it?''

How would you answer that question? You might begin by saying, ''I like it.'' This is a common answer. Many conversations about art begin with expressions of like or dislike. Unfortunately, many of these same conversations also stop there.

But suppose your friend, who hasn't had the benefit of an art education, asks another question: ''Well, I like it, too, but is it a good drawing? I mean, do you think it is well done?''

Many students have difficulty with questions of this kind. Much of that difficulty occurs because they don't know the language of art. This is especially true in discussions about the way a work is organized or put together. In these discussions, a knowledge of the **elements** and **principles of art**—the visual vocabulary—becomes essential.

THE VISUAL VOCABULARY

The elements of art are the ''building blocks'' the artist has to work with to express ideas. The elements are

■ *line,*

■ *shape,*

■ *form,*

■ *value,*

■ *texture,*

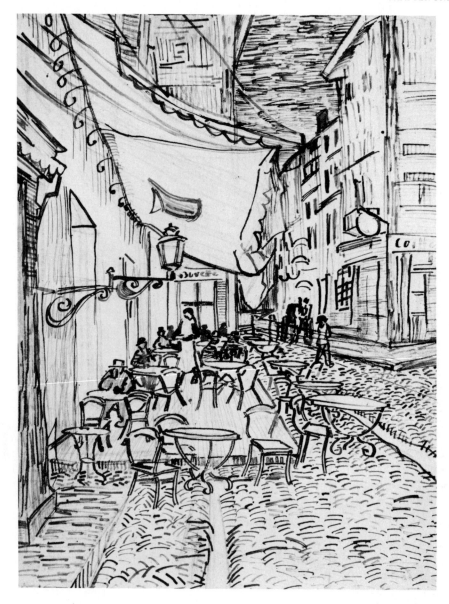

FIGURE 1.1 Vincent van Gogh, *Café Terrace at Night*, 1888. Reed pen and ink over pencil, 24⅝ × 18¾″ (62.5 × 47.6 cm). The Dallas Museum of Art, Dallas, TX. The Wendy and Emery Reves Collection.

- *space*, and
- *color*.

The ways the artist can use to blend the elements of art in a work are called *principles of art*. They include

- *balance*,
- *emphasis*,
- *harmony*,
- *variety*,
- *gradation*,
- *movement*,
- *rhythm*,
- *proportion*, and
- *space* (which can be both an element and a principle).

The elements and principles of art make up the *visual vocabulary*.

The visual vocabulary is as vital to the artist as the written vocabulary is to the poet. Without words, rhyme, and rhythm, there would be no poetry. Without colors, values, shapes, lines, textures, and spaces, there would be no drawing. And without a complete understanding of the various ways these elements and principles can be used in creating art, there would be few good drawings to enrich our lives.

You may be skeptical about the importance attached to this visual vocabulary. As one student put it, "I want to learn how to draw, not learn how to *talk* about drawing." That student failed to understand that learning how to talk about drawing is an aid to learning how to draw. Speech, after all, is our primary means of communication. How can you ask questions —or answer anyone else's questions—about your drawings if you don't understand the language you need? Without that vocabulary, the dialogue between you and your teacher, for instance, may be limited to those like-dislike statements mentioned earlier. Statements of that kind have little value in teaching or learning.

Understanding the language of art is also important when you want to learn from the drawings of master artists. A knowledge of the visual vocabulary helps you understand how those artists composed their works.

Look at Figure 1.1 again. What could you tell your friend about the *lines*, *shapes*, *forms*, *values*, *textures*, and *spaces* in this drawing? Would you refer to terms like *balance*, *emphasis*, *harmony*, *variety*, *gradation*, *movement*, *rhythm*, *proportion*, and *space* to explain how the elements have been used? Having a visual vocabulary consisting of these elements and principles of art would help you inform your friend about this drawing. But your friend would also have to know something about this visual vocabulary to understand your explanation.

Do you think a knowledge of how the artist used the elements and principles to design this drawing could help you make your own drawings? If your answer is ''Yes,'' then you realize that you can't learn in a vacuum. Your drawing now and in the future will be built upon what has already been done by other artists. If you ignore everything that can be learned from past and present art, you will limit your study of drawing and your improvement as an artist.

The rest of this chapter explains the elements and principles of art—the visual vocabulary. This information is essential to students who want to understand artworks created by others and to develop their own drawing skills.

THE ELEMENTS OF ART

In the months prior to his death, Vincent van Gogh painted and drew a variety of scenes observed in and around the city of Arles in southern France. Two of the best-known paintings from this period are café scenes. One of these shows the exterior of the Grand Café at night. Van Gogh wrote that it amused him to be able to paint an outdoor scene after dark. The work you have been looking at (Figure 1.1) is a drawing of that same café. (Figure 2 in the Color Section shows this drawing in color.)

It isn't known whether van Gogh produced this drawing before or after completing his painting of the same subject. A close examination, however, reveals that the drawing isn't a **sketch**, which is a drawing done quickly in preparation for a painting. It is instead a carefully designed, finished work of art. You can learn many things from it because of the way the artist used the visual vocabulary.

Observe how van Gogh made several kinds of lines in his drawing. He often used several pens with a variety of tips to achieve the results you see here. Working rapidly, as if he somehow knew his time was limited—he was to commit suicide in less than two years—he filled his paper to the edges with a pattern of contrasting lines. He created short and long, heavy and thin, straight and curved lines with powerful strokes.

Van Gogh used those lines to define space. He achieved a rich variety of textures that defined buildings, pavement, and sky. He created a sense of dramatic rhythm that expressed not only what he saw, but also what he felt about his subject. The light values used to identify the shapes of the café, terrace, and awning contrast with the darker values used to define the pavement, surrounding buildings, and sky. In this way, van Gogh suggested a bright, artificial light that attracts the viewer's eye to the most important part of the composition.

Clearly he wanted to emphasize the café, illuminated by a huge lantern and surrounded by the shadows of night. The pattern of contrasting lines and carefully balanced light and dark values result in a unified, appealing drawing.

ENRICHMENT

Vincent van Gogh

Few artists accomplished as much in so little time as Vincent van Gogh. His artistic career spanned just ten years. During this time, he received only one favorable review and sold only one painting.

This brief discussion of van Gogh's drawing illustrates how much you can learn from an artwork by identifying the elements and principles. To emphasize this point, reread the previous three paragraphs and list the elements and principles discussed.

You will find that reference was made to five elements (line, space, texture, value, and shape) and four principles (variety, rhythm, emphasis, and balance). You also discovered how the artist used these elements and principles to achieve an overall sense of unity or wholeness in the composition. This drawing shows how the elements and principles of art work together.

Let's examine each element and principle individually. Keep in mind, however, that they aren't used separately in a drawing. Even though the elements and principles work together in van Gogh's drawing and in all successful works of art, considering them separately will help you learn how each one functions in drawing.

Line

To draw, an artist moves a pointed instrument such as a pen, pencil, crayon, or brush over a smooth surface, leaving marks. The generally accepted name for these marks is **line**. Line is probably the oldest, and certainly the most direct, means of visual communication. It is also the main element of drawing, although other elements—such as value, shape, and texture—are also important.

Lines can be used in different ways, depending on the intent and the personality of the artist. Rapidly drawn lines can quickly capture a person's exact pose and attitude. An artist can use a more unhurried, controlled line to draw an exact likeness of a carefully posed model.

Paul Klee wasn't interested in capturing a gesture or in making a likeness in *The Mocker Mocked* (Figure 1.2). He used a single, unbroken line to draw a **portrait**, a picture of a person. His line scurries, turns, and twists across the page in a playful way before it finally comes to rest at the point where it started. Klee used what might be labeled a *consistent* line in his portrait. Notice that the line's thickness and value remain consistent along its entire length, although it curves in many directions.

Lines can change from dark to light or from thick to thin. They can be curving or straight, unbroken or interrupted. How the artist uses the element of line expresses feelings or ideas about a subject.

Shape and Form

An area that is determined by line, value, texture, space, or any combination of these other elements is a **shape**. Sometimes a shape may have exact, easily recognized boundaries. At other times its boundaries aren't clear.

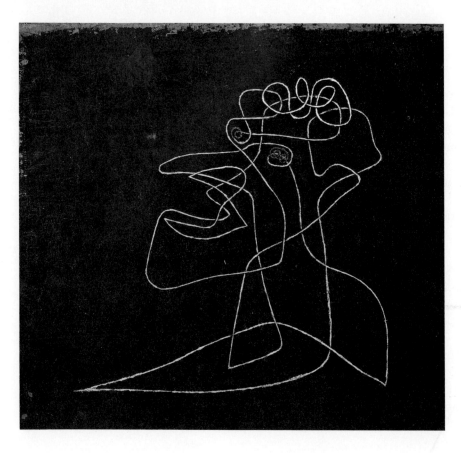

FIGURE 1.2 Paul Klee, *The Mocker Mocked*, 1930. Oil on canvas, 17 × 20⅝″ (43.2 × 52.4 cm). Collection, The Museum of Modern Art, New York, NY. Gift of J. B. Neumann.

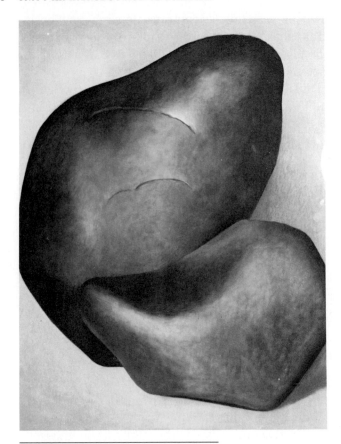

FIGURE 1.3 Georgia O'Keeffe, *My Heart*, 1944. Pastel on paper, 27½ × 21½″ (69.9 × 54.6 cm). The Museum of Texas Tech University, Lubbock, TX. Collection of the West Texas Museum Association.

When Georgia O'Keeffe was working on the drawing in Figure 1.3, she didn't think only about how to draw the dark **positive shapes**. She also directed attention to the empty or **negative shapes** that were created by placing the positive shapes on the paper (Figure 1.4). A positive shape is often called a **figure**, and negative shapes are referred to as **ground**. The negative shapes contribute as much to the overall effect of the finished composition as the positive shapes. What if O'Keeffe had decided to place the large positive shapes in the center of the page (Figure 1.5)? The resulting negative shapes would be quite different. The overall effect of the drawing would be less satisfying. (Figure 1 in the Color Section shows this drawing in color.)

Traditional drawings and paintings clearly separate positive and negative shapes. More recent artists, however, for a variety of reasons, don't worry about separating the two. Often the viewer can't

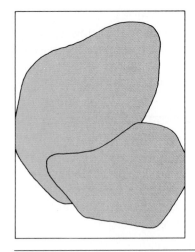

FIGURE 1.4 The shaded areas in this diagram of O'Keeffe's drawing are referred to as positive shapes or figures. The unshaded areas are known as negative shapes or ground.

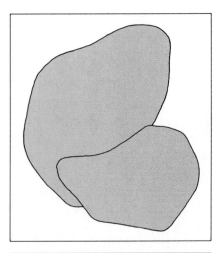

FIGURE 1.5 The placement of positive shapes in a drawing determines the size and configuration of the negative shapes. It also affects the overall design. Compare this diagram with the one in Figure 1.4. Which design provides more interesting negative shapes? Which one is more visually appealing?

FIGURE 1.6 (facing page) Peter Paul Rubens, *The Garden of Love* (right portion), c. late 1500s–early 1600s. Pen and brown ink over traces of black chalk touched with white, bluish gray, and green paint on paper, 18¾ × 27¾″ (47.6 × 70.5 cm). The Metropolitan Museum of Art, New York, NY. Fletcher Fund.

determine from the pattern of shapes which ones belong to the figure and which to the ground.

In some drawings, shapes appear solid and three-dimensional even though they are limited to two dimensions, length and width. The flat, two-dimensional appearance of shape sets it apart from **form**. Form has an implied third dimension, depth, in addition to length and width.

In drawing, artists usually suggest form through the use of **value gradation** or contrast. For value gradation the artist uses a gradual change from dark to light areas to create the illusion of roundness and solidity. This technique is used in Figure 1.3.

Overlapping parallel lines can also be used to create areas of differing degrees of darkness. This technique is known as **cross-hatching**. When the parallel lines are built on top of each other, a dense pattern of dark areas is created. By gradually reducing the density of these areas, an artist can add a sense of roundness to the forms. This is a type of value gradation. Sharp value contrasts are also used to make angular forms appear three-dimensional.

Value

The artist's use of light and dark areas in a drawing or painting is referred to as **value**. As noted earlier, gradual value changes can suggest the roundness of three-dimensional forms shown on a two-dimensional surface. Abrupt changes of value, on the other hand, can indicate planes at various angles to each other. Value is an element that can be used in many different ways.

Notice how Rubens used a change of values, from the dark figures in the **foreground**, or front, to the progressively lighter figures in the **background**, or back, to create the illusion of space in his drawing of a group of people celebrating a wedding (Figure 1.6).

Texture

"Be careful, the seat on that old bench is rough!"

"I really like the coarse feeling of this wool sweater."

"I'm going to sand the fender of that old Ford until it's as smooth as glass."

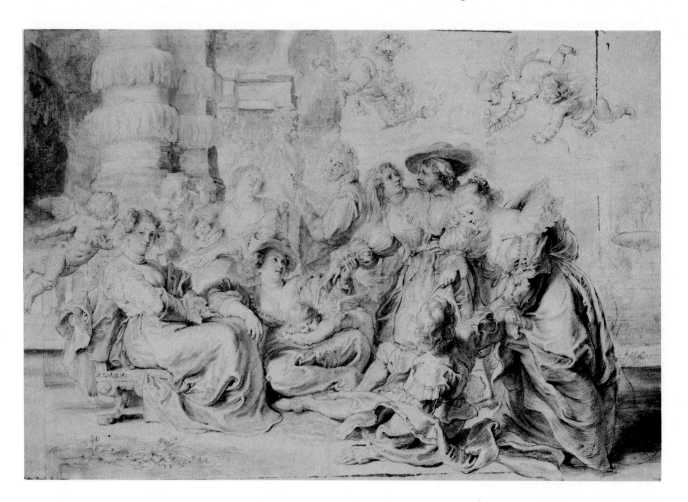

Whenever people talk about an object as being rough or coarse or smooth, they are referring to its **texture**. This is the element of art that appeals to the sense of touch.

When looking at paintings in a museum, you might have noticed that some are smooth and even. There is little to distract your eye as it glides over their glossy surfaces. In other paintings, however, artists have used heavy applications of paint that produced uneven surfaces of ridges and furrows. This technique adds to their tactile and visual impact. *Tactile* means appealing to the sense of touch.

The desire for a rich, tactile surface has caused artists to go beyond applying thick layers of color. Some have added sand, plaster, and other materials to paint to change its tactile quality. Others have pasted paper, cloth, and other items to their paintings and drawings to create another kind of **actual texture**. Actual texture is the kind that the viewer can touch.

Some paintings and drawings that are smooth to the touch can still suggest different kinds of texture. A suggested or implied texture is known as **simulated** or **visual texture**. Vincent van Gogh used a variety of pens to simulate different textures in his drawing of the café (Figure 1.1).

Space

The distance around, between, above, below, and within an object is **space**. In Giovanni Panini's drawing of the Spanish Steps in Rome (Figure 1.7), the artist has focused attention on the element of space. After examining this drawing, list the ways the artist has suggested space or distance on this two-dimensional surface.

How many were you able to identify? Actually, six different techniques can be found. They are explained briefly below.

Linear perspective. Notice how the lines of the building slant inward in Panini's drawing, making them appear to extend back into space. This technique, developed by artists in the fourteenth and fifteenth centuries, is called **linear perspective**. It shows the way these buildings would look if you actually viewed this scene. As the lines recede (move away), they seem to meet on an imaginary line known as the **horizon line** or **eye level line**. The point on the eye level line at which all of these lines meet is referred to as the **vanishing point**.

Size relationship. As your eye moves back into the picture, the objects become progressively smaller. This technique of making objects in the background smaller than those in the foreground also creates a sense of depth.

Placement of objects. Objects placed higher than others in the drawing appear to be farther back. This technique, especially when combined with a size difference, is an effective method for creating the illusion of space.

Overlapping of objects. Perhaps the basic technique for suggesting space is **overlapping**. This means placing one object in front of another, partially concealing the object behind. Observe how the figures overlap each other in Panini's drawing. This overlapping makes them appear closer. Some figures seem to be standing in front of others.

Value change. Did you notice that the figures in the foreground of this drawing appear to be darker in value than those in the background? This is a form of **aerial perspective**. In this technique the artist gradually lessens the value and value contrasts for objects that appear farther back in the composition.

Detail. The details of the figures in the distance are less clear than those of the figures in the foreground. Also, the contours of distant objects seem to blur just as they would if you were viewing these objects in nature.

Atmospheric perspective. Another technique for suggesting space should also be mentioned, although it isn't shown in the illustration. Where color is used in a landscape, objects in the distance are painted with hues that appear bluer and less intense or bright. When their values change, too—making these objects lighter—this technique creates the illusion of layers of atmosphere between the viewer and the distant objects. This technique is sometimes called **atmospheric perspective**.

Of course, artists don't always try to encourage the viewer to look back into their compositions. Many works are produced that provide little or no suggestion of depth. This is certainly the case with Ellsworth Kelly's drawing *Briar* (Figure 1.8). The picture consists of a flat pattern of shapes arranged on the **picture plane** (the surface of the drawing). The only suggestion of space is the single overlapping leaf. (This drawing is also an example of the effective use of line. How would you describe the lines Kelly has drawn?)

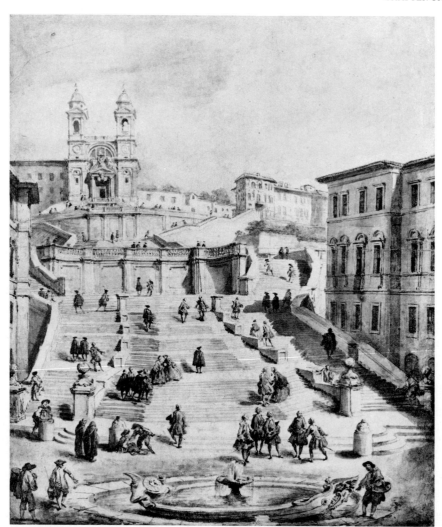

FIGURE 1.7 Giovanni Paolo Panini, *Spanish Steps*, c. 1730. Watercolor over black chalk, 13¹¹⁄₁₆ × 11⁹⁄₁₆″ (approx. 34.3 × 29.2 cm). The Metropolitan Museum of Art, New York, NY. Rogers Fund.

FIGURE 1.8 Ellsworth Kelly, *Briar*, 1963. Pencil on paper, 22⅜ × 28⅜″ (56.8 × 72.1 cm). Whitney Museum of American Art, New York, NY. Neysa McMein Purchase Award.

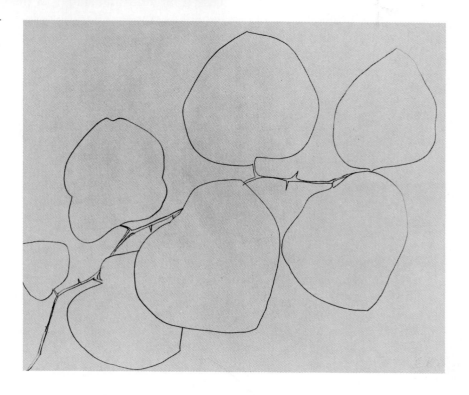

A Brief Comment About Color

A composition can be complete without using all of the elements mentioned. In drawing, the element of **color** is often not used. Beginning drawing students will probably want to wait to use color until they have developed their drawing skills with black and white materials. Therefore, the theory of color won't be considered at great length in this book, although color will sometimes be mentioned.

We see colors because objects reflect different wavelengths of light. A color wheel shows all the colors in the spectrum, which is white light separated into all of the different wavelengths it contains. Colors have hue (their spectral names), value (lightness or darkness), and intensity (brightness or darkness).

Colors can be combined in works of art in several ways. One common combination is the use of complementary colors, colors that are opposite each other (blue and orange, for example) on the color wheel. Another combination is analogous colors, colors located next to each other (like yellow-green, green, and blue-green) on the color wheel. Colors are sometimes divided into two groups: cool (green, blue, and violet) and warm (red, orange, and yellow).

THE PRINCIPLES OF ART

Each of the following principles describes a different way of using the elements of art discussed earlier. Knowing these principles should be helpful as you continue your education in art. As you know, this education includes studying others' artworks as well as practicing your drawing skills.

Balance

If you ride a bicycle, you already know that balance is important. Keeping your balance means that you won't fall off. Leaning too far to one side or the other could produce an imbalance; you and your bicycle could part company.

In art, **balance** refers to a way of combining elements to add a sense of stability to a work of art. Two kinds of balance are possible. The simpler kind is referred to as **symmetrical** or **formal balance**. In this kind of balance, similar shapes are repeated in the same manner on either side of a vertical, horizontal, or diagonal line dividing the composition in half. One half of the work mirrors the other half. You can

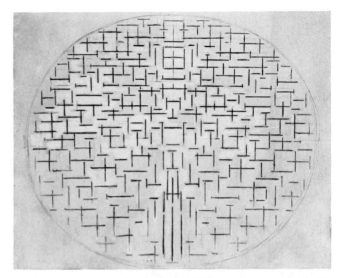

FIGURE 1.9 Piet Mondrian, *Pier and Ocean (Sea in Starlight)*, 1914. Charcoal and white watercolor, 34⅝ × 44″ (87.9 × 111.2 cm). Collection, The Museum of Modern Art, New York, NY. Mrs. Simon Guggenheim Fund.

see formal balance in Mondrian's drawing entitled *Pier and Ocean* (Figure 1.9).

A less stationary and usually more visually appealing type of balance is known as **asymmetrical** or **informal balance**. Balance of this kind is based on the apparent weight of the various objects in the work. Weight can be suggested by the colors, values, sizes, and shapes of the objects.

For example, in a drawing showing a man jumping on a train (Figure 1.10), Edward Hopper partially balanced the large, leaning railroad car at the left with the darker figures of the two men leaning in the opposite direction. The shape of the rock at the bottom of the drawing suggests that its largest and heaviest end is at the right. Along with the small house at the extreme right side of the drawing, the rock helps create the feeling of balance in this work.

Emphasis

Contrast is often used to achieve **emphasis**. It is a way of combining elements to point out their differences. In the process, the artist accents one or more elements to create points of visual interest. In this way the artist can direct the viewer's attention to the most important parts of a composition. In George Grosz's portrait of his mother-in-law (Figure 1.11), you can see how value can be used to achieve emphasis.

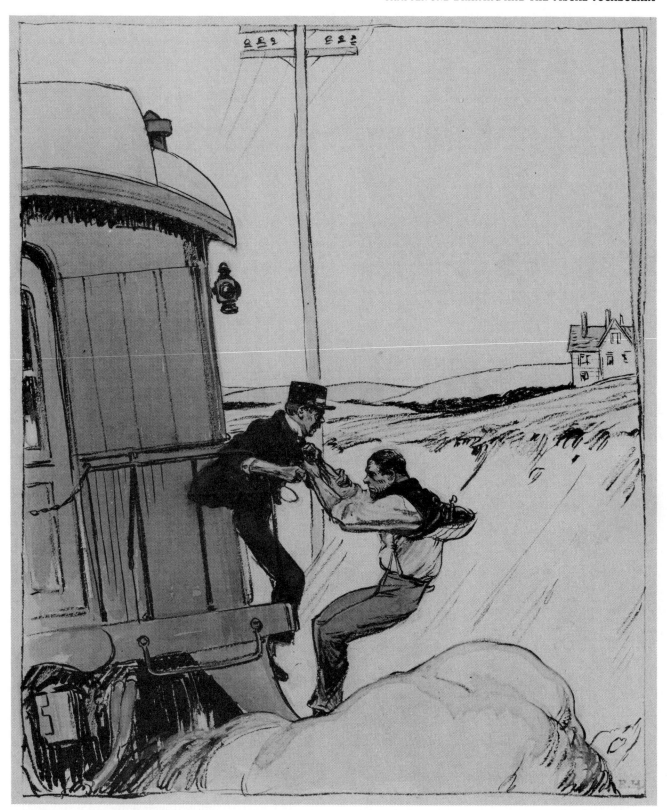

FIGURE 1.10 Edward Hopper, *Jumping on a Train*, c. 1906–14. Ink and wash on illustration board, 18¾ × 15″ (47.6 × 38.1 cm). Whitney Museum of American Art, New York, NY. Josephine N. Hopper bequest.

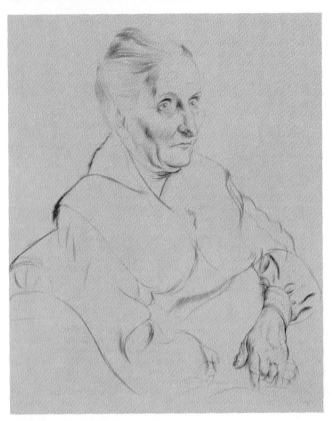

FIGURE 1.11 George Grosz, *Anna Peter*, 1926–27. Pencil, 27⅛ × 21¼″ (69 × 53.9 cm). Collection, The Museum of Modern Art, New York, NY. Gift of Paul J. Sachs.

Harmony

Mondrian's drawing *Pier and Ocean* (Figure 1.9) demonstrates the principle of **harmony**, as well as formal balance. Mondrian's repetition of horizontal and vertical lines throughout the drawing helps tie the composition together. Harmony can be thought of as a way of combining similar elements in a work to stress their similarities. When the artist decides to use repeated elements or make only subtle changes in elements, the artwork looks uncomplicated and even.

Variety

One way of combining elements to create complex relationships is the principle of **variety**. It is the principle artists use to increase the visual interest in their works. They must be aware, however, that too much variety can create visual clutter. The viewer could be confused. Variety must be balanced by harmony.

You can see both harmony and variety in a small drawing of a boy playing a flute, by the Japanese artist Katsushika Hokusai (Figure 1.12). There is variety in the long, flowing lines that are at some places dark and heavy and at others slight and thin. They suggest the differences between the boy's delicately pictured head, arms, and legs and the heavy folds of his garment. These long, flowing lines contrast with the short, abrupt lines that indicate the pattern and texture of the woven basket and the boy's unruly hair.

FIGURE 1.12 Katsushika Hokusai, *Boy with a Flute*, 1984. Ink on paper, 4½ × 6¼″ (11.4 × 15.9 cm). Freer Gallery of Art, Smithsonian Institution, Washington, DC.

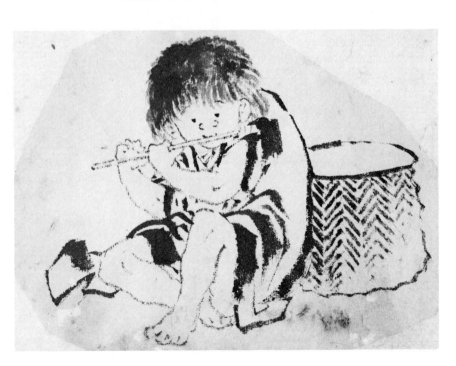

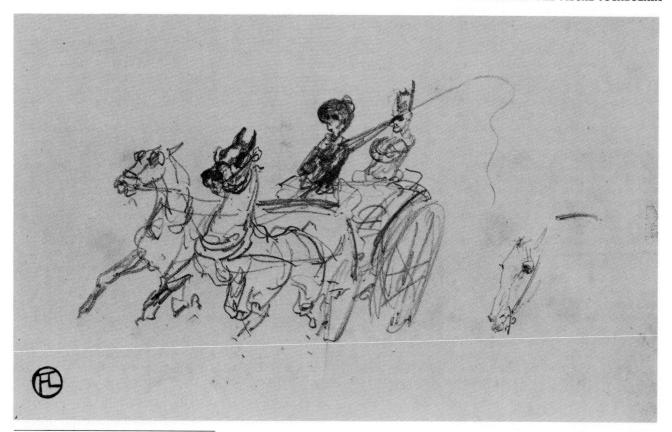

FIGURE 1.13 Henri Toulouse-Lautrec, *Toulouse-Lautrec Sketchbook: La Comtesse Noir*, 1880. Graphite on ivory wove paper, 6.3 × 10.1″ (16 × 25.6 cm). The Art Institute of Chicago, IL. Robert Alexander Waller Collection.

Value contrasts accent the hair and the decorative pattern of the boy's clothing.

Harmony in the Hokusai drawing was achieved through control. There are obvious contrasts of line, texture, and value, but they were carefully limited. The result is a drawing that is visually appealing.

Gradation

Using a series of gradual changes to combine art elements is called **gradation**. When an artwork has a series of shapes that gradually change from large to small, light to dark, or rough to smooth, the artist has used the principle of gradation.

You can see this principle in drawings with gradual changes from dark to light values. The changes suggest the appearance of rounded, three-dimensional forms. Several drawings you have already seen in this chapter use gradation. Georgia O'Keeffe's drawing (Figure 1.3) is one of these. How many others can you find?

Movement and Rhythm

In a sketch of a horse-drawn carriage (Figure 1.13) Toulouse-Lautrec used the principle of **movement** to create the look and feeling of action. The drawing conveys this sensation with hastily drawn lines. These lines capture the gait of the horses and the rapidly spinning wheels of the carriage. Placed at an angle, the carriage seems about to burst out of the picture as it rushes toward the viewer. Movement in this drawing was accented by the way the lines have been made. The hand of the artist must have dashed across the paper as he tried to record as quickly as possible the rapid movements of his subject.

Closely related to movement is the principle of **rhythm**. An artist often creates rhythm by carefully placing the same or contrasting elements throughout a composition. The repetition creates a visual tempo or beat. This tempo invites the eye to leap, skip, or glide from one element to the next.

The same shape or line, for example, might be repeated several times in a work. The shape or line would guide the viewer's gaze in a certain direction. Another possibility is for the artist to use visual contrasts of shapes or colors to lead the eye on a more irregular path. A series of large and small shapes, for

FIGURE 1.14 Charles White, *Preacher*, 1952. Ink on cardboard, 21⅜ × 29⅜″ (54.3 × 74.6 cm). Whitney Museum of American Art, New York, NY.

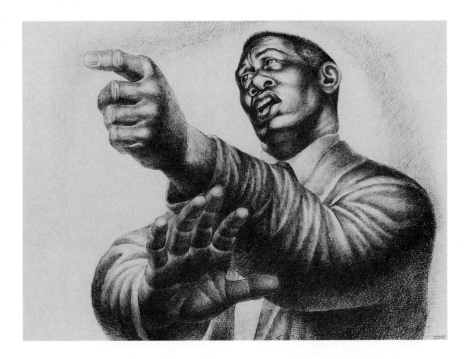

instance, could be placed so the viewer's eye is led forward, backward, then forward again through a work.

Proportion

The visual relationship of elements to the whole artwork and to each other is referred to as **proportion**. Often proportion is closely linked to another principle, emphasis. Enlarging objects or figures in a drawing not only shows the importance attached to them by the artist, but it also communicates this importance to the viewer.

Artists have used the principle of proportion for a long time. More recently artists have used **exaggeration** or enlargement of figures or objects in their works to communicate a certain idea or feeling. In Figure 1.14, Charles White exaggerated the sizes of certain parts of the figure to show the strength of a preacher delivering a powerful sermon. In this case, White made the head smaller and the gesturing hands larger than they should be. This exaggeration gives the preacher a more dramatic appearance.

Space

Space, you will recall, is one of the elements of art. You are probably surprised to see that space is also listed here as a principle. Sometimes the element of space, like the other elements, is controlled by the principles of art. So space can be balanced. Or it can be used to emphasize a certain part of an artwork, or to suggest a gradual movement into a work. Space can also be used, however, as a principle to control the other elements.

You have learned that shapes can be combined in a composition to create a feeling of symmetrical or asymmetrical balance. You have also learned that several contrasting shapes might be used to emphasize a certain part of a work. But shapes can also be created and arranged so that they seem to be placed at different distances in the work. In this case, the principle of space is used to manipulate the element of shape to create the illusion of depth. Space can be applied to any of the other elements to suggest a three-dimensional appearance in a work.

UNITY . . . AND BEYOND

When artists design their works, they must organize, in a unified way, the elements they have selected by using the principles of art. Some artists design their works deliberately and thoughtfully. Others work in a more spontaneous and intuitive manner. But, no matter how they choose to work, the result must be inviting and pleasing to the eye. Artists must skillfully blend the elements and principles to make all parts of a composition fit together in a visually appealing way. **Unity** can be thought of as the total visual effect achieved by carefully blending the elements and principles in a work of art. Without unity, a work could seem confusing and uninteresting.

It is impossible to create a formula or a list of rules for good design. If this were possible, you would only need to learn the formula or memorize the rules to become a successful artist. Good art would become common. Instead, you have to develop your own approach to good design. Doing this requires a knowledge and understanding of the elements and principles of art.

Students who acquire this knowledge and understanding are more likely to produce drawings that have unity. Achieving unity is by no means a simple task. Consider the enormous number of individuals who have attempted to create art. All of them had access to the same elements and principles. But only a few can boast of producing works of art that are recognized for their unity.

Also, even if an artist could consistently make unified artworks, there is no guarantee that those works would be thought of as good or successful. A good work of art must go beyond unity. Unless it does, it may be well composed, but it may also be boring, lifeless, and trivial. Unity must be combined with a sensitive and creative treatment of ideas, moods, and feelings. Then the artist can create works that are complete, unique, and exciting.

DRAWING AT WORK

Museum Artist: Mixing Art and Nature

Preparing exhibits for a natural history museum requires a unique combination of artistic talent and scientific knowledge. A museum artist may draw large background murals one week and prepare models of prehistoric animals the next week. Some jobs may even become a little tedious. For example, models of trees used in exhibits may take more than one thousand leaves that must be made and installed individually to create a realistic effect.

Stephen Quinn is senior principal exhibition preparator and artist at the American Museum of Natural History in New York City. Quinn has always been interested in both natural science and art. In high school he combined these interests by illustrating articles and magazine covers for a local Audubon Society as well as for fish and game magazines. While studying at the Ridgewood School of Art and Design in New Jersey, Quinn worked for two state park commissions, designing science exhibits.

Quinn's job with the museum is satisfying. As an artist, he enjoys the fact that the artistic medium he uses changes from project to project. In addition, he works with a variety of scientists.

Quinn's responsibilities are varied. He may make architectural or botanical models, draw scientific illustrations, or oversee a complete project from design to construction. Recently Quinn developed an exhibit on dinosaurs that has traveled to museums around the country. To create these prehistoric animals, Quinn studied bones and footprints to determine the probable ranges of movements. Scars on bones helped Quinn plot muscle masses. Studying living animals such as crocodiles, birds, and reptiles aided Quinn in making educated guesses about the behaviors and lifestyles of dinosaurs.

Drawing plays an important part in preparing exhibits. For example, Quinn drew and painted large murals as backgrounds for dioramas (three-dimensional displays) in the museum's Hall of Asian Peoples. One diorama depicts a Hindu wedding scene. The exhibit gives the viewers the feeling of standing among the wedding party on a hillside. The background is a landscape of India and includes a view of a typical village and distant fields.

This exhibit was created in stages. After doing his research, Quinn created preliminary drawings of the scene that included realistic details. From these sketches, he plotted the drawing onto a grid. Then he transferred these points to the larger areas in the diorama. This step involved careful adjustment to allow for the distortion caused by the curved backdrop of the exhibit. Next, he carefully drew the scene with charcoal. Finally, he finished the entire mural with paints.

The American Museum of Natural History trains three or four interns a year in the exhibitions department. The program offers talented young people an opportunity to explore the job of creating museum exhibits.

CHAPTER TWO

Aesthetic Qualities and Art Criticism

OBJECTIVES

After reading this chapter and doing the activities, you will be able to

■ explain the purpose of a theory of art;

■ explain the benefit of knowing and using more than one theory of art;

■ list and describe three theories of art;

■ list and describe three kinds of aesthetic qualities;

■ explain the difference between *looking at* and *seeing* works of art;

■ list the four steps in the art criticism process;

■ describe the literal qualities and identify the elements of art in drawings;

■ analyze artists' use of the elements and principles of art in drawings;

■ interpret the feelings, moods, and ideas that artists communicate in drawings; and

■ judge the success or failure of drawings and give reasons to support those judgments.

Three aestheticians (people concerned with what makes art successful) have gathered at a table in a small café. Jones, Smith, and Veeberholz are involved in an argument that began when they first met many years ago. They are trying to define art!

Pounding his fist on the table, Jones is claiming that a work of art must look lifelike to be successful. "When an artist draws a tree, then it must look like a tree, not a pot roast! And, if it doesn't look like a tree, it isn't art."

Shaking her head violently, Smith outshouts Veeberholz to state her point of view. "That's absurd! There is no reason why a work of art must look lifelike or real. But it must be carefully and effectively composed by the artist."

"And what exactly do you mean by that?" Jones asks.

"I mean that it must show a skillful arrangement of the elements of art according to the principles of art. The finished work must be unified and visually exciting. That's what I mean!"

Sensing an opening while Smith catches her breath and Jones covers his eyes in disbelief, Veeberholz leaps to his feet. "Both of you are wrong! A good work of art doesn't have to look real. It doesn't have to be well-organized. But it certainly must communicate an idea, a feeling, or a mood to the viewer. If it fails to do that, then it isn't art. It is as simple as that."

Jones and Smith lose no time standing up to protest. It is clear that the argument will end as it always does, with no winner.

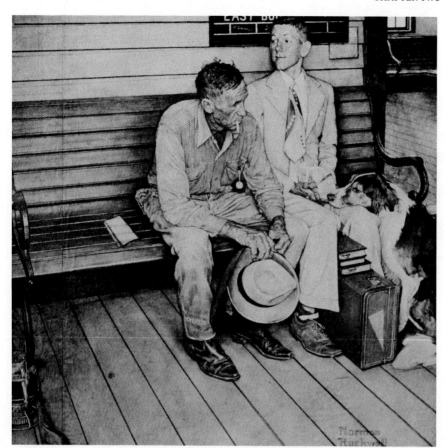

FIGURE 2.1 Norman Rockwell, *Off to College*, date unknown. Pencil drawing, 41¾ × 41″ (106 × 104 cm). Texas Tech University, Lubbock, TX. Collection of the West Texas Museum Association.

THEORIES OF ART

Although no conclusions were reached, this discussion is useful to us. Each of these aestheticians has a different theory of art. Theories of this kind have been proposed by aestheticians and philosophers for centuries. Not one theory, however, has emerged that satisfies everyone. Yet they are all alike in one way—each theory tries to define art according to certain qualities.

For example, Jones feels that a good work of art has to look real or lifelike. Smith thinks that it is more important that a work uses the elements and principles of art skillfully. And Veeberholz argues that it is necessary for a work to convey a message of some kind to the viewer. If they didn't enjoy arguing so much, Jones, Smith, and Veeberholz might recognize that there is some truth in all of these theories. Each one, however, is too limiting.

A single theory of art, you see, can point to *some* truths in *some* works of art. But it can't point to *all* truths in *all* works of art. Therefore, you need to become familiar with several theories of art rather than limiting yourself to accepting a single theory.

Together the theories of art can guide you in studying many different qualities in drawings. No serious art student approaches a work of art in a neutral way; some preconceived ideas are unavoidable. Your own experiences with art contribute to your approach. They affect how you look at drawings and determine what you see in them and how you respond to what you see. Knowing different theories of art, however, can broaden your experience of art. The theories can help you understand and appreciate not only drawings that are appealing at first glance, but also those to which you might at first respond negatively.

For example, it is unlikely that you would respond positively to each of the drawings in Figures 2.1, 2.2, and 2.3. One of these probably appeals to you more than the others. If this is so, ask yourself why. Do you think that one of these drawings is less successful than the other two? Why do you think it is less successful?

Ask yourself some final questions: Did you judge all three drawings by the same test? If you responded positively to the drawing in Figure 2.1 because it looks so real, did you respond negatively to either or both of the other drawings because they lacked that

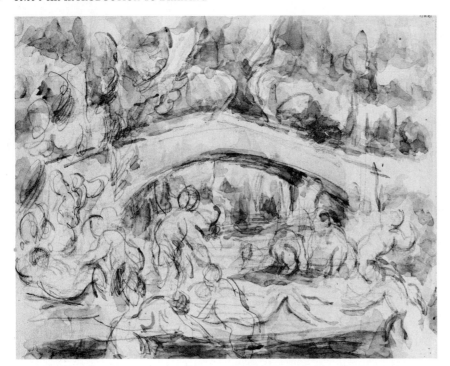

FIGURE 2.2 Paul Cezanne, *Bathers Under a Bridge*, date unknown. Watercolor over lead pencil on paper, 8¼ × 10¾″ (21 × 27.4 cm). The Metropolitan Museum of Art, New York, NY. Lizzie P. Bliss Collection, Maria DeWitt Jessup Fund.

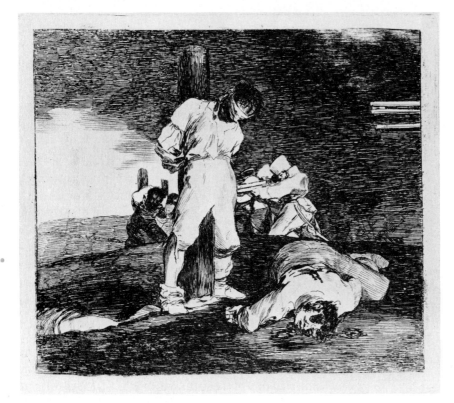

FIGURE 2.3 Francisco Goya, *Disasters of War*, c. 1812. Etching and aquatint. The Metropolitan Museum of Art, New York, NY. Mortimer Schiff Fund.

same lifelike quality? If this is the case, do you think it is right to judge all three drawings by the same standard?

After all, it should be clear that two of these artists didn't care about making their drawings look real. Assume that both were skilled artists who could draw in a realistic way if they wanted to. Since they chose not to do so, they must have been concerned with capturing something other than realistic appearances in their drawings. If you knew what they wanted to communicate—what theory of art these artists were using—you might respond differently to their drawings.

Theories of art can direct your attention to different qualities in drawings. Armed with that knowledge, you would be better prepared to understand and enjoy more types of drawings. You might even find that you could respond positively to all three of these drawings, but for completely different reasons.

In later chapters you will study three theories about the nature of art: **imitationalism, formalism**, and **emotionalism**. These theories will help you find different aesthetic qualities in drawings by other artists and make you more aware of those qualities in your own drawings. Imitationalism focuses on *literal* qualities, formalism on *visual* qualities, and emotionalism on *expressive* qualities. A brief introduction to these aesthetic qualities follows.

Imitationalism: The Literal Qualities

Qualities in a work of art that represent subject matter realistically are referred to as the **literal qualities**. Aestheticians who follow an imitationalist point of view (such as Jones) think that the value of any artwork is determined by how closely it imitates the real world. An imitationalist would probably respond favorably to Ingres's *Portrait of Count de Nieuwerkerke* (Figure 2.4). That same imitationalist, however, would probably react unfavorably, or at least indifferently, to Mondrian's *Self-Portrait* (Figure 2.5).

Look carefully at Ingres's drawing (Figure 2.4). Is there any doubt that this is exactly how this French count looked? A sensitive line barely indicates the coat and hands. Clearly, the focus of attention is on the face, which is carefully drawn with charcoal. Light areas give the head a feeling of roundness and volume.

Notice also how the artist gave clues about the personality of the count. What do the eyes, the mouth, and the facial expression tell you about the kind of person he was? Observe the pose, the clothes, and

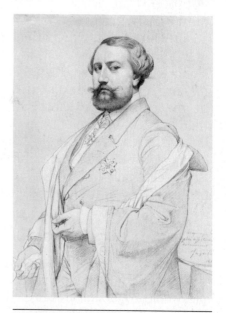

FIGURE 2.4 Jean Auguste Dominique Ingres, *Portrait of Count de Nieuwerkerke*, 1856. Graphite and white chalk on cream wove paper, 13.0 × 9.6″ (33.0 × 24.3 cm). The Harvard University Art Museums, Cambridge, MA. Bequest of Grenville L. Winthrop.

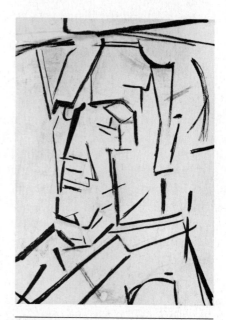

FIGURE 2.5 Piet Mondrian, *Self-portrait*, 1942. Ink and charcoal on paper, 25 × 19″ (63.5 × 48.3 cm). The Dallas Museum of Art, Dallas, TX. Foundation for the Arts Collection. Gift of the James H. and Lillian Clark Foundation.

the medal the man is wearing. What do these suggest about his wealth and importance?

If an imitationalist such as Jones looked at the Mondrian self-portrait (Figure 2.5), he would shake his head. "Surely the artist doesn't ask us to believe that he actually looked like this," he would say. "Why, there is nothing here but a series of hastily drawn lines—straight lines at that. I can see the general shape of a head and facial features. But the portrait isn't realistically drawn. No, in terms of the literal qualities, this drawing is unsatisfactory."

Formalism: The Visual Qualities

Another theorist might receive Mondrian's drawing more warmly. A formalist like Smith, for example, would argue that a work of art should be judged by its **visual qualities**, not its literal qualities. These visual qualities are the elements and principles of art. Formalists look at how successfully the artist used them to create a unified, interesting artwork. They aren't interested in whether or not a drawing looks real. Instead, they are concerned with how well the artist has used the visual vocabulary—the elements and principles of art.

As a formalist, Smith might say the Mondrian self-portrait (Figure 2.5) is successful. She would first point out the repetitious use of straight lines. These lines dominate this drawing and help to give it harmony. The way these lines were applied and arranged creates a sense of rhythm. The lines invite the viewer's eye to move from one to the next.

Small changes in the lines give the drawing variety. There are long, short, horizontal, vertical, diagonal, thick, and thin lines. This assortment is carefully organized to create a unified whole. The drawing would make Smith smile in appreciation, even though Lester would turn away with a shrug of indifference.

Emotionalism: The Expressive Qualities

Both imitationalists and formalists might respond positively to the self-portrait by Käthe Kollwitz in Figure 2.6, but for entirely different reasons. Imitationalists would point out the literal qualities, but formalists would emphasize the visual qualities.

Another group of theorists, however, would refer to different qualities to justify their positive response to the drawing. Emotionalists such as Veeberholz would say that it is successful because of its **expressive qualities**. By this they mean that the drawing effectively communicates a feeling or mood to the viewer.

Veeberholz might begin his study of this drawing by thinking about this woman's frame of mind. Does she appear to be happy and content, or depressed and sad? Notice the furrowed brow, the deeply set, staring eyes, and the straight, expressionless line of the mouth. It is unlikely that anyone, least of all Veeberholz, would suggest that the woman is happy and content. If she spoke, she would probably tell about suffering instead of joy. Will her frown pass and be replaced soon by a good-natured grin? Or is it as much a part of her appearance as her wrinkled brow and sorrowful eyes?

The drawing begs the viewer to ask questions of this kind. The answers help the viewer share for a moment the feelings of the woman who drew this self-portrait over fifty years ago. By focusing on expres-

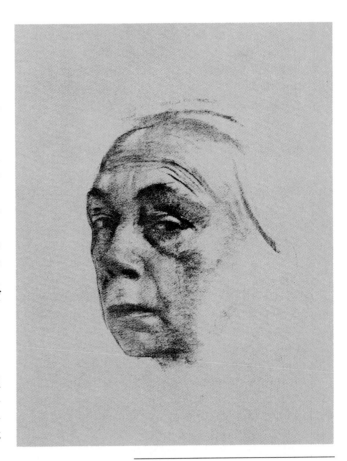

FIGURE 2.6 Käthe Kollwitz, *Self-portrait*, 1924. Lithograph, 9.8 × 10.0″ (25.0 × 25.5 cm). The Harvard University Art Museums, Cambridge, MA.

sive qualities, Veeberholz, or any other emotionalist, can discover and respond to the artist's message. What emotions does this drawing communicate?

LOOKING AT AND SEEING DRAWINGS

The theories of art point out the different aesthetic qualities in artworks. These theories show you what to look for. But you can identify these qualities more easily if you know not only how to *look* but also how to *see*.

You may be saying to yourself, "Everyone knows how to see art. People visit museums every day to look at art. Most of them have never been taught how to look" (Figure 2.7). All of this is true. People may not need to be taught how to *look*, but they probably need to be taught how to *see*. There is a difference.

For example, picture yourself walking into a large classroom. It is filled with familiar objects that have four legs, a seat, and a back. Of course you would know at once that these objects are chairs. Up to this point you have been looking. But in order to see, you must note the similarities and differences of the chairs.

You observe that some chairs are made of metal, some of metal and wood, and still others of plastic. Several are painted in bright colors. Other older chairs seem to have faded to a dull, neutral tone. Many chairs appear to be new, but some look as if they have been in use for a long time and badly need repair.

Each chair in the room is in some ways similar to and in other ways different from the others. By studying them carefully, you can see these similarities and differences.

Of course you could hardly be expected to observe this closely every time you encounter a chair or any other object. To do so would be highly impractical, even if it were possible. You save the capacity for observing and responding to an object's unique features for special occasions and special objects. If you were buying a chair, that would be a special occasion, and chairs would be special objects. You would try to find out which chair, out of all of those in the store, offered the best appearance, the most comfort, and the longest durability.

Among the objects that qualify for special observation and response are drawings. Learning from and about these works of art leads to understanding, appreciation, and enjoyment that enriches our lives.

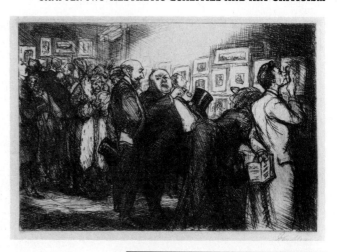

FIGURE 2.7 Why do you think these people are visiting the art gallery? John Sloan, *Connoisseurs of Prints*, 1905. Etching, 9⁹/₁₆ × 12½″ (24 ×32 cm). Collection of Whitney Museum of American Art, New York, NY.

To a drawing student, knowing both how to look at and how to see drawings is essential. Your art training shouldn't be limited to techniques for making your own drawings. It should also include lessons learned from studying drawings of the past and present.

Art criticism and *art history* are two different approaches to this study. As a drawing student you must have an understanding of the methods used in both of these approaches. When you are mainly concerned with identifying the various aesthetic qualities *within* drawings, you will use the art criticism approach. When you are mainly concerned with a search for facts and information *about* drawings and the artists who did them, you will use art history. You will begin to learn about art criticism here in this chapter. You will be introduced to art history in the next chapter.

ART CRITICISM

If you have never been involved in art criticism, you should realize from the start that it is not only easy but also enjoyable. Some beginning students mistakenly think that only those with a broad background in aesthetics, art history, or art production can critique art. It is true that such a background contributes to a more knowledgeable and sensitive response to art. But you can practice meaningful criticism while gaining that background. This book is designed to

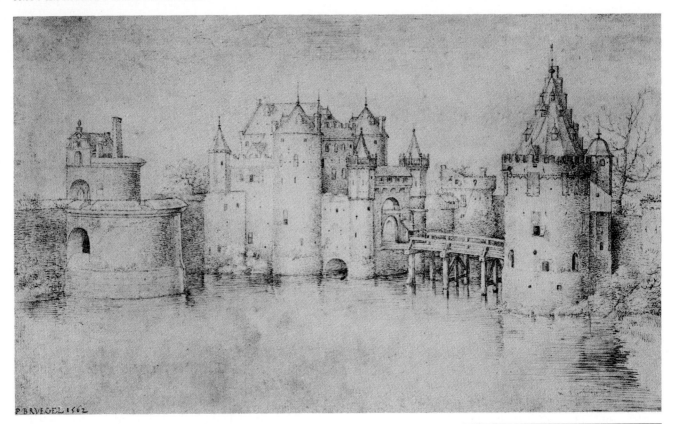

FIGURE 2.8 Jacob Savery, *The Amsterdam City Gates*, c. 1565–1602. Pen and two colors of brown ink over black chalk, $7\frac{1}{4} \times 12\frac{1}{8}''$ (18.3 × 30.5 cm). Courtesy of the Museum of Fine Arts, Boston, MA. Louis Curtis Fund.

help you learn how to respond to drawings through art criticism.

When you critique a drawing, you will use four separate but often overlapping steps or operations. These operations are

- description,
- analysis,
- interpretation, and
- judgment.

These steps help you ask different kinds of questions about a drawing. After you answer the questions, you will be able to

- identify everything in the drawing,
- determine how the drawing is organized or composed,
- explain what the drawing means, and
- make a personal decision about the drawing's degree of success.

Each of the art criticism operations identifies different aesthetic qualities in works of art. You will recall that these aesthetic qualities are

- the literal qualities,
- the visual qualities, and
- the expressive qualities.

Each operation for critiquing a drawing is explained below. You will soon find out that this approach will help you understand others' drawings. It will also help you critique your own drawings. *This process is essential in developing your skills as an artist.*

Description

Description, the first art criticism operation, involves asking and answering questions to discover everything in a drawing. It is the least difficult of the four steps, although the fact that it's easy doesn't mean that it isn't important. You should try to be as thorough as you can when you describe a drawing. You want to notice everything in the artwork.

Suppose you are observing a drawing done in an imitational style, such as the drawing in Figure 2.8. Begin by asking questions about the subject matter or literal qualities. If you haven't done this before, you may not know what to ask first. So begin with the most obvious question: *"What do I see in this drawing?"* Carefully study the drawing, noting everything in it.

Next, ask more specific questions, such as:

- How many buildings are included in the drawing?
- What are the buildings made of?
- Are there any windows in the buildings?
- Are there any people in the picture?

Answers to questions like these will help you learn a great deal about the drawing's literal qualities. You will begin to see things that you might have overlooked at first.

Of course there are many more description questions that should be asked in order to find everything in this drawing. Take a few minutes to study the drawing further, and try asking yourself some of these questions. When you become involved in the description process, you will think of questions quite easily.

But wait. This descriptive questioning process might work with an imitational drawing. But what happens when you look at an **abstract** or **nonobjective** work? This type of art doesn't have subject matter that looks real. How would you describe the work in Figure 2.9?

In a drawing like this, there are few literal qualities to describe. In this case, ask yourself, *"What elements of art can I identify in this drawing?"* As you know, elements, along with the principles of art, are the visual qualities stressed by formalism. You will think about how the principles are used in the next art criticism step. Study the elements of art, however, during the description operation.

You can also ask yourself more specific questions, such as:

- What *colors* can be identified (in color reproductions)?
- Are light and dark *values* used?
- What kinds of *lines* can I find in the work?
- How could I describe the *shapes* used?
- Are there areas of rough and smooth *texture*?
- How has the artist suggested depth or *space* in this drawing?

Actually, you should always ask questions about the elements of art when describing a drawing. If you are studying an imitational work, questions about the

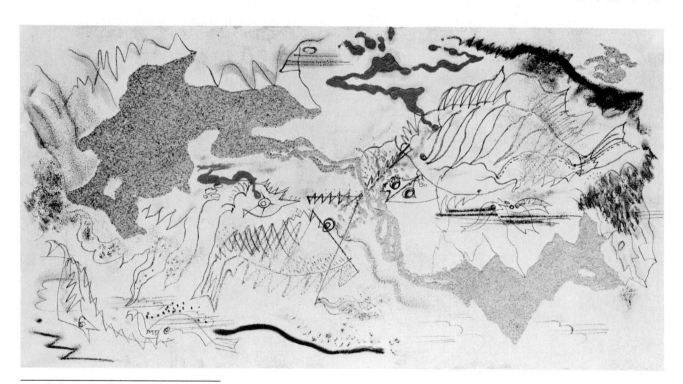

FIGURE 2.9 André Masson, *Battle of Fishes*, 1926. Sand, gesso, oil, pencil, and charcoal on canvas, 14¼ × 28¾" (36.2 × 73 cm). Collection, The Museum of Modern Art, New York, NY.

elements would follow those about the literal qualities. But if a work is abstract or nonobjective, begin the description process by asking questions about the elements of art.

Analysis

The second of the art criticism operations, analysis, is probably the most difficult. But this step may improve your drawing skills the most. During this operation you learn how a drawing is organized or composed. Your attention centers on the visual qualities. Since you identify the elements of art during description, focus during this step on the principles of art. The general question you need to ask yourself is *"Which principles of art are used to organize the elements in this drawing?"*

Students have found that a design chart, such as the one in Figure 2.10, can help when they analyze works of art. As you can see, the elements of art are listed vertically on the left side of this chart. The principles are listed horizontally across the top. The blank spaces show possible design relationships between elements and principles. These relationships may be important in the work's design.

One or more questions are suggested at each intersection of element and principle. For example, at the intersection of line and balance, you might ask, "Are the lines in the work balanced?" Or you might ask a question linking line with emphasis: "Is line used in this composition to emphasize one or more points of interest?"

To practice using the design chart, analyze Rembrandt's portrait of *Jan Cornelius Sylvius, the Preacher* (Figure 2.11). Remember, ask yourself the questions suggested at each intersection of element and principle.

The design chart in Figure 2.12 will help you get started. The Xs indicate three of the more obvious design relationships involving line in Rembrandt's drawing. The X at the intersection of line and variety means that the lines showing the chair and the book edge are wider and heavier than those used for the robe. Still thinner lines were used for the face, hair, and beard.

The X at the intersection of line and proportion refers to the relationship of these thick and thin lines. The thick lines of the book and chair make these objects look heavier than the robe, which is drawn with lighter lines.

The third X is placed at the intersection of line and space. The heavier lines in the drawing appear to be closer and the lighter lines farther away. These lines suggest different distances in the work.

DESIGN CHART		**PRINCIPLES OF ART**							
ELEMENTS OF ART		Balance	Emphasis	Harmony	Variety	Gradation	Movement/ Rhythm	Proportion	Space
Color	Hue								
	Intensity								
	Value								
Value (Non-Color)									
Line									
Texture									
Shape/Form									
Space									

UNITY

FIGURE 2.10 Design chart.

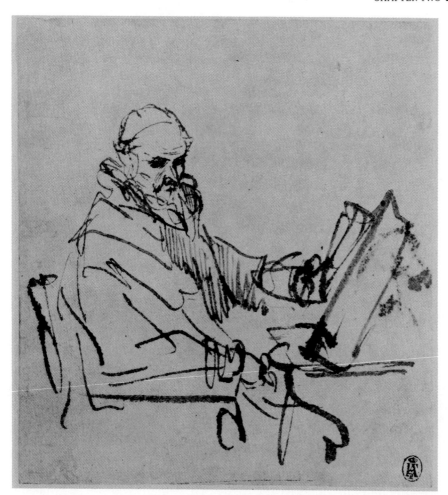

FIGURE 2.11 Rembrandt van Rijn, *Jan Cornelius Sylvius, the Preacher*, c. 1644–45. Pen and bistre drawing, 5.13 × 4.8″ (13.4 × 12.2 cm). National Gallery of Art, Washington, DC. Lessing J. Rosenwald Collection.

DESIGN CHART		PRINCIPLES OF ART								UNITY
ELEMENTS OF ART		Balance	Emphasis	Harmony	Variety	Gradation	Movement/ Rhythm	Proportion	Space	
Color	Hue									
	Intensity									
	Value									
Value (Non-Color)										
Line					✕			✕	✕	
Texture										
Shape/Form										
Space										

FIGURE 2.12 Partially completed design chart for Rembrandt's *Jan Cornelius Sylvius, the Preacher*.

Now complete the design chart. How many more design relationships can you identify? The number depends largely on your patience, determination, and powers of observation. Students with experience in analyzing art will probably find more relationships than other students. The more you analyze art, the more easily you can recognize design relationships.

Don't become discouraged if your first efforts seem difficult and unproductive. You certainly don't expect to learn to drive a car the first time you sit behind the wheel. So you shouldn't expect analyzing something as complex as a drawing to be easy the first time you try. You will get better at it with practice—just as your driving skills improve with practice.

Interpretation

The TV detective pauses dramatically before the roomful of suspects gathered in the library of the old von Sheckel mansion. He was asked to investigate the mysterious disappearance of old Baron von Sheckel. He has just finished presenting his collection of clues. Foul play is obviously involved. As the trench-coat-clad investigator has pointed out, each member of the Baron's family had opportunity and motive. One of them is guilty—but which one?

The camera slowly sweeps across the faces of the unfaithful young wife, the greedy sister, the hateful brother-in-law, stuffy Uncle Fenimore and his quiet but sinister wife, and kind Aunt Frieda. Except for kind Aunt Frieda, they all look guilty. You lean forward, eager to learn if you have identified the culprit. Suddenly, the detective whirls around and points an accusing finger at kind Aunt Frieda . . .

Interpretation is the third operation of art criticism. In many ways your role as a critic interpreting a work of art is similar to the role of the detective in the scene just described. Interpretation involves using the ''clues'' gathered during your investigation of a drawing to reach a decision about its meaning (or meanings). You consider everything you learned from a work during the description and analysis steps before you make this decision.

The expressive qualities are the focal point during this step. You will want to ask yourself, *''What ideas, moods, or feelings does this drawing communicate to me?''* Answering this quesion may be the most exciting part of the criticism process. In interpretation you express *your own personal decisions about works of art. There are no right or wrong answers.* Anything as complex as a drawing is open to many different interpretations. Interpretations often vary because they are colored by each person's unique past experiences. For example, a man born and raised in the jungles of Brazil, when seeing an airplane fly overhead for the first time, would interpret the sight much differently than a person born and raised in downtown Chicago.

Different interpretations of a drawing are acceptable, but they must be based on the clues found in the work. Try to avoid misjudging the clues. For example, to say that a picture of two snarling men wildly beating each other with clubs stands for peace and goodwill would be misreading the work.

Critiquing a drawing by Daumier (Figure 2.13) will give you an opportunity to test your skill in interpretation. Before you try to interpret it, however, be sure to describe and analyze the work as thoroughly as possible. In these steps you will gather the clues—literal and visual qualities—to use in making a decision about what the drawing means. (Don't read further until you have interpreted the drawing in Figure 2.13.)

Briefly review what you have learned from describing, analyzing, and interpreting the drawing by Daumier. During the description operation, did you identify the figure of a woman? Did you see that she appears to be gesturing wildly while leaning backward? During the analysis step, did you notice the variety of thick and thin lines used to suggest form and movement? When making your interpretation, did you use these and other literal and visual qualities to identify a woman who is

- happy and laughing hysterically?
- sad and weeping uncontrollably?
- frightened and reeling back in terror?
- angry and screaming loudly?

Of course, not all drawings will be as easy to interpret as this one. Some complex works might even be open to several different interpretations. In those cases you might find that your own interpretation (or interpretations) differs from those expressed by others. That is fine—a difference of opinion can lead to a lively exchange of ideas. Such a discussion can be stimulating as well as helpful to anyone interested in learning as much as possible from a drawing.

Remember that complete agreement is *not* the goal. Rather, you are asked to make a personal, care-

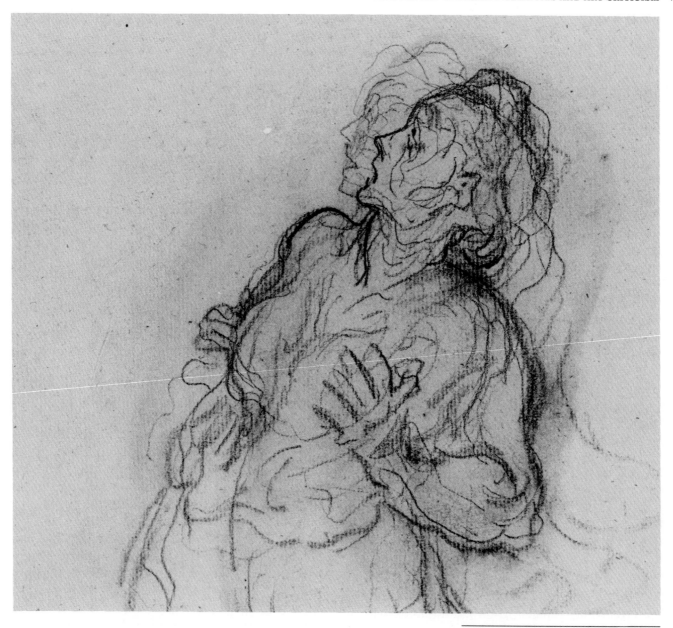

FIGURE 2.13 Honoré Daumier, *Fright*, 19th century. Charcoal over pencil, 8.0 × 9.2″ (20.3 × 23.4 cm). The Art Institute of Chicago, IL. Gift of Robert Allerton.

fully thought-out decision based on information gathered during a complete description and analysis.

The clues in Daumier's drawing are clear. Most viewers will decide that the figure in it is violently jerking backward in terror from some unseen threat. You may have missed one important feature, however, that affects the meaning. Did you notice the way the artist applied the lines in this drawing? Do these lines appear to have been made carefully after a great deal of thought? Or do they seem to have been done impulsively and wildly, like the frightened woman's instinctive and violent reaction to an unknown threat? The way this drawing was done helps reveal its meaning.

Honoré Daumier

Daumier's drawing of a woman in fright is all the more effective if you know something about the artist's tragic life. After a brief period during which he earned his living as a bookseller, Daumier became a political cartoonist. Eventually this occupation brought him into conflict with the king of France, Louis-Philippe. In 1832 an unflattering cartoon of the king cost Daumier six months in prison. His only complaints while in prison were that he didn't have enough ink with which to draw and that other prisoners were always asking him to draw their portraits. Daumier's fame as a cartoonist often hid the fact that he was a talented painter, although fellow artists recognized his abilities. Although he barely earned a living as a political cartoonist, he continued in this profession until he was in his seventies, when he lost his sight. The artist Camille Corot, a friend of many years, saved him from eviction from his modest cottage by buying it for him. When he died, Daumier was buried in a pauper's grave. The hundreds of drawings and paintings in the house were obtained by art dealers for almost nothing. Today, critics realize that Daumier's works foreshadowed modern art.

Judgment

After you have described, analyzed, and interpreted a drawing, you are ready to make an intelligent judgment about it. This is your chance to express your personal response to a work. It is here that you ask yourself, *"Is this a successful drawing?"*

Before answering that question, however, you must know the difference between a judgment and a statement of like or dislike. Judging a drawing isn't saying that you like or dislike it. Statements of that kind are emotional reactions to art. They are important, of course, but they don't have to be—and often can't be—backed up with clues from the drawing. Like-dislike statements are based on immediate and instinctive responses. You either like or dislike a work of art—period.

A judgment, on the other hand, is a thoughtful and informed response to a drawing. *This response must be supported by good reasons*. It isn't enough

to say that a drawing is good or bad; you must go on to explain *why* you think it is good or bad. When you have expressed a judgment and provided good reasons to support it, you have begun to understand and appreciate the drawing.

But, you ask, where do these good reasons come from? If you have carefully completed the first three art criticism operations, you already know them. These good reasons are everything you learned about a drawing during the description, analysis, and interpretation steps.

You might say that a drawing is successful because of its literal qualities ("It looks so lifelike!"). Maybe a drawing is successful because of its visual qualities ("The elements and principles are organized to create a unified whole.") Or you could judge the drawing positively because of its expressive qualities ("It clearly communicates a certain feeling, mood, or idea."). You could decide that a work is successful for one, two, or all three of these reasons.

During the discussion of the first three art criticism operations, you have studied several different drawings (see Figures 2.8, 2.9, 2.11, and 2.13). Now make a judgment about each of these drawings. Realize that no one else will make these judgments for you.

After making these judgments, study the drawing in Figure 2.14. Do each step of the art criticism process—description, analysis, interpretation, and judgment—for this work of art.

If you look in the back of the book for the "correct answers" to art criticism questions, you will be disappointed. There are no correct answers. You must make the judgments and offer support for them. In that way you will participate in art criticism just as you will participate in drawing. Actively participating in art criticism will help you develop both your aesthetic judgment and your drawing skills.

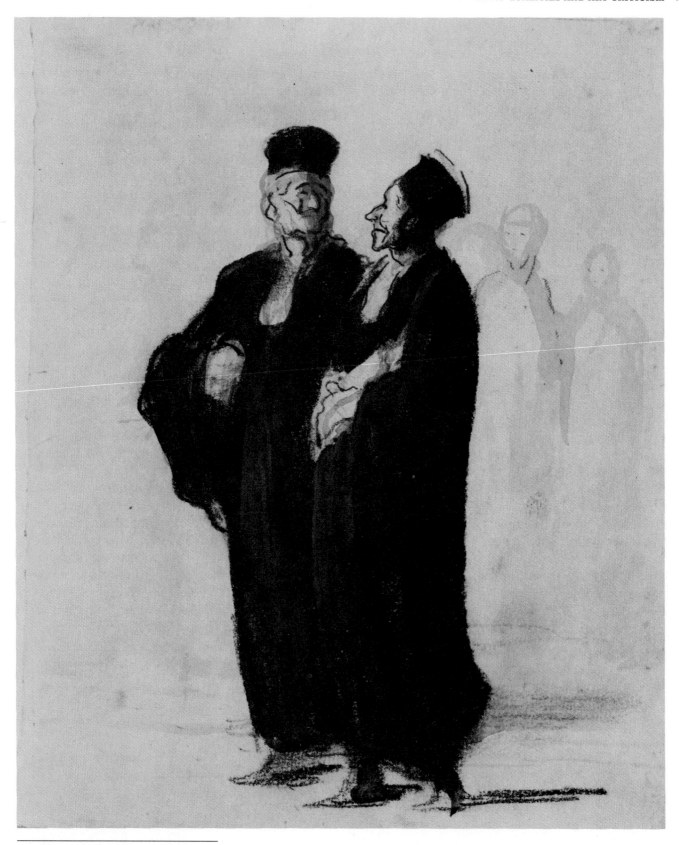

FIGURE 2.14 Honoré Daumier, *Two Law-yers*, 19th century. Charcoal and gray wash on laid paper, 9⁷/₁₆ × 7⁵/₈″ (24.0 × 19.3 cm). National Gallery of Art, Washington, DC. Chester Dale Collection.

DRAWING AT WORK

Art Teacher: Practicing What She Teaches

Secondary art teachers present a variety of topics. From art appreciation . . . to art history . . . to specific techniques, junior high and high school art teachers provide instruction and inspiration to students with wide ranges of artistic ability.

Sandy Archey has been an art teacher for fifteen years. She presently works in both junior and senior high classrooms in a small, rural Illinois school district. She especially enjoys providing creative outlets for her students because the small-town high school she attended didn't offer art classes.

Art has always been part of Archey's life. She and her twin sister, Sunny, were influenced by their artistic father. Both girls attended an adult art class while still in grade school. Later, in a high school without an art department, Archey found an artistic outlet by taking a class in shorthand and making her characters as decorative as possible.

During her junior year in high school, Archey entered an art competition sponsored by the local women's club. Her still life done in pencil won her a scholarship to a week-long art camp, which was at that time held at Allerton Park in Monticello, Illinois. That week at camp helped her decide to pursue a career in art. Both she and her sister graduated from Eastern Illinois University, Charleston, Illinois, with degrees in art education.

Archey uses a variety of approaches to teach drawing at the secondary level. As an introduction to drawing in junior high, Archey teaches a unit on Indian art. The students create bark paintings and ceremonial masks. She helps her students think about drawing in new ways by having them make thick and thin lines with sharpened sticks dipped in ink.

Another early unit in drawing teaches students how to use grids to transfer photographs into drawings. The grid is placed over the photograph, and the students use reference points to draw the picture freehand. This technique almost guarantees success for even the most inexperienced young artist. Later, the grid technique is used to show how drawings may be enlarged by doubling the size of the squares on the students' drawings. Students also receive instruction in figure drawing and perspective drawing using a variety of examples selected to fit individual students' abilities.

In addition to teaching art, Archey displays her own artistic efforts. Every month she designs, draws, and paints seasonal scenes that decorate the entrance to a stationery store. The bright and colorful pictures appear in four large, second-story window panels (48 × 84″) that can be seen for many blocks. Archey chooses the scenes to draw and coordinates the pictures with holidays to promote greeting card sales.

Archey enjoys drawing and painting, but teaching is her first love. She finds the best part of her job is working with young people. Sometimes students who haven't succeeded in other subject areas discover that they have artistic talent. Many take pride in their work for the first time and show their art projects to friends and relatives. Archey's greatest satisfaction is seeing this pride and self-esteem develop in her students.

CHAPTER THREE

Drawings and the History of Art

After reading this chapter and doing the activities, you will be able to

■ give reasons for studying art history;

■ explain how the study of art can help you create and improve your own drawings;

■ name and describe several different styles and periods of art;

■ identify characteristics of certain art styles and periods in drawings;

■ match individual artists and their works to the proper artistic period or style;

■ discuss the development of artistic styles as they relate to historical events and situations; and

■ discuss similarities and differences among works of art done in different historical periods or artistic styles.

In Chapter 2 you learned about three theories of art, each proposed by an imaginary art critic. You discovered that a drawing can be successful because of

■ literal qualities (it represents subject matter in a lifelike way),

■ visual qualities (it uses the elements and principles of art skillfully), or

■ expressive qualities (it communicates a feeling, mood, or idea to the viewers).

You also learned a process—the art criticism operations—for identifying these different aesthetic qualities in a drawing. You practiced the description, analysis, interpretation, and judgment steps by critiquing several drawings, and you learned a great deal from studying the artworks themselves.

But maybe you noticed that you haven't learned anything about the artists who created the drawings, or the drawings' context—how, when, or where they were made. You still have many unanswered questions, such as:

■ Who was Ingres, the artist who drew the lifelike portrait of the French count (Figure 2.4)? When and where did he live?

■ What circumstances caused Käthe Kollwitz to create the sad self-portrait in Figure 2.6?

■ What did Daumier (Figure 2.13) contribute to the development of drawing?

Questions like these are unavoidable after you have critically studied drawings and made judgments about them. Your curiosity is aroused, and you want to learn more about the artists who drew these works. Often, too, you want to compare your ideas with the ideas of people who have a greater knowledge and understanding of art than you do. But how do you get this information? How do you get answers to the questions that remain after the art criticism process is finished? The answer is *art history*.

WHY YOU SHOULD STUDY ART HISTORY

Often art criticism and art history are thought of as only vaguely related subjects. To understand one, however, you also need to understand the other. Both of these subjects concentrate on works of art, but they use different points of view. They often use the same processes, but gather different kinds of information.

Critics describe, analyze, and interpret information from a work of art before they decide if it is successful art (Figure 3.1). Historians may also describe, analyze, and interpret. But the information that concerns them is different (Figure 3.2). They try to find out who made the artwork, when and where the artist lived, and how the artist's personal style developed. Historians judge artists and their works by deciding how much they have influenced art history.

Students who want to expand their knowledge, understanding, and awareness of drawings must recognize the value of both art criticism and art history. They must learn to use both approaches. To ignore either one is like trying to ride a bicycle with one wheel missing—you aren't likely to go anywhere.

Students are usually eager to try art criticism. Perhaps they feel that it doesn't require the special knowledge associated with art history. Once they know what to look for (literal, visual, and expressive qualities) and how to look for it (the art criticism operations), they can immediately begin critiquing works of art. Art criticism also gives students the chance to become personally involved with a work of art. Students don't need an expert or an authority to help them decide how successful the art is.

To use the art history approach, however, students have to go beyond the artwork itself. They need to use the findings of art history scholars. From their discoveries, they get information about works of art and the artists who created them.

Some students may try to avoid art history because they think it doesn't have anything to do with developing their drawing skills. Art history, however, can offer valuable lessons to students who want to learn more about the process of drawing.

Learning about art history lets you take advantage of what other artists have discovered. Maybe you need ideas for subject matter for a drawing or for ways to show the subject matter you have selected. Maybe you need help in deciding how to use certain elements and principles of art to put an idea into visual form. Or maybe you would like to see what drawing media and techniques other artists have used to convey certain emotions.

Being familiar with the history of drawing can help you identify other artists who have already solved these problems. For example, a knowledge of art history would remind you that Daumier used subject matter to draw attention to problems in society. Ingres was a master of using line to create sensitive portraits. You could study Kollwitz's techniques for expressing emotions. The ideas and techniques of other artists can help you create more successful drawings, and knowledge of art history is the key to discovering these ideas and techniques.

The chronological outline on the following pages will help you study the history of drawing in Western art. Included with the outline are examples of drawings produced during different historical periods. The captions accompanying these drawings contain art criticism and art history questions to help you understand them. Study the outline and answer the questions about the artworks from each period. Doing this will help you learn how art history builds from one year, one decade, and one century to the next. As you become familiar with this outline, you will be better prepared to understand the historical context of drawings you encounter and create.

ART CRITICISM OPERATIONS	
Internal Clues	
Description	What is in the work, discovered through an inventory of the *subject matter* and/or *elements of art* found in the work.
Analysis	How the work of art is *organized* or put togther; concern centers on how principles of art have been used to arrange the elements of art.
Interpretation	Possible *feeling*, *moods*, and *ideas* communicated by the work of art.
Judgment	Facts relevant to making a *decision* about the degree of artistic merit in the work of art

FIGURE 3.1 Chart of art criticism operations.

ART HISTORY OPERATIONS	
External Clues	
Description	*When, where,* and by *whom* the work was done.
Analysis	Unique features of the work of art, compared to features found in other works, to determine its artistic *style*.
Interpretation	How artists are influenced by the world around them, especially by *time* and *place*.
Judgment	Facts relevant to making a *decision* about the work's importance in the history of art.

FIGURE 3.2 Chart of art history operations.

PREHISTORIC ART

Deep inside the caves of southern France and northern Spain are many drawings and paintings of animals. They are so well preserved and skillfully done that they have caused endless debate among scholars. Is it possible that prehistoric cave dwellers, working with the crudest instruments, could have produced such works of art (Figure 3.3)? Maybe they were produced by skilled artists as a fraud. On the other hand, if they are truly the work of prehistoric artists, why were they made and how did they survive?

Most scholars today agree that the works of art discovered at Lascaux, France, and Altamira, Spain, are the work of prehistoric artists. It is unlikely, however, that they represent humankind's first efforts in art. These works are too sophisticated for that. There must have been hundreds, perhaps thousands of years of slow artistic development before these works were created, even though we know nothing about it.

These drawings and paintings of bison, deer, boar, and other animals were done deep inside caves, far from living quarters at the mouths of the caves. They must have been used in some kind of magic ritual. Since our early ancestors depended on these animals for their survival, they probably had these ceremonies to bring them luck in hunting. Maybe prehistoric people thought that they were capturing the strength of these animals by making pictures of them. They may have thought that making these pictures would weaken the animals and make it easier to hunt them successfully.

Since the pictures were done far back in caves, they were well protected from wind and rain. These prehistoric works of art have survived to show us early man's powers of observation, artistic skill, and aesthetic sensitivity.

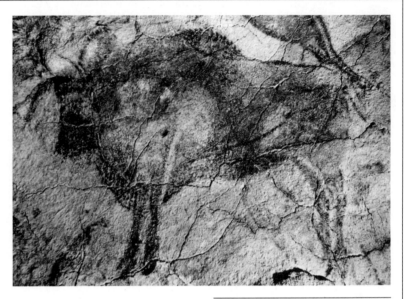

FIGURE 3.3 Standing bison, Altamira caves, near Santilla, Spain, c. 15,000–10,000 B.C.

Would you describe this work as lifelike? Can you identify the main features of the animal? What caused the controversy among scholars when works like this were discovered? Who is now given credit for creating these paintings? Why were they done? Why is it thought that these works don't represent humanity's first efforts at art? Do you agree with this point of view? Why or why not?

2686 B.C. to 332 B.C.

ANCIENT EGYPTIAN ART

Egyptian culture was based on a complex religion. Egyptians believed that the spirit came back to life after death. They thought that the spirit, or *Ka*, needed a body in which to live when it began a new life in the next world. They built elaborate tombs, the great pyramids, for the most important people in Egyptian society, the Pharaohs. These tombs were intended to protect the mummified bodies of the Pharaohs, who were thought of as both rulers and gods.

Even though the tombs were well guarded, they were often robbed and the bodies were damaged or destroyed. To make sure that the spirits would have bodies to live in, artists were employed to create substitutes—sculptures, drawings, and paintings—for bodies. The Egyptians thought that if a Pharaoh's body were destroyed, his spirit could live inside the carved, drawn, or painted substitute.

Since a drawing of a person was to take the place of that person's body, artists had to follow certain rules. Every part of the figure had to be pictured. Each had to be shown from the most familiar point of view. If an arm or a leg were hidden behind the rest of the figure, the Ka would have to live in an incomplete body.

For this reason, ancient Egyptian figure drawings combined front and side views. The head was always shown in profile, but the eyes were drawn as if seen from the front. The shoulders were also presented as if seen from the front. The legs and feet were shown from the side (Figure 3.4). Even though Egyptian artists had to follow these strict rules, they still made drawings that are visually appealing.

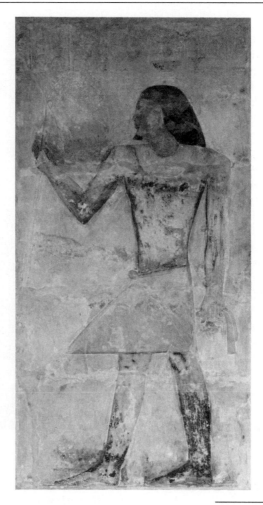

FIGURE 3.4 Egyptian, Old Kingdom, late V to early VI dynasty, *Relief from Ankh-Ni-Neswt's Tomb Chapel,* c. 2600–2500 B.C. Limestone, painted, 63 × 33″ (160 × 84 cm). Honolulu Academy of Arts, Honolulu, HI. Gift of Mrs. Charles M. Cooke.

Describe this figure. Does he appear to be an important person? If so, what makes you think so? Who was the Pharoah? Why was it necessary to build an elaborate tomb for the Pharoah? Why did ancient Egyptians create substitutes for the body after a person's death? Describe the rules that artists were required to follow when creating these substitutes for the body. Why were these rules imposed? Does this work follow these rules?

ANCIENT GREEK ART

Most of what we know about Greek drawing and painting has been pieced together from ancient writers' descriptions. Many Greek painters, however, were even more famous in their time than the Greek sculptors whose works are better known to us today.

Ancient writers tell us that a Greek painter's skill was measured by the literal qualities evident in his or her work. The more realistic the work, the more admired the artist was. Sculptors also tried to make their work look as lifelike as possible. We can show how successful the sculptors were by a story. A Greek citizen was asked why there were so few examples of Greek sculpture. He immediately answered that Greek sculptures were made to look so lifelike that as soon as the artists finished them, they jumped from their pedestals and ran away.

We can get some idea of what Greek painting and drawing may have looked like by looking at ancient Greek vases. As drawing developed, the figures on these vases became more and more lifelike and often told some kind of story (Figure 3.5). Greek artists were interested in good design, also. They drew their figures to fill the available space in a decorative, visually appealing way. The figures show accurate proportions, movement, and emotions that are never found in Egyptian art.

Besides being interested in visual accuracy and good design, Greek artists searched for the perfect combination of parts to make an ideal whole. Zeuxis, for example, was a Greek artist who tried to find a woman beautiful enough to be his model for a portrait of Helen of Troy. He finally selected five Athenian maidens with specific ideal features and combined these features in his painting.

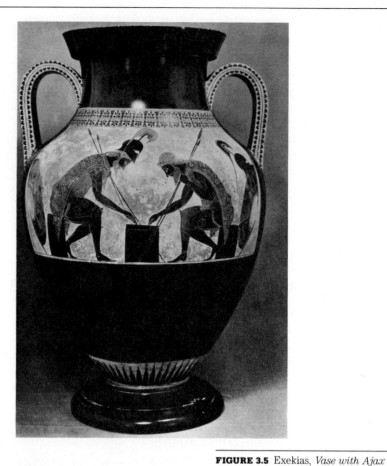

FIGURE 3.5 Exekias, *Vase with Ajax and Achilles Playing Draughts*, c. 540 B.C. Ceramic vase. Vatican Museums, Rome.

How many figures can you identify? How are they dressed? Describe the actions of the two figures. Are the lines in this composition used to achieve variety or harmony? How is value used to emphasize the figures? Is this an example of symmetrical or asymmetrical balance? How does the design of the painted composition complement the shape of the vase on which it is placed? What is happening in the scene? Is this a successful work of art? What aesthetic qualities would you point out to defend your judgment?

ANCIENT ROMAN ART

The Romans greatly admired and imitated Greek art, philosophy, literature, and science, but made few original contributions of their own. They were practical and were more interested in learning about architecture, engineering, law, and government. Roman artists are important to the history of art, however, because they preserved the Greek heritage and spread it throughout their empire.

Roman engineers used slave and army labor to construct over fifty thousand miles of roads, a feat that Europeans didn't match until the nineteenth century. This vast network of roads linked distant provinces and made possible the spread of Greek culture from Britain to India.

The Romans apparently didn't like to hang drawings and paintings on walls. Instead, they liked to paint and draw pictures directly on their walls. These murals (Figure 3.6) have several features that we find in the works of Italian Renaissance artists (pages 41–43).

For example, Roman artists used architectural forms to suggest both space and atmosphere. They had no exact knowledge of linear perspective, which was discovered and perfected by Renaissance artists. But Roman artists' sensitivity to aerial perspective was well developed. They also put figures in dreamy, imaginative landscapes that had either religious or secular themes.

What do you see in this picture? Are you able to identify any figures? List what you believe are the most important elements of art in this work. How is the illusion of space achieved? How does this work make you feel—happy, sad, or lonely? What contributes to that feeling? Is this a successful work of art? Why or why not?

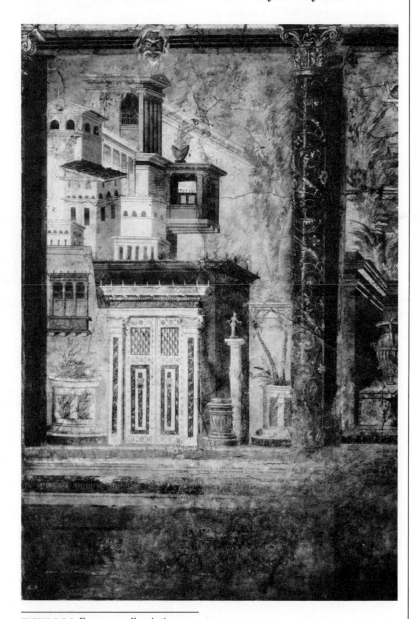

FIGURE 3.6 Roman, wall painting from Villa at Boscoreale (panel X from the Cubiculum), c. 50 B.C. Fresco. The Metropolitan Museum of Art, New York, NY. Rogers Fund.

476 to About 1050 ▷▷▷

EARLY MEDIEVAL ART

After the fall of the Roman Empire, the only stable organization left in western Europe was the church. Its influence was felt everywhere, and it gave the medieval period its special character.

The church saw that art could be used to inspire and teach its followers. Since most people couldn't read, they had to rely on visual images.

A limited number of handwritten books were produced for those few who could read, but the illustrations drawn and painted in these books were intended for the majority of people who couldn't read. The carvings on the facade or front of medieval churches also expressed religious teachings.

The task of teaching and spreading the faith belonged to monks. They were dedicated men living together under a strict set of rules in religious communities called *monasteries*. Besides being teachers and priests, these monks were among the leading artists and craftspersons of the period.

Among the tasks undertaken by monks was the production of religious books. There were no printing presses during the medieval period, so all books had to be copied painstakingly by hand. Monks who did this copying were often artists of great skill. They took pride in making beautifully proportioned letters and adding graceful miniature drawings.

The illustrated manuscript, or book (Figure 3.7), was the most important form of painting in western Europe from the fall of Rome around 476 until the fourteenth and fifteenth centuries, when easel painting and the printing press were developed. The drawings and paintings in these books may seem awkward and even crude to viewers who don't realize the depth and intensity of the artists' religious feelings. The monks sacrificed accuracy to express as clearly as possible their deepest religious beliefs.

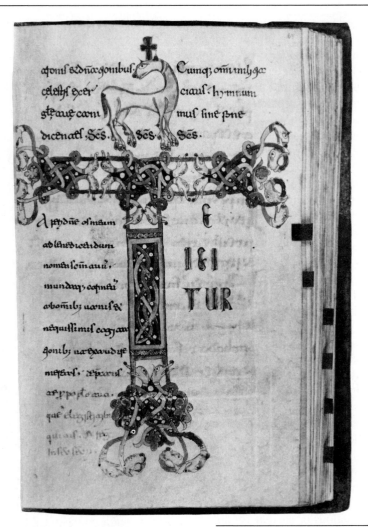

Who was responsible for the production of religious manuscripts? Why are the manuscripts considered to be so important today? If you were asked to describe this work, which two elements of art would you be certain to mention? What was the most important objective for the artists who created manuscript illustrations—the expression of physical beauty, a lifelike appearance, or the expression of religious feelings?

FIGURE 3.7 Southeastern Italy, *The Lamb of God Atop the Letter "T" of the "Te igitur,"* first half of the 11th century. Walters Art Gallery, Baltimore, MD.

ROMANESQUE ART

Miniature drawing and painting in religious manuscripts started in early Christian times and became more popular during the early medieval period. It continued to be an important artistic activity thoughout western Europe during the Romanesque period. The art of the early medieval period had been local, rarely reaching beyond the surrounding community. Romanesque art, however, gradually became more international in character. This international character resulted from the exchange of ideas due to the growth in trade and travel during the eleventh and twelfth centuries.

Romanesque paintings and drawings have a flat, two-dimensional look. Their brightly colored and richly patterned figures and objects look like they were cut from cardboard and laid one on top of the other. Romanesque artists made little effort to make their pictures look realistic. Instead, they used colorful shapes and dark lines to illustrate traditional religious stories.

A glance at one of these illustrations quickly brought the story to the viewer's mind. Then the viewer could meditate on the meaning of that story. For example, an illustration from a German prayer book (Figure 3.8) tells the New Testament story of the Annunciation. An angel informs Mary that she will be the mother of the Savior. The angel's right hand is raised to show that he is speaking. Mary turns toward him with open hands. This gesture suggests her willngness to accept the responsibility suddenly thrust on her.

The figures appear still and motionless; neither shows any sign of emotion. The viewer is left to imagine what is going on in Mary's mind at that moment. Clearly this illustration isn't a detailed, realistic drawing. Rather it is an uncluttered arrangement of familiar sacred symbols. Its purpose was to illustrate the story of the Annunciation heard over and over in medieval churches.

Describe the two figures in this manuscript illustration. Which of these figures appears to be speaking? How do you know this? What is the other figure doing? Who do you think these people are? What is happening here? Is there a sense of space in this composition? Which aesthetic qualities do you think are more important when examining this work—the literal qualities or the expressive qualities? Why?

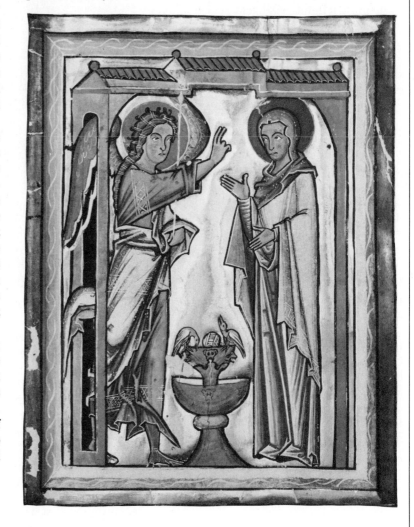

FIGURE 3.8 German, leaf of a breviary or missal, *Annunciation*, c. 12th century. Colors and gold leaf on vellum, 6 × 4¾″ (15.2 × 12.1 cm). The Metropolitan Museum of Art, New York, NY. Fletcher Fund.

1150 to About 1500

GOTHIC ART

At no other period in history were the visual arts so closely joined in a common effort than in the Gothic period. Drawing, painting, sculpture, and architecture were combined to create the Gothic cathedral or church, which featured pointed arches and weight-bearing pillars. Walls were only required to enclose and define space, so artists and craftspersons began designing walls made of stained glass.

The designs used for stained glass windows greatly influenced the style of drawing and painting used in manuscript illustrations. Gothic manuscript illustrations often showed slender, graceful religious figures in flowing costumes placed inside frames like those of cathedral windows. Solid gold backgrounds were used to emphasize the spiritual importance of the scenes.

Tempera paintings on wooden panels used similar designs to decorate the altars inside churches. This elegant style of painting became so popular throughout western Europe that it came to be known as the *Gothic International style.*

Because the Gothic style of architecture didn't spread to Italy until later, Italian artists could still paint religious pictures on interior church walls. First, the artist made a charcoal drawing on the wall. Then a thin coat of plaster was applied, and the charcoal lines were traced. Paint mixed with water and egg whites was applied. This process gave the painting technique its name, *fresco.* The paint and wet plaster mixed together to form a permanent surface when they dried.

The painting had to be done quickly while the plaster was still wet. The technique required confidence, boldness, and skill. One extraordinary artist, Giotto di Bondone, had all of these traits. Giotto's concern for realism shaped the course of art history for centuries. In his *Madonna and Child* (Figure 3.9), Giotto captured the love between mother and son.

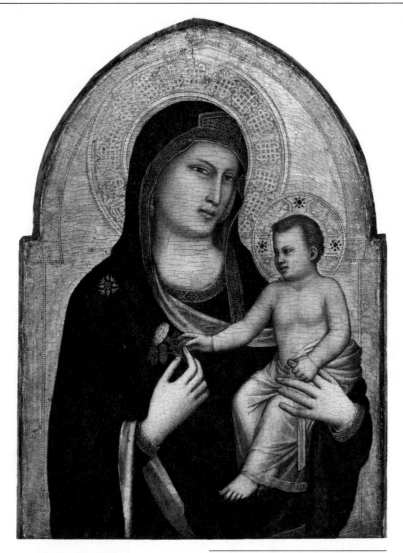

FIGURE 3.9 Giotto, *Madonna and Child*, c. 1320–30. Wood, 33⅝ × 24⅜″ (85.5 × 62.0 cm). National Gallery of Art, Washington, DC. Samuel H. Kress Collection.

Do these figures look realistic to you? How do they differ from the figures in Figure 3.8? Would you describe these figures as round and solid, or flat and thin? How has the artist expressed the love between these two figures? Do you think this is a successful work of art? Did your decision take into account the historical importance of this artist?

1400 to 1520 ▷▷▷

THE ART OF THE RENAISSANCE IN ITALY

During the medieval period, people were mainly concerned with living in a way that would assure their eternal reward in the next world. Gradually people became more interested in the present world and their place in it. This change of attitude, the period in which it occurred, and the ways in which it was demonstrated in art, literature, and learning are called the *Renaissance*.

The Renaissance began in Italy during the fourteenth century and reached its peak in the fifteenth and early sixteenth centuries. One reason it began in Italy was that the tradition of classical art and culture was never entirely lost in this country.

Studying the classics encouraged artists to look for subject matter outside of religion. It also made realism more important. In drawing and painting, artists developed rules of perspective and the science of using light and dark values to obtain amazingly realistic effects. Artists also studied anatomy to try to make their drawings of figures look more lifelike.

Up to the Renaissance, the history of art is mainly the history of styles and ideas to which many unknown artists contributed. But after the fifteenth century, the history of art deals mainly with the lives and accomplishments of individual artists. Leonardo, Michelangelo, and Raphael were three artists who made up the most astonishing trio of geniuses who ever lived at the same time in the same place.

Leonardo da Vinci wanted to learn everything possible about a subject before trying to recreate it in art. This effort, however, took up so much of his time that the amount of art he finished is rather small.

The human body was just one of Leonardo's many interests. He estimated that he filled 120 notebooks with his figure drawings (Figure 3.10). These drawings were surrounded by explanations and reminders to himself about other subjects that interested him.

(continued on next page)

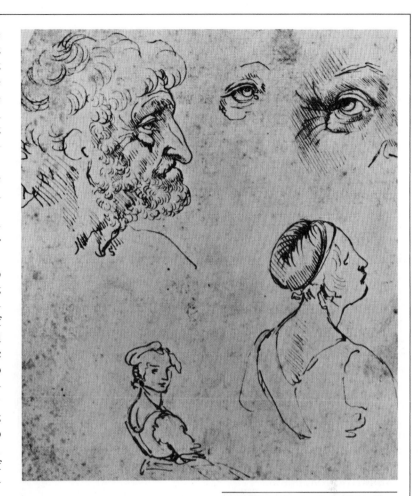

FIGURE 3.10 Leonardo da Vinci, *Figure Studies*, c. 1470–80. Pen and brown ink over traces of black chalk, 6.5 × 5.4″ (16.4 × 13.8 cm). The Armand Hammer Collection, Los Angeles, CA.

Why did the Renaissance begin in Italy? What new techniques were developed at that time to make works of art appear more lifelike? Why was Leonardo's artistic output so small? Did he create many drawings? What does this tell you about the importance he placed on drawing?

THE ART OF THE RENAISSANCE IN ITALY

Michelangelo is known for his painting and sculpture, but he depended on drawing skills to design his works. Imagine that you meet him at the foot of a huge scaffold in the Sistine Chapel over five hundred years ago . . .

The artist peers upward at the dim corner of the ceiling 68′ (20 m) above where he will paint a twisting female figure. He reaches for his sketch paper and a piece of red chalk and begins to draw.

Then he returns to his small studio. Michelangelo takes out a fresh sheet of paper and begins to draw a model, concentrating on the model's feet, hand, and torso. All of these drawings are crowded onto a single sheet (Figure 3.11). All of the available space is used because paper is expensive.

The artist has been drawing a male model, since female models weren't used in the sixteenth century. So Michelangelo makes another drawing at the bottom corner of the paper, changing the face of the figure to look more like a woman's.

Michelangelo is tired. It seems as if the Sistine Chapel ceiling will never be finished. He has food sent up to him on the scaffold, so he doesn't have to stop work. He leaves the scaffold for a few hours of sleep only when he is too weary to continue.

Painting the ceiling seems like a waste of effort. The walls in the chapel are already decorated with great works by well-known artists. Who will bother to stop admiring these paintings and look up at the ceiling?

Unexpectedly the artist reaches for a pen and begins to write, perhaps to express some of his frustration and disappointment.

"When will the nightmare be over?
My chin is growing into my stomach,
My beard has become part of my arm,
My face is a mosaic of color,
Now I drink and breathe only paint.
My body is twisted backward in a circle,
and my sanity is completely gone.
I hate this place.
Why am I here? I'm not even a painter!"

(continued on next page)

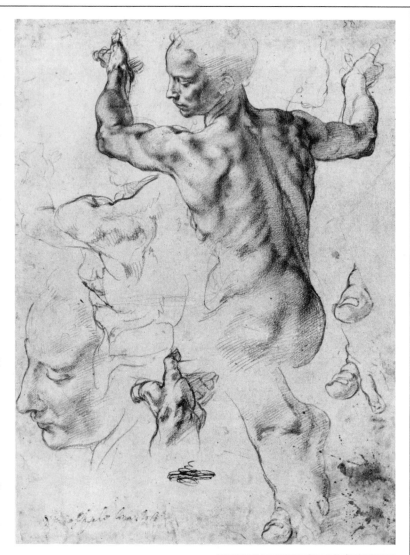

FIGURE 3.11 Michelangelo, *Studies for the Libyan Sibyl*, c. 1511. Red chalk, 11⅜ × 8⅜″ (28.9 × 21.3 cm). The Metropolitan Museum of Art, New York, NY. Joseph Pulitzer bequest.

Why have so few drawings by Michelangelo survived to the present time? Why were drawings like this done? What do these drawings tell you about the artist? Do you think drawings like this should be regarded as successful works of art? Why or why not?

1400 to 1520

THE ART OF THE RENAISSANCE IN ITALY

The next day Michelangelo would begin drawing and painting the new figure on the ceiling. It would be one of 342 figures he created on the chapel's ceiling. The task demanded all of his waking hours for four years. But as an eyewitness later reported, when the artist was finally finished and the Sistine Chapel was opened to the public, the whole world rushed to Rome to stare in wonder at the ceiling.

Michelangelo wanted to keep his creative process a secret. He gathered up and burned as many of his sketches as he could before he died. Only a few survived. One of these is shown in Figure 3.11.

Twenty-two years after painting its ceiling, Michelangelo Buonarroti returned to the Sistine Chapel to paint his version of *The Last Judgment* on the altar wall. Like the figures he designed earlier for the ceiling, the figures in the painting were carefully planned in detailed drawings. When he was finished with the huge fresco, he signed it simply *Michelangelo, Sculptor*.

Raphael Sanzio didn't invent new techniques, as Leonardo and Michelangelo did, but he was able to perfect their techniques to create what is referred to as the *High Renaissance style*. His figures skillfully blended Michelangelo's sense of movement and full, well-rounded forms, and Leonardo's soft modeling with light and dark values. But even though he borrowed freely from these and other artists, Raphael maintained his own identity by adding his own charm and grace. These qualities are especially apparent in a drawing he made of the Madonna and Child with the infant St. John (Figure 3.12).

Describe the figures in this drawing. What is each of these figures doing? Is the artist successful in suggesting three-dimensional form in this drawing? If so, what combination of element and principle is used to accomplish this? Would you describe these people as happy, sad, thoughtful, bored, or angry? Is there anything about this drawing that reminds you of Leonardo (Figure 3.10) and Michelangelo (Figure 3.11)? Is this a successful work of art? What aesthetic qualities—literal, visual, or expressive—would you note in defending your decision?

FIGURE 3.12 Raphael, *Madonna and Child with the Infant St. John the Baptist*, c. early 1500s. Red chalk, $8^{13}/_{16} \times 6^{1}/_{4}''$ (22.4 × 15.9 cm). The Metropolitan Museum of Art, New York, NY. Rogers Fund.

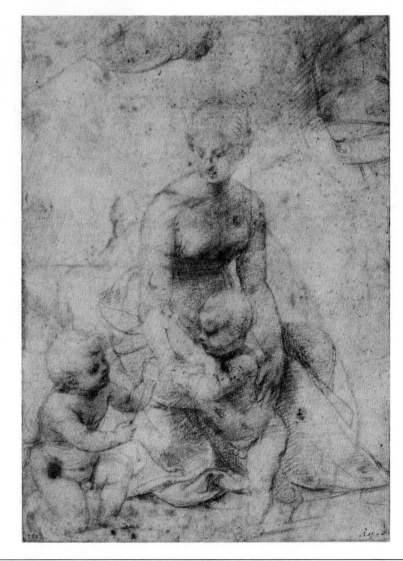

THE ART OF THE RENAISSANCE IN NORTHERN EUROPE

The art produced in the countries north of Italy during the fifteenth century followed the traditions of the late medieval period. Northern European artists showed little interest in the art of ancient Greece and Rome. Instead, they kept on developing the Gothic International style by making it more realistic.

The northern European artists could add more details to their works because a new oil painting technique was developed at this time. Oil paints consisted of dry pigments, oils, and sometimes varnish, making the drying time for oil paintings longer than for fresco paintings. Oil paints gave artists the opportunity to work at a more leisurely pace.

Jan van Eyck is often credited with developing this new oil painting technique. Using the Gothic International style as a starting point, van Eyck created a new painting tradition, showing scenes as they actually looked. He was a master at suggesting atmosphere through subtle gradations of light.

His paintings showed every detail. In his picture of *The Annunciation* (Figure 3.13), every strand of hair appears to be painted individually with a fine brush or a quill pen.

Rogier van der Weyden was van Eyck's great contemporary, but added some new ideas of his own to van Eyck's style. A popular artist during his lifetime, van der Weyden was especially admired for his strong designs and elegant figures. His works were also noted for their refined, dignified emotionalism.

The new styles of Jan van Eyck and Rogier van der Weyden became less important by the end of the fifteenth century because of the effects of the Italian Renaissance. Italian influences were introduced into the drawings and paintings of northern Europe. This strange mixture continued into the sixteenth century, when it finally evolved into a style called *Mannerism*.

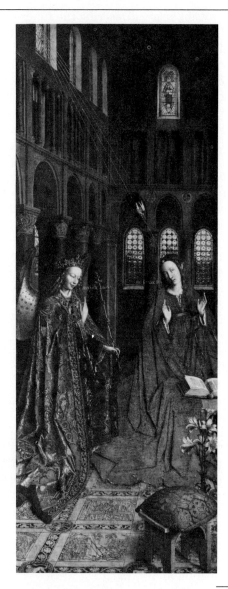

FIGURE 3.13 Jan van Eyck, *The Annunciation*, c. 1434–36. Oil on wood transferred to canvas, 36½ × 14⁷/₁₆″ (92.7 × 36.7 cm). National Gallery of Art, Washington, DC. Andrew W. Mellon Collection.

List everything you see in this work. What makes this work seem so realistic? What new painting technique enabled this artist to include so much detail in his work? How did this technique differ from the fresco technique? What perspective technique did the artist use to suggest space in this composition?

1520 to 1600

THE ART OF THE SIXTEENTH CENTURY IN ITALY, SPAIN, AND GERMANY

The artists of the island city of Venice combined the lights and colors reflected in surrounding waters with a Renaissance concern for reality. Their style was noted for its brilliant use of color, light, and texture; its swirling, full-bodied figures; and its dream-like atmosphere.

The first of the great Venetian artists was Giorgione. Although only a few of his pictures still exist, he is regarded as one of the greatest painters in history. His work changed the way people thought about paintings because his paintings weren't just drawings filled in with color. He put areas of color next to each other without using many lines.

When Giorgione died, Titian became the most important Venetian painter. From Giorgione, Titian learned how to use **landscape** to create moods. Landscapes are works of art that use natural scenery as subject matter. Although he drew and painted every subject you can imagine, Titian was most famous for his skillful portraits of kings, popes, philosophers, and military leaders.

The last great Venetian artist of the sixteenth century was Tintoretto. Tintoretto's figure drawings (Figure 3.14) used the same full-bodied form and sense of movement in space as those by Michelangelo.

In his paintings, Tintoretto emphasized the emotional aspects of a story rather than illustrating it accurately. His highly unique painting style used contrasting light and dark values to suggest a flickering movement. He stretched out the proportions of figures and often showed them making exaggerated, theatrical gestures.

The church welcomed this style of dramatic painting because it was experiencing disorder and change. Martin Luther had started the Protestant Reformation in 1517. Many people were leaving the church. Its leaders valued the art of Tintoretto and others because it appealed to the emotions of the people, reminding them that the church was still there to help them find salvation. This

(continued on next page)

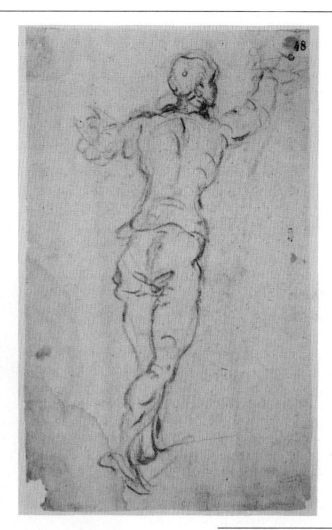

FIGURE 3.14 Jacopo Tintoretto, *Standing Youth With His Arm Raised, Seen From Behind*, date unknown. Black chalk on laid paper, 14¼ × 8⅝″ (36.3 x 21.9 cm). National Gallery of Art, Washington, DC. Ailsa Mellon Bruce Fund.

Does this figure seem to be still or in motion? How would you describe the line used in this drawing? Point to places where the line seems to be darker and more clearly defined. Do the same for lines that appear to be more sketchy and lighter in value. How do these differences in line quality add to the illusion of movement? Name some possible activities this figure might be performing.

1520 to 1600

THE ART OF THE SIXTEENTH CENTURY IN ITALY, SPAIN, AND GERMANY

emotionally charged art later came to be known as *Mannerist* art.

The most striking Mannerist painter lived in Spain. His name was Domenico Theotocopoulos. Since most people had difficulty pronouncing his name, he came to be known simply as *The Greek* or *El Greco*.

El Greco arrived in Spain from the Greek island of Crete after having spent a number of years in Venice and Rome. El Greco settled in Toledo, Spain, where he spent the rest of his life.

Other Spanish artists were still concerned with representing reality. El Greco, however, was daring enough to express his own inner visions. All of his figures, even in his portraits, were creatures formed by his unique imagination.

El Greco's unfinished painting of St. Jerome (Figure 3.15) illustrates his methods. The figure of the saint was drawn with bold, dark contour lines. The figure was deliberately distorted to suggest the godlike grace of saints. El Greco didn't intend his St. Jerome to look real; he meant him to look supernatural.

Albrecht Dürer was the only German artist of his time to use all the ideas of the Italian Renaissance in his work. In 1494 he returned to his native Germany from a trip to Italy determined to draw and paint in the new Renaissance style. He studied perspective and anatomy and then applied what he had learned to his art (Figures 7.5 and 7.6).

Other German artists, however, weren't as willing as Dürer to accept the new Renaissance ideas from the South. Matthias Grünewald, for example, chose to use Renaissance techniques only to increase the emotional impact of traditional Gothic subjects such as the Crucifixion.

How did El Greco differ from other Spanish artists of this period? Why did he use distortion when drawing and painting figures? What name is applied to the style of art practiced by sixteenth-century artists such as Tintoretto (Figure 3.14) and El Greco? Why was this style valued by the church? In judging this work, would you be inclined to place more value on the literal qualities or the expressive qualities?

FIGURE 3.15 El Greco, *Saint Jerome*, c. 1610–14. Oil on canvas, approx. 5′6″ × 3′7″ (1.68 × 1.11 m). National Gallery of Art, Washington, DC. Chester Dale Collection.

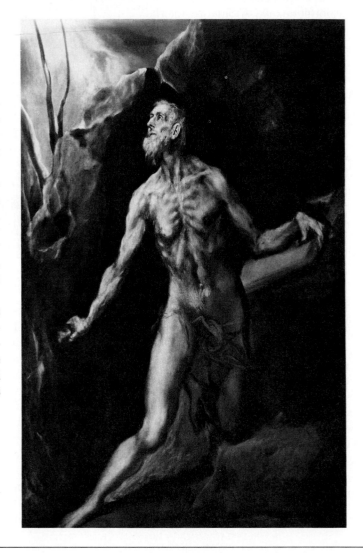

THE ART OF THE SEVENTEENTH CENTURY

By the beginning of the seventeenth century, the church had regained much of its influence in Italy and was involved in a large-scale program of building and decoration. A new style of church construction known as *Baroque* featured a sculptured, dynamic look.

The unique character of the Italian Baroque painting style was due largely to the efforts of one man, Caravaggio. Caravaggio was curious about how things actually looked and drew his inspiration from carefully observing things around him. Later, his style changed to include a greater use of a bold, strong light. His figures looked human, not spiritual or supernatural as they did in Mannerist paintings. Caravaggio's style of combining light and realism had an impact on the entire European art world.

Perhaps the only Italian artist of this period worthy of being ranked alongside Caravaggio is the Bolognese painter Annibale Carracci. He shared Michelangelo's belief that artistic perfection could only be achieved through drawing. His later works used a line quality powerful enough to be compared with Michelangelo's. But Carracci could also use a firm, clear, sensitive line to create a scene of great warmth and charm (Figure 3.16).

Peter Paul Rubens was the greatest Flemish painter of the seventeenth century. While still a young man, Rubens spent eight years in Rome. The drawings he created at that time show that he studied classical ruins, the works of Renaissance masters, and the works of leading contemporary artists, including Caravaggio. Rubens's later drawings and paintings were noted for their grandeur and flowing rhythm (Figure 1.6).

Anthony van Dyck, Rubens's greatest follower, gained fame as a portrait painter. His fashionable portraits were noted for their elegance, dignity, and skillful portrayal of rich materials. Besides his famous portraits, van Dyck also made some remarkably fresh landscape studies in watercolor and in ink.

The first great Dutch seventeenth-century artist was Frans Hals. He painted portraits

(continued on next page)

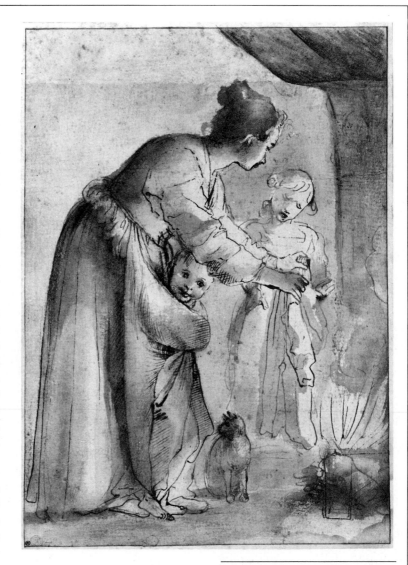

FIGURE 3.16 Annibale Carracci, *A Domestic Scene*, early 1580s. Pen and black ink, gray and brown wash, 11.4 × 9.2″ (29 × 23.3 cm). The Metropolitan Museum of Art, New York, NY. Mrs. Vincent Astor and Mrs. Charles Payson gift. Harris Brisbane Dick Fund and Rogers Fund.

What does the woman in this drawing hold in her hands? Why do you think the child has wrapped himself in his mother's apron? What has the artist done to make these figures look round and solid? Is space suggested in this work? How is this done? Is this an event of great importance?

THE ART OF THE SEVENTEENTH CENTURY

with such dazzling brushwork that he is regarded as one of the most skilled technicians in the history of art.

While other Dutch artists specialized in painting portraits, landscapes, or scenes from everyday life, Rembrandt used every subject. He also painted these subjects with such brilliance that he is recognized as one of the supreme artistic geniuses of all time.

Although he didn't follow the lead of many other Dutch artists who visited Italy, Rembrandt went to art auctions and collected engravings that were modeled on the works of earlier masters. His drawing based on Leonardo's *Last Supper* (Figure 3.17) is one of three he did that were inspired by an engraving. In this drawing, he created an asymmetrical composition by adding a canopy behind and to the left of the seated Christ. The informality of the asymmetrical balance is enhanced by the quickly drawn chalk lines. These lines suggest the meaning of the scene in which Christ has just announced that he will be betrayed.

Little is known about the life of Jan Vermeer, also from the Netherlands, and only a few of his paintings survive. Even so, this painter ranks with Rembrandt and Hals as one of the greatest Dutch artists. Vermeer was skilled in handling detail, color, and light to reproduce the exact appearance of his subject.

Diego Velázquez was one of a group of gifted artists who contributed to Spain's golden age of painting in the seventeenth century. As the court painter for King Philip IV, he used sensitive brush strokes to capture the movement of light on figures.

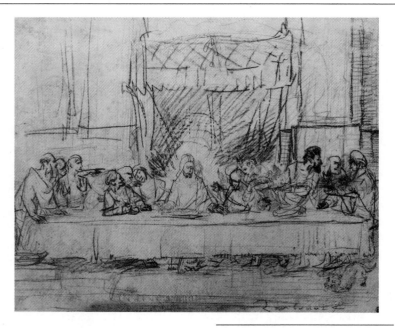

FIGURE 3.17 Rembrandt, sketch after Leonardo's *Last Supper*, c. 1635. Red chalk on paper, 14 × 18¼″ (36.5 × 47.5 cm). The Metropolitan Museum of Art, New York, NY. Robert Lehman Collection.

Would you describe this drawing as highly detailed? Point to the most important figure in this work. What has the artist done to emphasize this figure? Why do you suppose the artist chose not to place this figure under the center of the canopy? Would you refer to this work as formal and dignified, or informal and lifelike?

THE ART OF THE EIGHTEENTH CENTURY

At the beginning of the eighteenth century a new, lighter style of art, inspired by the work of Rubens and the great Venetian masters of the sixteenth century, appeared in northern Europe. This style used a free, graceful movement; a playful application of line; and rich colors. The label attached to this new style is *Rococo.*

Antoine Watteau, a Fleming by birth, developed the Rococo style to its highest level. His drawings and paintings, a haunting combination of grace and sadness, present a make-believe world in which trouble-free young aristocrats pursue pleasure and romance. Watteau valued his drawings more than his paintings because the drawings had qualities that he couldn't render in paint. Often relying on three colors of chalk, he drew figures with a confidence and delicacy often missing from his paintings (Figure 3.18).

The man who continued Watteau's style was Jean-Honoré Fragonard. Fragonard, like Watteau, was a court painter. Fragonard's gay, romantic subjects were well suited to a painting style that featured delicate color and sound drawing (Figure 5.6).

Before the middle of the eighteenth century, the Protestant Reformation had caused hostility to religious art, and not much art was created in England. The artist who was largely responsible for increasing the prestige of English painting was Sir Joshua Reynolds. He was successful in painting the portraits of the aristocracy and became the undisputed leader of his profession.

Thomas Gainsborough was Reynolds's equal as a portrait painter, although Gainsborough maintained that he preferred landscapes. The colors in Gainsborough's paintings sparkle when viewed from a distance. Viewers are surprised when they move closer to discover the sketchiness of his painted surfaces. Gainsborough created this effect by sometimes painting with brushes attached to handles measuring as long as six feet. Using these enabled him to place him-

(continued on next page)

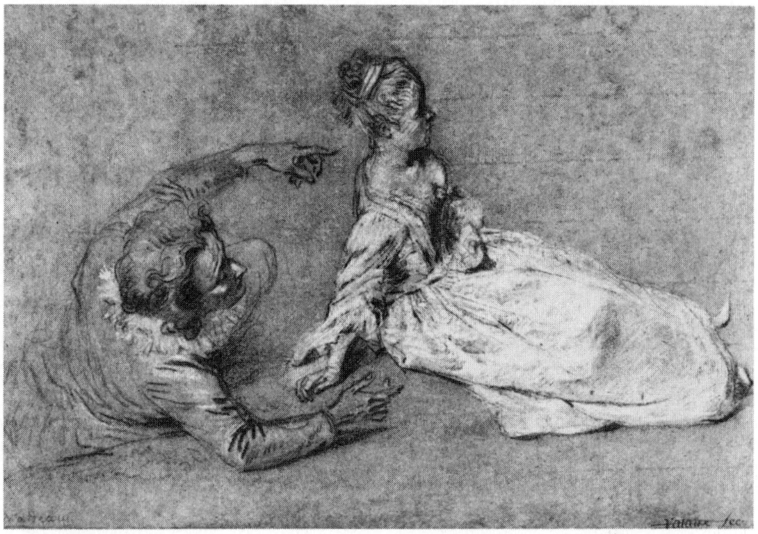

FIGURE 3.18 Antoine Watteau, *Couple Seated on a Bank*, c. 1716. Red, black, and white chalk on buff paper, 9½ × 13¾″ (24.1 × 34.9 cm). The Armand Hammer Collection, Los Angeles, CA.

What is the name of the art style that Watteau is credited with developing? What are the main features of this style? Which earlier artists inspired the development of this new style? In addition to Watteau, name another important artist who followed this style.

1700 to 1800

THE ART OF THE EIGHTEENTH CENTURY

self at the same distance from his model and his canvas.

Another famous eighteenth-century artist was William Hogarth. Many of his paintings were picture stories told in several scenes. They revealed the immoral conditions and foolish customs of his time.

The most significant artist in Spain during this period in history was Francisco Goya. Goya's early works showing the aristocracy at play are similar to Watteau's and Fragonard's paintings done in the Rococo style. But later his style changed dramatically. In a series of etchings entitled *Disasters of War*, Goya recorded the horrors associated with the invasion of Spain by French troops in 1808 under Napoleon (Figure 2.3).

The outstanding Italian artist of the eighteenth century was Giovanni Battista Tiepolo. Constantly commissioned to make paintings, he created ceiling and wall frescoes filled with airborne figures and fleecy clouds. In his studies for these frescoes, he used broad sweeps of light values over the barest suggestion of chalk rendering to suggest three-dimensional forms.

Francesco Guardi, brother-in-law of Tiepolo, is the best-known member in a family of Venetian artists. He is famous for his pictures showing various views of Venice. Guardi's drawings are free and expressive. They suggest rather than describe, hint rather than declare.

Canaletto, another Venetian artist, used canals, churches, bridges, and palaces as subjects. You can see his detached, detailed style in a drawing of a festival (Figure 3.19). As in many of Canaletto's works, the subject is seen from a distance in order to include as much of it as possible. Even though Canaletto didn't communicate much feeling in his work, during his lifetime he was Italy's most popular artist.

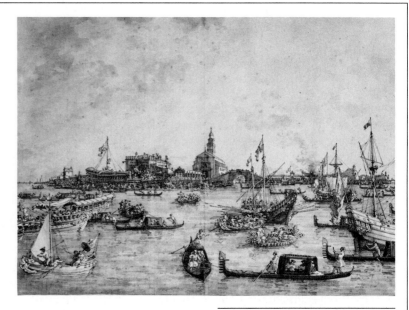

How would you describe this artist's style: spontaneous, precise, or expressive? What advantages are there in drawing a subject at a distance? Do you think the expressive qualities should be an important consideration when evaluating this work? During his lifetime, Canaletto was Italy's most popular artist. Why do you think he was so popular?

FIGURE 3.19 Canaletto, *Ascension Day Festival at Venice*, 1766. Pen and brown ink with gray wash, heightened with white, over graphite on laid paper, 15³⁄₁₆ × 21³⁄₄″ (38.6 × 55.7 cm). National Gallery of Art, Washington, DC. Samuel H. Kress Collection.

1800 to 1850

THE ART OF THE EARLY NINETEENTH CENTURY

The first half of the nineteenth century saw the rise of three successive and important art styles: Neoclassicism, Romanticism, and Realism. Neoclassicism was a reaction to the earlier Baroque and Rococo styles. Rejecting traditional subject matter, artists turned to the classical art of ancient Greece and Rome and the Renaissance masters for their inspiration.

Among the foremost artists to work in this new Neoclassic style were Jacques-Louis David and Jean A. D. Ingres. Ingres is considered to be one of the great drafters of history. He was forced for a time after the defeat of Napoleon to make a living by drawing pencil portraits of wealthy English tourists. Ingres developed a style marked by a keen eye and sensitivity for line (Figure 2.4).

Théodore Géricault is usually credited with creating the Romantic style, which emphasized a spontaneous approach to drawing and painting. At Géricault's death, Eugene Delacroix assumed the leadership of the Romantic movement. A trip to north Africa in 1832 exposed him to the colorful life of the Arabs. One of his drawings, showing an Arab being attacked by a lion (Figure 3.20), clearly illustrates Delacroix's ability to capture furious action.

Around the middle of the nineteenth century, a new style known as *Realism* became prominent. Artists practicing this new style expressed little interest in exotic, romantic subject matter. Instead, they looked closely at the objects and events around them to find worthwhile subjects for their art.

One of the first artists to use the Realistic style was the caricaturist, painter, and sculptor Honoré Daumier (Figures 2.13 and 2.14). Although Daumier may have wanted to create more paintings, poverty forced him to spend much of his time making lithographs for publication. Lithographs are prints made from inked stones or metal plates. Many of the four thousand he produced criticized the social and moral injustices of his age. Daumier's drawings show us that he was one of the great drafters of all time.

(continued on next page)

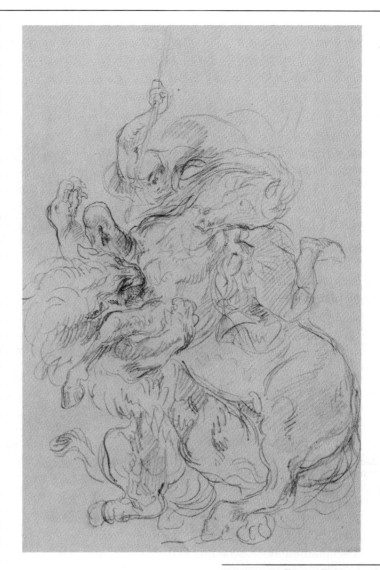

FIGURE 3.20 Eugene Delacroix, *An Arab on Horseback Attacked by a Lion*, 1849. Graphite on tracing paper, 18.1 × 12.0″ (46.0 × 30.5 cm). The Harvard University Art Museums, Cambridge, MA. Bequest of Meta and Paul J. Sachs.

Neoclassic artists such as Ingres and David turned to classical Greek and Roman artists and Renaissance artists for their inspiration. Can the same be said for this artist? Compare and contrast this work with the work of Ingres shown in Figure 2.4. What is the name given to Daumier's style? Which artist is credited with being the originator of this style? Do you consider this to be a successful work of art? What aesthetic qualities did you consider when making your judgment?

1800 to 1850 ▷▷▷

THE ART OF THE EARLY NINETEENTH CENTURY

Gustave Courbet was the acknowledged leader of the Realist movement in France. Courbet believed that artists should use direct experience and paint only what they had seen and understood.

Since he exhibited his paintings with Courbet's, Edouard Manet was considered to be a part of the Realist movement. His work, however, is actually a bridge between Realism and the art movement that followed, Impressionism. Much of Manet's work was inspired by his study of the old masters, including Raphael, Giorgione, Titian, Velázquez, and Hals.

Manet's work influenced the next generation of French artists, who came to be known as the *Impressionists*. Using the contemporary scene, as Courbet and Manet did, the Impressionists tried to reproduce an *impression* of what the eye sees at a specific moment in time—not what the mind knows is there. They were attracted most often to the landscape, with or without people.

The best known of the Impressionists was Claude Monet. Working outdoors, Monet became fascinated by constantly changing colors. He often painted the same subject under different light conditions.

Auguste Renoir, another Impressionist, carefully arranged his compositions. His subjects were posed to look as if the viewer had encountered them accidentally. His works show a love of warm colors, appealing subjects, and sun-drenched landscapes.

Berthe Morisot's figures live in a world of warm summer afternoons and pleasant, carefree moments. No less an artist than Claude Monet regarded Morisot's painting achievements as equal to those of any of the other Impressionists.

Edgar Degas agreed with the Impressionists' views, but he didn't regard himself as a Impressionist. Rather than paint outdoors, he remained in his studio. He maintained that drawing wasn't recording what the artist sees, but making others see.

(continued on next page)

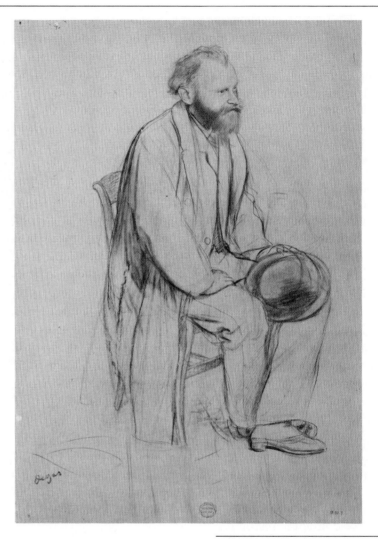

FIGURE 3.21 Edgar Degas, *Study for a Portrait of Edouard Manet*, c. 1864. Black chalk and estompe, 13 × 9⅛″ (33 × 23.2 cm). The Metropolitan Museum of Art, New York, NY. Rogers Fund.

Do you think this drawing provides a faithful representation of the subject? What has the artist done to give the figure a solid, three-dimensional appearance? In what ways did this artist differ from the Impressionists? Do you think an imitationalist would regard this as a successful work of art? How do you think a formalist would react to it?

THE ART OF THE EARLY NINETEENTH CENTURY

Degas also preferred to draw and paint figures rather than landscapes. Degas's affection for drawing, which was inspired by his admiration for Ingres, also separated him from the Impressionists. His study for a portrait of Edouard Manet (Figure 3.21) is an excellent example of his drawing style.

Mary Cassatt, an American, pursued a painting career in Paris and became an Impressionist through her friendship with Degas. Although she never married, Cassatt often created enchanting scenes of motherhood (Figure 9.6).

Two unique landscape painters, John Constable and J. M. W. Turner, charted the direction that art was to take throughout the nineteenth century in England.

John Constable tried to create a feeling of the momentary, a glimpse of nature at a particular moment. For this reason he focused attention on color, light, and atmosphere. For Constable, the sky with its moving clouds was the focal point of any landscape. Working outdoors, Constable completed countless sketches of the English countryside which were the basis for his large, six-foot wide paintings.

Joseph Mallord William Turner is regarded as one of the most original landscape painters. Like Constable, he was fascinated by light and atmosphere. But he combined this fascination with an active imagination. In his paintings, the forms seem to dissolve in the golden glow of light.

On his many travels, Turner filled sketchbooks with studies of every kind. Space and light dominate in his pencil drawing of the Scottish highlands (Figure 3.22). In this drawing you can see the barest hint of a landscape beyond the darker figures of herdsmen and their livestock.

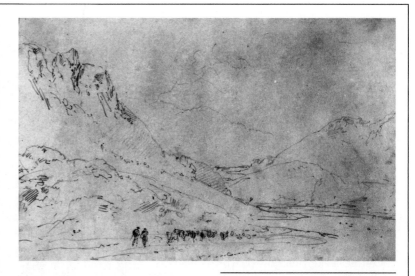

FIGURE 3.22 Joseph Mallord Turner, *Scotch Highlands*, date unknown. Pencil drawing, 10⅜ × 16¼″ (26.4 × 41.3 cm). Courtesy of the Museum of Fine Arts, Boston, MA. Gift of Dr. William Norton Bullard.

Carefully describe the literal qualities in this drawing. What appears to be most important here: the landscape, the people, the livestock, or the space and light? If you were evaluating Turner's sketchbook, what grade would you assign to this sketch? What comments would you pass on to your "student"?

THE ART OF THE LATE NINETEENTH CENTURY

As the nineteenth century entered its final quarter, a number of artists, including Georges Seurat, Paul Cezanne, Vincent van Gogh, Henri de Toulouse-Lautrec, and Paul Gauguin, tried to solve the problems they associated with Impressionism. Their efforts greatly influenced artists in the next century.

Georges Seurat developed a style of art known as *Neo-Impressionism* or *Pointillism*. He deliberately applied tiny, uniform dots of pure color to his canvases instead of using a more uneven color pattern of dabs and dashes. Seurat was also a splendid drafter. He is noted for drawings done in black conte crayon (Figure 3.23).

While the Impressionists were concerned with the appearance of objects under different light conditions, Paul Cezanne was interested in the structure of those objects. His paintings seem to be made out of cubes of color that turn in a variety of directions (Figure 2.2).

In 1886 Vincent van Gogh moved first to Paris and later to Arles in the south of France to develop his artistic skills. His style is characterized by vibrant colors, twisting lines, and heavy applications of paint (Figures 1.1 and 7.8). An increased emphasis on drawing separated him from the Impressionists. His lack of realistic accuracy and smooth, finished technique aroused critics.

Paul Gauguin began his artistic career in his middle years after leaving his family and a high-paying position as a stockbroker. In his work he distorted or exaggerated ordinary natural forms and colors. Seeking exotic subject matter, Gauguin spent much of his career in the South Seas. An ink drawing with watercolor (Figure 3.24) shows the way he used flat shapes to make decorative patterns.

Although he didn't belong to any group of artists or art movement, Henri de Toulouse-Lautrec also contributed significantly to the development of modern art. A brilliant drafter, Lautrec was able to capture a scene, a character, even an emotion with a few quick strokes of pencil, pen, or brush (Figure 1.13).

(continued on next page)

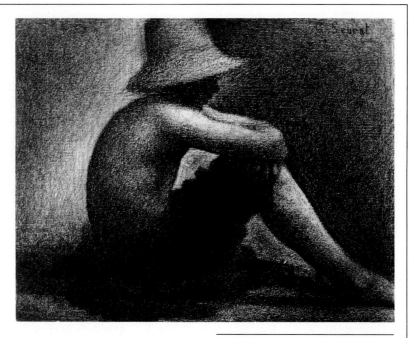

FIGURE 3.23 Georges Seurat, *Seated Boy with Straw Hat*, 1882. Conte crayon drawing, 9½ × 12¼″ (24.1 × 31.1 cm). Yale University Art Gallery, New Haven, CT. Everett V. Meeks Fund.

How does this seated figure differ from the seated figure by Edgar Degas (Figure 3.21)? Explain how the principle of gradation is used to create the look of three-dimensional form. How is harmony achieved in this drawing? What creates variety? What do you consider to be the most impressive feature about this drawing?

1850 to 1900

THE ART OF THE LATE NINETEENTH CENTURY

Lautrec often visited a cabaret (or night club) owned by a friend, Aristide Bruant. Bruant wrote songs about the painful, often desperate lives of the people who came to his cabaret. In 1887 one of his songs was published, accompanied by an illustration drawn by Lautrec. You will study this drawing later in this book (Figure 9.5).

By the close of the nineteenth century, the United States had become a world leader. The country's change and growth were reflected in American art. The art of this period is best represented by the works of three artists—Winslow Homer, Albert Pinkham Ryder, and Thomas Eakins.

Homer's work reflects his lifelong affection for saltwater, ships, and sailors. He was largely self-taught and worked for many years as a lithographer before directing his energies to serious painting. Often his pictures show man opposing the powerful forces of nature.

Albert Pinkham Ryder's small paintings show that he ignored technique. He layered on paint to thicknesses of one-quarter inch and often returned to work on a picture while it was still wet. As a result, his paintings have cracked and faded with age. Even so, Ryder achieved a position as one of the dominant American painters. His imaginary subjects were painted in a simple style using large areas of color and texture.

Thomas Eakins valued precision and accuracy so much that when he was painting a crucifixion he strapped a friend to a cross for a model. When drawing or painting a surgical operation (Figure 5.4), Eakins didn't try to soften the impact of the scene. Works showing such harsh subjects in such startling detail were often excluded from exhibitions.

This drawing by Gauguin reveals his unique style. Describe the main features of that style. How are line and value used to organize this drawing? Would you describe the shapes used here as round and three-dimensional, or flat and decorative? What prompted this artist to spend much of his career in the South Seas?

FIGURE 3.24 Paul Gauguin, *Nave Nave Fenua*, c. 1894–1900. Watercolor, 16.5 × 10.2″ (41.9 × 26 cm). National Gallery of Art, Washington, DC. Lessing J. Rosenwald Collection.

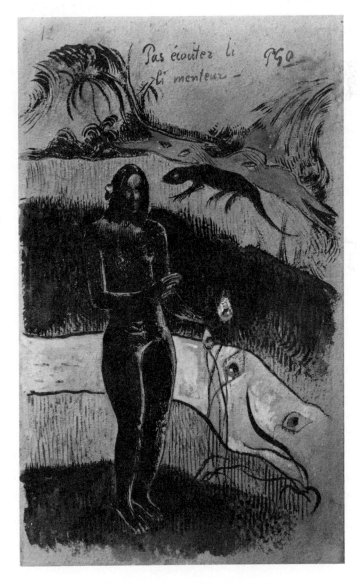

THE ART OF THE EARLY TWENTIETH CENTURY

Artists like Goya, Cezanne, van Gogh, and Gauguin were leaders of a revolution in art that began in the nineteenth century and came to dominate art in the twentieth century. Inspired by the creative efforts of those earlier painters, twentieth-century artists used their personal visions to produce unique works of art.

During the early years of the century, a group of French artists who became known as the *Fauves* (French for *wild beasts*) appeared. Their approach to painting ignored realism and used a heavy, bold application of brightly colored paint to express emotion. One of these artists was Henri Matisse. Matisse is often referred to as the first modern artist. He saw the world as simple, flat shapes of pure color.

Matisse's approach to drawing was similar to his approach to painting. He carefully examined the subject of a drawing to determine the essential shapes and lines to be included in the work (Figure 7.7). In his compositions, the figures are presented as flat, decorative shapes and are defined and decorated with lines.

An art movement known as *Expressionism* was important in the first quarter of the twentieth century. It stressed the artist's need to communicate to viewers his or her emotional response to a subject.

Ernst Ludwig Kirchner, a leader in the Expressionist movement, used flat, brightly colored shapes in his early works. Later he used unusual contrasts of colors; large, simple shapes; and distortions to express his feelings and moods. In 1937, Kirchner's art was condemned in Germany by the Nazi Party, and six hundred of his works were seized.

Another artist associated with German Expressionism is Käthe Kollwitz. Although human tragedy, suffering, and death are themes of many of her powerful works (Figure 2.6), Kollwitz is also known for her sensitive portrayals of motherhood. Her own experiences as a mother were tragic; her son Peter was killed in World War I.

(continued on next page)

What style of art is represented by this drawing? Which earlier artist inspired artists like Picasso to develop this style? How would you describe this style of art to someone who had never heard of it? What elements and principles of art are especially important in this work? Do you think this drawing achieves unity?

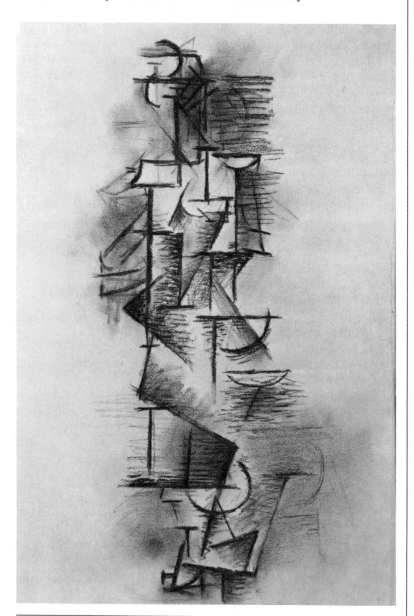

FIGURE 3.25 Pablo Picasso, *Nude*, 1910. Charcoal, 19¹/₁₆ × 12⁵/₁₆″ (48.6 × 31 cm). The Metropolitan Museum of Art, New York, NY. The Alfred Stieglitz Collection.

1900 to 1925

THE ART OF THE EARLY TWENTIETH CENTURY

The Expressionists were influenced not only by the Fauves but also by Vincent van Gogh and a Norwegian artist named Edvard Munch. On a visit to France while he was still in his twenties, Munch encountered the work of Gauguin and was impressed with Gauguin's simplified shapes of intense color. It was then that Munch recognized how he could use such shapes in his own art. When his powerful compositions were first displayed in France, they caused so much controversy that the exhibition was closed within a week. The controversy, however, made him famous overnight.

Vasily Kandinsky completed his first works in his native Russia; experimented with Impressionism, Fauvism, and other styles in France; and then joined the Expressionist movement in Germany. His approach to expressing inner feelings eventually led him to abandon subject matter in his work. Kandinsky is generally regarded as the first nonobjective artist.

Another important movement, known as *Cubism*, was inspired by Cezanne's paintings. His works were composed of cubes of color arranged to create the illusion of solid form. Pablo Picasso took this concept further. In a figure drawing (Figure 3.25, opposite page), he presented the subject from a variety of viewpoints and made a fragmented form out of interlocking planes or shapes.

Picasso didn't extend Cubism into complete nonobjectivity, but other artists did. One of these artists, Piet Mondrian, studied Cubism and eventually rejected any attempt to represent subject matter. His works were composed of a limited visual vocabulary, consisting of the primary colors along with black and white, square and triangular shapes, and straight lines (Figures 1.9 and 2.5).

At the beginning of the twentieth century, the most celebrated portrait painter was the American John Singer Sargent. Sargent enjoyed great success as a painter of fashionable portraits. He was also well known for his excellent watercolors.

(continued on next page)

Would you describe this scene as accurate and lifelike? How has the artist used value to create a sense of space in this drawing? How has value been used to create the look of three-dimensional form? What has been done to emphasize the most important parts of this composition? What name was given to the group of artists to which Sloan belonged? What kind of subject matter was preferred by the artists in this group?

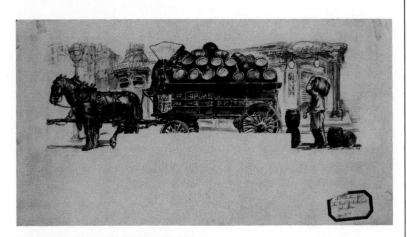

FIGURE 3.26 John Sloan, *Medusa Beer Truck*, 1908. Pencil, black crayon, brush and black and gray ink with gray wash on board, 11.6 × 21.8″ (29.4 × 55.3 cm). National Gallery of Art, Washington, DC. John Davis Hatch Collection; Avalon Fund.

1900 to 1925

THE ART OF THE EARLY TWENTIETH CENTURY

One group of early twentieth-century artists resisted traditional European styles and subject matter. Because these artists wanted to draw and paint the American scene—the streets, alleys, cafés, and theaters—they were laughingly referred to as members of the Ashcan School of art. One of the leading artists in this group was John Sloan.

Sloan wanted to portray the colorful views of everyday, lower-class life in the big city. His drawing of a man loading a beer truck (Figure 3.26, preceding page) is characteristic of his vivid, accurate style and common, working-class subject matter.

George Bellows sympathized with the views expressed by Sloan and other members of the Ashcan School. His lifelong love of sports is reflected in paintings that capture the frenzied action of the boxing ring with slashing brushwork. Bellows was also capable of creating sensitive, engaging portraits (Figure 3.27).

On the evening of February 17, 1913, a huge exhibition of European and American art opened in New York City. The International Exhibition of Modern Art, more commonly known as the *Armory Show*, introduced the American public to the most advanced movements in European art. It also motivated many American artists to start the experiments that began the modern era in American art. This exhibition dramatically changed the direction of art in the United States.

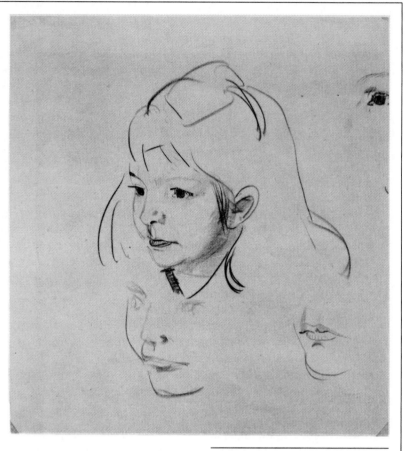

FIGURE 3.27 George Wesley Bellows, *Studies of Jean*, c. 1920. Black crayon, $10^5/_{16} \times 9^3/_8''$ (26.1 × 23.9 cm). National Gallery of Art, Washington, DC. John Davis Hatch Collection; Avalon Fund.

What adjective would you use to describe this drawing—precise, objective, or sensitive? What two elements would you be sure to mention when describing this drawing to a friend? Which facial feature seems to be emphasized in this drawing?

ART TO THE PRESENT

After World War I, Europe experienced a period of pessimism and unrest. Artists associated with a movement known as *Dada* felt that European culture no longer had purpose or meaning. To them, art objects should no longer be beautiful or meaningful, but ordinary and meaningless.

Although the Dada movement ended in 1922, it had an impact on later artists who were attracted to its imagination and humor. Surrealism, a new art movement, became a significant force in Europe throughout the 1920s and 1930s. During the Second World War, it spread to the United States.

Surrealist artists tried to express the world of dreams and the workings of the mind with pencil and brush. One of these artists was the Spaniard Joan Miró. In drawings like *The Kerosene Lamp* (Figure 3.28), Miró tried to record on paper the fantastic sights he encountered in his dreamworld.

Miró shared a mischievous, childlike humor with the Swiss artist Paul Klee. Klee was a small, gentle man who often worked on as many as six pictures at the same time. Klee thought of painting as a magical journey into the realm of the fantastic (Figures 1.2 and 9.4).

Giorgio Morandi chose not to associate himself with any movement or group of artists. He remained in his native Italy and became famous as a still-life artist. For his compositions, he needed only a few simple objects, which he defined first with a variety of crisp and soft lines.

Henry Moore's reputation was built mainly on his strength as a sculptor. But some of his most popular works are drawings of people seeking protection in underground shelters during the World War II London blitzes, or air raids.

Contemporary art in the United States appears to be developing in every direction at once. In this overview, we can only emphasize the diversity that is largely responsible for the vitality of today's American art.

(continued on next page)

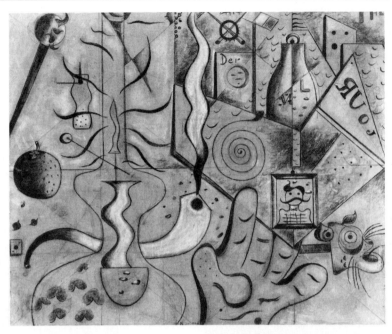

FIGURE 3.28 Joan Miró, *The Kerosene Lamp*, 1924. Black and white chalk with touches of pastel and red pencil on canvas, 31.9 × 39.5″ (81 × 100.3 cm). The Art Institute of Chicago, IL. Joseph and Helen Regenstein Foundation, Helen L. Kellogg Trust, Blum-Kovler Foundation, Major Acquisitions Fund, and gifts from Mrs. Henry C. Woods, Members of the Committee on Prints & Drawings, and Friends of the Department.

Describe this work by listing the recognizable objects. Discuss the elements and principles of art used. What style of art is represented by this drawing—Romanticism, Impressionism, Cubism, or Surrealism? Where did artists who practiced this style turn for their subject matter? Would it be appropriate to search for logic or meaning in this work? Why or why not? Do you think this is a successful work of art? What aesthetic qualities would you refer to if asked to defend your judgment?

1925 to the Present

ART TO THE PRESENT

Edward Hopper's works reflect America during the Great Depression. In some ways, Hopper's drawings and paintings are related to those produced by the Ashcan School artists. He was also concerned with portraying the American scene realistically. His pictures are remembered for showing the emptiness, alienation, and loneliness of contemporary life (Figures 1.10, 5.2, and 9.1).

The Great Depression was soon overshadowed by World War II. The destruction and suffering caused by that conflict is recorded in works by many American artists. One of these was the German-born American illustrator, painter, and caricaturist George Grosz. In drawings and paintings he pictured the horrors of war.

As a storyteller Grosz is surpassed by Jacob Lawrence. Lawrence learned his art in Harlem during the 1920s in a government-sponsored workshop. Today Jacob Lawrence is considered to be among the foremost black artists in America. His colorful, simplified tempera paintings, often accompanied by written explanations, focus on the lives of his people.

During and after the war years, abstract and nonobjective art became popular in the United States. Artists working in New York in the 1930s and 1940s used media and visual qualities more freely to create works with little emphasis on recognizable subject matter. This new art movement was known as *Abstract Expressionism*. Under the leadership of Abstract Expressionists, New York replaced Paris as the art center of the world after the Second World War.

Arshile Gorky, who immigrated to the United States in 1920, was one of the first Abstract Expressionists. In the 1940s, he created works in which brilliant washes of color were contained by or freely flowed out of curving shapes defined by thin, black lines.

Gorky's use of flowing, delicate lines can be contrasted with the wide, slashing lines of Franz Kline. In his huge paintings, ragged black lines overlap and enclose areas of white.

(continued on next page)

What style of art is represented by this drawing? Where do artists who practice this style turn for their inspiration? Why do these artists choose to work on a large scale? What ideas or feelings are communicated by this work?

FIGURE 3.29 Claes Oldenburg, *Drawing for Stake Hitch*, 1983. Pastel and watercolor on paper, 40 x 29³/₁₆″ (101.6 × 74 cm). The Dallas Museum of Art, Dallas, TX. General Acquisitions Fund and a gift of The 500, Inc.

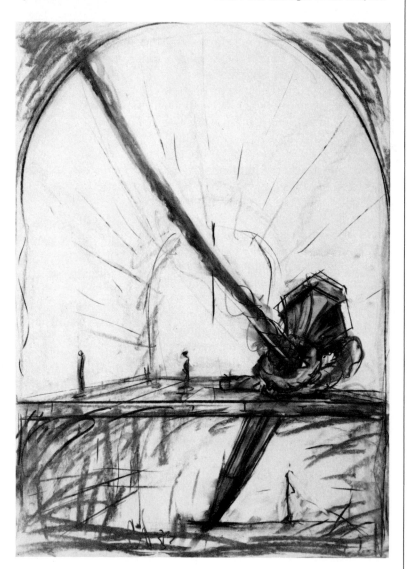

ART TO THE PRESENT

They suggest the dramatic outlines of modern bridges or the framework of skyscrapers.

No artist represents Abstract Expressionism better than Jackson Pollock. Laying a large section of unstretched canvas on the floor enabled Pollack to work on a painting from all directions. He then used a variety of instruments to make a pattern of lines, colors, and textures.

Abstract Expressionism, like all artistic movements, didn't escape the threat of new ideas and approaches. In the 1950s and 1960s many artists again became interested in realism. Responding to the popular culture around them, they based their art on comic strips, magazine advertisements, billboards, and supermarket products. Labeled *Pop artists*, they focused attention on the unimportant products of contemporary culture.

Claes Oldenburg's drawing of a stake hitch was done in preparation for a huge, three-dimensional creation installed in the Dallas Museum of Art (Figure 3.29, opposite page). The figures show the intended scale of the metal stake and rope. Like other large Pop art creations, it is designed to force viewers to see these familiar objects in a new way.

Another kind of realism is practiced by Andrew Wyeth. He may be America's best-known artist. A pencil drawing (Figure 3.30) demonstrates Andrew Wyeth's ability to record detail and express feelings at the same time.

This story of art history could continue indefinitely. New artists and new movements are constantly appearing on the scene. We couldn't hope to keep up with the continuously changing events in the art world. It is an exciting time for knowledgeable viewers of art—and a stimulating and challenging environment in which new artists can learn and practice their art.

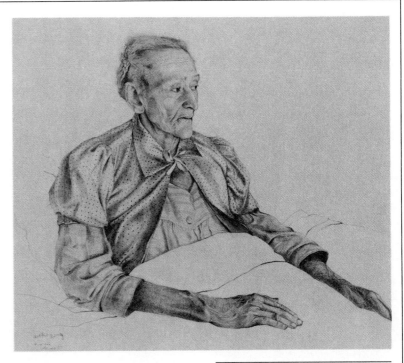

FIGURE 3.30 Andrew Wyeth, *Beckie King*, 1946. Pencil on paper, 30 × 35″ (76.2 × 88.9 cm). The Dallas Museum of Art, Dallas, TX. Gift of Everett L. DeGolyer.

The artist who drew this portrait is skilled at recording details. What else can be said about his work on this drawing? What is the woman doing? Does she look well cared for? What might she be thinking? How do you feel about this woman? Defend the argument that literal, visual, and expressive qualities should all be considered when viewing and judging this work.

CHAPTER FOUR

Entering the Studio

OBJECTIVES

After reading this chapter and doing the activities, you will be able to

■ name the most important factor in making successful drawings;

■ make gesture drawings;

■ make contour drawings;

■ demonstrate the use of different drawing tools and media;

■ demonstrate the use of basic drawing techniques;

■ make hinged mats for presenting your drawings;

■ list several reasons for using a sketchbook;

■ list sources of ideas for making drawings; and

■ explain the difference between plagiarism and originality in art.

When you enter the studio to make a drawing, your pencil is *not* the most important thing to take with you. Neither is your paper or your drawing board.

The most important thing is not even a strong and honest desire to make a drawing. Your wish to have a good likeness of someone or something won't help you. In fact, this wish can get in your way unless you really enjoy taking part in the *process* of drawing.

The one thing you need to be successful is the *desire to draw.* Your attitude is your most important equipment.

This doesn't mean that the drawings you make aren't important. They are. But they are important to a large degree because they are the record of an act. People have considered the act of drawing important since the dawn of history.

The other things that make drawings important are their physical characteristics, aesthetic qualities, and uses. We talk about these subjects in other parts of this book. But your first concern is your involvement in the act of drawing—the process.

Do you find that it matters only a little what you are drawing? Does it seem that the time you spend drawing goes much too fast? If so, you can probably become a successful artist. A bit of talent helps, of course, but it isn't nearly as important as most people think. A moderately talented student with self-discipline and a desire to draw will be much more successful than an extremely talented student without self-discipline or much interest in the drawing process. If you are willing to practice and enjoy the *pro-*

cess, the *product* will take care of itself. You don't need outstanding talent.

The activities in this chapter introduce basic drawing techniques. Drawing **media**, or materials, and how to use them are explained in activities throughout *Creating and Understanding Drawings*. Items shown at the bottom of the activity pages are described more fully in the *Media Handbook*, which lists the tools and media used in the activities, in the back of the book.

GESTURE DRAWING

Drawing gestures or movements of the body is called **gesture drawing**. Since gestures require movement, you have to operate like a camera when you draw gestures and freeze the movement. You also need a person to make the gesture. At this point, you aren't expected to draw the **figure**, the human form. You are just expected to draw what the figure is doing. This is called the *gesture*.

It is impossible, of course, to draw an action without indicating the person doing the action. You will probably show the figure somehow. But let that happen as a result of the drawing process—not because you are trying to draw a figure.

Doing lots of gesture drawings will help improve your drawing skills in several ways. In the first place, they force you to see the model and the model's movement as a single image, not one detail at a time.

Second, gesture drawings help you forget your childhood habit of outlining all of the shapes in a drawing. You probably think that outlining is always the right way to begin a drawing. But outlining isn't used for gesture drawing. Outlining can be slow, stiff, and frustrating. Persuade yourself to ignore the outlines, and make the shapes by ''scribbling'' them.

Third, gesture drawing helps you overcome your fear of the blank page as you put expressive marks on paper. And finally, gesture drawing is a good way to become acquainted with various art-making media. You will try several in the gesture drawing activities.

If you have an easel in your **studio**, or art room, use it and work standing up. Standing will let you be free to make the almost athletic movements required in gesture drawing. It is a good idea to put the easel slightly to one side of what you are drawing. This is true any time you are drawing at an easel. You don't want to have to stand on tiptoe to peer over the top

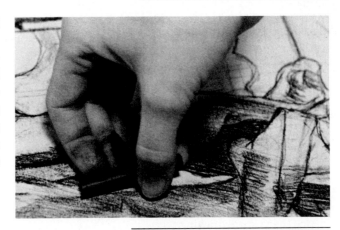

FIGURE 4.1 Note that the drawing instrument isn't held like a writing tool while drawing large shapes or doing gesture drawings.

of the paper at the objects or **model**, the person who poses for a drawing. When you place the easel at an angle so the model is observed by looking across your drawing arm, the paper will be high enough to reach easily. You won't have to turn your head very far to see your drawing.

Also, don't hold the drawing instrument as if you were writing. See Figure 4.1 for the correct grip. You can't do gesture drawings with the small muscles in your fingers, as if you were writing a letter. You must use the large muscles in the whole arm. Using your whole arm helps you become involved in the action of drawing. It also removes the temptation to start out drawing details instead of looking for the single image.

ENRICHMENT

Gestalt

Seeing the thing you are drawing as a whole rather than just as a collection of parts results in more successful drawings. The fact that we naturally see things as a whole was discovered in Germany in 1912 by a psychologist named Max Wertheimer. He founded a branch of psychology called *Gestaltism*. The German word *gestalt* means *pattern* or *form*. According to Gestalt psychology, we only recognize objects by seeing total patterns or forms, not by adding up the individual parts we see. In making most drawings, do the large shapes first. Add the details later. Think in terms of the gestalt view of life.

easel

STUDIO

Gesture Drawings of a Still Life

MATERIALS

Vine charcoal, newsprint

Look at the drawings in Figures 4.2 and 4.3. Soon you will try to make drawings like these, but first practice the gesture drawing technique on a **still life**, a group of nonmoving objects. Make several drawings of a three-object still life from various positions around it.

For these drawings, use vine charcoal and newsprint. Vine charcoal is a soft, lightweight, black drawing medium made by cooking sections of vines in a kiln, or drying oven, until nothing remains but carbon sticks. The newsprint pad on which you will work is simply a pad made of the same kind of inexpensive paper on which newspapers are printed. The pad should be at least 17 × 22″ (43 × 56 cm) in size so you can get two or three drawings on a sheet. Use spring clips to hold the pad on a Masonite or wooden drawing board.

Since the still life can't move, you could take your time drawing it. Even so, spend only about twenty seconds on each drawing. With three objects in the composition, the time divides into five seconds on each object and a little over two seconds to change from one object to another. Try to define the stance, or direction, and the shape of each object *without outlining it*. Do this in a single, continuous series of strokes without raising your charcoal from the paper except between objects. See Figure 4.4 for a typical still-life **setup**, or group of objects arranged for drawing. See Figures 4.5 and 4.6 for a look at the drawing process.

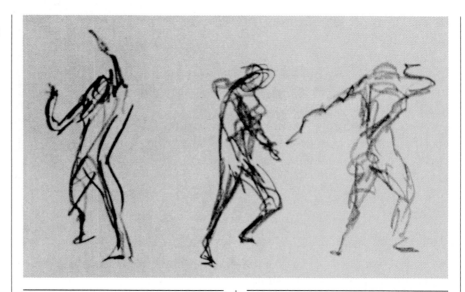

FIGURE 4.2 (above) These small gesture drawings by student Damon Six were created in fifteen seconds each.

FIGURE 4.3 (below) These larger gesture drawings were finished by student Rob Wilson in about twenty seconds each.

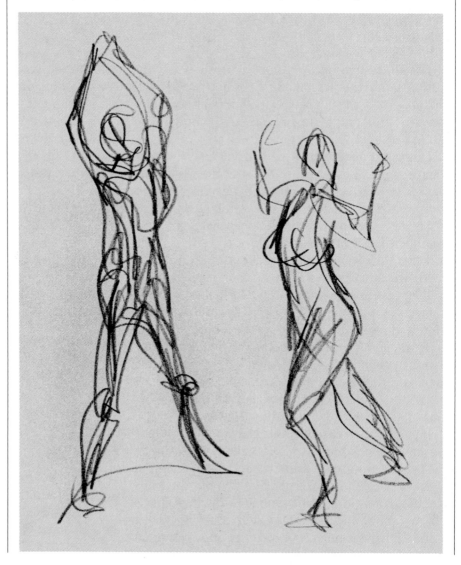

vine charcoal
newsprint
drawing board

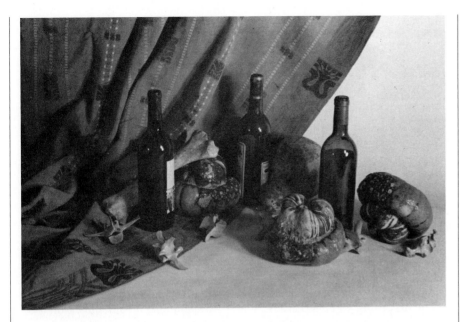

FIGURE 4.4 Objects can be put together in many ways for a still-life drawing setup.

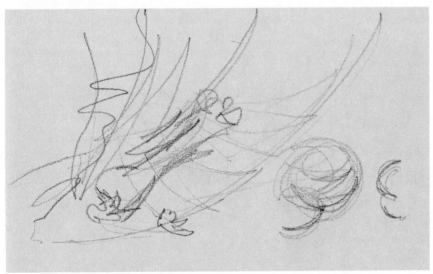

FIGURE 4.5 The start of an expressive gestural approach to still-life drawing.

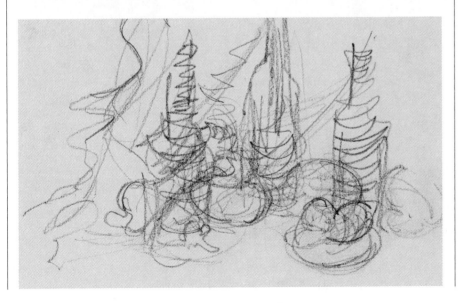

FIGURE 4.6 Finished version of the drawing in Figure 4.5. Note that the artist treated all objects as though they were transparent. This is necessary in good gesture drawing and desirable in all preliminary drawings.

Notice in the drawing in Figure 4.6 on the preceding page that every object in the composition is drawn as though it were transparent. If objects in the setup overlap each other, the hidden parts are drawn just as though the artist could see through the overlapping object. Drawing objects as if they were transparent is a good idea, not just in gesture drawing but in all drawing.

In gesture drawings, always try to exaggerate the differences in size, shape, and direction. And remember: don't outline.

STUDIO

Gesture Drawings of a Model

MATERIALS

Vine charcoal, newsprint

After you have practiced gesture drawing with a still life, you should be ready to tackle the real gesture drawing of a person. Have a model assume five poses for twenty seconds each. Draw the gestures in the same way you drew the still life.

The first thing you need is a person to make a gesture. Dancers are good models for gesture draw-ing, or class members can take turns. The model should take active poses. Each action should look as if it were interrupted or photo-graphed in mid-motion with a still camera. Actions such as

- the more active dance motions,
- bending to tie a shoe,
- lifting a heavy load,
- making a baseball umpire's "Safe!" sign, or
- placing something on a high shelf

are all good ones for your model to try. You can request some of the more difficult poses for this activity since the model will need to hold them for only twenty seconds.

Remember: *no outlines*. Don't think about the figure—draw what the figure is doing. A good way to

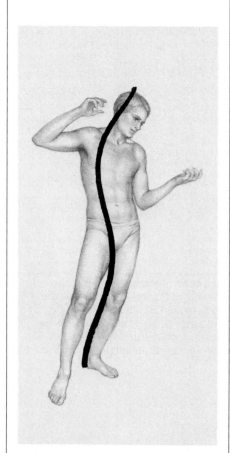

FIGURE 4.7 Start the gesture drawing by quickly drawing the gesture of the axis through the figure.

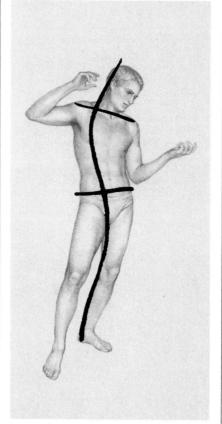

FIGURE 4.8 A good second step in gesture drawing is to locate the position and tilt of the hips and shoulders.

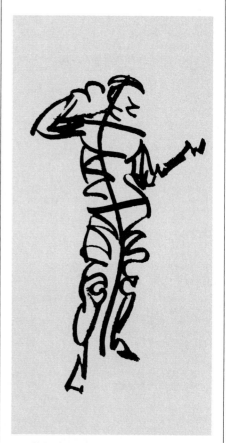

FIGURE 4.9 Finish your gesture drawing by scribbling lines around and across the form.

start your drawing without using outlines is shown in Figure 4.7. Start with the **vertical axis** of the overall motion of the figure. This axis is an imaginary line dividing the figure in half vertically. Then get the tilt of the shoulders and hips. Finally, fill out the shapes by scribbling across the axis (see Figures 4.8 and 4.9).

Make each drawing at least 8″ (20 cm) high. You can get three or four on a page of newsprint. Do at least ten of these drawings a day.

STUDIO

Large Gesture Drawings

MATERIALS

Compressed charcoal, newsprint

Make some big gesture drawings of a model. Fill a whole page with a single drawing using a stick of compressed charcoal. Compressed charcoal is carbon, like vine charcoal, that has been ground up and compressed into a larger square or round stick. It is very black.

STUDIO

Brush and Ink Gesture Drawings

MATERIALS

Brush, black India ink, watercolor paper

Make several gesture drawings of a model in black India ink, which is a wet medium. Make each drawing the same size that you used for the vine charcoal drawings, 8″ (20 cm). You can put three or four of them on a sheet. To apply the ink, use a soft, round brush, #2 to #5.

The most commonly used ink for drawing with a brush is called *India ink*. This ink is almost waterproof, so try not to get it on your clothes or spill it. The pigment or colored powder may separate from the liquid in the bottle, so shake the bottle before you start. You want the ink to make dark marks when you draw with it.

You will need a working surface heavier than newsprint for drawing with ink. The best paper is probably a moderately good grade of watercolor paper that isn't too rough. A watercolor block is easy to use for gesture drawing.

A watercolor block is a pad of watercolor paper for sketching. The sheets are glued down on all four edges so that the paper will stay flat. The pad is stiff enough not to need the backing of a drawing board. To remove a sheet, run an object such as a plastic ruler around the block underneath the sheet's edge. If you don't use a watercolor pad, put watercolor paper on a drawing board.

Drawing with a brush and ink is different from drawing with dry media. Practice some straight and curved strokes and some squiggles with your brush until you learn how to control it. Some of the strokes may look like oriental calligraphy or handwriting. The brush has been used as a writing instrument for a long time in various Eastern countries.

You can make an expressive drawing with a brush when you are working rapidly to describe a gesture. Learning to control a brush is a little more difficult than learning to control a pencil or charcoal stick, but the extra range of expression is well worth the effort.

TECHNIQUE NOTE

Caring for Brushes

Before you use a new brush, wash out any glue placed on the tip to protect its shape.

While you are drawing, stop often to swish your brush around in water so that the medium you are using won't dry in the brush hairs. Then blot the brush with a rag, tissue, or paper towel. If you blot the brush, the medium won't be diluted when you dip your brush into it again.

When you are through with the brush for the day, wash it with soap and water until the rinse water comes out clear. Rinsing the brush will keep the medium from building up under the metal ring that holds the hairs. If ink or paint collects there, the brush hairs will fan out.

---

compressed charcoal
India ink

brush
watercolor block

CONTOUR DRAWING

Drawing the edges, or contours, of figures or objects is called **contour drawing**. While gesture drawing is quick, contour drawing is slow and painstaking. While gesture drawing records an action all at once, contour drawing is more concerned with shape and structure. While gesture drawing may capture the entire image, contour drawing also explores the smallest details.

Outline Contour Drawing

The first kind of contour drawing we will explore is outline contour drawing. The **outline contour** is the line that shows the overall shape around the outer edge of an object that you are viewing from a particular spot. Of course the shape's outline would change as you move around the object, viewing it from different angles.

The only kind of object whose shape wouldn't change in an outline contour drawing is a sphere. Imagine or look at a sphere, such as a globe or a smooth rubber ball. If you drew the outline contour from three different views, what shape would all three contours be? This shape could be drawn with the compass you use in geometry class.

When you are drawing more than one object, outline contours are more complex. For example, the shape formed by the pile of boxes in Figure 4.10 has an exterior contour line that outlines the shape of the whole pile. The pile also has interior contour lines that outline the shape of each box. Outline contour drawings show the outline contours of a subject as a whole and of all the shapes within it.

A good way to learn to draw outline contours is to practice blind contour drawing. Blind contour drawing is an exercise in a valuable but limited way of seeing things. It is perhaps the only kind of drawing that doesn't use the gestalt principle of drawing the overall image first.

As you know, in gesture drawing you disciplined yourself not to outline. In blind contour drawing, you should discipline yourself *never* to look at the drawing until it is complete. This is why it is called *blind* contour drawing.

If you cheat by looking at your paper out of the corner of your eye while you draw, you will defeat the purpose of blind contour drawing. When comparing your drawing with those of your classmates, every-

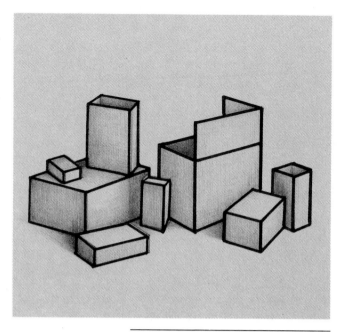

FIGURE 4.10 This pile of boxes has both outline and interior contours. Both the exterior and the interior contours are shown by the lines drawn on the drawing.

one will know that you cheated. This won't be because your drawing will be any more accurate than theirs, but it will be stiffer, less detailed, and less sensitive.

While you are drawing, imagine the point of your drawing instrument actually moving slowly, like an ant crawling over the giant landscape of the model or objects. Move inch by inch along the edge of the shapes, over the bumps and hills, and into the cracks and valleys. Don't lift your drawing instrument from the paper until you finish. In most cases, this shouldn't be for at least ten or fifteen minutes. If you finish sooner, you have not been observing as closely as you should.

Blind contour drawing helps you accomplish two things. First, you will be closely observing the structure of the object or person you are drawing by feeling your way around all of the shapes with your drawing instrument. This observation will make you more sensitive to detail. Second, as you capture proportions, you will develop a connection between your drawing hand and the part of your brain that causes you to see the whole image of your subject. You will be trying to estimate the size, direction, and arrangement of all of the parts of what you are drawing.

Blind Contour Drawings of a Still Life

MATERIALS

Charcoal pencil, graphite pencil, fiber-tipped pen, newsprint

Make blind contour drawings of a still life in three media: charcoal pencil (a soft one of the wooden kind), graphite ("lead") pencil (also soft), and a fiber-tipped pen (sometimes called a *fine-line marker*) that makes a medium-weight line.

The charcoal pencils recommended for this activity are the wooden kind, just like graphite pencils. Don't confuse them with the charcoal pencils wrapped in paper that is peeled off before they are sharpened. These paper-wrapped pencils are similar to the large compressed sticks you used in gesture drawing.

Blind contour drawings are usually used to practice figure drawing, but, like gesture drawings, they can be made from any object or setup. Start by drawing some objects that have interesting shapes, such as chairs, fireplugs, or perhaps a piece of an old, gnarled tree. Set up your easel and drawing board just as you did for gesture drawing.

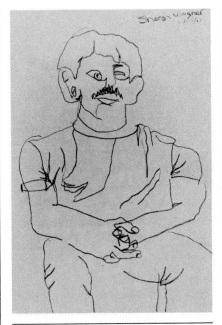

FIGURE 4.11 Student blind contour drawings from a model are often humorous, but like this one by Sharon Wagner, they can also reveal character.

Blind Contour Drawings of a Model

MATERIALS

Charcoal pencil, graphite pencil, fiber-tipped pen, newsprint

After you have practiced drawing inanimate objects, find a subject who is willing to sit still for fifteen minutes and practice some more blind contour drawing. Use charcoal pencil, graphite pencil, and fiber-tipped pen on newsprint. Do some blind contour drawings of a model each day for the whole semester.

Blind contour drawing of people will produce some humorous results. But when you look more closely, you will also see the beautiful line quality and the searching analysis that gives these drawings character.

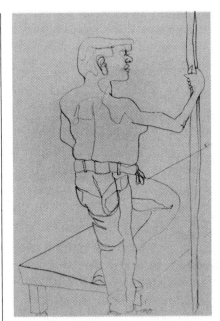

FIGURE 4.12 Blind contour drawings like this student effort by Kristie Smith have effective formal qualities due to the diversity and analytical character of the line.

Figures 4.11 and 4.12 show some good blind contour drawings created by students. Note how facial features, clothes, and clothing wrinkles are all treated as outlined shapes.

charcoal pencil
graphite pencil
fiber-tipped pen

STUDIO

Modified Blind Contour Drawing

MATERIALS

Charcoal pencil, graphite pencil, fiber-tipped pen, newsprint

After a few weeks of blind contour drawing, your drawings should begin to have better proportions. You will have learned to estimate size and distance without looking at your paper. If this is the case, you are ready to try some modified blind contour drawing.

As you have probably guessed, modified blind contour drawing is just like blind contour drawing except that you pause about once every minute to look at your paper for a few seconds. This technique will produce interesting drawings. You can draw compositions that are much more complex and more realistically proportioned than the compositions you create by doing completely blind contour drawing.

With modified blind contour drawing, you can use a model along with objects such as a table, chairs, and a pitcher with glasses. If you are sports-minded, you could set up a pose with a batter, catcher, and umpire. In any case, don't forget to draw the figures and objects transparently—as if you could see right through them where they overlap. (See the modified blind contour drawings by students in Figures 4.13, 4.14, and 4.15.)

Using this see-through vision will add some interesting complexity to the lines of the drawings. You will also develop your analytical skill about parts of images you can't see. Drawing transparently will be useful when you start creating realistic drawings because most of the things we see in the natural world overlap something else.

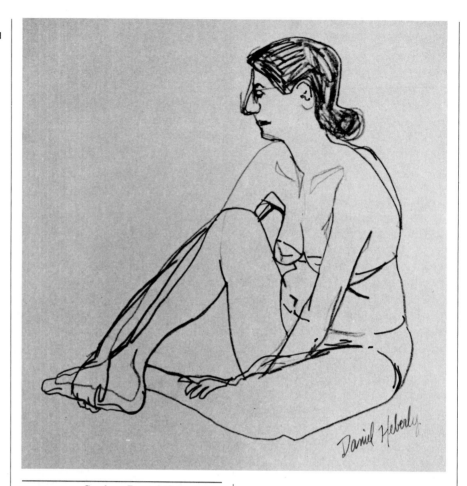

FIGURE 4.13 Student Daniel Heberly's modified contour drawing from a model.

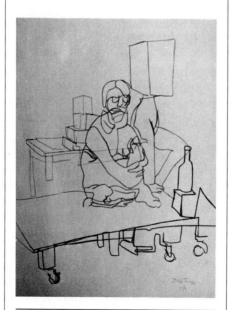

FIGURE 4.14 Modified blind contour drawing of a model and objects by student Brad Fuoss.

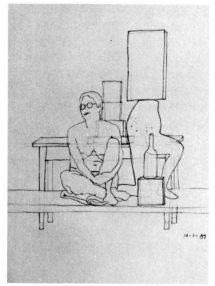

FIGURE 4.15 This modified blind contour drawing by student Ben Rodriguez is a different view of the model seen in Figure 4.14.

Cross-Contour Drawing

Up to this point, we have been talking about the outline contours of shapes. The other kind of contour line most people recognize is often called the **cross contour** of a form. An outline-contour line follows the shape of a form, flattening it. A cross-contour line runs across the form or around it to show its volume or to give it depth. This kind of line creates the illusion of a third dimension, depth, in addition to width and height.

One of the best examples of cross-contour lines is found in United States Geological Survey maps. The fragment of the Wheeler Peak Quadrangle shown in Figure 4.16 allows you to peer down like an eagle on the highest point in New Mexico.

By reading the contour lines on the map, you can see the highest point—the peak of the mountain. Then you can see the shape of the mountain by looking at the cross-contour lines. These lines show levels that are each about 40′ (12 m) lower than the previous one. They look like rubber bands slipped down over the peak or bandages around a mummy, each parallel to the one above it.

Now look at the drawing in Figure 4.17. The student who did the drawing did more than show the hollow outline of the objects. She also wrapped the objects with cross-contour lines to show the ins and outs, bumps and bulges of all the shapes. Notice where darker values are located. How did the artist use cross-contours to create these areas?

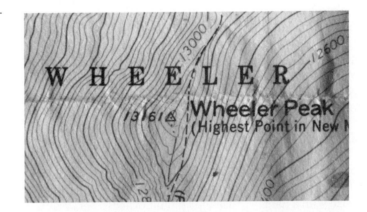

FIGURE 4.16 If you have ever hiked in the wilderness, you may have used a map like this one. A geological survey map is basically a cross-contour drawing of the wrinkles on the earth's surface.

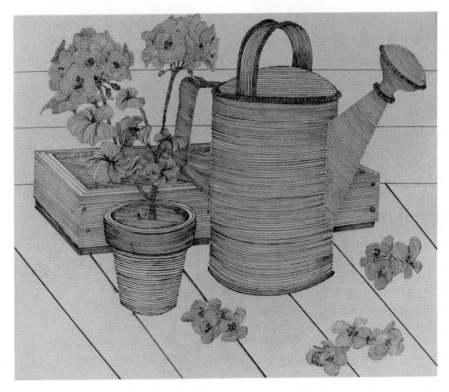

FIGURE 4.17 Student Cylinda Baker did this charming back-porch still life using cross-contour lines to analyze the three-dimensional shapes.

Cross-Contour Drawing of Natural Forms

MATERIALS

Graphite pencil, fiber-tipped pen, any paper except newsprint or other absorbent paper

Now try cross-contour drawing. Start out simply. Remember that this time you aren't doing a blind contour drawing. You may look at your drawing as often as you wish.

Make a cross-contour drawing of natural forms, such as two carrots and a potato. Look at the photograph of the potatoes with the cross contours drawn on them (Figure 4.18). As you can see, the contour lines can be drawn either vertically or, as on the mountain in the map, horizontally. In either case, contour lines will define the form and shape of what you draw.

It's a good idea to start by drawing the objects full size with a hard pencil. Later you can go over the light pencil lines you want to keep with a fiber-tipped pen. After that, you can easily erase the pencil lines, leaving only the ink drawing. Make the drawing about 15 × 11″ (38 × 28 cm).

Start by holding an object in your nondrawing hand close to the paper on which you are working. Do you remember making a drawing of your hand when you were a child? You laid your hand on a sheet of paper and traced around it. You can't trace around most objects, but you can hold an object close to the spot where you will draw it and reproduce its size and outline fairly accurately. Remember not to press too hard. You need to keep the pencil lines light.

After you have drawn the outline of one form lightly in pencil, draw the others. Let at least two of

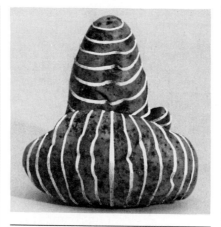

FIGURE 4.18 Almost any three-dimensional object can be defined by cross-contour lines like the ones drawn over the photograph of these potatoes.

the three overlap. Making at least two of the objects touch each other improves the unity of your composition by using the principle of harmony.

Now that you have your composition outlined, you can add cross-contour lines with the pencil. You can draw them as close together or as far apart as you wish. You can use the amount of space between lines to create different values. For example, draw the lines closer together for the dark potato and wider apart for the light carrots. Of course, if the lines are too widely spaced, you will lose the image altogether.

After you have roughed in the cross-contour lines in graphite, darken them with a pen, making any necessary corrections. Darken only the cross contours, not the outlines of the shapes. Don't forget to follow the details closely as you did in blind-contour drawing. Each little ''hill'' or ''gully'' is an important feature.

After you have inked the cross contours, erase all of the pencil lines, including the outlines. The cross-contour lines should be spaced closely enough to define the form by themselves so that an outline isn't needed.

Cross-Contour Drawing Using Gradation

MATERIALS

Graphite pencil, brush, black India ink, two-ply bristol board

Draw a setup similar to the one in Figure 4.19. Make your drawing about 22 × 17″ (56 × 43 cm). Notice that the cross-contour lines in this drawing aren't all the same thickness. Thinner lines are used on the parts of the forms that are closer to the viewer. This gradation gives the forms an added illusion of volume because we are used to seeing **highlights**, or at least to seeing more light on prominent areas of a form, under certain light conditions. Highlights show the areas of a surface reflecting the most light. They can be created by using gradation. The designer of the American Telephone and Telegraph logo in Figure 4.20 turned a circle into a sphere—that is, gave a two-dimensional shape the illusion of volume—by using gradation.

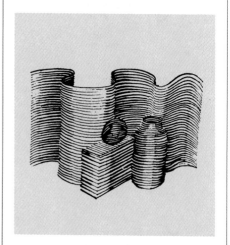

FIGURE 4.19 In this drawing, the student artist chose to vary the weight of the cross-contour lines to show highlights on the closer parts of the objects.

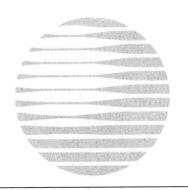

FIGURE 4.20 The graphic designer has used cross-contour lines to turn a circle into a sphere in this famous AT&T logo.

You can use heavy cloth or bend some wrapping paper for the background draping. Work with a pencil first, then a #2 or #3 round brush and ink. You don't need to draw every cross-contour line in the preliminary pencil drawing. Draw only enough of them to indicate direction and frequency before you use ink. Don't forget to shake your ink before you start.

A brush is a good drawing tool to use for thick-to-thin gradations. If you use a pen for this drawing, you should thicken the lines by building them up with repeated strokes. The brush is a little harder to control, but it is faster because you don't have to go over your lines as many times. Two-ply bristol board paper with a *kid*, *vellum*, or *medium* finish will provide the right texture to use with the brush and ink.

Cross-Contour Drawing Using Shadows

MATERIALS

Charcoal pencil; graphite pencil; brush; black tempera paint, designer's gouache, or acrylic paint; drawing paper

In this cross-contour activity, you will be drawing shadows. Since this drawing is a bit more involved, you might wish to make it a little smaller than the one in the last activity to save time in finishing it. Leave a margin for matting the drawing if you wish. Directions for matting begin on page 76.

Use a hard pencil for the preliminary work for this drawing. Pick something interesting outdoors to draw. Work on your drawing in early-to-mid-morning or mid-to-late-afternoon sunshine. There should be distinct shadows, both on the forms and on the

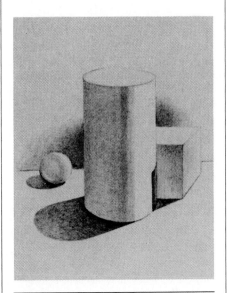

FIGURE 4.21 Demonstration of careful shadow rendering that shows the soft edge and core of form shadows and the hard edge and value change in cast shadows.

ground. In your pencil drawing, lightly outline the shapes of the shadows on your paper. You can return to the studio to do your **rendering**, or finished artwork.

If it isn't practical to do your preliminary drawing outdoors, set up something interesting in the studio. Put a strong light on it from above and on one side. If your studio isn't equipped with floodlights, you could use a clip-on light and reflector. You can purchase the light and reflector for a few dollars at a local supermarket or discount hardware store.

Look at the shadows in the pencil rendering in Figure 4.21. There are two kinds of shadows: **form shadows** and **cast shadows**. Form shadows are the shadows on the side of forms away from the light source. Form shadows on curved surfaces have soft or fuzzy edges. This is because a curved form turns *gradually* away from the light. The sharp corners of angular forms, of course, define the edge of the shadows at the corners where the forms turn *abruptly* away from the light.

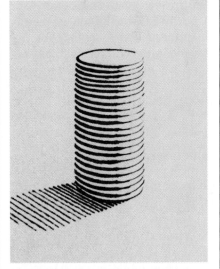

FIGURE 4.22 Although it is hard to show very subtle value changes with cross-contour lines, edge differences between form and cast shadows are evident in this drawing.

Cast shadows are the shadows cast by shapes onto other surfaces. They have hard, distinct edges unless the surfaces are rough or fuzzy. Look at Figure 4.22 (preceding page) to see how to define the edges of the two different kinds of shadows with contour lines.

Before rendering this drawing in paint, do a small shadow study. Do this **rough**, or practice drawing, with charcoal pencil to establish the gray-to-black values of all of the major shadows. To make it easier, treat the cast shadows as if they were uniformly black. Actually, some areas of cast shadow are darker than others.

Rough in the overall value of each object. Try to show clear separation between lighter and darker objects. Finally, darken the form shadows. Make their values consistent with the overall values of the objects on which they are found. After completing these steps, you should have a useful plan for your finished drawing.

For this drawing, you can try using black tempera paint, designer's gouache, or acrylic. Any of these paints produces a flat, black coverage with fewer coats than most inks do. Do the finished rendering as a cross-contour line drawing. Allow the lines to thicken noticeably in the shadows. The white areas will be squeezed into narrow bands.

ENRICHMENT

Dimensions Used in Printing

When commercial printers speak of the dimensions of a page, they usually give the width first and then the height, even if the page is wider than it is high. They also list the width first when they speak about illustrations to be printed on these pages. This is useful to know if you want to become an illustrator or a photojournalist.

In the last two activities, you made *horizontals*—drawings that are wider than they are long. Drawings that are taller than they are wide are referred to as *verticals*.

Printers in the United States usually give page sizes in inches, though this measurement may be changed as the international metric system becomes more widely used. When printers talk about widths of columns of printing, however, they usually refer to printing measurements, using the word *picas*. There are six picas in an inch, and each pica can be broken down into tiny measurements called *points*.

12 points = 1 pica
6 picas = 1 inch
72 points = 1 inch

STUDIO

Color Cross-Contour Drawing

MATERIALS

Graphite pencil, colored pencils, tracing vellum or layout paper, drafting tape

Considerable life can be added to a drawing by using color. In Chapter 6, we will study the realistic use of color. But color can also be used simply as a design element. In this activity you will use colored pencils to make the contour lines and draw an outdoor scene or an odd combination of objects. Not only will each color contour line define the forms, but the lines will also help unify the composition with gradation. You will change the color from a warm, medium dark color (red-violet, for example) on the closest part of each object to lighter values and cooler colors (such as a light tint of blue) as the lines move away into the picture.

You can use either tracing vellum or layout paper for this drawing. Tracing vellum is a tough, **translucent**, white or blue-white paper used mainly by mechanical drafters for making plans and working drawings of buildings or machines. Translucent paper allows some light to pass through it. Don't confuse this paper with what is usually called *tracing paper*, which is too lightweight for your purposes in this activity. A layout pad has paper similar to tracing vellum, but its surface is often a bit rougher. You will need a pad that is at least 17 × 22" (43 × 56 cm).

Both tracing vellum and layout paper have enough tooth to be used with dry media. *Tooth* refers to a slightly rough quality of the surface that strips the particles of color from pencils.

Start the drawing by finding an outdoor scene or making a setup that interests you. Then draw outlines of the objects fairly heavily in pencil. Use one or two large, important objects in the composition and add some smaller objects for variety; don't forget to overlap some of them.

A good size for your working area with this medium is about 17 × 22" (43 × 56 cm). Fill most of the working space with objects, leaving only a little negative space (sky or background). Limiting the negative space will make the rendering easier and produce a more unified composition.

Shift objects around and change the composition until it suits you. You can do this by overlapping your

---

tempera paint
designer's gouache
acrylic

colored pencils

tracing vellum
layout paper
tracing paper

drawing with another sheet of paper and tracing what you want to keep. You can rearrange, remove, or add objects. Keep a sheet of white paper or cardboard under the tracing vellum or layout paper as you work. The paper or cardboard will reflect the light up through the vellum or layout paper so you can easily see the drawing underneath.

After you are satisfied with the design of your preliminary drawing, you are ready to start the colored pencil drawing. If you have been working in a fairly heavy graphite line, you can see it easily through another sheet of layout paper or tracing vellum. Simply tape your first drawing to a drawing board with drafting tape. This tape is similar to masking tape, but not as sticky. It won't tear the paper when you peel it off.

Now tape a second sheet over the first. Use two or three fairly long strips of tape at the top to hold the sheet firmly. Use two or three short strips at the bottom so you can lift them easily to slip an **opaque** sheet of paper between the graphite drawing and the colored pencil drawing. Opaque paper doesn't allow light to pass through it. This extra sheet will let you check your colors and value contrasts by blocking out the graphite outline contour.

When you render the lines in color, make the ones on nearer objects a bit thicker for more contrast. Use progressively thinner contour lines on objects farther back in the picture. Remember to gradually change values for the contour lines. This gradual change involves gradation, one of the principles of art. Use the high contrast of a warm, medium-dark color at the closest point to the viewer. Use a lighter, low contrast color in spaces or edges that are farther back in the picture.

See Figures 4 and 5 in the Color Section. Note that the students who made these drawings had to

thicken contour lines to achieve gradation when using color. These lines might even be called *contour bands*.

You may want to create a feeling of deep space behind the objects in the drawing. If so, fill in the negative areas (or sky, if you are drawing an outdoor scene) with a dark value of a cool color, such as dark blue, blue-green, or blue-violet.

If you want the objects to emerge more subtly from the working surface, fill in the negative spaces with a light value of a cool color. The cool color should be analogous to the colors of the cross-contour lines that are farthest back in the picture. (Analogous colors are located next to each other on the color wheel.) These lines will almost blend with the ground (or surface) at their lightest and coolest end, but they will seem to emerge and come forward as they get darker and warmer.

The paper you are using is light and translucent. When you mount it on the backing for a hinged mat, be sure that the backing is clean and white. Also, make sure there is a margin of a few inches around your drawing so the mat can easily hold the drawing down flat. Directions for matting begin on page 76.

Directions for matting begin on page 76.

TECHNIQUE NOTE

Sharpening Pencils

To get the most from pencils, proper sharpening is important (whether the pencil is graphite, charcoal, or colored). Ordinary pencil sharpeners don't leave enough lead exposed. Some studios have a drafter's pencil sharpener that removes only the wood and none of the lead. If your studio doesn't have one of these, sharpen the pencil by grasping the pencil and knife as shown in Figure 4.23.

Use the muscles in the hand holding the knife to guide the knife,

not to push it. Push the knife with the thumb of the hand holding the pencil. Using this thumb will give you more control as you remove the wood. Shape the exposed lead to a sharp point or any other shape you need with fine sandpaper.

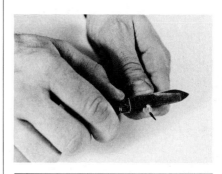

FIGURE 4.23 Hold the knife in one hand to guide it. Push the knife with the thumb of the hand holding the pencil.

SAFETY NOTE

Sharpening Pencils Safely

For better control and safety, use a small, sharp knife, such as a mat knife, an Exacto knife, or a penknife, to sharpen pencils. A small, sharp knife is always safer than a large, dull one.

Never use a kitchen knife or a razor blade to sharpen pencils.

Always push the knife blade away from your fingers or body.

drafting tape

PRESENTING YOUR DRAWINGS

Since you may have already produced a good drawing by doing the activities in this chapter, let's discuss the presentation of your drawing. *Presentation* means how your finished artwork is prepared to be shown to someone else. You may be showing it to your teacher or to the public at an art gallery. If you become a designer or an illustrator, you will show your work to an art director or a client.

No one will have much respect for your artwork if you don't present it properly. On the other hand, if you present it as if you care about it, most people will give your art close attention. You can't disguise a poor drawing with a showy presentation, but because of a poor presentation, sometimes a good drawing is overlooked. You can prevent your drawings from being overlooked by presenting them well. Matting your drawings is a good way to present them.

Matting a Drawing

MATERIALS

Mat knife with replaceable blades, metal ruler, hard graphite pencil, art gum or Pink Pearl eraser, mat board, backing sheet, masking tape

Matting means framing a picture with a border. Matting of drawings is usually required even in exhibitions whose rules don't require framing of artwork. Drawings included in an artist's **portfolio** are also matted. A portfolio is a collection of samples of an artist's work. The artist shows the portfolio to people who might buy the art or pay for the artist's services.

The standard form for presenting drawings for both exhibitions and portfolios is a hinged mat (or border) on a backing with outside dimensions equal to those of the mat. Look at the mat in Figure 4.24. You can see how it is hinged to the backing with a strip of masking tape at the top on the inside.

There are various methods for mat cutting, but the following procedures seem most useful. (See Figures 4.25, 4.26, and 4.27.)

First, clean the drawing surface with a soft eraser to take away any remaining pencil lines or fingerprints.

Use your pencil to mark on the mat board where the corners of the

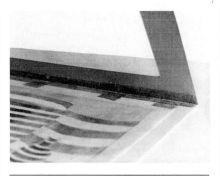

FIGURE 4.24 Student Genevieve Smead made this neatly hinged mat. It is obvious that she wanted to present her work effectively.

mat window or frame will be (Figure 4.25). A standard-sized sheet of mat board is 40 × 32″ (102 × 81 cm). Use pebble-grained, double-sided (gray and white) board.

The size of the window will vary with the size of the drawing. The width of the frame around the drawing may vary, but in general the frame should not be less than 3″ (8 cm) wide. The frame should be equally wide on all sides unless you want a slightly wider bottom piece for more visual stability.

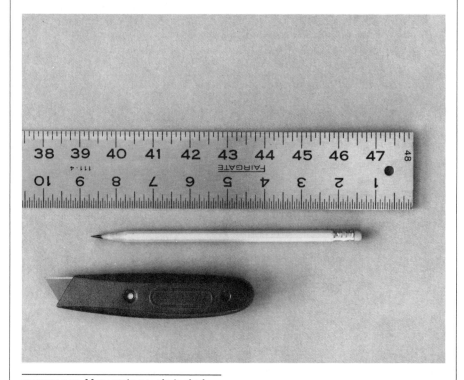

FIGURE 4.25 Mat cutting tools include a mat knife (or utility knife) like this one, a metal ruler, and a pencil. Don't use a T square or triangle as a guide for cutting lines.

mat board

The inner edge of the mat window should usually cover about ¼" (6 mm) of the ragged outer edge of the drawing.

If the edge of the drawing isn't ragged, you can leave this amount of space—or a little more—between the outer edge of the drawing and the inner edge of the mat. This practice adds interest to the framing without being too visually competitive with the drawing.

Use a mat knife (sometimes called a *box knife* or *utility knife*) to cut through the mat board. It is important to keep a sharp blade in the knife. Paper dulls blades rapidly, so be sure to replace the blade when necessary. You will cut the lines on the inside edge of the mat window. Put a piece of scrap cardboard under each line before you cut. The cardboard will protect the tabletop and keep the blade from being turned by the wood grain when you cut through the mat.

Lay the ruler along the outside edge of the first line. Hold it with your thumb and two fingers of one hand. With your cutting hand, hold the knife blade against the ruler. Don't let it lean left or right. Cut the board with several strokes in the same groove. (See Figure 4.27.) Don't try to cut the mat in one or two strokes by using muscle. Cut the other three lines in the same way. (See the Safety Note below.)

Erase any marks left on the surface of the mat. Then trace around the outside of the mat onto the backing sheet and cut the backing sheet the same size as the mat. You can use corrugated box board as backing for your classroom drawings. A sheet of Fome-cor, a thin sheet of styrofoam sandwiched between two layers of cardboard, makes an even better backing board. You could also use another sheet of mat board as backing for a small drawing. Common poster board or card stock isn't stiff enough.

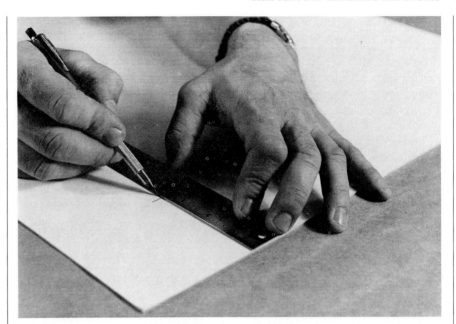

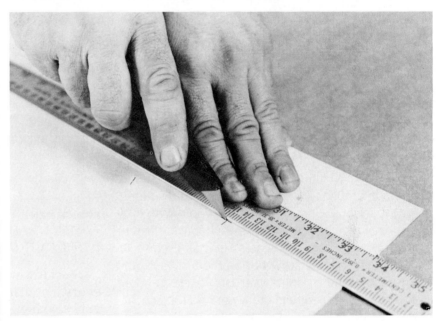

Lay the mat facedown, and hinge it to the top of the backing board with masking tape as shown in Figure 4.24. Lay the drawing faceup on the backing and close the mat on it. Then adjust the drawing to its best position. Hold it there while reopening the mat.

Fasten the drawing at the top of the backing with three or four short strips of tape so the drawing simply hangs loose against the backing. Leaving the drawing loose will prevent it from warping when

FIGURE 4.26 (top) Mark only the corners of the mat window to save erasing unnecessary pencil lines.

FIGURE 4.27 (bottom) Exert muscle power in the hand holding the ruler—not the one holding the knife. Use several strokes of a sharp knife, and don't cut on a bare tabletop. Watch out for the fingers!

mat knife
mat backing

the humidity of the air changes. (If you cut the strips of tape first and stick them lightly to your shirt-front, you won't need a third hand while you are trying to hold down the drawing.)

To protect your matted drawing, wrap it in some clear, thin acetate, a kind of plastic film. You can usually buy acetate for a few cents per foot at your local art supply or hobby shop. Cut the acetate a few inches larger than the drawing. Lay the acetate on a clean surface, and make sure there are no eraser shavings or bits of lint on the acetate or the drawing. Lay the drawing on it, facedown. Then fold the acetate over the back, and tape it to the backing board with masking tape. Fold it as if you were wrapping a package.

The acetate wrapping will make your drawing look finished and will protect it in your portfolio or at home. It will, however, make the drawing a little harder to see because of reflections in the acetate. Ask your teacher whether you should wrap drawings before you hand them in or after they are returned.

THE SKETCHBOOK

A first-rate art critic once said, ''There can be no end to drawing. It is the fundamental and continuing activity of the artist.'' Part of that activity takes place in a **sketchbook**.

A sketchbook is just a small pad filled with a moderately good grade of drawing paper. It can range in size from $4 \times 5''$ (10×12.5 cm) to four times this size, or larger. It comes in every form from a simple, unbound notepad to an elegant, hardbound volume.

Most serious artists and many people who only make art for recreation keep sketchbooks. Sketchbooks are also used by artists such as architects, interior designers, illustrators, graphic designers, and industrial designers. One way artists use sketchbooks is to try out ideas before making works of art (see Figures 3.10 and 3.22 in Chapter 3). This type of drawing is called *sketching* or *making a rough*.

The sketch in Figure 4.28 was done by the student who completed the oil painting next to it. The preliminary sketch helped the student in several ways. For instance, it allowed her to make a trial composition to see how much of the working surface she wanted the images of the still-life objects to cover. Obviously she decided to fill the space more fully with the objects when she made the painting.

The sketch also allowed her to practice drawing the objects and to draw them in a faster way than she could with paint. As a matter of fact, she probably did several sketches for practice before even starting the painting.

Finally, the sketch helped her decide about the light and dark values for the objects in the still life. It was important for her to know what values to use. Even though the objects are painted in color, a large part of their contrast depends on the amount of light reflected by the colors.

ENRICHMENT

Pure Imitationalism

Very few works of art fall into a single style category. For instance, a mainly imitational painting may also have powerful formal characteristics as well as strongly expressive qualities. The student painting in Figure 4.28, however, comes about as close as any work ever does to pure imitationalism.

The student's intent was to do nothing more than copy what was in front of her as faithfully as possible. She didn't make the setup. She had little choice of the angle from which she viewed it, and she wasn't allowed to alter or move any of the objects in the composition. This is an art school painting made over thirty years ago as an exercise in the careful copying of shapes, colors, values, and texture.

acetate

A sketchbook can also be used to record information in the form of diagrams of things you see. It can be used as a visual diary of your ideas for compositions and design problems. Or it may just be used for drawing practice.

The illustrations in Figures 4.29 through 4.34 are examples of sketches made for various purposes. Figures 4.29 and 4.30 are both shadow studies. The students used a strong light on the model to help them define the shadows. Figure 4.29, the study of a whole human form, was done rapidly with vine charcoal. Figure 4.30, the head study, is larger and more detailed than the study for the whole form. It still qualifies, however, as a sketch used for practice and for recording shadow information to be used in more finished works. It was done with a charcoal pencil. Why do you suppose the sketch of the whole body is smaller than the study of the woman's head?

A fiber-tipped pen or fine-line marker was the instrument used in the sketchbook drawing of the stereo headset in Figure 4.31. Like the head drawing in Figure 4.30, it is almost life-sized. It also was probably done for practice and to save information. In this case, though, the structure and the relationship of hard and soft forms were more important to record than the light and shadow pattern. Why do you think the artist selected a pen to do this drawing?

The drawing in Figure 4.32 is a sketch of a chair that the artist did in a hospital waiting room. It was done with a ballpoint pen on a paper towel. Obviously it isn't a chair one would see in a hospital, so the artist must have imagined it. It represents a fantasy idea about chairs that the artist wished to record. Do you think the artist should have waited until materials other than a paper towel and a ballpoint pen were available?

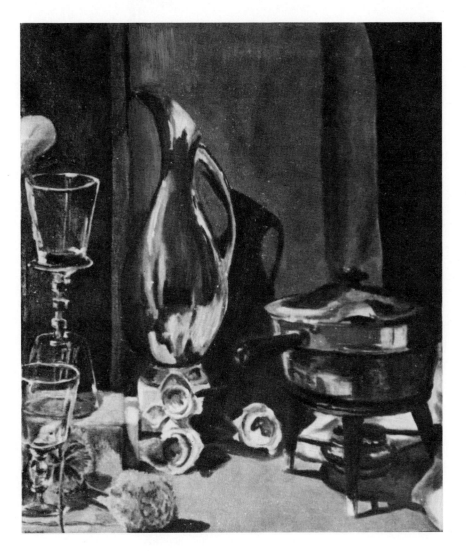

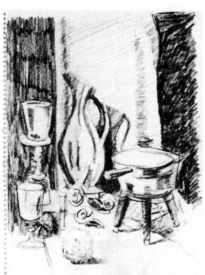

FIGURE 4.28 What changes did student Rebecca Naejgnik make from the sketch (above) to the finished painting (at the left)?

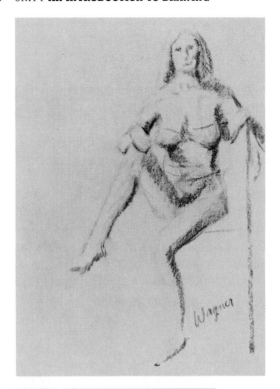

FIGURE 4.29 Nothing gives a more rapid or graphic indication of overall form than a bold, flat shadow study like this one by art student Sharon Wagner.

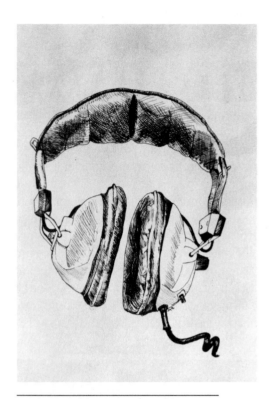

FIGURE 4.31 Many common objects have shapes worth sketching. This sketch by student Jeff McMillan clearly reveals the interesting qualities of a stereo headset.

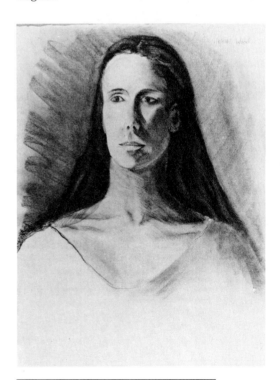

FIGURE 4.30 This head study by student Richard Wood also deals with shadows, but in a larger, more detailed form.

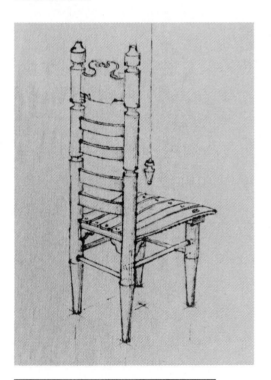

FIGURE 4.32 This sketch was found in a hospital waiting room. Surely the artist wasn't looking at a chair like this while drawing. It is obviously an imagined chair. The sketch was drawn on a paper towel. What do you think the carpenter's plumb line means?

The tiny sketches in Figure 4.33 on page 82 are called **thumbnail sketches** because they are almost small enough to have been drawn on a thumbnail. Thumbnail sketches are small sketches drawn quickly to record ideas and information for finished drawings. Actually each little drawing is about 5 × 5″ (13 × 13 cm). They were done with pen and ink. Jane Cheatham, the artist who did these expressive little sketches, used them to plan a series of paintings of animal totems, or symbols of ancestry.

Because they are thumbnail sketches, the artist could get many ideas recorded rather rapidly. They reminded this fine artist of visual ideas and creative subject combinations on which she based the finished art. Graphic designers and illustrators use thumbnail sketches to record ideas and also to show ideas to other artists, art directors, and executives. If you would like to see a finished painting by the artist who did the thumbnail sketches in Figure 4.33, look at Figure 6 in the Color Section.

Artists who create three-dimensional works also use sketches. The sketches in Figure 4.34 on page 82 were done by Keith Owens, the artist who made the whimsical sculptural construction in Figure 7 in the Color Section. Note how Owens visualized the sculpture from several viewpoints. Are all his sketches exactly like the finished construction?

ENRICHMENT

Finished Art

Finished art in a gallery or on a wall means art in which the idea is expressed to the artist's satisfaction. It is completed with care in a medium of the artist's choice.

Finished art to an advertising art director, story illustrator, or a publisher of books means art that is ready to be reproduced by printing. It is sometimes called *camera-ready* art because it will be photographed to make a printing plate, the surface from which copies are printed.

Let's return to the questions about the examples. The student who sketched the shadows on the model shown in Figure 4.29 was interested in speed. She worked small since this was one of several practice sketches she made. This sketch showed her the overall shadow pattern that defined the form. She was practicing the good habit we mentioned of working with the general, large areas first and saving the details for later.

The student who did the almost life-sized head in Figure 4.30 was also concerned with shadows. He, however, needed more detail since he had already practiced general shadow structure. So he had to work larger and spend more time.

The student who drew the stereo headset in Figure 4.31 probably selected a pen for aesthetic reasons. He may have liked the way the pen lines expressed his emotions about drawing or about the object at that time (emotionalism). Or he may have liked the way the pen lines had to be overlapped into a dense texture to make the light-to-dark gradations (formalism).

The artist who made the chair sketch in Figure 4.32 obviously chose media for the wrong reason. He used a ballpoint pen and a paper towel to get his idea recorded because they were the only materials he had at the moment. A ballpoint pen marks on only certain kinds of surfaces. It isn't the best drawing tool, and a paper towel isn't a good drawing surface. But the artist was right to use these media. If he had waited until he had better materials, he would have lost his idea. At least he could save the sketch to tape into his sketchbook or put in a file of ideas. A better option for him would have been to carry the right equipment at all times.

Many art teachers consider the sketchbook to be an important tool that students should take with them everywhere, along with a drawing instrument. You may find that one of your first assignments is to keep a sketchbook and practice in it every day. Look for things you like that are also interesting to draw.

Try to stay away, though, from drawing what everyone else draws. Nearly all beginning artists draw their teddy bear, or their tennis shoe, or a comic book character. Instead, why not find the city's oldest manhole cover for a portrait, or draw a square foot of earth with leaves and twigs, or go to an import shop and sketch wicker furniture?

After you have sketched for several weeks, you will have accumulated quite a few pages of drawings in your sketchbook. You can use those ideas for the drawing activities in this book.

FIGURE 4.33 Jane Cheatham's tiny thumbnail sketches were done in ink. They are sketches for a group of nine small paintings to be hung as a unit of three rows of three. The paintings are concerned with animal symbolism.

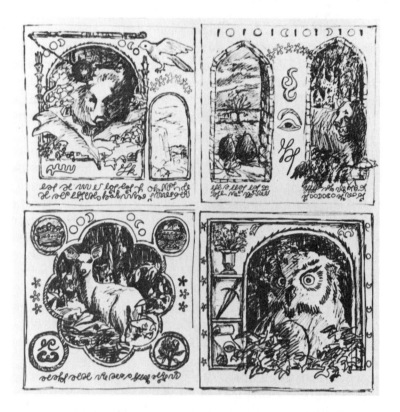

FIGURE 4.34 This sketch in graphite pencil was drawn by Keith Owens for his wood and clay construction called *The Serpent's Portal.* Note the tiny, multiple-view studies.

Courtesy of the artist.

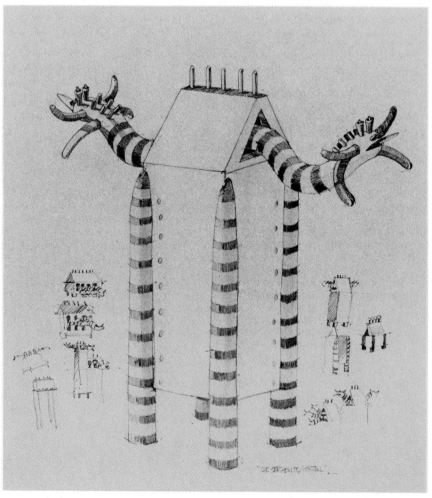

MAKING YOUR DRAWINGS ORIGINAL

In addition to the more-or-less mechanical application of skills, the drawing process involves *ideas*. If you are like most art students, you are already aware of the importance of creative ideas in the drawing process. Many art students aren't aware, however, that creative thinking is a skill that can be learned just as students learn to manipulate drawing tools and to closely observe what they draw.

Where do our ideas come from? They come from our experiences and our unique personalities. The people we know, the places we have seen, the books we have read—all our experiences generate ideas. For an artist, the experiences that he or she has had experimenting with various media are especially important in the creative process.

Look at Ken Dixon's three-panel drawing in Figure 4.35. As you look at this work, think about how Dixon's personal experiences might have led to his original idea for the work. Can you see that even something as personal as his handwriting is an important factor in the design? Figures 8 and 9 in the Color Section are other drawings by Dixon. The fact that he has used gum bichromate (a photographic printing medium) in all these works indicates how his experiences with media have contributed to his ideas. The use of the gum bichromate along with the more standard media, such as colored pencils, gives Dixon's work distinctive surface qualities.

For most people, family backgrounds can provide a rich source of drawing material. For example, Jeff McMillan had an idea for portraying his father as a fantasy character as much unlike his father's actual personality as possible. Figure 10 in the Color Section shows McMillan's father as an underworld figure from Central America, while in real life McMillan's father is a college administrator.

As you become more involved in the drawing process, you will find that ideas tend to generate other ideas. Look at Jeff McMillan's montage (combination of several images into one) in Figure 4.36 on the next page. McMillan's idea of showing his mother riding an off-the-road vehicle was the extension of his idea for the fantasy drawing of his father.

The multimedia drawings in Figures 11 and 12 in the Color Section are part of a series based on the personal images of John Wilson. An art student who is also a musician, he is interested in giant cetaceans (especially, as you can see in the drawings, the killer whales). Wilson rendered the threatening teeth of the killer whale in brightly colored, stuffed fabric in the first composition. In the second composition, he used a group of jazz musicians to repeat the direction of

FIGURE 4.35 Ken Dixon's three-panel work is called *Passing Through*. What do you think his sources were for this drawing?
Courtesy of the artist.

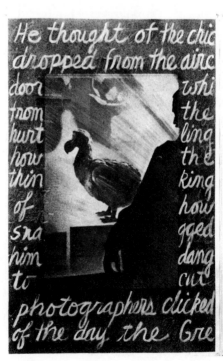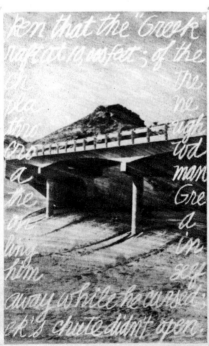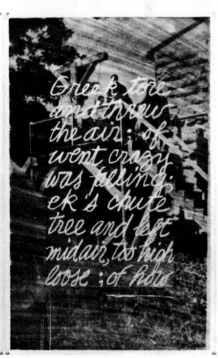

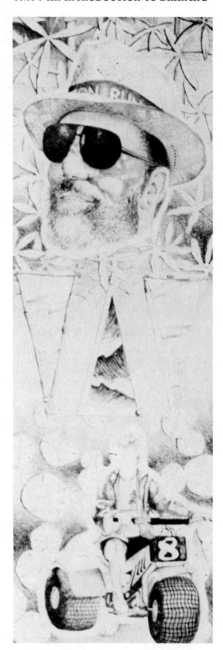

FIGURE 4.36 This drawing by student Jeff McMillan extends his idea for *Father Popcorn* (Color Section, Figure 10).

the row of whale's teeth to make a visually exciting and amusing drawing.

You can stimulate your own creative thinking in several ways:

■ Be curious about everything and develop many strong interests. Take drawing ideas from things that interest you.

■ Research your subject extensively. The library, your friends, government agencies, and professional societies are just a few of the many sources of information.

■ Make many sketches to obtain information and experiment with a composition.

■ Discuss your ideas with friends.

■ After experimenting with a new idea, leave it alone, ''sleep on it'' for a while. Then come back to the idea with a fresh approach.

Your best ideas will probably come to you when you are alert but relaxed—and probably when you least expect them.

In looking for ideas, do you think it is ever good practice to draw what someone else has already drawn? There are only three reasons for reproducing anyone else's drawing. One reason is to explore a technique to discover how the artist did it. Another reason is to record information that the work was meant to give; for example, from a technical illustration in an encyclopedia. The third reason is to honor a famous work with commentary or an extension of the artist's idea.

Copying the work of a photographer is a little like using someone else's drawing. You can draw mechanical or factual information if the photograph's purpose is to make that information available.

It is definitely wrong to copy, however, if you are stealing the artist's or photographer's *idea* and presenting it as your own. This kind of copying is called **plagiarism**, and it is unlawful and unethical.

Using the same subject as another artist doesn't always mean you are plagiarizing, though. There are subjects that are universal—the property of everyone in our culture. Every artist has a right to draw these, and many of them have done so.

An obvious example of a universal subject is the event in Christian history called the Last Supper. No one knows how many artists have interpreted this scene, but at least five famous interpretations were made in the century and a half between 1450 and 1600. (See Figure 3.17 in Chapter 3.) Of the interpretations made in the twentieth century, the version by Salvador Dali is probably the best known, but there are many others.

A wise teacher named Richard Sears once advised, ''Quit worrying about being different and worry about being good. *That will be different enough!*'' He went on to explain, ''I mean there is vir-tually nothing that has not been done at some time in the history of art; so the only truly original thing you bring to your work is *yourself*. You are one of a kind; and if you express yourself honestly in your ideas, your uniqueness will be evident; and if you learn to express yourself well in your craft, you will be a member of a small and select company.''

DRAWING AT WORK

Fashion Designer: Patterns for the Future

The fashion designer is the key person in the garment industry. Whether creating designs for clothing, accessories, or jewelry, the fashion de-signer must keep pace with changing trends and styles. Many of the over twenty thousand designers and assistant designers working in the United States are employed by manufacturers of paper patterns. Dora Latorre has worked for Butterick, Inc. in New York City for over three years. Latorre designs for Vogue, a department of Butterick, which carries over ten lines of clothing.

Designing for Vogue enables Latorre to combine three of her primary interests: drawing, sewing, and fashion. She was able to find a career that suited her so well by taking a mini-course at the Parsons School of Design in New York City. Parsons conducts a month-long course in fashion design in the summer to allow interested students to explore fashion as a career. Students take classes in illus-tration, draping, patternmaking, and drawing.

These mini-courses also give prospective stu-dents a true picture of the extreme demands made on the students at Parsons. One teacher told Latorre that while at the school, ''You eat fashion, you drink fashion, you think fashion.'' This state-ment turned out to be true. But Latorre was will-ing to work hard because she discovered after the summer course that she wanted to pursue a career in fashion designing. She continued her studies and graduated from Parsons.

Latorre has never regretted her decision. Her job with Vogue is both exciting and challenging with a variety of duties. The design process begins with a new idea for a garment. These ideas may be suggested by the merchandising director, who has the latest news about styles, or by the individ-ual designers themselves. Part of Latorre's job is attending fashion shows in New York to stay in-formed about what is happening in the field.

When a particular ''look'' has been chosen, Latorre sketches three views of the garment. One view may have a long skirt, another may show the same garment with a shorter skirt, and the third view may change the design of the sleeves.

The next step is to have the garment made up in muslin, a cotton fabric. A garment may look strik-ing in a drawing, but the designer must also con-sider the specific needs of the construction process. After the adjustments are made to the muslin gar-ment and the final design is approved, the design is sewn in an inexpensive material in all three views.

Latorre's work isn't finished when a design is approved. She oversees the patternmaking process, coordinates her design with other departments, and supervises the artist who creates the drawing for the pattern catalog. She is responsible for the total look of the design—from what zipper to rec-ommend to the consumer to the accessories pic-tured on the pattern package.

It should be noted that the work of the fashion designer is different from that of the fashion illus-trator. It is the illustrator's job to picture the already finished clothing in a glamorous way to help sell it in magazines, newspapers, and mail-order catalogs. The work of a fashion illustrator is shown in Figure 10.17.

Latorre feels that her job allows her to develop design skills. She came to Butterick with drawing talent, design training, and a sense of fashion, and now she has learned the logic behind garment construction. Her job is as exciting as next year's fashion fad.

UNIT I

━━━━━━━━━━━━━━━━━━━━━━━━━━━━━   ━━━━━━━━━━━━━━━━━━━━━━━━━━━━━

Evaluation and Review

MEETING YOUR OBJECTIVES

By answering the following questions and doing the exercises, you will demonstrate your ability to meet the learning objectives listed at the beginning of Chapters 1, 2, 3, and 4.

Chapter 1

1. Why is it important to learn the visual vocabulary?
2. List the elements of art.
3. Study the drawing in Figure 1.14 carefully. Then write one statement about each element you observed in the drawing. Underline the element.
4. List the principles of art.
5. Again look at Figure 1.14 carefully. Now write as many statements as you can that combine an element of art with a principle. Underline both the element and the principle in the sentence.
6. Write a detailed paragraph about Figure 1.14. Begin the paragraph by saying either ''I think this drawing shows unity because . . . .'' or ''I think this drawing fails to show unity because . . . .''

Chapter 2

1. What purpose does a theory of art serve?
2. What is the advantage of knowing and using several theories of art rather than just one theory?
3. Name the three theories of art discussed in Chapter 2. Write one sentence that describes each.
4. List the three kinds of aesthetic qualities described in this chapter. For each of the three qualities, write one sentence that describes that quality.
5. What is the difference between *looking at* and *seeing* works of art?
6. List in the proper order the four steps in the art criticism process.
7. Write as many sentences as you can describing the literal qualities in Figure 2.1.
8. Analyze Cezanne's use of the elements and principles of art in *Bathers Under a Bridge*, Figure 2.2. Do this by placing checkmarks in the design chart to indicate at least three design relationships. Then write one sentence about each relationship.
9. Give your interpretation of Francisco Goya's *Disasters of War*, Figure 2.3. Write one sentence for

each idea, mood, or feeling that Goya's work communicates to you.
10. Earlier you told why you thought Figure 1.14 was or was not a unified drawing. Now judge the overall success or failure of that work. Give reasons for your judgment.

Chapter 3

1. List at least three ways that studying art history might help you improve your drawing skills.
2. Pick five periods or styles of art discussed in Chapter 3. For each style or period, write one paragraph describing its identifying characteristics.
3. Pick three drawings from Chapters 1 and 2 and write the titles on a sheet of paper. Next to each title write the name of the artistic period or style to which that work belongs. Then point out as many characteristics as you can find in the work that make it representative of that style or period.
4. For each of the following artists, give the name of the artistic period or style with which he or she is most closely associated: Jacques-Louis David, Giotto, Claus Oldenburg, El Greco, Joan Miró, Michelangelo, and Berthe Morisot.
5. For each of the following works from Chapters 1 and 2, give the name of the artist and the related artistic period or style discussed in Chapter 3: Figures 1.1 (period), 1.2 (style), 1.6 (period), 1.13 (period), 2.4 (style), and 2.14 (style).
6. Give at least three examples of artistic styles that were affected by historical events and situations.
7. Compare Figure 2.13 to Figure 3.20. These works are examples of two different styles of art. Write one or two paragraphs describing the differences and similarities between these two works.

Chapter 4

1. What is the most important factor in making successful drawings?
2. Do a small (about 8 × 10″) gesture drawing of a model in charcoal.
3. Do a small (about 8 × 10″) cross contour drawing of a still-life setup. Do the preliminary work in graphite pencil and finish the work with a fiber-tipped pen.

4. Do a cross contour drawing as described in number 3 above. In this drawing, however, use color and value to make the cross-contour bands advance and recede into space.
5. Make a list of all the drawing tools and media you used in doing the studio exercises in Chapter 4.
6. Make a list of all the drawing techniques you learned and used in Chapter 4.
7. Make a hinged mat and mount the drawing you created in number 4 above.
8. Give four possible uses of a sketchbook.
9. List at least three sources of ideas for your art projects.
10. Write one or two sentences explaining how it's possible to get ideas from the works of other artists without plagiarizing their work.

LEARNING DRAWING TERMS

You encountered several new drawing terms in this unit. The most important terms are those printed in heavy, bold type, such as **harmony** and **variety** on page 12. Write all the terms in heavy, bold type on a sheet of paper. Then, without looking in your book, tell what each term means in your own words. If you are not sure of a meaning, use your book to write a definition.

EXPERIENCING DIFFERENT MEDIA

Each new drawing medium is listed at the bottom of the page on which it is first mentioned. Review your experiences with all the media, comparing strengths, weaknesses, and personal preferences. Then write a report summarizing your experiences with these media.

SEEING YOUR ENVIRONMENT

Learning to see the world around you as it really is is one of the first steps to improving your drawing skills. Doing the following exercises and others like them will help get you in the habit of seeing your environment more closely.

1. Find two examples of line in your environment. Make sketches showing the different types, widths, and directions of the lines in both examples.
2. Notice negative shapes in your environment. Pick two or three objects in your environment and make drawings that emphasize the negative shapes.

3. Identify an example of rhythm in your environment. It could be sounds you hear while studying, or the patterns you notice as cars pass you on the way to school. Try to recreate the rhythm.

EVALUATING DRAWINGS

1. Evaluate the drawing you did for number 3, Chapter 4, under "Meeting Your Objectives." Rate yourself from 1 to 10 for two categories: 1) craft and composition and, 2) variation in cross contour lines to emphasize volume or depth.
2. Use the art criticism steps you learned in Chapter 2 to evaluate the drawing you critiqued above.

EXPANDING YOUR HISTORICAL KNOWLEDGE

Learning about the history of art will help you improve your drawing skills. It will also increase your understanding of your own culture and the cultures of others, both past and present. Answering the questions below indicates that you are learning art history. You will be able to answer most of the questions by referring to the Enrichment sections and to Chapter 3. To answer the last question you will probably need to refer to art history books, such as those listed in the Bibliography at the back of this book.

1. Artists from which period of art are important because they helped preserve the Greek heritage?
2. Artworks from what period are characterized by a flat, two-dimensional look, with brightly colored and richly patterned figures?
3. What style of art was inspired by Cezanne?
4. What 17th century artistic style featured a sculptured, dynamic look in its architecture?
5. What art movement focused on the world of dreams and the workings of the mind?
6. During which important period in history did people become more concerned with the real world, while the artists began to use perspective and other techniques to create more realistic works?
7. Pick two artists whose works you find appealing. Skim Chapter 3 for ideas. Then study several works by each artist. Identify the techniques, subjects, or media that make those artists two of your favorites. Then write a paragraph about each artist telling what you think you can learn from the artist.

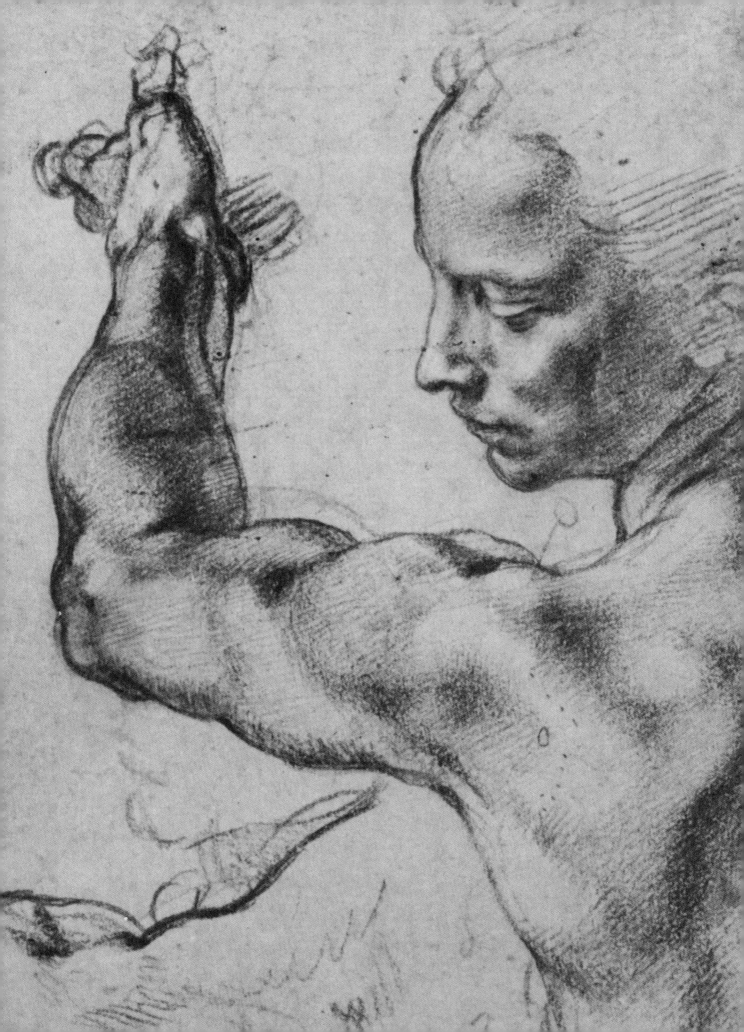

Realistic Drawing

In Unit II you will learn about drawings done in a realistic style. You will focus on the literal qualities, which are considered the most important aesthetic qualities by imitationalists.

To find out how other artists have used the literal qualities, you will imagine that you are attending an opening of an exhibition at a local art gallery. No matter which of the theories of art you personally prefer, in Chapter 5, ''Understanding and Judging Literal Qualities,'' you will assume the role of an imitationalist critic. You will use the art criticism process to describe and judge several drawings to decide how successful they are by how well they imitate reality.

In Chapter 6, ''Making Imitational Drawings,'' you will use what you have learned through art criticism and history about literal qualities to create your own realistic drawings. As you learn techniques for creating proportion, perspective, and shadow, you will be able to make drawings that look lifelike. Human forms are often included in realistic drawings. Chapter 6 closes with techniques for drawing the human figure.

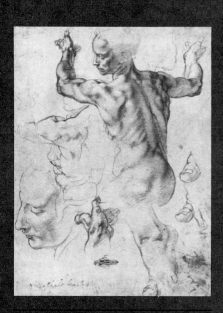

Michelangelo. *Studies for the Libyan Sibyl*. c. 1511. Red chalk. 11⅜ × 8⅜ (28.9 × 21.3 cm). The Metropolitan Museum of Art, New York. (Joseph Pulitzer Bequest.) (detail at left)

Understanding and Judging Literal Qualities

OBJECTIVES

After reading this chapter and doing the activities, you will be able to

■ explain how an imitationalist judges drawings;

■ describe the literal qualities in drawings; and

■ judge drawings based on their literal qualities and give reasons for your judgment.

In Chapter 2, you learned about three theories of art: imitationalism, formalism, and emotionalism. Each of these ideas about what makes an artwork successful focuses on different qualities. You discovered that:

■ An imitationalist measures drawings by their *literal qualities* or subject matter.

■ A formalist measures drawings by their *visual qualities* or the elements and principles of art.

■ An emotionalist measures drawings by their *expressive qualities* or how well they express meaning or feelings.

In this chapter we want you to think like an imitationalist. Responding to literal qualities in drawings will prepare you to create drawings of your own that emphasize these qualities. *As an imitationalist, you will describe everything you see in drawings.*

You should find that acting like an imitationalist isn't difficult. In fact, you may already be an imitationalist without knowing it. If you are, that should make the role even easier to play. All you must do is respond to works of art the way you always have. If you are an imitationalist, you are convinced that literal qualities are the most important ones in drawings. They are the standard by which you judge all art.

If you aren't an imitationalist, you are asked to act like one while you read this chapter. This pretending may seem awkward at times, but it will focus your attention on the literal qualities. You will play other roles in later chapters, and these may be more to your liking. For now, remember that you aren't concerned with the visual qualities or the expressive qualities of drawings. You are much too busy judging works of art by how real their subject matter looks.

As you read, you will find questions that you should ask yourself as you respond to drawings in your role as an imitationalist. Often these questions won't be followed by answers.

You can react to these unanswered questions in one of two ways: ignore them and read on, or try to answer them before reading further. If you want to develop your understanding and knowledge of drawing, you should try to answer the questions. They serve two important purposes: to stimulate your thinking and, more important, to bring out your personal opinions, feelings, and ideas.

A final comment is needed about responding to drawings. As you read and reread this chapter—and the rest of the book—don't become alarmed if you find yourself wanting to change some of your answers to the questions. Changing your mind shows that you are thinking your way through this book instead of just flipping through the pages to finish your assigned reading.

It is now time for you to take on the role of an imitationalist. You are to respond most favorably to drawings rendered in a realistic style. Among the works displayed at a local gallery opening are drawings done in this style. Having learned this fact, you look forward to seeing the drawings and make plans to attend the opening . . .

Gas

EDWARD HOPPER

The gallery is jammed with people. They are all voicing their opinions about the wide assortment of artworks on display (Figure 5.1). The room becomes silent when you enter; everyone is eager to see how you will react to the drawings. People edge closer as you pause before a black conte crayon drawing by the American artist Edward Hopper (Figure 5.2 on the next page). They all watch as you study it closely. (Don't read further until you have completed a thorough description of the drawing *Gas* in your role as an imitationalist. To do this, make a list of everything you see in the work.)

Several of the more impatient onlookers interrupt your examination. They urge you to give your opinions about the drawing. What will you mention first? Will you begin by describing the work in a general way and then point out the details? If so, you might say

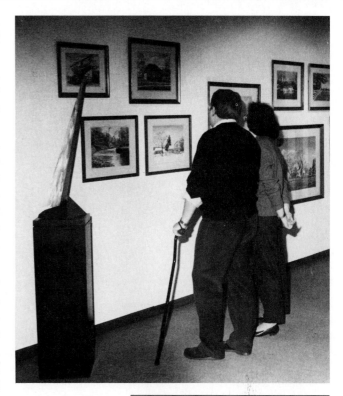

FIGURE 5.1 People examining works of art in a gallery.
Photo by Vicky Kee.

that the drawing consists of a gas station located at the side of a narrow country road. Maybe you describe the dreary station, the three gas pumps, and the solitary figure in the foreground.

Will you also mention the road? It looks hardly wide enough for two cars to pass each other. A row of dark trees keeps the eye from moving back into the distance. This barrier emphasizes the isolation of the small gas station.

The figure at the gas pumps seems to be performing some kind of job (Figure 5.3). What is he doing? It is impossible to say for certain. There is no car waiting for service, and there is none in sight on the road that might need attention. So there seems to be little need for the attendant to be doing anything at the moment.

Someone in the group interrupts to ask if you think the drawing is successful. Remember that you think the literal qualities just described are the most important in a drawing. How will you respond? Does the drawing show this scene in a realistic way?

You might answer that the drawing is quite descriptive, even though there aren't many details. The artist held his imagination back. He must have been determined to include only the most important

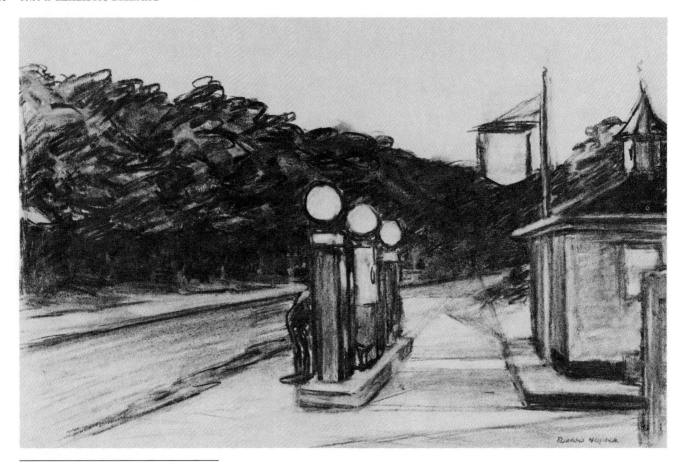

FIGURE 5.2 Edward Hopper, drawing for painting *Gas*, 1940. Conte and charcoal with touches of white paint on paper, 15 × 22⅛″ (38.1 × 56.4 cm). Whitney Museum of American Art, New York, NY. Josephine N. Hopper bequest.

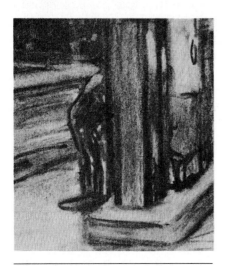

FIGURE 5.3 Edward Hopper, drawing for painting *Gas* (detail).

features. He wanted to draw a specific place at a certain moment in time. Several people listening to your comments look again at the drawing and then nod in agreement. They also are convinced of the drawing's success. (You can see Hopper's painting *Gas* in Figure 3 in the Color Section.)

Gross Clinic

THOMAS EAKINS

Another drawing across the gallery (Figure 5.4) catches your attention. You make your way through the crowd to look at it more carefully. (Don't read further until you have made a complete list of everything in the drawing *Gross Clinic*.)

You think of a number of questions as you look at this drawing:

■ Where is this scene taking place?

■ How many people are pictured?

■ What is each person doing?

■ How do the actions of the single female figure set her apart from everyone else in the drawing?

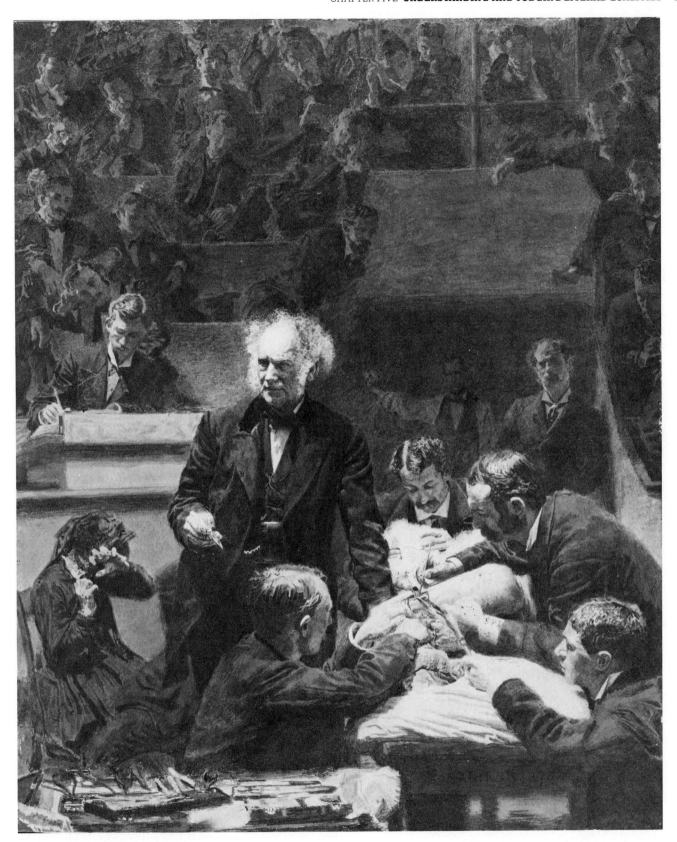

FIGURE 5.4 Thomas Eakins, *Gross Clinic*, 1875. India ink wash on cardboard, 23⅝ × 19⅛″ (60 × 48.6 cm). The Metropolitan Museum of Art, New York, NY. Rogers Fund.

- Who is the most important person in the drawing?
- How is this person's importance emphasized?
- To whom is this person speaking?
- How are the people dressed? Are their clothes appropriate for the occasion?
- Where does the light come from? What is its purpose?
- Finally, is this a successful work of art?

ENRICHMENT

Thomas Eakins

Any discussion of Eakins must begin with his constant devotion to imitationalism. This loyalty kept him from becoming a popular painter. It isolated him from everyone but his family, students, and a few friends.

Eakins was twenty-seven years old when he returned to his native America after studying art in France. He found that the most successful American artists were producing dull landscapes and sentimental scenes of daily life. He certainly had the skill to paint similar pictures and if he had painted them, he would probably have been popular and wealthy. But Eakins stubbornly insisted on painting life exactly as he saw it.

What could have inspired such loyalty to an artistic style? Why did Eakins choose a life of disappointment and frustration? While in Europe, Eakins had seen and been impressed by the works of Gustave Courbet (Chapter 3, page 52) and other leading contemporary French artists. These artists, known as *Realists*, had rejected subject matter that glorified the past or romanticized the present. They painted everyday events the way these subjects really looked.

But it was the work of the masters of the seventeenth century—Diego Velázquez, Franz Hals, and Rembrandt van Rijn—that Eakins never forgot. These artists were his teachers. The lessons he learned from their works affected every drawing and painting he did during a career of forty years.

Eakins studied geometry, perspective, and anatomy to be able to draw accurately. In one drawing that he did as preparation for a painting, he used perspective to reproduce as accurately as possible the reflections in rippling water (Figure 5.5). But Eakins valued anatomy the most. He even required his students at the Pennsylvania Academy of Fine Arts to dissect human corpses.

Imitationalism is clearly shown in the drawing *Gross Clinic* that Eakins completed in 1875, four years after his return to the United States. The subject fascinated him so much that he did a large painting of it as well. It is often called his greatest work. The clinic was a natural subject for Eakins since he was interested in anatomy and knew many of the staff at the clinic.

The drawing shows a hushed operating room filled with attentive students. They are listening to a highly respected physician explain a surgical procedure. There is a momentary pause in the lecture. A woman, shielding her eyes with an arm, starts sobbing. She is a relative of the patient. The law at that time required a relative to be present during surgery. The doctor, ignoring her, stands with his back to the patient, still holding the scalpel with which he made the incision.

Many people objected to the blood on the scalpel and on the surgeon's hands. They said that showing the blood was tasteless and unnecessary. They didn't listen when Eakins explained that the blood was a part of the scene. The blood had to be shown exactly as he saw it.

The following year Eakins was humiliated when his painting of the Gross Clinic was rejected from the Philadelphia Centennial Exhibition. The painting was eventually put on display, but not with the other works of art. Instead, it was included with the Centennial's medical exhibits!

The realism that was responsible for isolation during his lifetime still sets Thomas Eakins apart, but in a completely different way. Today, he is widely regarded as one of America's most important artists.

Self-Portrait at Age Twenty-Two
ALBRECHT DÜRER

As you continue to stroll through the crowded gallery, you are fascinated by what you can learn from drawings by studying their literal qualities. You pause a moment to look at a small ink self-portrait by Albrecht Dürer (Figure 7.5 on page 143). This drawing looks so lifelike that it must have been completed while the artist was studying his own reflection in a mirror. This fact would explain the unusually large

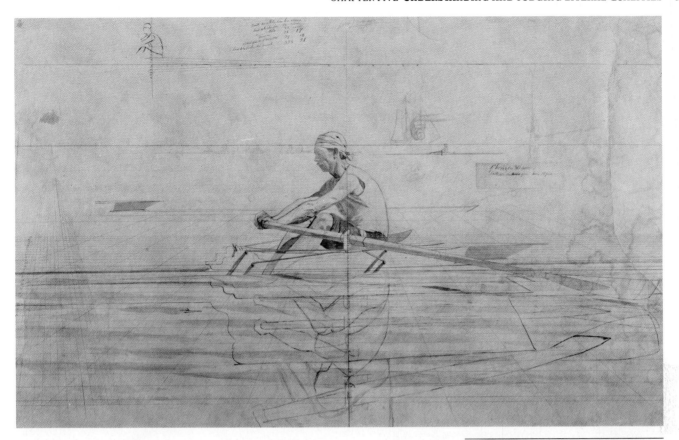

FIGURE 5.5 Thomas Eakins, *Perspective Drawing for John Biglen in a Single Scull*, date unknown. Pencil, pen, and wash drawing, 27⅜ × 45³/₁₆″ (69.5 × 114.6 cm). Courtesy of the Museum of Fine Arts, Boston, MA. Gift of Cornelius V. Whitney.

hand delicately balanced as if he were holding a mirror in front of his face.

While you are admiring the precision in this drawing, you suddenly notice something quite surprising. Unless you had carefully studied the drawing, you would have missed it. You tell the people standing next to you to look at the drawing of a pillow included on the same sheet of paper.

They look puzzled, so you urge them to look at it more closely. ''What do you see?'' you ask. As they, too, see something in the pillow, they begin to smile. There, hidden among the wrinkles and shadows, are several strange face-like images.

Head of a Girl with Braids
HENRI MATISSE

What's this? Some people are waving to you and pointing to still another drawing. They want your opinions about it, so you hurry over to examine it. Clearly this drawing (Figure 7.7 on page 145) is unlike any of the others you have looked at so far. As an imitationalist, how will you respond to this work? Can you say that it is lifelike, accurate, or detailed?

It is a drawing of a girl with braids, but it is clearly not supposed to look like her. It is little more than a simplified outline. The artist hasn't tried to show volume or realistic detail.

You are disappointed with the drawing. It obviously lacks the literal qualities that you think are necessary in a successful drawing. It isn't surprising, then, that you reject it as unimportant.

The Last Respects
HENRI DE TOULOUSE-LAUTREC

The next drawing on display (Figure 9.5 on page 175) also seems unsuccessful to you. Although it is more realistic than the last work, it also doesn't have enough detail to look lifelike. But you still pause a few moments to look it over. Parts of the picture at least suggest reality. The face, for example, with its furrowed brow, heavy eyelids, and drooping mustache,

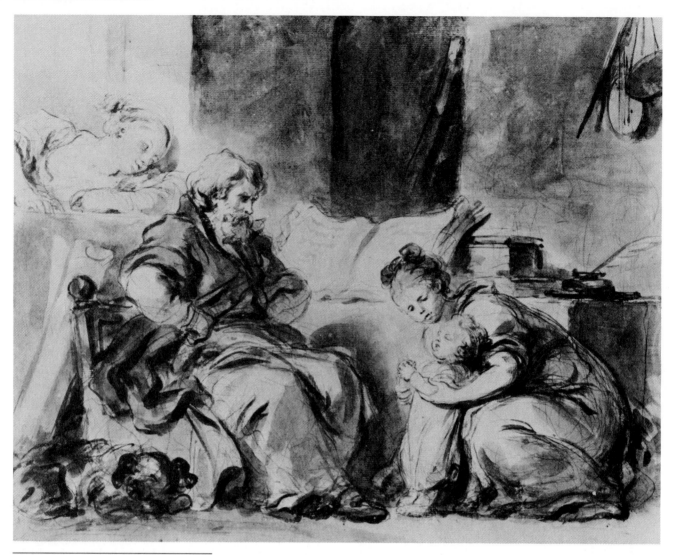

FIGURE 5.6 Jean-Honoré Fragonard, *Grandfather's Reprimand*, c. 1770–80. Gray-brown wash over black chalk, 13½ × 17¾″ (34.3 × 45.1 cm). The Armand Hammer Collection, Los Angeles, CA.

belongs to a specific person who is grieving. But the face hasn't been drawn with light and dark values. As a result, it doesn't look three-dimensional as a real face does.

You find another drawing in the gallery that is appealing because of its exciting use of literal qualities (Figure 5.6.) Study it closely and describe its literal qualities. Based on these qualities, make a personal judgment about the drawing. (Don't read further until you have described and judged the drawing in Figure 5.6).

Glancing at your watch, you find that it is still quite early. If you hurry, you will have enough time to return to your studio to work on drawings of your own—imitational drawings, of course.

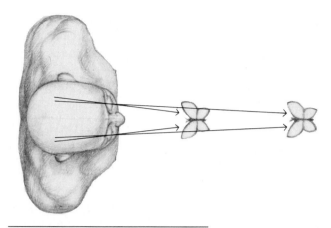

FIGURE 6.1 This diagram isn't biologically accurate, but it shows how stereoscopic binocular vision helps us judge distances.

PROPORTION

In making drawings that look real, one of the first things to consider is proportion. We say that items in a composition are *proportional* if their sizes look real when we compare them. Each object in a drawing must be the correct size in relation to all the other objects.

The size of a person's hands should be correct in relation to the face. The size of a brick in a wall should be correct in relation to the wall's height. The size of a house far away on a hill should compare correctly with the size of a daisy that is right in front of us.

The girl in the student sketch in Figure 6.2 looks believable because most of the proportions are correct. Though we may not immediately recognize all of the items in the still life in Figure 6.3, we decide it shows a real setup because the popcorn popper, the pitcher, and the branch seem to be the right size in comparison with each other. That is, the proportions look correct. The shapes and forms are the correct size.

How can we make things in a drawing look the right size? We measure their proportions, and then we place the objects or figures in the right positions.

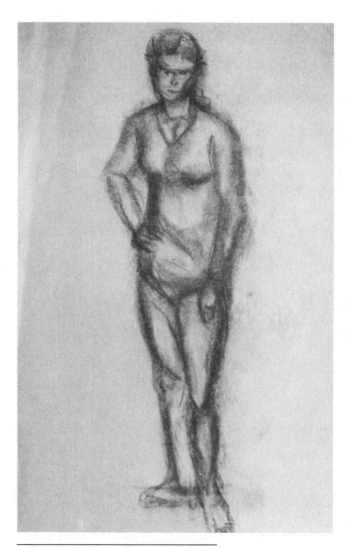

FIGURE 6.2 Although art student Bryon Stamets drew this figure rapidly in charcoal, he didn't neglect correct height proportions.

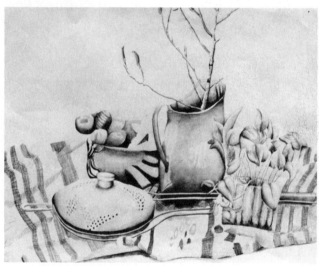

FIGURE 6.3 This drawing was done in rubbed graphite pencil by student Kevin Gentry.

Binocular Vision

No photographic technique has been able to duplicate the human brain and eyes in creating images of objects in space. Stereoscopic photography, which combines two images into one, captures some of the illusion, but this photography is limited because it requires a controlled viewing position. The principle of binocular vision has also been used to design optical range finders for mapmaking and tank gunnery. Your local camera dealer will have stereoscopic cameras and viewers and books on double-image photographs.

Double-image (or 3-D) movies are another example of the use of the principle of binocular vision. These movies are produced by making one print of the film in warm colors and one print in cool colors. These prints are shown side by side. The audience is given glasses that filter out the warm colors for one eye and cool colors for the other eye. Because of binocular vision, the brain lays one image on top of the other so that viewers see a third dimension, depth.

Holograms

Holograms, three-dimensional pictures produced by lasers, also try to duplicate human vision. They succeed to a degree because the image changes as the viewer moves from side to side. Holograms are still limited, however, because they can't capture images of moving objects or adequately portray natural color.

Measuring Proportions

MATERIALS
Pencil

Let's try checking the proportions of some things in the room using a pencil as a measuring tool. Look at Figure 6.4. The student artist is using the pencil as a ruler to measure height or width. She is holding the measurement by using a thumbnail as the marker. Note that she holds the pencil at full arm's length from her eyes.

Lean a large book against the studio door, and step back a few feet. Using your pencil to measure, find out how many ''books'' high the door is when it is seen from where you are standing. Start by sighting down your arm and holding the pencil just as the student in Figure 6.4 is holding it. Be sure to extend your arm fully. Place the top of the pencil in line with the top of the book; then slide your thumbnail down the pencil without moving the pencil until the thumbnail marks the bottom of the book. Hold this measurement.

Extend your arm again. Now start at either the top or bottom of the door, and see how many books high it is.

Suppose you were making a drawing of the book and the door from where you were standing. You could decide how much of your paper you wanted the door to cover. Then, by dividing this height by the number of books it contains,

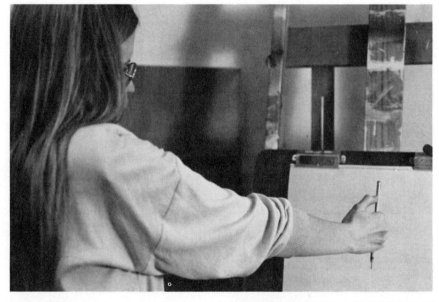

FIGURE 6.4 Making comparative measurements with a pencil is a helpful technique. Remember always to keep your arm straight when sighting along the pencil.

you would know how tall to make the book. Of course, width comparisons may be made the same way.

In fact, you can use the measurement of one object in a drawing (like the book's height) as a unit to measure everything in the drawing. As long as you are consistent

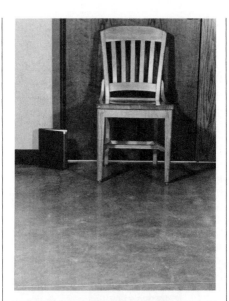

FIGURE 6.5 Notice that the chair is much closer in the second photograph. You can tell this because the chair seems much larger and has moved downward in the picture.

in using it, you can even make up your own unit of measure and mark it on a pencil or brush.

Now put a chair next to the book and door. Return to your drawing **station point**, the viewpoint from which you made your first measurements, and find out how many books high the chair is. Then move the chair to a point halfway between your station point and the door. What happens to the measurement?

Remember the discussion in Chapter 1 about the principle of proportion? If you changed the proportion (number of books of height) of the chair in a drawing, you would change the element of space by moving the chair closer. See Figure 6.5 for a photograph of how the chair changes proportions and placement in the drawing when it is moved closer.

Check the photograph in Figure 6.5 again. Notice that you could also use the book to measure the distance between objects, or the distance of an object from the edge of the drawing. For example, when the chair was moved closer, it

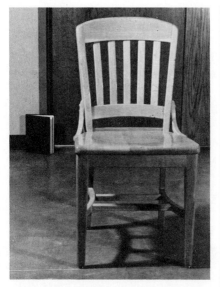

became taller, but it also had to be moved down on the page.

How many books is the chair from the bottom of the page in its new position? How many books from the right-hand edge? You can answer these questions by laying the edge of a piece of paper next to the book in the diagram, marking its length, and then seeing how many times this length can be fitted into the distance you are trying to measure. Of course, the measurement won't always come out even. Sometimes you will have to add a fraction to the measurement.

You can use your pencil as a measuring stick whenever you draw. But remember: always remain at the same station point while you are measuring, and

always measure with your arm fully extended. Ignoring these two rules will make your estimates meaningless.

STUDIO

Proportional Drawings of a Still Life

MATERIALS

Soft graphite or charcoal pencil, newsprint

Make a still-life setup of three simple objects on a table. Using the measuring technique you have just learned, make an outline drawing of the shapes. Make them no bigger than 6″ (15 cm) in their largest dimension.

Then make a drawing of the same objects after moving one of them much closer to you. Now move one of the other objects much farther away, perhaps to another table, and make a third drawing. See the examples in Figure 6.6.

FIGURE 6.6 Making several drawings of a group of simple objects with some of the objects moved to different distances will help you learn to draw illusions of deep space.

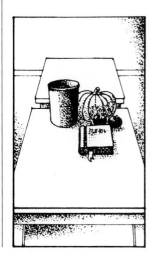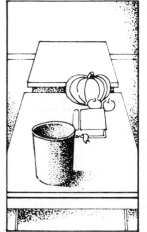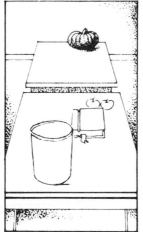

NEGATIVE SPACE

Besides measuring, another good way to establish correct proportions is to carefully study the negative space around and between the shapes of things you want to draw.

Look at the photograph of a typical still-life setup (Figure 6.7). Then look at the tracing of the negative spaces in the picture. If you can accurately draw the spaces where there are no objects, you can easily fill in the objects using correct proportions and placement.

In fact, even if you don't fill in the objects, it will often be obvious what they are. When you start figure drawing, using negative space to check proportions can be particularly helpful. Start now making a habit of checking the negative spaces. Space is an element of art, and it is important in all drawings.

FIGURE 6.7 The drawing over the photograph of the still-life outlines some of the negative areas.

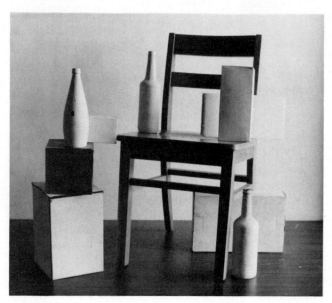
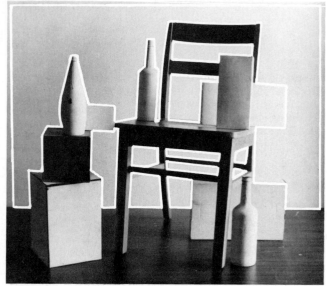

STUDIO

Sketchbook Charcoal Drawing of Negative Spaces

MATERIALS
Soft charcoal pencil, sketchbook

Practice drawing negative spaces in your sketchbook for a still-life setup. Make each drawing fill a page. Working too small will cause you to overlook important details. Do five or six drawings.

STUDIO

Large Charcoal Drawing of Negative Spaces

MATERIALS
Vine charcoal, newsprint

Do a large drawing of the negative spaces for a collection of objects or an outdoor scene. If the negative shapes between some objects overlap those between objects farther away, don't worry about it; draw all of the negative shapes transparently (as though you could see through them). Now go back to find the outlines of the positive shapes of the objects in the picture, and darken them. They should emerge clearly from overlapping negative shapes.

The purpose of this exercise is to practice proportion and placement for making imitational drawings. However, if you do the exercise carefully enough, you can produce an interesting formal drawing like the one in Figure 6.8.

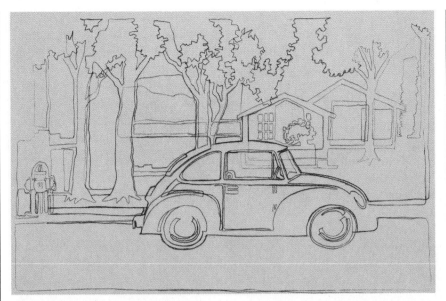

FIGURE 6.8 Even an outdoor scene like the one in this student drawing can be rendered by drawing the negative shapes first.

STUDIO

Eraser Drawing of Negative Spaces

MATERIALS

Compressed charcoal; vine charcoal; sand pad; felt pad or tissue; kneadable eraser;chamois skin; one-ply bristol board; drafting tape

For this negative space rendering, you will cover an entire sheet with a middle value of gray and then erase the areas where the positive shapes would be, leaving only the negative spaces. Use a still-life setup or objects from an outdoor scene for your subject.

First, rub the compressed charcoal against the sand pad. A sand pad is a small paddle with sheets of fine sandpaper attached at one end. Tap the sand pad lightly against a sheet of paper or into a shallow dish. Repeat this process until you have a small pile of carbon dust.

Use a sheet of paper at least 17 × 22″ (43 × 56 cm) for this drawing. Fasten your paper on the drawing board at the corners with drafting tape. Sprinkle the paper lightly with carbon dust; then smooth the dust to an even coating of gray with the felt pad, a small pad of felt cloth or tissue.

Next, squeeze your kneadable eraser into a ball. A kneadable or dough eraser can be squeezed into any shape. Transfer the eraser to your non-drawing hand, and continue to knead or squeeze it occasionally to keep it soft while you draw.

Now start drawing with your finger wrapped in the chamois skin. Chamois is a soft, flexible leather. It will pick up carbon dust from the paper almost like an eraser. Feel out the shapes of the objects in your drawing. The chamois will leave only the negative areas dark gray.

Focus on the positive shapes. Shape your kneaded eraser to a point and draw the lightest lights on the positive shapes. Pick up more dust on the corner of your felt pad, and use the dust to build up darker darks where you see them. Finally, use vine charcoal to fill in the darkest darks in your drawing.

When your drawing is finished, spray it with fixative. (See the Technique Note and Safety Note below.)

TECHNIQUE NOTE

Using Spray Fixative

Spraying drawings with fixative protects them from smearing. Drawings in just about any dry medium will be damaged by rubbing against other surfaces if they aren't sprayed.

Spray fixative is sold both in aerosol cans and in small bottles with atomizers. Fixative in a bottle is applied by blowing through the atomizer.

Test the spray first on a piece of scrap marked with the same medium used in the drawing. Don't get the spray device too close to the drawing. Hold the spray device 12 to 18″ (30 to 46 cm) from it. Keep the sprayer moving. Several light coats are better than one heavy one. Fixative dries rapidly.

For your purposes, spray fixative labeled *workable* is best. This term means that after you spray an area of a drawing lightly, you can still draw on it.

SAFETY NOTE

Using Spray Fixative Safely

Always use spray fixative outside the studio in a well-ventilated area—outdoors, if possible. Breathing fixative over a long period of time can be lethal. Try to hold your breath during the few seconds of each spraying. If you are using a mouth atomizer, remember to blow out instead of breathing in.

sand pad

felt pad
kneadable eraser
chamois

fixative

PERSPECTIVE

Another major tool we use in making imitational drawings is linear perspective. It is often called simply *perspective*.

As you will recall from Chapter 1, Renaissance artists developed the technique of perspective because of their increased interest in making drawings more lifelike. The goal of perspective drawing is to portray objects and figures the way they appear to the viewer's eye—to re-create the way the viewer actually sees what is being drawn. As you learned in Chapter 1, perspective is one way artists suggest the element of space. It creates on a flat surface the illusion of depth or volume for three-dimensional objects.

In Chapter 11, you will learn details about making accurate perspective drawings using special measuring tools. Architects, industrial designers, and engineers use accurate perspective to make plans, sketches, and technical drawings. In this chapter, you will learn how perspective works so that you can make realistic drawings using careful estimation instead of exact measurements.

Perspective Drawing on Glass

MATERIALS

Lithograph pencil or china marker; glass or acrylic plastic

A German Renaissance artist named Albrecht Dürer (Chapter 3, page 46) made perspective drawings on a piece of glass. You can do the same thing. Go to a window, and pick a scene some distance away that includes constructed objects such as sidewalks, fireplugs, part of a building, or a parked car.

Position yourself so that you can see this scene without moving your head. Ask an assistant to stand behind you and place a hand on either side of your head to help you avoid moving.

Now simply trace the scene on the glass with your lithograph pencil or china marker. A lithograph pencil is actually a waxy, greasy crayon. A china marker can also be used to draw on glass. Your tracing is a perspective drawing. (See Figure 6.9.)

If your studio has no windows, use a piece of glass or heavy acrylic plastic in a picture frame. Make a tabletop still-life setup, and have two people hold the "window" steadily in front of it while you draw.

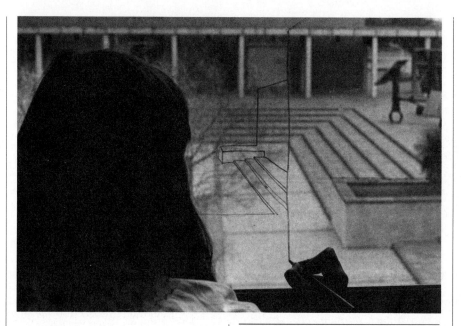

FIGURE 6.9 This girl has traced the outline of some steps she sees through the window. She could continue to draw the whole scene on the glass (or picture plane).

Perspective Drawings on Windows

On the viewing deck at the top levels of the World Trade Center in New York City, the windows overlooking the city have small perspective drawings like the ones Albrecht Dürer—and you—made. The drawings on clear sheets fastened to glass help the viewer locate the outlines of points of interest like famous buildings and bridges.

Handling Glass

Never attempt to hold a piece of unframed glass unless the edges have been carefully taped all the way around. Glass cuts are painful.

lithograph pencil
china marker

PERSPECTIVE DRAWING

Having made a perspective drawing, you are a magician of sorts. You have created an illusion. A perspective drawing is the illusion of three-dimensional objects and spaces projected on a two-dimensional plane—the picture plane. Your goal, of course, is not to create a three-dimensional illusion by drawing on glass—though some beautiful drawing is done by etching or scratching a design on glass (see Figure 13 in the Color Section). Your goal is to create this illusion on paper. The paper becomes the picture plane.

For **freehand drawing**—drawing done without measuring tools—you must know how to estimate proportion the way you did in the still-life drawings you made earlier. You also must know how to relate objects to the horizon.

The Horizon

As you know, the horizon is that line in the far distance where the earth and sky seem to meet. From most station points, or points of view, the horizon is hidden from us by trees, hills, or houses. You may have seen the horizon, however, while you were at the beach looking out to sea or when you were in the country on flat land. We see the horizon only because the earth is a ball and always curves downward away from where we are standing. Look at the diagram in Figure 6.10.

One important thing to remember about the horizon is that it always seems to be at eye level—that is, at the height of our eyes above the ground. If you move, it moves. You can prove this simply by looking at something outdoors that is a bit taller than you are and doesn't have any obstructions around it. The horizon will seem to pass behind the object. If you step up on a ladder and look over the object, the horizon will seem to move up to a point above the object. The

horizon will always be *at your eye level*. That is why another name for the horizon line is *eye level line*.

If your eye level (the horizon) is above an object, you can see the top of the object. If your eye level is lower than the top of an object, you can't see its top. You can, however, see the underside of some things, like the eaves of a house (Figure 6.11). If you are drawing a person from a low eye level, you can see the undersides of the eyebrows, nose, lips, and chin (the darkened areas in Figure 6.12).

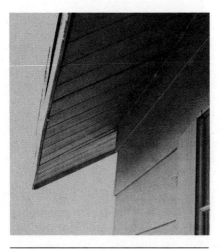

FIGURE 6.11 This picture was shot with a fairly low horizon or eye level so that you can see the underside of the eaves on the house.

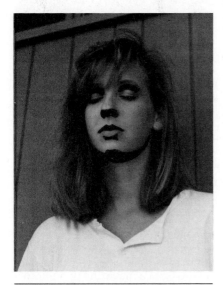

FIGURE 6.12 The shaded areas make the model's face look odd, but they show that you can see the undersides of nose, chin, and eye sockets because the horizon is low.

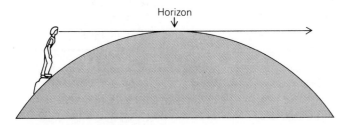

FIGURE 6.10 This little figure on a greatly reduced earth shows the curvature that causes us to see a horizon.

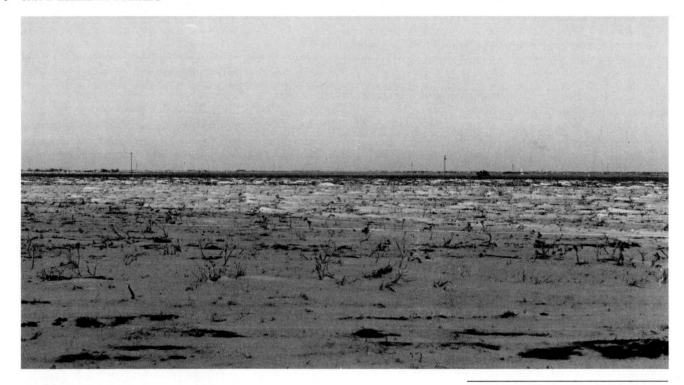

FIGURE 6.13 The horizon in this flat countryside is about 36″ (1 m) high because that was the height of the camera that ''saw'' it.

The second important thing about the horizon is that it passes behind every person and every object in a scene *at the same height above the ground*. To create the illusion of deep space believably, you must be consistent in placing people and objects in relation to horizon height. In the example in Figure 6.13, the horizon is about one yard (1 m) above the ground. This is the eye level of viewers who are squatting down and, in this case, the height of the camera taking the picture.

STUDIO

Adding Figures to a Photograph

MATERIALS

Photographs, ruler

Cut out a full-length figure from an old photograph. Use either a picture from a magazine or a photograph you have taken. Avoid photographs taken from extremely high or low angles. The figure can be either standing or seated. Now find a second figure a bit larger or smaller in another photograph, and cut it out. In this exercise, you will place these figures on the photograph in Figure 6.13 so that they are in correct perspective with the rest of the photograph and with each other.

We have noted that the horizon line (eye level or camera level) in Figure 6.13 is about one yard above the ground. Ask a friend who is about the same size as one of the people in the photograph you have cut out to help you. Ask your assistant to stand or sit as the figure is doing. Then use a ruler to measure from the floor up to the horizon line height—the same height it is in the photograph—on the body of your assistant.

Note lightly with a pencil mark on your cutout figures where this horizon line height would be on their bodies. Now lay the cutouts on Figure 6.13 so that the horizon passes behind their bodies at this height—the same height you located on your assistant. The figures will be in perspective with each other and with the rest of the picture.

The cutouts will be in perspective even if one is over ten inches tall and covers almost the whole photograph. If this is the case, just move that figure a little to the right or left along the horizon until you can see some of the photograph. Then the cutout figure becomes what is sometimes called an *interrupting plane*, which we look past into deep space. Just remember, however, that the horizon must pass behind the figure at the required one yard above the ground. Otherwise, the figure will be either floating in air or standing in a hole!

Of course, a figure in an imitational drawing could be floating (coming down in a parachute, flying a hang glider) or standing in a hole (or ditch or gully). Also, the ground in a realistic scene could be hilly or sloping. Even so, the height of the true horizon will always be at our eye level and will pass behind everything in the scene—including the hills—at our eye level. The horizon height stays the same even though some of the people or objects in the picture may be above or below our eye level and will appear above or below the horizon. (See Figure 6.14.)

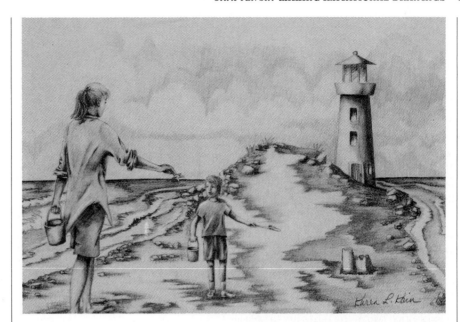

FIGURE 6.14 In the drawing by Karen Kain, the horizon passes behind all objects and figures in the scene at the same height no matter what their height is. The horizon is at eye level.
Courtesy of the artist.

Vanishing Points

To understand perspective further, we must next consider vanishing points. Vanishing points are the places on the horizon where parallel lines going away from us into the picture would finally come together if we extended them that far.

Study the diagram in Figure 6.15 on the next page. You will see that the lines defining the front edges of the box in the center of the drawing are parallel to the picture plane. They are also parallel to the horizon, so they are called *horizontal* lines. These lines, if they were extended, would never come together or vanish at any point on the horizon.

On the other hand, the lines that form the right and left edges of the box, moving away from us at a ninety-degree angle to the picture plane, will come together at a central vanishing point on the horizon. The box to the left of the center box is sitting parallel to it, so its receding lines will vanish to the same vanishing point.

The receding lines of the box on the right, however, vanish to a set of *two* vanishing points because none of this box's sides are parallel to the horizon. Neither of its two vanishing points can be the same as that of the first box. There can be as many sets of vanishing points in a drawing as there are objects set at different angles to the picture plane or horizon. See Figure 6.16 for an example of a drawing using several vanishing points. Which two boxes have edges that recede to only one vanishing point? Which two other boxes are sitting at the same angle?

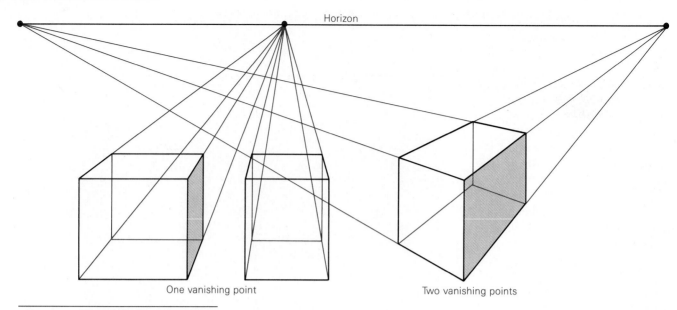

Horizon

One vanishing point

Two vanishing points

FIGURE 6.15 Two of the boxes are in one-point perspective, so they vanish to the same point on the horizon line. The third box is in two-point perspective because it is turned at an angle to the picture plane and the viewer.

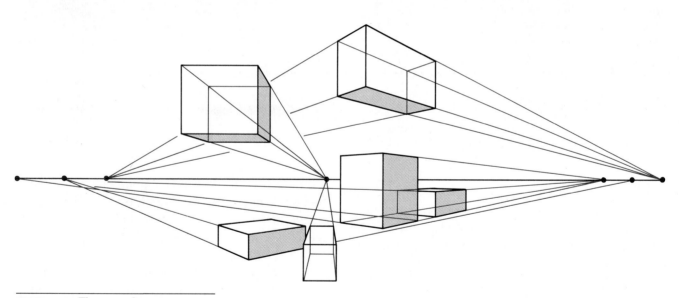

FIGURE 6.16 There can be as many different sets of vanishing points as there are objects at different angles to the viewer.

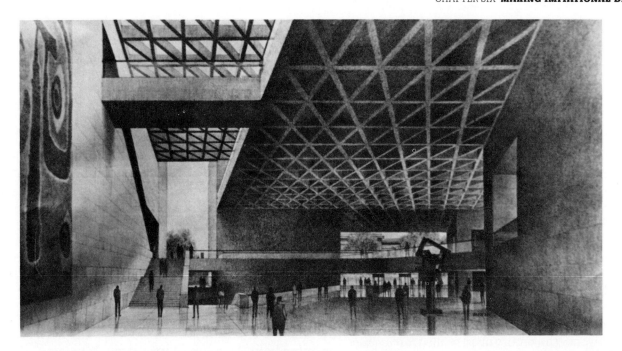

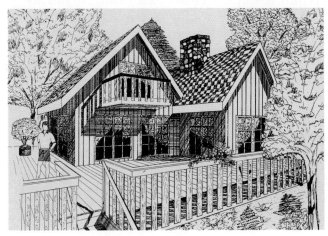

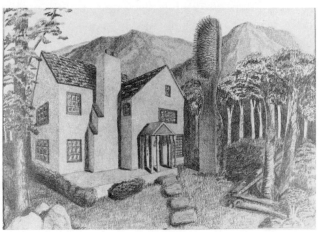

FIGURE 6.17 (top) Paul Stevenson Oles,
for I. M. Pei and Partners, Architects.
East Building, National Gallery of Art,
1970. Courtesy of the artist and the
Department of Architecture, Texas Tech
University.

FIGURE 6.18 (above left) Rebecca
Berry showed the exterior of this
home with a dramatically exaggerated
two-point perspective.
Courtesy of the artist.

FIGURE 6.19 (above right) Student Holly
Holt's fantasy features a house with
exaggerated perspective and a gigantic
toothbrush. It was done in charcoal
pencil.

Although many artists like to play with perspective to create special effects, it is a basic tool for making imitational art. As we mentioned earlier, perspective is often used by designers to show how a finished product will look. Figure 6.17 is an example of an architect's perspective drawing of interior space. This rendering shows an addition to the National Gallery of Art in Washington, DC. Designing interiors requires concern for the effective and satisfying use of space. An architect also relies on perspective to draw building exteriors like the one in Figure 6.18.

Perspective is also used in fine art drawings like the one in Figure 6.19. In this student drawing, the perspective is exaggerated, and an out-of-proportion object (the toothbrush) is included to create an imitational fantasy drawing. How many vanishing points do you think this artist used?

One-Point Perspective

The simplest kind of perspective is the kind you see if you are standing in the middle of a long, straight road, sidewalk, or railroad track. The lines formed by the sides of the road, walk, or track seem to come together at a vanishing point on the horizon. This point is also the **center of vision**, and what you are seeing is called **one-point** or **parallel perspective** (like the drawing of the center box in Figure 6.15).

In a one-point perspective drawing, all receding lines meet at one vanishing point. One-point perspective presents a dramatic view of deep space. The sides of objects facing the viewer are parallel to the picture plane. The sides of these same objects that move away into space seem to converge at a central point on the horizon directly in front of the viewer.

One-point perspective was popular during the Renaissance (Chapter 3, pages 41–44) and later with a group of twentieth-century artists called *Surrealists* (Chapter 3, page 59). It is also popular with interior designers because it allows them to make renderings for their clients that show three walls of a room's interior. See this kind of rendering in Figure 6.17.

Look again at Figure 6.18. Is this architectural rendering a one-point perspective? How do you know it isn't? Is the drawing in Figure 6.19 a one-point perspective?

ENRICHMENT

The Nearness of the Horizon

In geometry, we learn that parallel lines will never meet, no matter how far they are extended. In linear perspective, they meet at the horizon. We consider the horizon to be at an infinite distance from the viewer. So we allow parallel lines to converge at an infinitely distant vanishing point.

This idea works with some accuracy in drawings, but in real life the horizon is seldom far away. If you are sitting in a chair at the beach with your eyes about 4′ (1.22 m) above sea level, the horizon is only about 2½ miles (4 km) away. If you are on a mountain and your eyes are one mile (1.61 km) high, on a clear day you can see about 96 miles (153.6 km) before the horizon cuts off your vision.

STUDIO

One-Point Perspective Drawing of Boxes

MATERIALS

Hard graphite pencil, art gum or Pink Pearl eraser, fiber-tipped pen or technical pen, ruler, lightweight bristol board

For this first one-point perspective drawing, use some rectangular boxes of different sizes as your subject. You will need a sheet of drawing paper that is about 17 × 22″ (43 × 56 cm). Tape it on your drawing board so that it forms a vertical rectangle 22″ (56 cm) high.

Place the boxes on a table, grouping some together and separating one or two from the rest. Place them so that the sides of each box are parallel to the sides of the table.

Do your drawing looking squarely at the middle of one of the four sides of the setup, but with your body and drawing board turned a little to the side. Then you won't have to peer over the top of the drawing board.

If you stand up to draw, stay back from the table about 10′ (3 m). If you draw seated, leave only half of this distance between yourself and the table. In any case, make sure your eyes are at least 17″ (43 cm) higher than the tabletop.

Raise the paper on your easel until your eyes are level with a point about two-thirds to three-fourths of the height of the paper (one-third or one-fourth of the way down from the top). Use your ruler and pencil to draw the horizon. Don't forget that the horizon line represents your eye level. In fact, in this case, it *is* your eye level.

Mark a point in the center of it. This point will be your center of vision and also the single vanishing point.

You have used your ruler for the last time on this drawing. You need to learn about drawing in perspective freehand—without the use of instruments other than your pen, pencil, eyes, and brain.

Using your pencil, draw the horizontal line for the front of the table as far down on the paper as it seems to be below your eye level (or horizon line). Make it extend almost from edge to edge of your paper. From each of the ends of this line, which are the front corners of the table in your drawing, draw a line to the vanishing point (center of vision).

These are the lines of the edges of the table that are going away from you toward the other end of the table. You can think of these lines as going *to* the vanishing point, but it will be easier to draw them if you pull them *from* the vanishing point downward toward the corners.

Even if you draw lines toward the corners, you will probably make them crooked the first two or three times. Just be patient; use a soft eraser, like an art gum eraser or a Pink Pearl eraser, and correct them until you have two lines extending like railroad tracks to the horizon.

Of course, your table doesn't extend to the horizon, does it? So where should you cut if off? You will need to measure proportions. Select a unit of measure (perhaps the height of one of the boxes), and measure the length of the table by the pencil-sighting estimation method. Then draw another horizontal line cutting off the table at the proper distance up on your paper. If you have been somewhat accurate, you should have a good representation of the rectangular tabletop in one-point perspective.

Now draw the boxes with your pencil, using your eraser as needed to make corrections. Start by looking at the boxes as though you could see through them to their bottoms resting on the table; draw these rectangular bottoms just as you drew the tabletop.

Of course, these rectangles will be smaller and will be placed differently, but their edges that are parallel to the receding edges of the tabletop will vanish to the same vanishing point. Again, use the proportional measuring technique to locate the corners of the boxes on the table. Draw lines to the vanishing point, and cut off the boxes to the right length.

Next, raise vertical lines from the front corners of the boxes. Measure the front verticals of each box, and cut them off with the horizontal top edge. Then extend the top receding edges to the vanishing

point. These edges are parallel to the receding edges of the table. The lines will cross the verticals you raised from the back corners of the boxes, and the boxes can be completed with one more horizontal. Each line you draw may need some corrections.

Since you have been carrying lines to the vanishing point and drawing transparently, many of your light pencil lines aren't a part of the objects you have been drawing. They are part of the total drawing, however, and they make it more interesting. Leave them undisturbed.

To complete your drawing, locate all of the lines defining edges of the table and boxes that are actually visible from your point of view. Darken these lines with either a fiber-tipped pen or a technical pen, such as a Rapidograph. A technical pen is usually used for **mechanical drawing** (drawing done with measuring tools), but it is also becoming popular with artists. Technical pens are fairly expensive, so read the directions carefully before using one.

TECHNIQUE NOTE

Using the ''Basic Box'' in Perspective Drawing

Before doing any perspective drawing, you should learn three important procedures:

1. *Put each object in the drawing in a basic box.* This basic box should be square or rectangular and just large enough to contain the object that you want to draw. The farthest extended points of the object should just touch the sides of the box.
2. *Draw the shape of each basic box and each object on the ground or floor first.* You can

raise vertical lines from the corners of the box, which you have drawn in perspective on the ground or floor. Put a lid on the top, and start drawing the object inside.

3. *Draw everything transparently.* Drawing the lines and shapes that would normally be hidden by other shapes is a good idea in any drawing because it makes you understand the structure of objects. This technique is required to make an accurate perspective drawing so that you can find correct proportions of objects defined by a basic box.

STUDIO

One-Point Perspective Drawing of a Scene

MATERIALS

Hard graphite pencil, art gum or Pink Pearl eraser, higher contrast drawing medium of your choice, ruler, lightweight bristol board

For a more advanced exercise in one-point perspective, pick a section of street or the interior of a room you want to draw. Stand a bit behind a point you have chosen as your picture plane.

Put your horizon at a height you think is appropriate. A low horizon will make more objects overlap and cause objects to tower over the viewer, making a more dramatic picture. A high horizon will keep some objects from overlapping, sometimes making them harder to combine in a unified way, but it will allow for a larger view of the ground area being drawn. For an example of a student's one-point perspective, see Figure 6.20.

art gum eraser
Pink Pearl eraser

technical pen

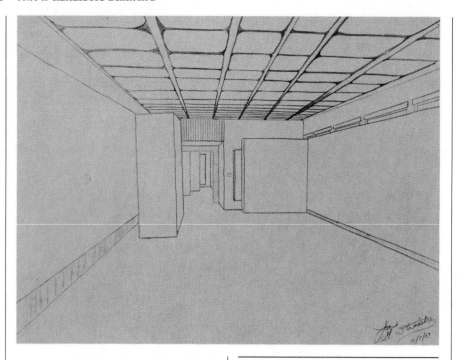

For this drawing, use pencil first, as before. Finish the drawing in a higher contrast medium with which you have had some practice, like a softer graphite pencil or a fiber-tipped pen.

FIGURE 6.20 This is a one-point perspective of an interior art gallery space done by Jon Strmiska in a freehand drawing class.

Two-Point Perspective

Look again at Figure 6.16. Note that each box that isn't parallel to the horizon and picture plane has *two* vanishing points. Also, these vanishing points can't be used for any other box unless the two boxes are parallel to each other. Each of these boxes is drawn in what we call **two-point** or **angular perspective**.

Two-point perspective is often used by illustrators. It lets them show things the way we usually see them—at odd angles, from various points of view—rather than facing all of the rectangular objects in a picture squarely at a ninety-degree angle.

Two-point perspective uses all of the rules of perspective we have talked about so far. The parallel edges or sides still come together at common points. These points are still on the horizon, and they are still called *vanishing points*. The horizon is still at eye level and still has the center of vision on it. But the center of vision isn't a vanishing point, as it was in one-point perspective.

The best way to observe two-point perspective is to look at the corner of a rectangular box that is sitting diagonally to your picture plane. Figure 6.21 is a rare three-point perspective of a box on which even the lettering is in perspsective.

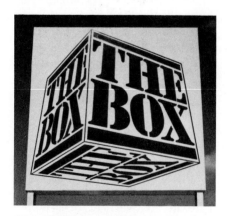

FIGURE 6.21 This box is on a sign in front of a store in Plainview, Texas. Can you find three vanishing points?

Two-Point Perspective Drawing of a Box

MATERIALS

Hard graphite pencil, art gum or Pink Pearl eraser, fiber-tipped pen or technical pen, ruler, lightweight bristol board

Now make your own two-point perspective drawing, using a rectangular cardboard box as a subject. Put the carton on the table with one corner nearest to you. Remember that the horizon is at eye level. You will be able to see that the top and bottom edges of each side would seem to come together if they were extended to points on the horizon. There are two vanishing points—a right one and a left one—as in the diagram in Figure 6.22.

But what is wrong with the box in Figure 6.22? It is distorted. The parallel edges come together too rapidly. The front corner looks as though it is about to fall right out of the picture toward us.

This kind of distortion makes the drawing look like a photograph shot with a wide-angle lens. Sometimes you will want to use this kind of exaggerated perspective for dramatic effect—but not if you are

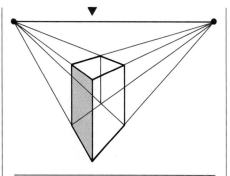

FIGURE 6.22 This box is distorted because the vanishing points are too close together.

trying to draw imitationally. This drawing is distorted because each of the vanishing points is much too close to the center of vision—and to the other vanishing point.

In Figures 6.22 through 6.25, the center of vision is indicated by a small vertical mark on the horizon above the box. If you look again at the box you are drawing, you can tell that the vanishing points in your drawing should be much farther apart than the ones in Figure 6.22. Getting vanishing points too close together is a common error for beginners and, unfortunately, for some more experienced artists, also.

For your drawing, you will first draw the box in light pencil lines. Put in the horizon and vanishing points, and in your first drawing place the box well below the horizon. If you turn the paper sideways,

you may have enough space to get both vanishing points on the paper where you can see them. If not, tape two sheets together.

How do you know where to locate the vanishing points? If you look at Figure 6.23, you will see that the nearest corner of the box has a dial like a clock face over it. With the lower front corner of the box in the center of the clock, the right bottom line recedes toward the horizon at a point between two and three o'clock. The left bottom line goes back at an angle between nine and ten.

You can look at your box and make the same kind of estimate. Then draw the lines from a point where you have decided the corner should be all the way to the horizon. Now you have located the right and left vanishing points.

To help you estimate the proper angles, you can cut a 4″ (20 cm) circle in a piece of cardboard and put marks along the edge of the circle like those on a clock face. You can then look through the circular hole, centering the corner of the box in the circle, and estimate the angles

FIGURE 6.23 It is helpful when sketching a basic box or rectangular object to use an imaginary clock face at the nearest corner. This technique is derived from a system recommended by Boston artist Dick Freeman and explained by Steve Oles in *Representation* magazine.

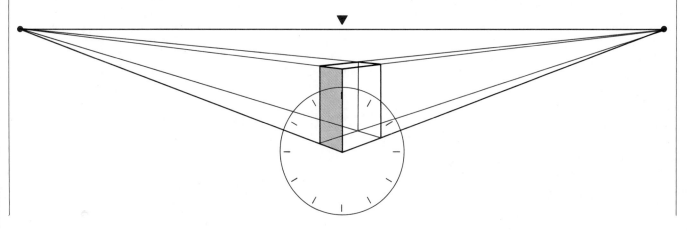

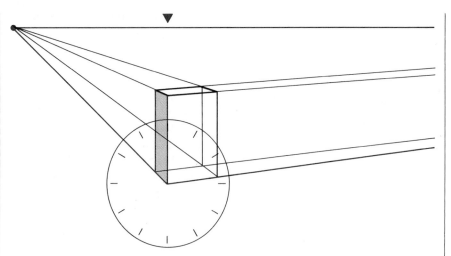

FIGURE 6.24 When the box is turned at a different angle to the viewer, the edges ''tell a different time'' on the clock face.

at which the lower edges of the box recede. Remember to hold the circle straight up and down while you look through it.

Now check the drawing you are making, and ask yourself if you will be seeing the box at an angle you like. Will you be seeing enough of the side you want to see, or does it need to be turned a little? Finding the right angle would be important if you were drawing a house with doors, windows, and other details on the sides, or if the box you are drawing has lettering on one side that you want to be readable in the drawing.

The box in Figure 6.24 is the same size as the one in Figure 6.23, and the center of vision is in the same spot. But the box in Figure 6.24 has been turned farther to the right (or clockwise if you were seeing it from above).

This angle has pushed the right vanishing point far out to the right. It went off the page, in fact. Of course, at the same time the left vanishing point came in closer to the center of vision. The right and left vanishing points are still the same distance apart, and the box is still seen in undistorted perspective. Now, however, we see a broader view of the right side of the box, while the left side has decreased in size. How has the angle of the front corner changed in the clock dial?

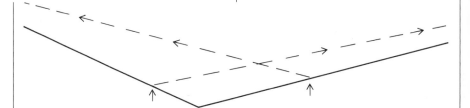

FIGURE 6.25 To find the back of the box, cut off the lines that extend to the vanishing points.

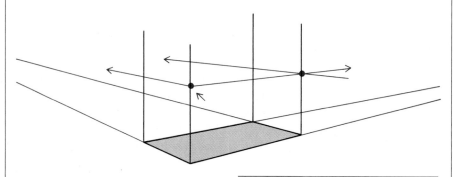

FIGURE 6.26 With the floor laid, verticals can be raised at the corners of the walls.

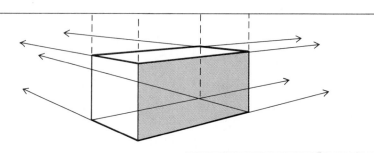

FIGURE 6.27 Completed box in two-point perspective.

After you have decided that you have your box at the right angle and the horizon is at the height you want, draw the outline of the box where it rests on the table. Pick a spot for the front corner, and estimate the angle of the corner. Extend lines to the vanishing points.

Use your pencil to measure the proportional distance along the bottom edge of the box to the rear corners on each side. You can use any unit of measure you wish as long as you use it consistently. Stay in the same spot to measure everything.

Now raise verticals from the corners of your box in the drawing. Remember that you are making a transparent drawing. Measure the height of the front corner of the real box with your pencil. Cut off the vertical lines at the front corner of your drawing at the correct proportional height. From this height you can extend lines to the right and left vanishing points that will automatically locate the

top rear corners of the box in your drawing. Look at Figures 6.25 through 6.27 for step-by-step illustrations of this process.

When your drawing is complete, leave all of the pencil lines visible. Darken with ink the lines defining the edges that you can see on the real box.

STUDIO
━━━━━━━━━━━━━━━━━

Two-Point Perspective Drawing of a Building

MATERIALS
Charcoal or soft graphite pencil, drawing paper

For a more challenging two-point problem, draw a house or some other building that interests you—maybe your own home. Make sure the building is based on rectangles. You should be able to see enough of the building to have some idea of its plan. You will need to estimate and draw an outline of where the building rests on the ground.

After drawing the house, add trees, shrubs, fireplugs, and anything else in the environment you would like. Try to observe and draw all of the interesting details, keeping them in correct perspective.

Remember: work from the ground up, put everything in a basic box, and work transparently. Start lightly, and darken the visible lines later. Note that the top of the basic box for the building will be above your eye level (the horizon). The lines from the top of the nearest corner will angle *down* to the vanishing points instead of up (as for the box you drew in the previous activity). Leave a little margin because you may wish to mat this drawing.

Atmospheric Perspective

Atmospheric perspective creates the illusion of decreasing contrast in colors and values across areas of deep space or distance. It can be achieved in an imitational work of art by gradually reducing the contrast in rendering objects that are farther away from the viewer.

For an example from nature, think about the way distant mountains look. They seem to be blue-gray and almost disappear into the sky. This effect is caused by layers of atmosphere between the viewer and the mountains.

For an example of an atmospheric perspective, look at the detail of the Peter Rogers mural (Figure 6.28, next page). This mural, which is in the foyer of the museum of Texas Tech University, is one of the largest India ink and wash drawings we know of. A **wash drawing** is made with a brush and ink or paint thinned with water. This drawing is an excellent example of imitational art that uses both linear and

atmospheric perspective. Note the reduction in value contrast as the eye moves from the foreground logs, rocks, and grass to the distant mesas at the right side. This technique created atmospheric perspective—the illusion of distance. The more air between the viewer and distant objects, the more they seem to fade. The mesas appear blurrier and less distinct than the objects in the foreground. This kind of perspective works with the linear perspective, which was created by reducing the size of the distant man and horse in the left middle ground.

You can also make atmospheric perspective work in drawings that don't involve deep space. Look at the fine student rendering of two blue-jean-clad figures in Figure 6.29 on the next page. See how the figure closer to us contrasts with the background as well as with the figure behind. This contrast seems to move the figure forward. You can use the same technique in your drawings.

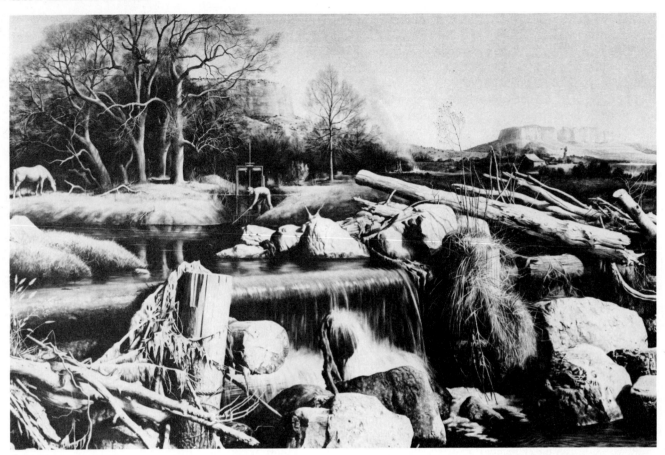

FIGURE 6.28 This detail of Peter Rogers's remarkable ink and wash mural shows the atmospheric perspective in the fading contrast of the distant mesas.
Courtesy of the Museum of Texas Tech University, Lubbock, TX.

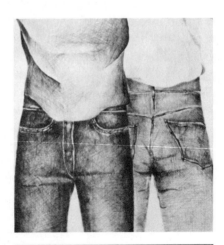

FIGURE 6.29 Atmospheric perspective can be used even for short distances. Art student Ann Pikoraitis decreased the contrast for the more distant figure.

ENRICHMENT

Reducing Contrast to Create Atmospheric Perspective

There is a difference between reducing contrast and making things darker. In speaking of atmospheric perspective, we don't say that things in the distance get *darker* or *lighter*. They may do either one.

Losing contrast means that distant objects are less clearly separated by value or color from their surroundings than things in the foreground. As the atmosphere affects the light rays reflected back to us by distant things, their colors become less intense or more neutral—closer to black or white. The color of their surroundings gets less intense, too. And since all distant objects also become more alike in value, everything seems to blend and lose detail in the far distance. Since we are used to seeing this effect in nature, we accept it easily as an indicator of depth in drawings even for short distances.

FIGURE 1 See page 6 for discussion.
Georgia O'Keeffe, *My Heart*, 1944. Pastel
on paper, 27½ × 21½″ (69.9 × 54.6 cm).
The Museum of Texas Tech University,
Lubbock, TX. Collection of the West Texas
Museum Association and the Museum of
Texas Tech University.

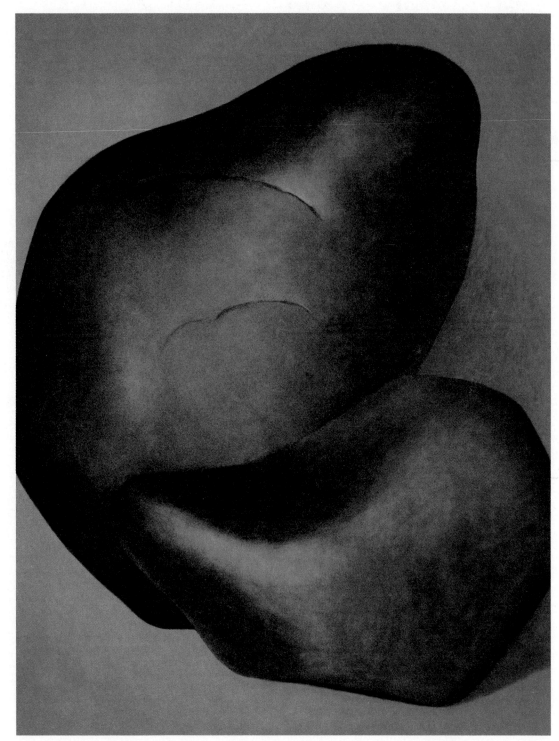

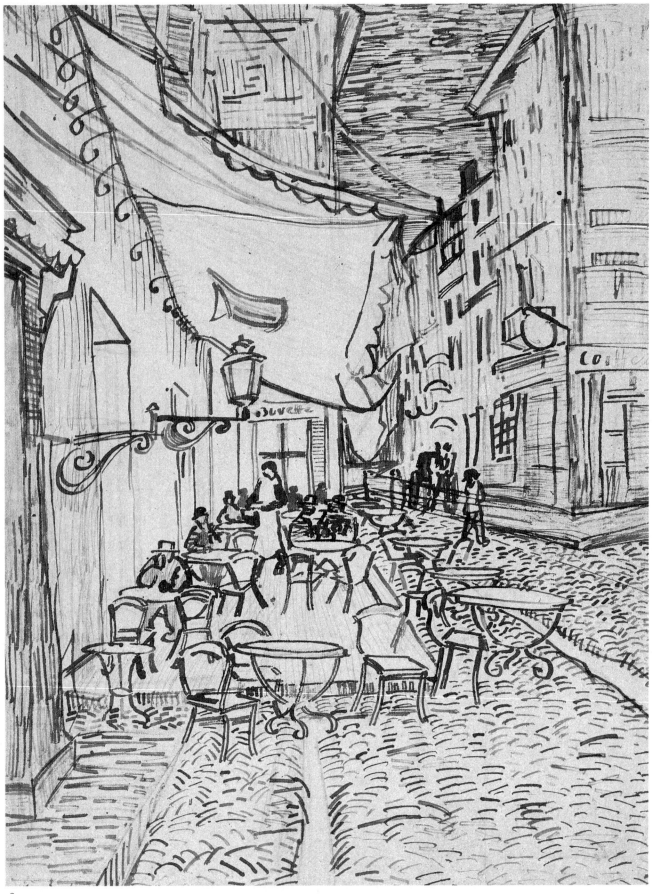

FIGURE 2 See page 4 for discussion.
Vincent van Gogh, *Café Terrace at Night*,
1888. Reed pen and ink over pencil, 24⅝
× 18¾″ (62.5 × 47.6 cm). The Dallas
Museum of Art, Dallas, TX. The Wendy
and Emery Reves Collection.

FIGURE 3 See page 91 for discussion.
Edward Hopper, *Gas*, 1940. Oil on canvas,
26¼ × 40¼″ (66.7 × 102.2 cm). Collection, The Museum of Modern Art, New
York, NY. Mrs. Simon Guggenheim Fund.

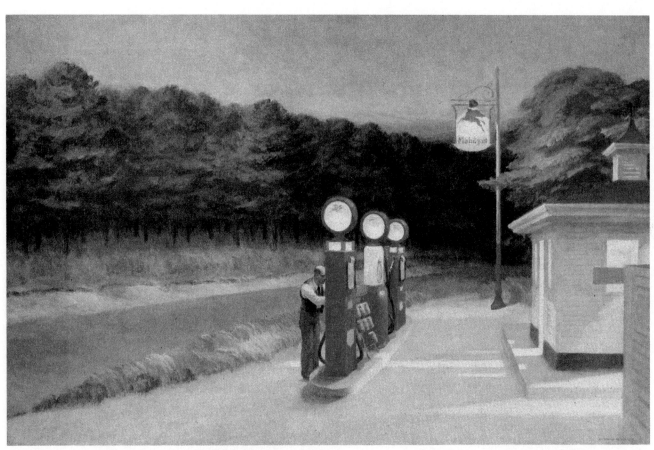

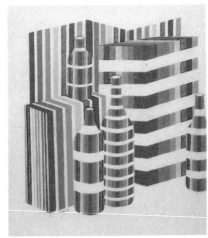

4

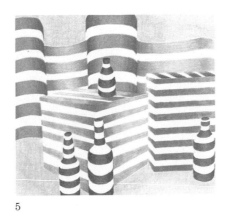

5

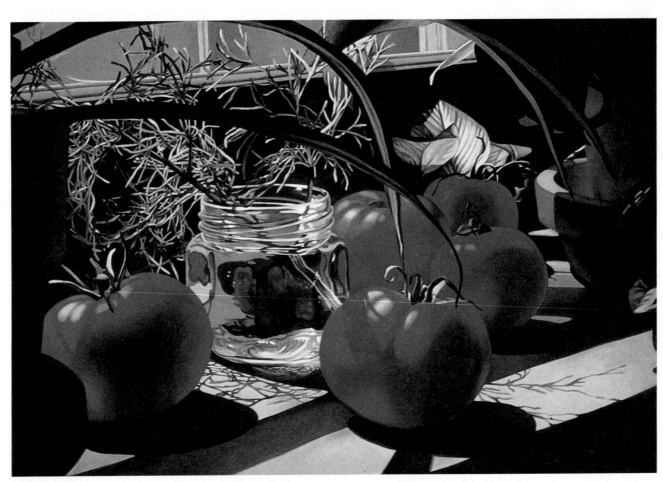

6

FIGURE 4 This colorful cross-contour drawing by student Melody Owen takes some liberties with the shapes, but it is an effective formal study. See page 75 for discussion.

FIGURE 5 Student Jay Lemon's drawing required several hours of effort. In this still-life work, cross-contour lines were widened into bands. See page 75 for discussion.

FIGURE 6 The precise finished quality of this large painting by Jane Cheatham, *July Window*, bears little resemblance to her thumbnail sketches in Figure 4.33, but the painting preserves the vitality of the sketches in light and dark values and color. See page 81 for discussion.
Courtesy of the artist.

FIGURE 7 This whimsical construction of wood and clay, *The Serpent's Portal*, is by Keith Owens. It is about 2 feet tall. Compare the finished work with the sketch in Figure 4.34. See page 81 for discussion.
Courtesy of the artist.

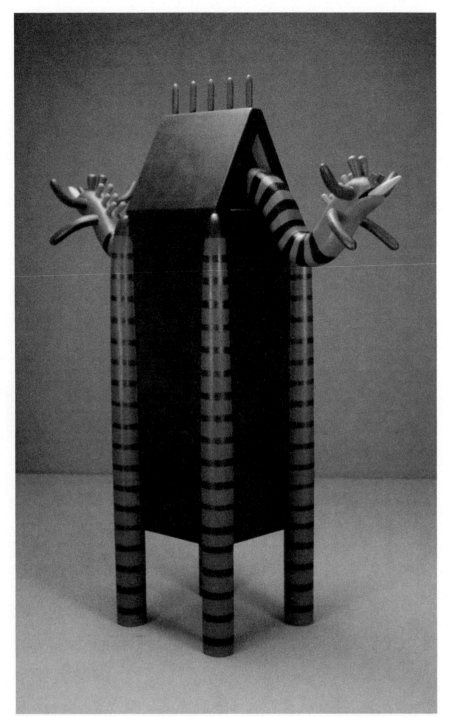

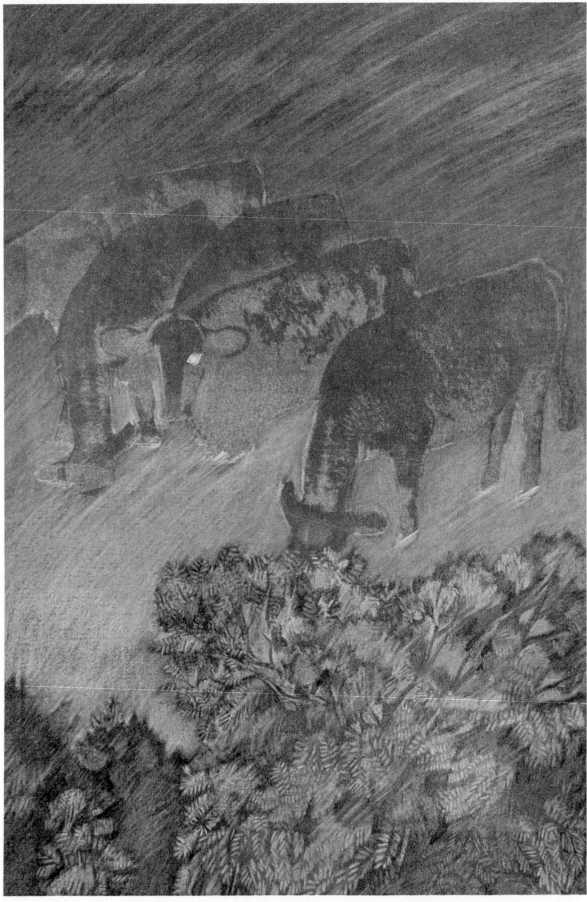

FIGURE 8 Ken Dixon's work called *Origin of the Evening Star* uses gum bichromate. The artist drew on the sensitized surface with colored pencils. See page 83 for discussion.

Courtesy of the artist.

FIGURE 9 This work by Ken Dixon is called *Reading the Signs—Blue Skies Again*. What do you think were the sources of the ideas for this drawing? See page 83 for discussion.

Courtesy of the artist.

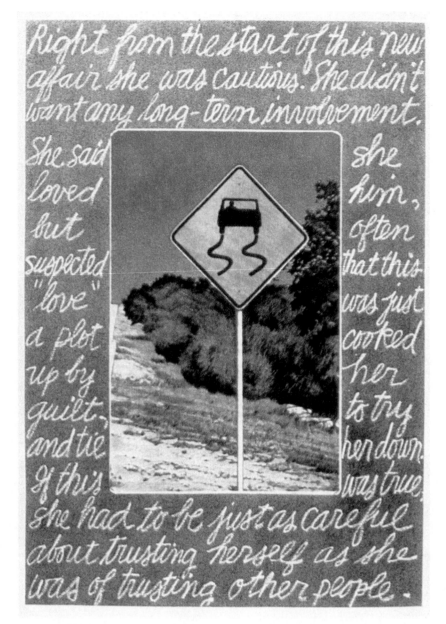

9

FIGURE 10 Student Jeff McMillan's drawing *Father Popcorn* shows his father as a fantasy character. See page 83 for discussion.

FIGURE 11 Note the formal use of cone-shaped objects in student John Wilson's drawing *Teeth*. These objects were derived in part from the teeth of a killer whale. See page 83 for discussion.

FIGURE 12 Using directional repetition and variation for interest, student John Wilson introduced some musicians into his composition called *Teeth and Musicians*. See page 83 for discussion.

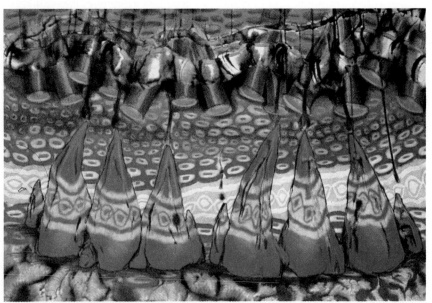

11

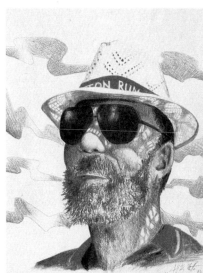

10

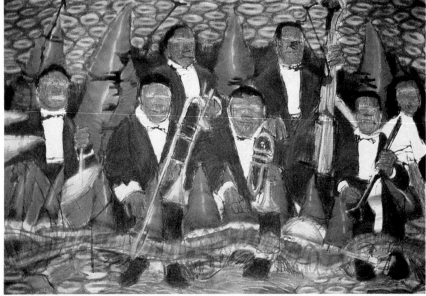

12

FIGURE 13 This lion was engraved on the crystal bowl by Paul Hanna. See page 162 for discussion.

Courtesy of the artist.

FIGURE 14 Artist Terry Morrow's *Tejas Kid* is a fine example of a formal fantasy rendered in colored pencil. See page 119 for discussion.

Courtesy of the artist.

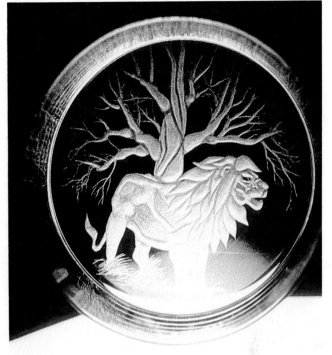

13

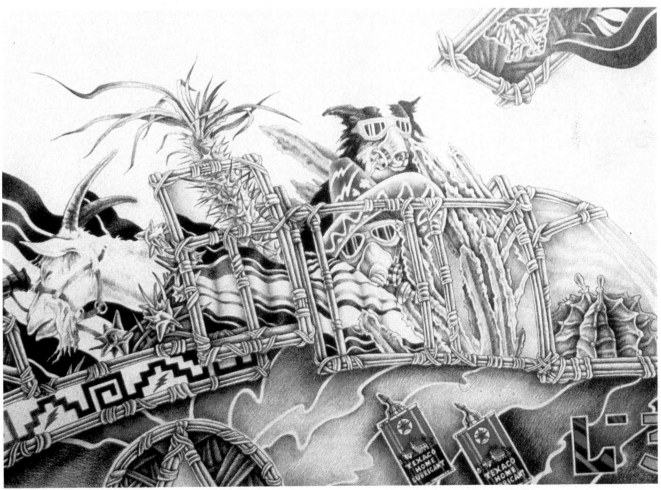

14

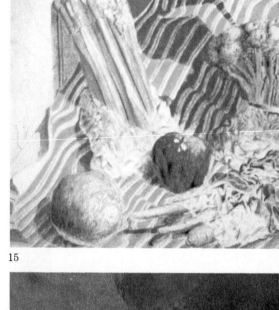

15

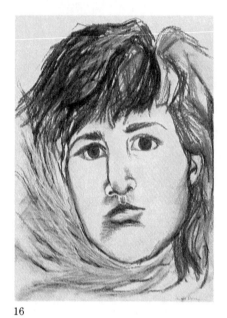

16

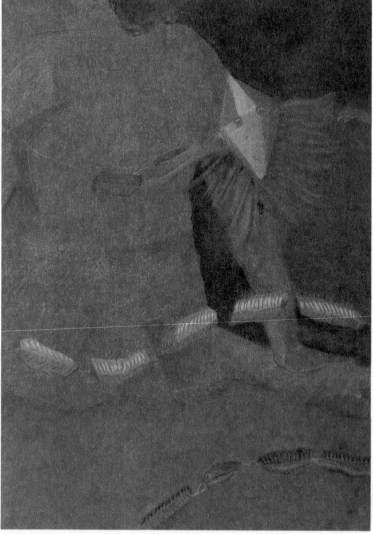

17

FIGURE 15 Student Mike Barrett's still life. How did he render shadows? See page 125 for discussion.

FIGURE 16 In this expressive self-portrait, you can see the corrections student Christa Moser made in the finished work from the sketch in Figure 6.54. See page 131 for discussion.

FIGURE 17 How has art student Shelley Settle changed the structure of the real-life images she used as sources for her drawing? See page 156 for discussion.

FIGURE 18 Annette Berlin is the drawing student who produced this fantasy still life using an old department store mannequin, a catcher's mask, and other objects. See page 159 for discussion.

FIGURE 19 Student Nicole Brints used extreme enlargement in scale of small objects and textures to emphasize structure in this work. See page 161 for discussion.

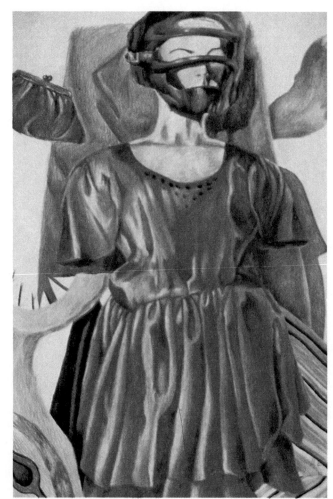

18

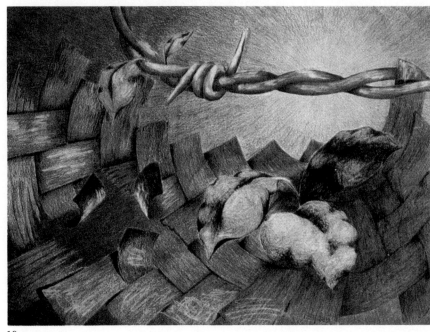

19

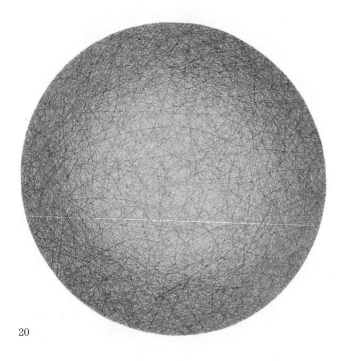

20

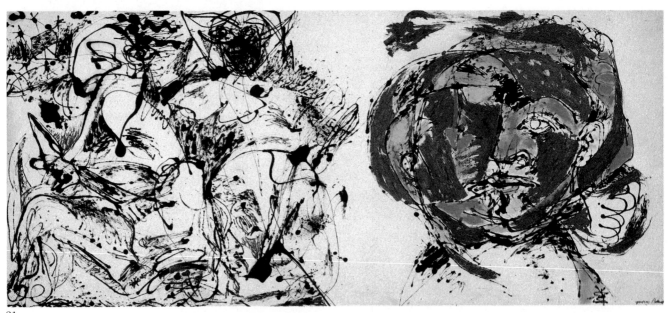

21

FIGURE 20 Paul Hanna's linear acrylic painting is called *Querencia No. 14.* It implies vast energy, but structurally it is carefully controlled. See page 162 for discussion.

Courtesy of the artist.

FIGURE 21 See page 61 for discussion.

Jackson Pollock, *Portrait and a Dream*, 1953. Enamel on canvas, 4'10" × 11'2¼" (1.5 × 3.4 m). The Dallas Museum of Art, Dallas, TX. Gift of Mr. and Mrs. Algur H. Meadows and the Meadows Foundation Incorporated.

FIGURE 22 What emotions are expressed in this mixed media drawing by Linda Kennedy ? Are these emotions related to a person or situation, or to the drawing process? See page 179 for discussion.

Courtesy of the artist.

FIGURE 23 Student Philip Ford produced this pastel drawing, *The Courtship,* based on childhood memories and the *commedia dell'arte* theater. What characteristics does this drawing share with the drawing of the old man in Figure 10.18? See page 182 for discussion.

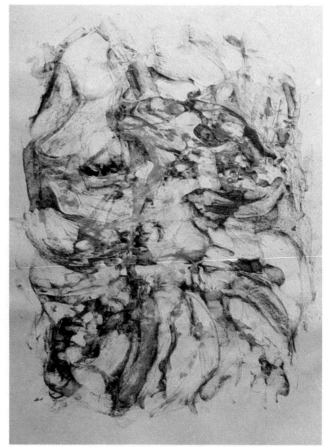

22

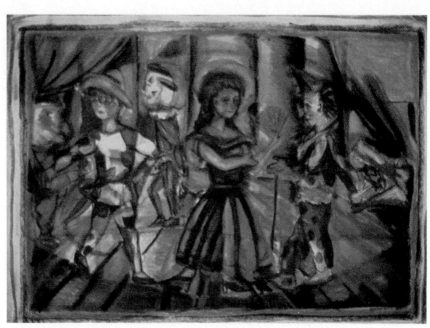

23

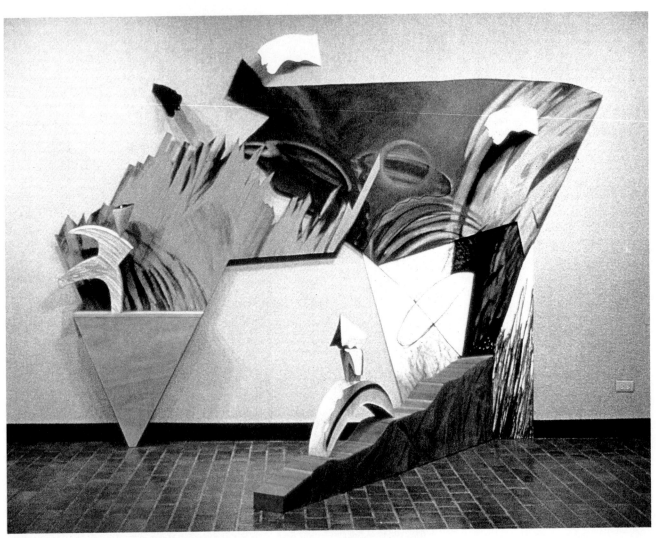

24

FIGURE 24 Compare this mixed media work by Sara Waters called *Crossing . . .* with her drawing in Figure 10.8. What are the similarities and differences? See page 183 for discussion.

Courtesy of the artist.

FIGURE 25 This woodcut print by Paul Hanna is called *Owl and Heart Flower.* What makes the use of color so dramatic? See page 190 for discussion.

Courtesy of the artist.

FIGURE 26 This drawing by student Kathy Hicks was done in watercolor wash. See page 192 for discussion.

Courtesy of the artist.

FIGURE 27 Do you think Kathy Hicks made many wash drawings like this one? Was this drawing done slowly or rapidly? How do you know? See page 192 for discussion.

Courtesy of the artist.

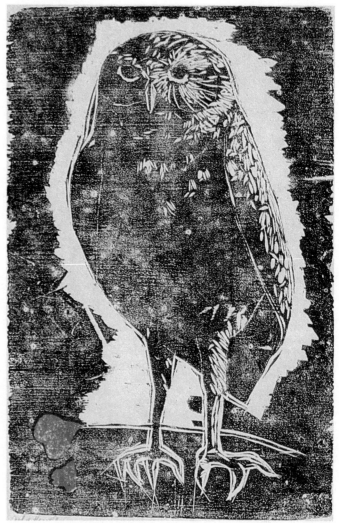

25

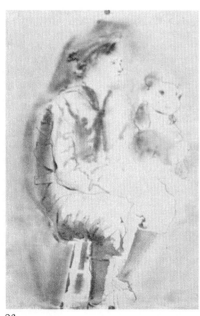

26

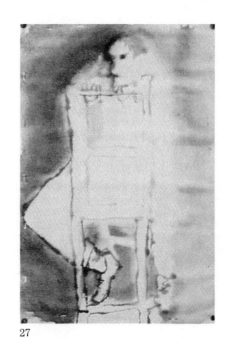

27

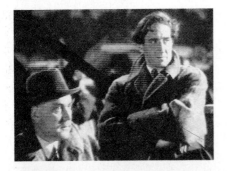

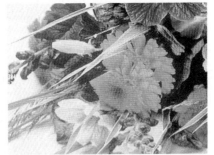

FIGURE 28 Colors are selected for each object, costume, and figure in a scene, and the computer adds color to each frame. It may take up to four hours to ''colorize'' one minute of black and white film. See page 242 for discussion.

Frame from *Sherlock Holmes and the Secret Weapon* (1942). Courtesy of Hal Roach Studios, Inc. and Colorization, Inc.

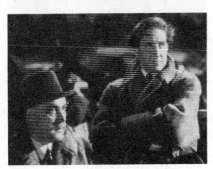

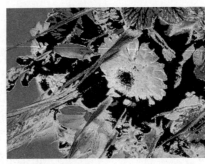

FIGURE 29 The natural colors of these flowers have been changed by a software operation called pseudo-coloring. See page 249 for discussion.

Courtesy of Gould Inc., Imaging and Graphics Division.

FIGURE 30 These images show how an artist constructs a drawing step-by-step using computer hardware and software. The image illustrated a business magazine article about big and small businesses. See page 249 for discussion.

James Dowlen, *Big Bun*, 1986. Produced on a customized IBM PC using Lumena software by Time Arts, Inc., Santa Rosa, CA.

28

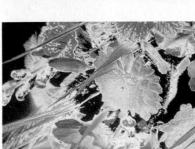

29

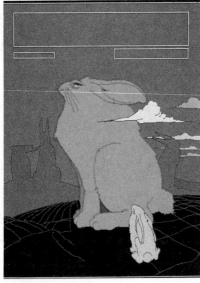

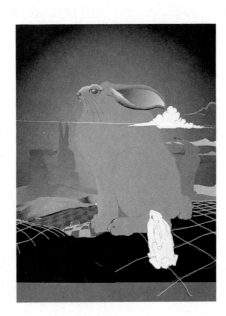

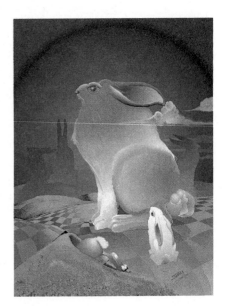

30

Peter Rogers

Peter Rogers (Figure 6.28) is a New Mexico artist. Most of his paintings are more formal and expressive than this one. This particular mural is also highly imitational. It is painted on the wall of a museum associated with the International Center for Arid and Semi-Arid Land Studies. It illustrates the importance of water as a natural resource.

Stippling is one technique used to create atmospheric perspective. Stippling means rendering light and dark gradations in a drawing by making a pattern of dots. The dots are spaced closer together or farther apart to show value changes. A variation of stippling is called *patterned rendering*. Tiny shapes are used instead of dots.

Figure 6.30 is an example of a stippled drawing by a student. Notice how the man in the foreground stands out because of his contrast in value with the background bushes. Also notice how the background building doesn't contrast much with the snowy evening sky. This lack of contrast is a use of atmospheric perspective.

Look also at the stippling in Figures 6.31 and 6.32. The first drawing is a detail from an illustration for a newspaper advertisement. Figure 6.32 isn't totally realistic, of course. It is a student's formal drawing of a female head. It is, however, a good example of patterned rendering.

Stippling makes it easy to render atmospheric perspective because you can work all over the drawing at once, adding more dots where they are needed. Remember, though, that it is easier to add dots than to remove them, so it is a good idea to make sketches just to decide where to place darker values.

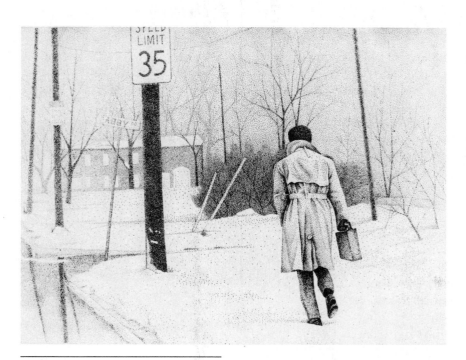

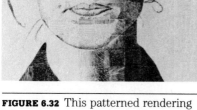

FIGURE 6.32 This patterned rendering is by art student Christina Konen.

FIGURE 6.30 (above) Art student Mike Cherapek chose stippling to render atmospheric perspective in this evening snow scene.

FIGURE 6.31 (at right) Stippling is an appropriate technique for reproduction in newspaper advertising.
Courtesy of *The University Daily*, Texas Tech University.

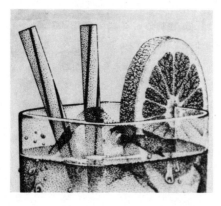

Atmospheric Perspective Drawing Using Stippling

MATERIALS

Graphite or charcoal pencil, tracing vellum, drafting tape, hard graphite pencil or ballpoint pen, any wet drawing medium, bristol or illustration board

For this activity, choose a scene involving deep space, with objects or people in the foreground, middle ground, and background as subject matter. You will create atmospheric perspective by using stippling.

It is a good idea to do some sketches to practice showing values before starting the rendering. You don't have to use stippling in the sketches, though. A preliminary drawing on tracing vellum will also help you design your finished work. There should be no lines left in a stippled rendering because they would be out of character with the rest of the drawing. You can transfer the lines lightly from your practice drawing to bristol or illustration board (another type of heavy drawing paper) and erase them later.

To transfer a drawing, turn the preliminary drawing into carbon paper by rubbing graphite or charcoal on the back. Or if you don't want to damage your preliminary drawing, you can rub carbon all over the back of a third sheet. Then slip the third sheet between the preliminary drawing and the paper to be used for the finished rendering.

In either case, tape the preliminary to the finish sheet firmly at the top with drafting tape. Use only a few strips of tape at the bottom so you can lift the preliminary occasionally to check the transfer. Trace the lines of the preliminary drawing with a hard pencil or a ballpoint pen. Remember to place the carbon-rubbed side *down* against the surface of the paper for the finished rendering.

After making the transfer, start rendering the lights, darks, and gradations with a wet medium. Stippling is usually done with ink, but almost any wet medium will work. Use a fiber-tipped pen or any instrument you can use with paint or ink. Whatever tool you choose, practice stippling on the side to see how to make good light-to-dark gradations.

With single-sized dots, only the space between them controls the value. With dots that vary in size, the control of transition from light to dark is easier. Of course, when the dots get close enough to blend, you have white dots on a black ground—and, finally, solid black.

Don't make the dot pattern too important by letting the dots get too large and obvious. In that case, a formal element would be overpowering the subject matter. Look at the formal drawing in Figure 6.32 (the patterned rendering) again. In imitational drawing, the subject matter shouldn't be overpowered by any formal element.

In working with atmospheric perspective, remember that you can stipple in negative spaces as well as in positive shapes to control contrast. Look again at Figure 6.30.

You may want to mat this drawing, so leave a small margin.

SHADOW

Light and shadow allow us to see objects as three-dimensional shapes that have volume—a vital ingredient of imitational art. (We see objects as volumes because there are no true lines in nature. Lines are considered one-dimensional, and in our three-dimensional universe, objects must have width and depth as well as length. What we call *lines* that define the edges of shapes actually have width, even if it is only the width of a pencil lead, and depth, even if it is only the depth of a grain of carbon dust.) We don't see people and objects because they have lines around them as they do in drawings. We see them only because they reflect light. The amount of light they reflect from a particular side tells us which side is toward the light and which side is in shadow, or turned away from the light. Shadow gives us a clue about objects' thickness or volume or the space they occupy.

In this text, we won't try to deal with the effects from multiple light sources. For most imitational drawing, a single light source like sunlight is adequate for a convincing illusion. Once you learn to use light from a single source to create shadows, using more than one light source is fairly easy to learn.

As you discovered in Chapter 4, there are two basic kinds of shadows: form shadows and cast shadows. *Form shadows* appear on any form on the side that is away from the light. *Cast shadows* fall on a surface that is shielded from the light by another object.

illustration board
ballpoint pen

Sketching Form and Cast Shadows

MATERIALS

Graphite pencil, sketchbook

Reproducing form and cast shadows is important in creating the illusion of reality. Make sketches and notes as you observe these shadows.

Roll a sheet of fairly stiff white paper into a cylinder about 4″ (10 cm) in diameter. Glue the edges together, and set the cylinder on end in the sun on a sheet of white cardboard. Drop a plastic sandwich bag with some sand in it down the center to keep the cylinder from blowing over. You can clearly see the shadow on the cylinder on the side away from the sun. This is the form shadow.

Also, you can see the shadow the cylinder makes on the cardboard. This is the cast shadow. Notice that the cast shadow starts at a point on the ground at the side of the cylinder right where the form shadow on the cylinder begins.

Notice also that the cast shadow as a whole is darker than the form shadow, though neither of them has an area that is really black. A cast shadow will always be darker than a form shadow as long as both the object and the surface on which its shadow falls are about equal in value and there is light from only one source.

Now notice and record that the edge of the form shadow on the cylinder is soft and fuzzy. In other words, the shadow begins gradually as the cylinder turns away from the sun. Just inside this soft edge, however, you can see a darker area, usually called the *core* of the shadow.

The core extends the full height of the cylinder just inside the edge of the form shadow. But as the form shadow wraps around the cylinder, this core rapidly fades back to the general gray value of most of the shadow. As the shadow continues away from the sun, it may seem to get slightly darker again.

Now observe the cast shadow. Unlike the form shadow, it has a hard or sharp edge—not a fuzzy one. Also, the cast shadow has no core inside the edge. In fact, the edge generally looks a little darker than the rest of the shadow.

The most important thing to know about rendering the cast shadow, however, is the fact that it is darkest close to the object that casts it. It fades steadily to a lighter value as it moves away from the object. You can exaggerate this difference when drawing, even for cast shadows that aren't very long, such as the shadow cast by a nose onto a cheek.

Cast shadows should cross every detail of the surfaces on which they fall. The edge of a cast shadow is like a cross-contour line, defining the form of the surface it crosses.

Hold another object so that its shadow falls across the cylinder's shadow. Is there a darker shadow where they cross? No. The two shadows simply disappear into each other. A darker shadow could only be caused by two sources of light, one stronger than the other.

Drawing Cylinders and Their Shadows

MATERIALS

Soft, medium, and hard charcoal pencils; sketchbook

After collecting information about form and cast shadows during the previous activity, return to the studio and make a drawing of two cylinders in the sunlight. Draw one of them standing on end so it casts its shadow across the other one, which is lying down.

Make sure to sand a sharp point on each of your pencils. Stop to resharpen them as often as necessary. To do this drawing well, you must keep sharp points on your pencils. For this drawing you can use your sketchbook or almost any other white drawing paper with a little tooth.

For a good example of rendering with the points of pencils, look at the part-imitational, part-formal colored pencil fantasy by Morrow in Figure 14 in the Color Section. Figure 6.33 on the next page is a detail of a black and white drawing that you can use to study the inter-action of the pencil point with the surface of the paper. Before you start drawing, practice a bit with the points of your pencils. Try to get the same kind of interaction between pencil point and paper surface that the artists who made these drawings used.

Do some thumbnail sketches to decide where to place the two cyl-inders and the light source. The light's location determines where the shadows will be, of course.

As you are doing these roughs, look at Figures 6.34 and 6.35 on the next page to see how to draw cylindrical objects. The drawings began as basic boxes. Then the

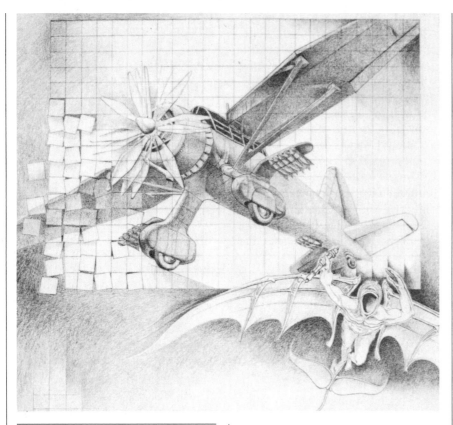

FIGURE 6.33 A rendering like this requires several weights of pencils. All of them must be kept sharp.

objects were sketched in perspective, and everything was drawn transparently. If the horizon had been drawn, it would have been about twice the height of the standing cylinder so we could easily see the top of the basic box. The location of the vanishing points for each box was estimated. By estimating where the vanishing points were, the sides of the boxes could be drawn more believably than if they had been ignored.

Once the boxes were drawn, it was easy to find the centers of each square end by drawing an X from corner to corner. (See the first drawing in Figure 6.36.) Then, by drawing a line through the center toward the vanishing points, the midpoint of each side of the square was located. This is shown in the second drawing in Figure 6.36. The midpoints are the points on each side of the square where the arcs of the circle would touch. Of course, since the circle is in perspective now, it has become like an ellipse.

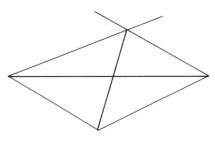

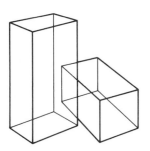

FIGURE 6.34 Drawing cylinders in perspective requires drawing basic boxes first.

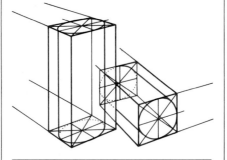

FIGURE 6.35 The cylinder—like any other object drawn in perspective—completely fills the basic box. Although we followed the right steps, the freehand ellipses for the standing cylinder are a little distorted. Where did we miss our estimate on the basic box?

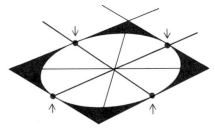

FIGURE 6.36 This diagram shows the steps for drawing an ellipse starting with the "floor" of the box. Draw an X from corner to corner in the square to find the center; then take lines from the vanishing points to find the center of each side.

The ends of an ellipse are short, fat curves, and the top and bottom are long, flat curves.

In the first drawing in Figure 6.37, you can see one of the mistakes made most frequently when drawing circles in perspective. If you are trying to draw them accurately in a realistic way, don't make their ends pointed. That is, don't shape them like footballs or eyes. Notice in the rest of the circle drawings in Figure 6.37 that, no matter how narrow the ellipses get, they all have rounded ends.

Naturally, as the ellipses get higher toward the horizon, they get narrower. What happens to an ellipse that is right on the horizon at eye level? Cut a circle out of cardboard and check. When it gets above eye level, what do you see? The bottom of it, of course.

With a little practice, you can lightly draw the cylinders and very lightly indicate the shadow edges with line. Then start shading with your pencil point. Study the pencil technique in Morrow's drawing (Figure 14 in the Color Section) and the drawing in Figure 6.33 again. Try to create the subtle changes and surface quality of these drawings when rendering your shadows.

For shadow structure, look also at the sketches by Peter Hurd in Figures 6.38 and 6.39. In Figure 6.38 the light source is in front of the model. You can see the broad treatment of light and shadow on the model's left arm. In your drawing, do the large, broad areas first in a flat value with no gradation. This technique will define the light and shadow sides of the big forms and establish the total image of the cylinder. Then return to the form to add the details of the darks and lights.

FIGURE 6.38 Peter Hurd's sketch of publisher James Lorenzo Dow is a preliminary drawing for a large fresco. A fresco is a painting on the wet plaster of a wall.
Courtesy of the Museum of Texas Tech University, Lubbock, TX.

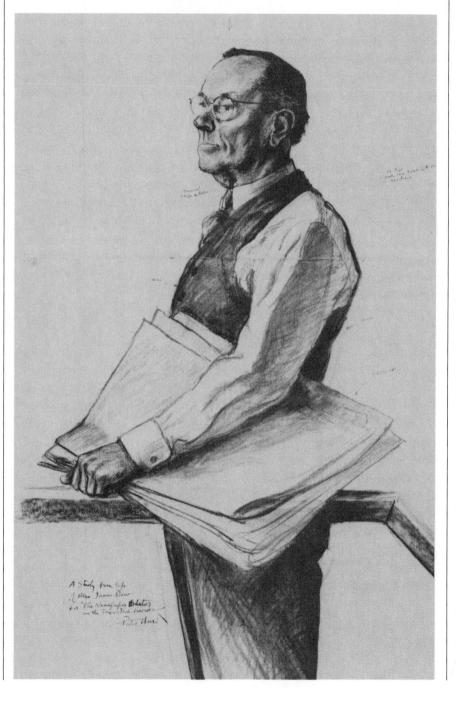

— Eye level —

FIGURE 6.37 The first ellipse is incorrect. It is pointed like a football. In the stack of correct ellipses, none are pointed, no matter how thin they become.

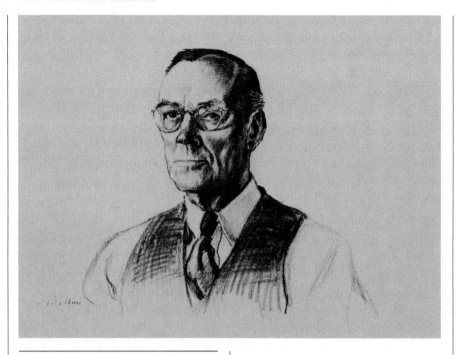

FIGURE 6.39 In Peter Hurd's sketch of Dow's head, which shadows are form shadows and which are cast?
Courtesy of the Museum of Texas Tech University, Lubbock, TX.

Also refer to Peter Hurd's second sketch of James Dow in Figure 6.39. In this sketch, the light source is from the upper left. Note the darker core of the form shadow on Dow's temple and the hard edges of the cast shadows projected under the nose and from the glasses onto his cheek.

ENRICHMENT

Peter Hurd

The late Peter Hurd was a well-known Southwestern artist who once did a portrait of President Lyndon B. Johnson. President Johnson is reported to have commented about it, "That's the ugliest thing I ever saw!" A new artist was found to paint the portrait.

Hurd was much more successful, however, with some of his other works. The sketches in this book from the life of James Lorenzo Dow, a pioneer newspaper editor, and of Dora Nunn Roberts, a rancher and oil field owner, are charming and skillful works. They are studies for figures in a large fresco. It is interesting, though probably not obvious in the small reproduction, that the artist's notes about details like windows and necktie colors were written on the drawing in Spanish, a language he used with as much ease as his own.

STUDIO

Value Studies of Crumpled Paper

MATERIALS

Soft graphite or charcoal pencil, drawing paper

To practice with shadows, crumple a large piece of paper and do some sketches of it from various angles, showing values. Now do a more finished rendering using a floodlight. See Figure 6.40 for an example.

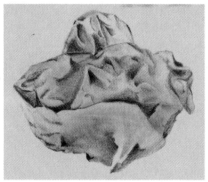

FIGURE 6.40 Art student Alison Howze defined the planes and curves of crumpled paper in this shadow exercise.

STUDIO

Drawing of an Open Paper Bag

MATERIALS

Soft graphite or charcoal pencil, drawing paper

Wad up a paper bag; then open it and lay it on the floor with its mouth facing the light. Now draw the receding space inside it in values of shadow.

Drawing of Perspective, Shadows, and Reflections

MATERIALS

Soft, medium, and hard charcoal pencils; tracing paper or tracing vellum; drafting tape; hard graphite pencil or ballpoint pen; medium-surface bristol board

Think of a subject for a drawing with perspective, shadows, and reflections. You can use a setup with fruit, cylindrical objects, and drapery, like the one in Figure 6.41, or a single ordinary object like the toothpaste tube in Figure 6.42. Another possibility would be to draw a one-point perspective with furniture and figures, like the detail of a graphite pencil drawing in Figure 6.43 on the next page. Still another possibility would be to choose your own subject matter. Use either a still life with different objects, textures, and reflections; a small object, enlarged to show details; or an interior with objects and figures in which you use low eye level and reflections on a floor, pool, or mirror.

Rough out your ideas first in thumbnail sketches using different points of view, placement of objects, and placement of light sources. Make sketches even if you are working from a setup.

FIGURE 6.41 (top) Drawing student Annette Berlin showed unusual skill with the charcoal pencil in this drawing.

FIGURE 6.42 (at right) A dramatic view of a small object made to fill the working area by art student Mike Cherapek.

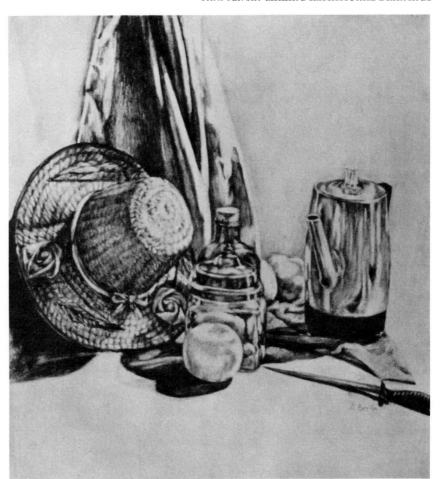

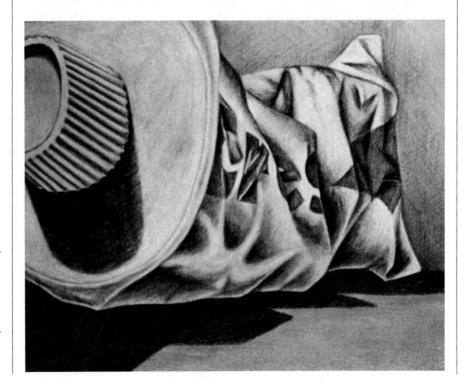

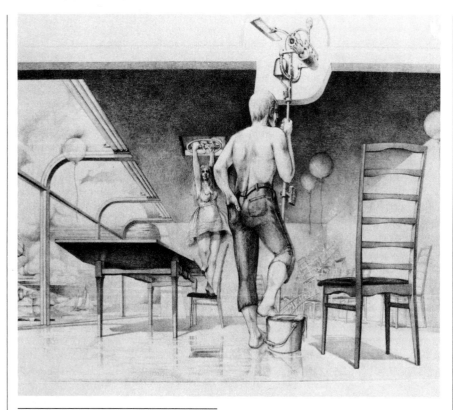

FIGURE 6.43 Detail of a graphite pencil drawing on white tracing vellum.

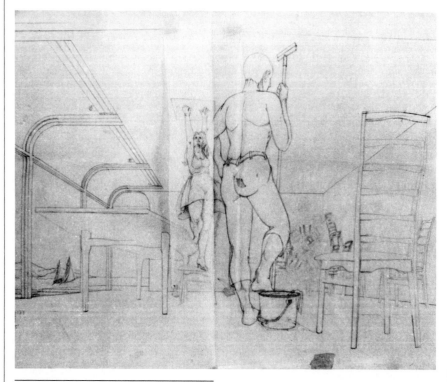

FIGURE 6.44 Preliminary tracing paper overlay used in composing and correcting the drawing in Figure 6.43.

Keep the design flexible until you are ready to start the final drawing. Be willing to move or change items to create a better composition. If you use overlays of tracing paper or vellum, you won't be tied to a certain composition. You can easily make changes until you are satisfied with the design (see Figure 6.44).

When you are satisfied, transfer the overlays to the final drawing as you did for the stippling activity (see page 118). Render the design with shadows and reflections. Remember to work all over the rendering, doing large, major areas of shadow first, then the details.

To learn about reflections, get a mirror in the studio, and put objects next to it or on it. Then look at a curved reflective surface, such as the coffee pot in Figure 6.41, or a rippled one like the floor in Figure 6.43. See how these surfaces reflect the objects. Don't try to draw reflections in window glass and showcases until you have had some experience with "pure" reflective surfaces like the mirror. Glass partly reflects images, but it also partly transmits images of whatever is on the other side. The mixture of two images is harder to render.

STUDIO

Color Shadow Drawing

MATERIALS

Colored pencils or chalk; white bristol board or heavy layout paper; felt pad, chamois, tissue, or paper stumps (optional)

Select an outdoor scene or make a still-life setup for the subject of this drawing. If you draw a setup, illuminate it with a floodlight so that the shadows won't move.

Use colored pencils (described in the Color Cross-Contour Drawing activity in Chapter 4) or chalks. There are various kinds of colored chalks. The common blackboard variety works best on chalkboards and is of little interest to you. The small, hard, square sticks called *layout chalks* are sometimes used by graphic designers, art directors, or illustrators for making rough sketches. They are also made in pencil form.

For this drawing, you can also use soft pastel chalks, called simply *pastels*, that come in large square sticks and in pencil form. They are brilliant in color and were the favorite dry medium of some of the Impressionist painters who lived in France in the late nineteenth and early twentieth centuries.

Pastels may be used to mix colors by putting small dots of different colors close together. They can also be blended by using a felt pad, chamois, tissue, or paper stumps to get color gradations. Paper stumps, which can be purchased in a variety of thicknesses, are tube-shaped and have pointed ends.

Remember to practice first before using any new media. Also, when working with color, always keep a piece of scrap handy from the same paper stock you are using. Then you can try color combinations before you use them on your drawing. Pastels are hard to erase cleanly without damaging the surface of your paper.

If you wish to work in patterns of dots or short strokes, study the Impressionists' paintings. If you are interested in smooth blends of color, look at Figure 1 in the Color Section. This Georgia O'Keeffe pastel could be mistaken for a painting.

Note the sunlight shadows in Jeff McMillan's *Father Popcorn* (Figure 10 in the Color Section) for exaggeration of soft form shadows and sharp cast shadows. Note also the warm colors used in even the strongest shadow areas. Some color was used because shadows tend to be darker values of the color of the surface on which they are cast. Also, some reflected light from the red shirt could tint the shadow. In any case, the warmth of the shadows helped unify the red of the shirt and the red of the hatband.

Mike Barrett's visually active still life (Figure 15 in the Color Section) is also well unified, in this case by the striped cloth that runs behind the fruits and vegetables. The artist used the stripes as cross-contour lines to define the folds and the form over which the cloth is draped.

Both of these student artists did several sketches in color before attempting these finished drawings. You should do the same. Don't be afraid to experiment. For imitational work, though, don't forget the importance of the overall shadow pattern or the difference between form and cast shadows.

DRAWING THE HUMAN FIGURE

In any chapter about imitational drawing, there needs to be a section on the human figure because so many imitational drawings have people in them. On the other hand, there are many good figure drawing texts and books on the structure of the human form already available. For any detailed study, we recommend these. In this section, we will tell you how to get started drawing human figures and explain the most important human proportions.

When measuring proportions of figures, it is both traditional and practical to use the head as a unit of measure. This doesn't include the hair or a beard. In real life, most of us are about 7½ heads tall. (Remember using a book as a unit of measurement when you sighted along your pencil? To draw figures, you will use the head to make similar length and width to measure proportions.)

Look at Peter Hurd's sketch of Dora Nunn Roberts in Figure 6.45 on the next page, and measure the model's head. Divide her overall height (head to toe) by the head measurement. You will find that she conforms to the 7½-head standard. (The faint lines in the background of Hurd's sketch don't relate to measuring the height of the figure. They relate to a proportional grid used in transferring the figure to the large-scale mural.)

Even though the real-life human figure is 7½ heads tall, we suggest that you take a hint from ancient Greek sculptors and use an 8-head figure. Using eight heads as the standard would make only about a ½″ (12 mm) difference in the head size of the model. This amount translates to less than ¼″ (6 mm) on the head size of an 18″ (46 cm) figure in a drawing.

The Greeks used eight heads to make what art historians call the **heroic figure**, a figure that appears a little taller than life-sized. Their sculptures of human figures represented their ideal of a body with perfect proportions. The heroic figure is an example of using exaggeration to express an idea. The other reason for using an eight-head figure is that eight is an even number. The halfway point between the top of the head and the ground becomes four heads. You can see the measurement on the chart with the sketch in Figure 6.46.

colored chalks
layout chalks

pastels
paper stumps

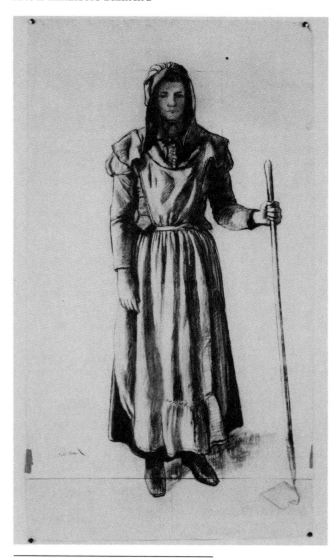

FIGURE 6.45 In this sketch of pioneer rancher, oil producer, and philanthropist Dora Nunn Roberts, Peter Hurd adheres to correct head and height proportions.
Courtesy of the Museum of Texas Tech University, Lubbock, TX.

You can find this halfway point on your own body by pushing a finger into the side of your hip, low on the pelvis, at the point where the big bone of the leg, called the *femur*, is fastened. The projection you feel at the top of this bone is called the *greater trochanter*. It is the midpoint of your body.

Knowing the midpoint of a standing figure is useful when you are drawing. Many people think the waist is the middle of the figure. If you believe this, your drawings of people will look like the one in Figure 6.47.

On the other hand, if you want to put a man of about average height (6′ or 182 cm) in a drawing with a horizon or eye level 32″ (80 cm) high, you know exactly how to place him. The horizon will pass behind him about 4″ (10 cm) below the projection of his hip, the great trochanter. One-half of 6′ (182 cm) is 3′ (91 cm), which is 36″ (91 cm) and 4″ (10 cm) above the horizon at 32″ (80 cm).

Another look at the chart in Figure 6.46 will tell you that on the mature female figure the center of the chest is 2 to 2½ heads down from the top. On the mature male, the line below the large, flat chest muscles called the *pectoralis majors* is down about two heads, or slightly more, from the top.

Although the waist averages about three heads down from the top of the figure, its location varies. When we refer to some people as *long-legged* or *short-legged*, we are usually referring to the height of their waists. People with high waists look as if their legs are long, but the fact is that legs take up about the same proportion of the figure on all of us. Check the comparison in Figure 6.46.

When a person's arms are hanging naturally at the side of the body, the tips of the fingers are somewhere near mid-thigh. This location varies, though, because people with high waists often have slightly shorter arms. The elbows usually line up with the waist.

Again, refer to the chart in Figure 6.46. Measure the legs from the bottom of the figure to the point where the knees bend. That point is just below the *patella*, or kneecap. The knees are about halfway between the greater trochanter and the ground, six heads down (or two heads up) on the classic figure.

Most of these vertical figure measurements are averages that can vary a little from person to person. The two that seem to be constant are the 7½-head height of the figure (which is exaggerated to eight heads in drawing) and the midpoint location of the greater trochanter.

In our years of teaching figure drawing, we have found only two models who varied from this norm, and they didn't vary by much. One of them had the classic eight-head figure you are using. The other had a long skull that made him only about seven heads high.

Width proportions vary so greatly that averages are almost meaningless. They depend on such things as the shoulder muscles (*deltoids*), the muscles that wrap around the sides of the rib cage (*latissimus dorsi*), and the amount of fat on the body. Individual differences in body width can always be measured by using the head as a proportional unit.

Even when we stand erect, our necks aren't held straight up and down. We all carry our heads a little forward. Our faces are vertical, but the axis of our necks tilts sometimes as much as thirty degrees.

There are subtle differences between male and female figures. Even though many women now concentrate on muscular development, the average male skeleton and muscles are heavier, and the male is somewhat more angular. On the whole, men are also somewhat taller than women. Also, the male figure's hips are narrower than shoulder width, while the female's hip and shoulder widths are often about the same.

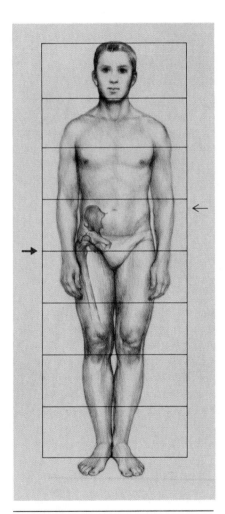
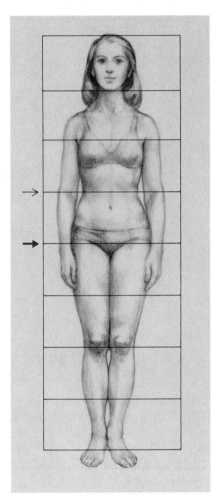
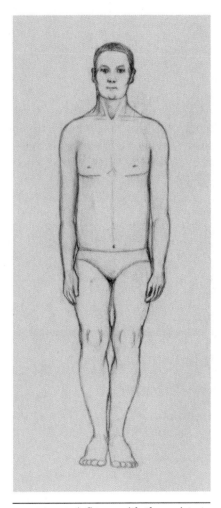

FIGURE 6.46 These figures are eight heads tall. The greater trochanter (indicated by the large arrow) is at the halfway point. The woman is what some would call "shorter-waisted" or "higher-waisted" than the man (see the smaller arrows).

FIGURE 6.47 A figure with the waist at the halfway point.

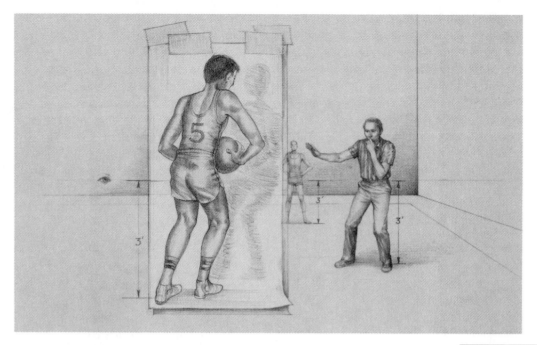

FIGURE 6.48 The horizon is about 3′ (91 cm) high. No. 5 is about 6′8″ tall. The referee is about 5′8″. The referee and background players are on the finished drawing. No. 5 started as a gesture drawing on a tissue overlay just like the player guarding him. The figure was then traced and corrected on another overlay. The eye symbol is on the horizon.

Figures to be placed in drawings can be drawn first on an overlay. They can then be refined while being traced on another overlay. Finally, they can be transferred onto the working surface in correct relation to eye level. (See Figure 6.48.)

Working on overlays instead of making corrections by scrubbing things out with an eraser allows you to draw more freely. You won't put anything on the surface of your finished drawing until you think it is ready, so you can start with a free, expressive sketch.

STUDIO

Proportional Chart of a Model

MATERIALS

Medium soft graphite pencil, ruler, graph paper with one-quarter-inch squares or drawing paper, charcoal pencil or vine charcoal (optional)

For your first attempt at accurate figure drawing, make a proportional chart for a model. The model should relax, but stand erectly. You will need the model to pose for two sessions of fifty minutes each. Give the model a five-

minute break after each fifteen or twenty minutes.

If you want to work larger than the graph paper with one-quarter-inch squares will allow, use your pencil and ruler to divide a sheet of 17 × 22″ (43 × 56 cm) paper into one-half-inch squares. On paper with these larger squares, draw with a charcoal pencil or vine charcoal. Use a medium-soft graphite pencil to draw on graph paper.

Draw the model using a head height measurement of four squares. Use your pencil or ruler to sight while making proportional estimates. Don't rely on the chart in Figure 6.46 to make the drawing. Your model may vary from this chart in several ways.

Start by marking the head on the chart; then mark the midpoint at the greater trochanter. Use a slightly short head measurement when measuring the model because you are using an eight-head figure. Remember, don't be fooled by the hair. As you draw, note all of the head units of measure at the side of the figure and the anatomical features at those points.

Don't forget that when you have located the height of a part of the body, you also need to measure how many heads wide the figure is at that point. The head width is different from the head height.

Drawing the Head and Face

Study the drawing of the woman in Figure 6.49. It is marked with the basic proportions of the head and facial features. The basic structural proportions of the head don't vary much from one person to another. The surface features, however, vary a great deal.

First, you must draw the basic proportions and the gesture of the head correctly. The gesture of the head is the way the person holds it. Drawing the surface features—eyes, nose, mouth, ears—will be easier after you have drawn the basic proportions of the head. Amusement park artists, who draw **caricatures** for a few dollars each, humorously exaggerate these features and ignore the basic structural proportions.

When you measure the vertical proportions of a face, you will find that the nose isn't at the halfway point. The *eyes* are. Between the highest point on the head and the underside of the chin, the center of the eyes is the halfway mark. Remember, we don't count the hair on the top of the head or any beard.

Look at Figure 6.49 for illustrations of the following dimensions.

Forgetting the whole head for a moment and considering just the face, let's look at vertical dimensions. The face extends from the hairline to the bottom of the chin. The place we are talking about when we refer to *hairline* is the place where the top of the head turns downward to become the facial plane. The hairline isn't always the actual starting point for the hair.

The face divides vertically into three equal areas. One is from the hairline to the browline (the bony ridge over the eyes where the eyebrows are). The middle area is from the browline to the bottom of the nose, where it joins the upper lip. The bottom third is the rest of the face. These measurements hardly ever vary from face to face.

The length of the ears and the distance between the eyes don't vary, either. Ears are the length of that center third of the face between the brow and the base of the nose. (There are exceptions. See the Enrichment feature on facial dimensions.) The distance between the eyes is the width of one eye opening, corner to corner.

The rest of the face measurements do vary from one person to another, but we can at least give averages. One of the varying measurements is the width of the mouth. On the average, the corners of the mouth are directly under the center of the eyes. The

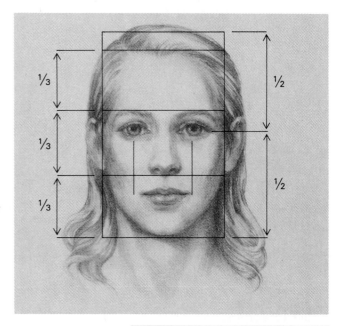

FIGURE 6.49 The most basic proportions of the head are usually the same. The eyes are halfway down. The facial plane is divided into thirds, with the brow and the base of the nose as dividing lines. The corners of the mouth are usually under the centers of the eyes. The ears are the length of the middle third of the face.

mouth opening is often a third of the way down between the nose and the bottom of the chin. It is also often lower than this, but seldom higher.

The distance between the outer corner of an eye and the outer point of the cheek bone is usually no greater than an eye's width. Of course, this distance varies with the size of the eyes and the width of the skull across the cheek bones.

The shape of the eye opening varies, but it is usually not shaped like an almond or like a football with points at both ends. On the average, the eye opening is arched at the top. The bottom line is somewhat straighter and usually turns up a little at the outer end.

The upper eyelid covers about the top third of the iris, the colored portion of the eye. The bottom of the iris meets the line of the lower lid. The upper lid often overlaps the lower lid at the outer corner, and the little notch of the tear duct may be seen at the inner corner. (In extremely old or ill people, the lower lid droops, exposing white beneath the iris. In amazement, joy, or fear, the eyes may be opened enough to expose white all around the iris.)

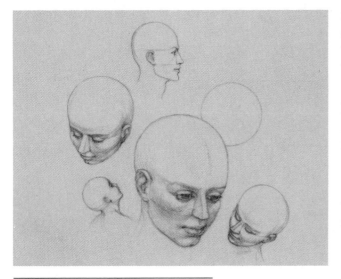

FIGURE 6.50 Starting the sketch with a ball for the cranium is a good way to capture the head gesture.

Although the method isn't entirely accurate, a general way of constructing the head and capturing its gesture is to draw a ball for the cranium, the portion of the skull enclosing the brain, then hang the frontal and lateral (side) planes on it. You can see examples in Figure 6.50.

After this, the horizontal lines are added. They define the location of the eyes, from outer corner to outer corner; the base of the nose; and the mouth, from corner to corner. These lines pass through the skull—not around it—and they must all be parallel to each other. Otherwise the head you are drawing will look bent.

Notice that these horizontal lines seem to get closer together when the head is tilted forward or backward. In Figure 6.51, the first sketch of the child's head is corrected by the second one, which makes the horizontal lines parallel to each other. The finished drawing shows how close the lines seem to each other and how the nose overhangs the upper lip because the head is tilted forward. The characteristic smallness of a child's features in relation to the cranium is also evident.

ENRICHMENT

Facial Dimensions of the Elderly and Children

The ears of older people may be longer than the center third of the face because the skull compresses, but the ears don't shrink. The length of the lower third of the face may actually decrease in old people—particularly for those who can't take advantage of modern orthodontics and dentures. Young children have features that are small, close together, and not well defined.

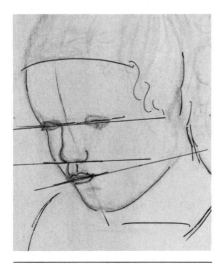
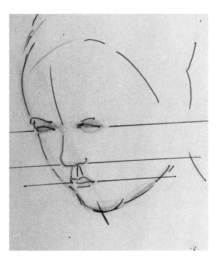
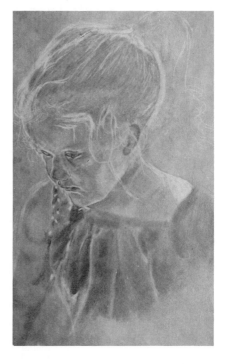

FIGURE 6.51 To construct the final drawing at the right, student Julie Miller used preliminary sketches to correct the important alignments of eyes, nose, and mouth. She used graphite and white conte on toned paper.

STUDIO

Sketchbook Head Drawing

MATERIALS

Charcoal pencil or conte crayons, sketchbook

Fill a page with drawings of heads. Use 3″ (76 mm) spheres for the craniums. Draw the heads from as many angles as you can.

The conte crayons you might choose for these drawings are small, square, hard, and somewhat waxy. The most popular colors are black, sepia (grayish brown), and rust. Often these colors are used together. Hold a crayon like a drawing tool, not like a writing instrument.

Even in your busiest moments, you can carry a small sketchbook and a stick of conte. You can capture the gesture of the heads of people you see while you are waiting at the bus stop or in a supermarket checkout line.

Remember to start with a quick circle, then hang the face structure on it. Soon you will be putting a nose on the face, then lines for the mouth and eyes.

These little heads fit well on gesture drawings of the body.

Drawing Portraits and Self-Portraits

Before starting a portrait or self-portrait, look at these good examples made by students.

The student who drew the girl in Figure 6.52 certainly had the inspiration of a beautiful model. The drawing is an excellent example of a graphite and white conte rendering on gray charcoal paper. Also, you can see the careful measurement of proportion in the features and the parallel alignment of the eye axis, base of the nose, and mouth.

Steven Haynes's excellent graphite rendering (Figure 6.53, next page) is a Scholastic Art Award winner. He deserved an award for the richness of surface, the emerging character of the form, and the interaction of line and value. It is definitely a portrait made to look like someone. But it also has formal overtones, so we can assume that some of the distortions are deliberate. We show it here in a chapter on imitational drawing so you can compare the basic head structure of a realistic head with this one with its slightly misaligned features, widely spaced eyes, and shortened forehead.

Christa Moser's sketch (Figure 6.54, next page) is another drawing that has as many expressive qualities as imitational ones. The finished self-portrait is shown in Figure 16 in the Color Section. Note in these drawings that even with the exaggerations and expressive pastel chalk strokes, the anatomical proportions of the head are correct.

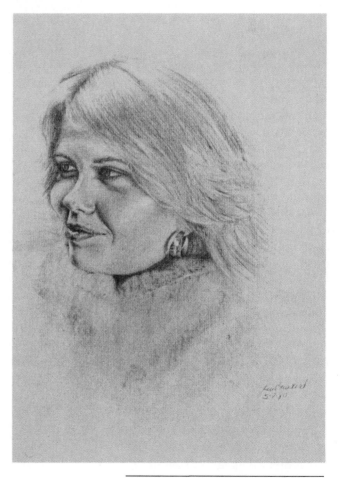

FIGURE 6.52 This drawing was done by student Ken Bussard with graphite and conte on toned paper.

conte crayons

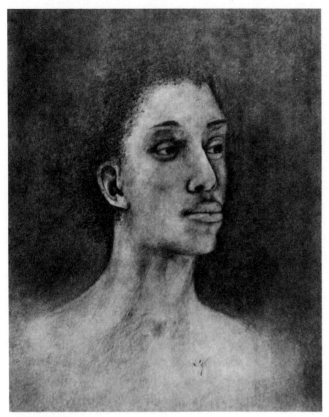

FIGURE 6.53 Art student Steven Haynes distorted certain structural aspects of the head to make an expressive portrait.

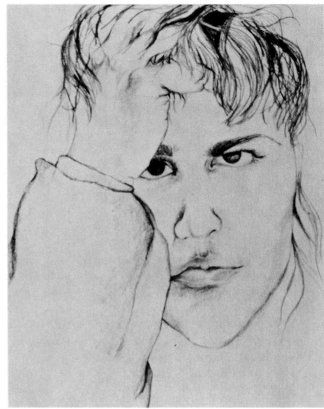

FIGURE 6.54 Christa Moser is the art student who did this sketch for a self-portrait. It is expressive but accurate.

Conte Crayon Self-Portrait

MATERIALS

Black and red (rust) conte crayons, drawing paper

Draw a self-portrait. Make an 8–10″ (20–25 cm) head, which will be about life-sized. Put the head on a neck and shoulders. Set up a mirror so you can see yourself without turning too far each time you look. Put a strong light on your face at an angle that will give interesting shadows, but don't let the light shine directly in your eyes.

Start by drawing the basic gesture and outline with the red conte crayon. Then, with the same crayon, lightly rough in the three horizontal guidelines at the correct locations for the browline and the base of the nose. Locate the horizontal axes for the eyes, the base of the nose, and the mouth. Keep rechecking as you work to see that these axes remain parallel to each other.

Before you put in more lines, start making the major areas of shadow on the side of the head, under the chin and nose, at the side of the nose, and in the eye sockets. Use the black crayon, but don't mark too heavily at first. Apply the crayon evenly. Use the red conte crayon in areas of lighter shadow, and use both black and red to make lines where you need them.

Now build up line and shadow details. You will alternate line with shadow so that they blend into a unified whole. The details will define the anatomy of your head— and, we hope, a little of your character.

Don't worry, however, if your first self-portrait doesn't look too much like you. The important thing is to get the structure right. After establishing the structure, the surface features become easy to draw.

Full-Color Head Drawing

MATERIALS

Pastel chalks or pencils; drawing paper; felt pad, paper stumps, or tissue

For a more advanced head drawing, do a self-portrait or a portrait of a model in full color. Try the Impressionists' stippling technique, or blend colors by rubbing them with a felt pad, paper stumps, or tissue. Pick an appropriate paper for pastels. Be sure to spray your drawing when you are finished.

ENRICHMENT

Mechanicals

Production artists are people who carefully and accurately assemble drawings, photographs, and type. They paste them together on single sheets before they are sent to the printer. These sheets are called *mechanicals.*

Editors and production artists often use light blue pencil for putting instructions on mechanicals. These pencil marks won't photograph in black and white printed reproduction. In fact, there is a Berol pencil color called *non-repro blue.* Sometimes cartoonists and illustrators also use light blue pencil for preliminary drawings.

Charcoal Drawing of a Model Using a Proportional Window

MATERIALS

Graphite, light blue, or tan pencil; ruler (optional); charcoal pencil; drawing paper

Make a careful and accurate charcoal pencil drawing of a model by using the procedure that follows.

The length of the model's head is a convenient unit of measure. By measuring with your pencil or ruler, determine how many heads high and how many heads wide your drawing must be. These are the proportions of an imaginary "window" in space whose outer edges would just enclose your

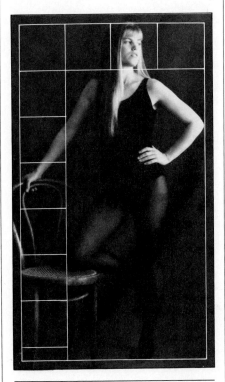

FIGURE 6.55 Proportional "window" drawn over the model with head-length marks measuring the rectangle.

drawing. The outermost points of the drawing will touch this frame. See Figure 6.55 for a photograph of a model with a proportional window placed over it.

Lightly draw a proportional window on your paper, making it large enough to almost fill the working area. If you like, use a lighter blue or tan pencil for preliminary work. (See the Enrichment feature titled "Mechanicals.")

Draw the sides of the window first. Then measure the distance between the sides, and divide this distance by the number of heads wide your model is. This will give you the length of one head as the unit of measure for your drawing.

Use this head unit to measure the height of your proportional window up to the number of heads tall your model is. (A seated model won't be eight heads tall.) Lightly draw in the top and bottom of your proportional window. Mark off the head units on the top, bottom, and sides. Make a grid over the whole

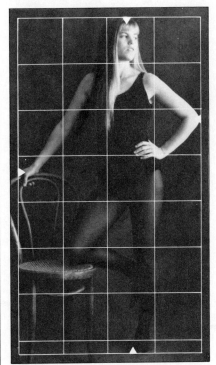

FIGURE 6.56 Completed grid over the model.

proportional window by connecting these marks. (See Figure 6.55 for marks and Figure 6.56 for the grid.)

All of this measuring can be done by careful estimation using a pencil. If you have used your ruler for these measurements, however, finish the drawing without it.

If you have done a careful and accurate job of making a proportional window and head unit grid, you now have a frame your drawing will fill. Next, you can figure out where the drawing should touch the edges. When you start, if the drawing doesn't touch the edges, you will know it needs some proportional correction.

To determine these contact points on the frame, again use your pencil to measure the model. See how many heads up the left side of the frame the first contact point is, and mark it. Label it with the part of the body that touches the frame there. Do this with all contact points on both sides and the top

and bottom of the window. There probably won't be more than six to eight of these points. There may be only four. (See Figure 6.56.)

Lightly sketch the outline and gesture of the model's head. Make it one head high, of course, and measure to make sure you get it in the right place. Then roughly sketch in other parts of the body where they touch the edges of the window. Don't worry about details. Try to get the total image in proportion. (Check Figure 6.57.)

Now use your pencil to determine alignments. You will discover that if you hold your pencil between your eye and the model, you can align the pencil with some nearly straight edges or imaginary lines that are implied by the model's anatomy. Some of these lines might be the axis or center line of the torso, the edge of the upper arm, or the edge of a *tibia* (shin bone).

You will discover that if you extend these lines, some will align

with other lines on the figure. Others will point to specific places on the model or the model's clothing that you can mark or label on your drawing. This procedure will help you draw the model's gesture accurately. Use head units to measure the distances along these lines to locate various points. (See Figure 6.58.)

Most of the hard work is now complete. You can enjoy finishing the drawing with charcoal. See Figure 6.59 for final steps. Remember to look at the negative spaces while you draw.

If this procedure seems long and difficult, don't be fooled. It actually saved you time in making an accurate imitational drawing. As you become more experienced, you may leave out some of these steps—or you may do them in your head instead of on paper. But for now, this procedure will help you learn to draw figures imitationally.

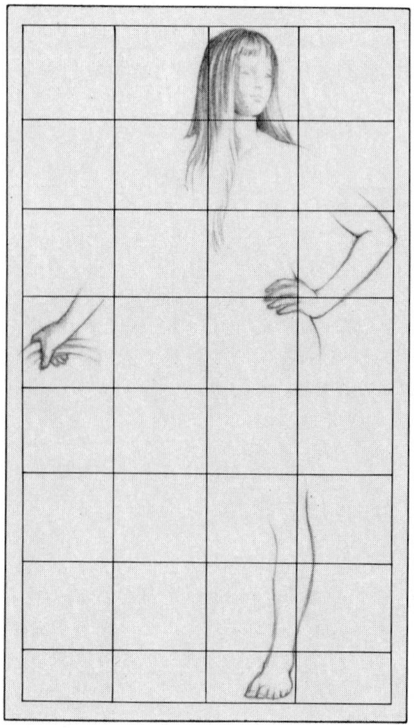

FIGURE 6.57 Removing the photograph of the model, we indicated the points at which parts of her anatomy would touch the grid.

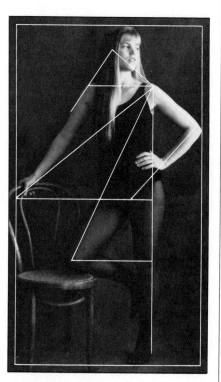

FIGURE 6.58 Lines were drawn to show alignment relationships in the figure composition.

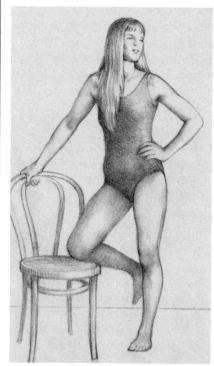

FIGURE 6.59 With preliminary planning, the gesture and outline contours are easy to draw.

Landscape Architect: Creating Vital Environments

Landscape architects work to combine beauty and usefulness when designing projects as varied as parks, industrial centers, urban plazas, historical restorations, and even whole communities. As president and director of design of Land Design/Research, Inc., Columbia, Maryland, Donald Hilderbrandt is involved in all aspects of environmental design.

Hilderbrandt's interest in painting and courses in advanced art in high school helped influence his choice of architecture as a major at Pennsylvania State University. While at Penn State, he specialized in landscape architecture. After graduation, Hilderbrandt earned a master's degree in landscape architecture from the University of Michigan. He worked as associate and senior designer and then as chief landscape architect for other firms before founding LDR in 1971. A Fellow of the American Society of Landscape Architects, Hilderbrandt has gained national recognition for several of his projects, including Pennsylvania Avenue in Washington, D.C., and the Hyatt Regency Hotel in Chicago, Illinois.

At the beginning of any job, a landscape architect talks with the client in order to clearly understand the purpose, the specific needs, and the funds available for the project. Then he must study the site itself and map features such as the slope of the land, existing plants and trees, and any other special features.

The next step is to prepare preliminary drawings that combine creativity with technical competence. This is one of Hilderbrandt's favorite parts of his work. In this step Hilderbrandt uses triangles, scales, and a circle template or pattern as well as aerial photographs and slides to create plans to show the client. Hilderbrandt considers graphics to be an effective form of communication: ''A perspective sketch can convey a design concept quickly and clearly and often can stimulate someone's imagination, which is important in the design process.'' You can see an example of an architect's sketch in Figure 11.2.

While satisfying the client is a high priority to Hilderbrandt, ultimate personal satisfaction comes from contributing to the quality of our environment, both natural and man-made. Hilderbrandt manages over twenty projects at a time. A typical day may find him working on two or three projects, supervising designers and graphic artists, or traveling to projects as far away as Montreal, Bermuda, Hawaii, Venezuela, or Wales. But Hilderbrandt works close to home, too. He especially enjoyed working on the master plan for the new town of Columbia, Maryland, where he lives.

UNIT II

████████████████████ ████████████████████

Evaluation and Review

MEETING YOUR OBJECTIVES

By answering the following questions and doing the exercises, you will demonstrate your ability to meet the learning objectives listed at the beginning of Chapters 5 and 6.

Chapter 5

1. How do imitationalists judge drawings?
2. Pick one drawing from each of the first four chapters in this book. Describe the literal qualities in each drawing.
3. From Chapter 3 select one work that you think an imitationalist would regard as *unsuccessful*. Write one or two paragraphs telling why you think the imitationalist would judge this work unsuccessful.
4. From Chapter 3 select one work that you think an imitationalist would regard as *successful*. Write one or two paragraphs telling why you think the imitationalist would judge this work successful.

Chapter 6

1. Make a drawing of a room in your house or school. Use your comparative measuring skill to insure that doors, windows, and objects in the room are in correct proportion to each other.
2. Use a fixative to preserve the drawing you did for number 1 above.
3. Draw a one-point perspective of a scene you have observed in your neighborhood. Make sure the horizon is at your eye level. Leave the lines for basic boxes and the lines going to the vanishing point lightly visible in the drawing. Darken the visible lines of actual objects and figures.
4. Do a rendering in full color and value of a two-point perspective. This perspective drawing must involve at least one major manufactured object (a machine, piece of furniture, vehicle, etc.). Use colored pencil or chalk.
5. Do a stippled rendering that has atmospheric perspective. Do several preliminary drawings to help you design your finished drawing. The scene you choose to draw should involve deep space.
6. Do a drawing of a still life setup. Use colored pencils to create the natural colors of the objects in the setup. Pay special attention to the form and cast shadows. Mount and mat your finished drawing.
7. Do a two-point perspective drawing that includes at least three human figures. The figures should be in correct proportion and perspective. Develop the figures by sketching from a model. Do the figures on a tracing vellum overlay and refine them on other overlays. Transfer them to the finished drawings in proper relation to the horizon. Render them in colored pencils or chalks. Mount and mat your finished drawing.
8. Make a list of the drawing tools and media you used in doing the studio exercises in Chapter 6.
9. Make a list of the drawing techniques you learned and used in doing the studio exercises in Chapter 6.

LEARNING DRAWING TERMS

You encountered several new drawing terms in this unit. The most important terms are those printed in heavy, bold type. Write all the terms on a sheet of paper. Then, without looking in your book, tell what each term means in your own words. If you are not sure of a meaning, use your book to write a definition.

EXPERIENCING DIFFERENT MEDIA

Each new drawing medium is listed at the bottom of the page on which it is first mentioned. Review your experiences with all the media, comparing strengths, weaknesses, and personal preferences. Then write a report summarizing your experiences with these media.

SEEING YOUR ENVIRONMENT

Learning to see the world around you as it really is is one of the first steps in improving your drawing skills. Doing the following exercises and others like them will help you get in the habit of seeing your environment more closely.

1. Look for scenes in your day-to-day routine where it seems that parallel lines come together at a vanish-

ing point. Try to draw these scenes as you see them.
2. Go to the nearest art museum or gallery and find the most realistic work you can. Take your time and study the work closely. Then make a list of all the literal qualities in that work.
3. Look for interesting and varied arrangements of shadows. Fill several pages in your sketchbook with realistic sketches that include the shadows.
4. Find examples of the principle of harmony in the natural world. Make sketches of the scenes you observe.

EVALUATING DRAWINGS

1. Evaluate the drawing you did for number 7, Chapter 6, under ''Meeting Your Objectives.'' Rate yourself from 1 to 10 for four categories: 1) proportions of figures, 2) perspective (spatial illusion and procedure), 3) believability of shadows, and 4) color and value relationships.
2. Use the art criticism steps you learned in Chapter 2 to evaluate the same drawing you critiqued above.
3. Use the art criticism process to evaluate the drawing on this page. Compare the drawing to one of the drawings in this unit. Discuss both differences and similarities.

EXPANDING YOUR HISTORICAL KNOWLEDGE

Learning about the history of art will help you improve your drawing skills. It will also increase your understanding of your own culture and the cultures of others, both past and present. Answering the questions below indicates that you are learning art history. You will be able to answer most of the questions by referring to the Enrichment sections in this unit and to Chapter 3. To answer the last question you will probably need to refer to art history books, such as those listed in the Bibliography at the back of the book.

1. Explain how Egyptian spiritual beliefs affected Egyptian art.
2. Give one reason why the Renaissance style of art began in Italy.
3. How were the geographic conditions of Venice realized in the works done by painters of that city?

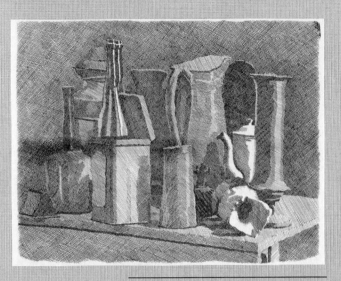

Giorgio Morandi, *Large Still Life with Coffee Can*, 1934. Etching on paper, 11.7 × 15.4″ (29.8 × 39.0 cm). The Harvard University Art Museums, Cambridge, MA.

4. Explain how the problems facing the Catholic Church in the early 16th century helped popularize the Mannerist style of art.
5. How might the events of World War I have affected the aesthetic qualities found in the works of artists such as Kathe Kollwitz?
6. The work of which later American artist—Jackson Pollock or Edward Hopper—would most resemble the work of Thomas Eakins? Explain.
7. On page 94 the names of four artists who influenced Thomas Eakins are mentioned. Pick one of these artists. Find three good sources of information in addition to Chapter 3 about the artist and his work. Then write several paragraphs comparing the artist and his work to Eakins and his work. You may also want to read more about Eakins and study several more pieces of his work.

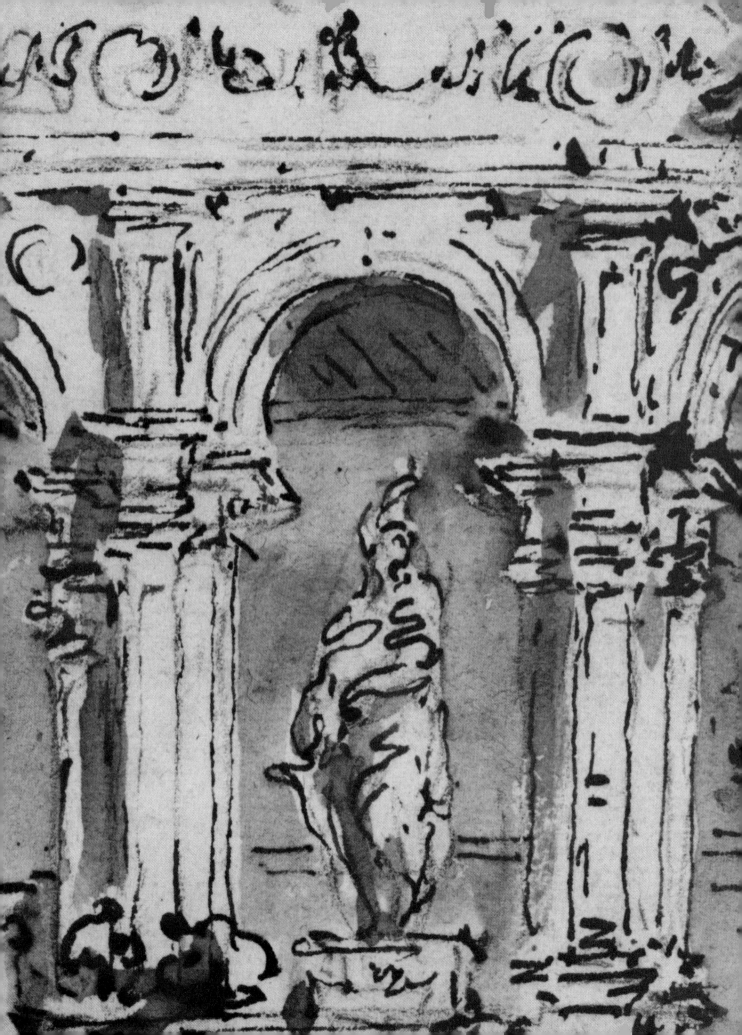

Structural Drawing

Unit III emphasizes the visual qualities, which are the aesthetic qualities valued most by formalists. As you learn to understand and create structural drawings, you will study how other artists have used the elements and principles of art to produce drawings with effective structure.

In Chapter 7, "Understanding and Judging Visual Qualities," you will imagine that you are returning to the art gallery you visited in Chapter 5. But this time you will play the role of a formalist critic. You will analyze several drawings and make judgments about them based on their visual qualities.

When you return to the studio in Chapter 8, "Making Formal Drawings," you will use what you have learned through art criticism and history to create structural drawings. All types of drawings—including those whose purpose is to imitate reality or express emotion—rely on effective formal qualities. As you create drawings in this chapter, you will discover ways to organize visual qualities. You will also learn methods for finding visual ideas for formal drawings and use media that emphasize the elements and principles of art.

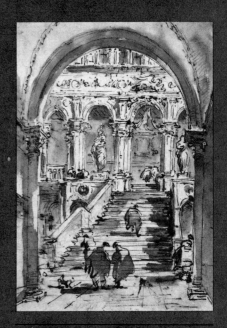

Francesco Guardi, *Stairway of the Giants in the Ducal Palace*, 18th century. Pen and wash over red chalk, 10⅜ × 7⁵/₁₆″ (26.3 × 18.6 cm). The Metropolitan Museum of Art, New York, NY. Rogers Fund (detail at left).

Understanding and Judging Visual Qualities

OBJECTIVES

After reading this chapter and doing the activities, you will be able to

■ explain how a formalist judges drawings;

■ analyze drawings to determine how artists have used the elements and principles of art; and

■ judge drawings based on their visual qualities and give reasons for your judgment.

In Chapter 5 you were asked to assume you were an imitationalist. You were supposed to describe and judge several drawings you saw at a gallery opening according to their literal qualities. Were you comfortable in that role? Or did you experience some uncertainty as an imitationalist? You might have been uncertain because you knew that imitationalism overlooks many important qualities of art.

In this chapter, you are invited to become an inflexible formalist—and you may become uneasy again. You are asked to focus on certain aesthetic qualities and ignore any others. *As a formalist, you will consider only the visual qualities—the elements and principles of art—as you analyze and judge drawings.* (You might want to briefly review the discussion of these elements and principles in Chapter 1.)

Being a formalist won't be easy, but don't get discouraged. You will become more skilled at analyzing the elements and principles in drawings with practice. You may even surprise yourself by being able to see how artists use these elements and principles to organize their compositions.

The design chart on the next page will help you judge drawings as a formalist would. You can use it to identify the elements and principles and the ways they are combined in the drawings.

Because you are a formalist, you like works of art that emphasize visual qualities. From an article in the local newspaper you learn that drawings of this kind will be displayed at a nearby gallery. You decide at once to attend . . .

Gas

EDWARD HOPPER

The gallery is jammed with people. They are voicing their opinions about the wide assortment of artworks on display. The room becomes silent when you enter; everyone is eager to see how you will react to the drawings. People edge closer as you pause before a black conte crayon drawing by the American artist Edward Hopper (Figure 5.2 on page 92). They watch as you study it closely. (Don't read further until you have completed a thorough analysis of the drawing *Gas* in your role as a formalist. To do this, use the design chart in Figure 7.1.)

Several of the onlookers are waiting for your reactions to the Hopper drawing. What will you mention first? Certainly you won't refer directly to the drawing's subject matter. No, as a formalist you are much more concerned with the way the drawing is put together. You might begin your analysis by stating that the artist used the principles of *harmony*, *emphasis*, *variety*, and *gradation* to organize the elements of *shape*, *value*, *line*, and *space*.

Of course you are ready for the puzzled looks on the faces of some in your audience. After all, not everyone is familiar with formalism. So you decide to go into more detail. You will explain how different combinations of elements and principles create a sense of unity in the drawing.

You begin your explanation by pointing out the three white circular shapes on top of each gas pump. These same circular shapes are repeated in the contours of the two dark areas (trees) to the far left. This repetition creates harmony (Figure 7.2, next page). The artist has also enhanced harmony by repeating rectangular shapes in the gas pumps, curbs, sign, and building (Figure 7.3, next page).

When everyone understands how the principle of harmony has been used to organize the element of shape, you ask if anyone can identify the most important shapes in the drawing. Most members of your audience find these shapes easily. Several immediately point to the gas pumps.

Then you ask how the artist emphasized these gas pumps. After a pause, one member of the group observes that their light and dark values contrast with the dark and light values behind them. Someone else suggests that the gas pumps are important because they are placed directly in the center of the composition. By emphasizing the gas pumps, the artist pointed out the function of the isolated building beside the narrow road. It couldn't be mistaken for a grocery store, a fast-food restaurant, or a motel.

DESIGN CHART		**PRINCIPLES OF ART**							
ELEMENTS OF ART		Balance	Emphasis	Harmony	Variety	Gradation	Movement/ Rhythm	Proportion	Space
Color	Hue								
	Intensity								
	Value								
Value (Non-Color)									
Line									
Texture									
Shape/Form									
Space									

UNITY

FIGURE 7.1 Design chart.

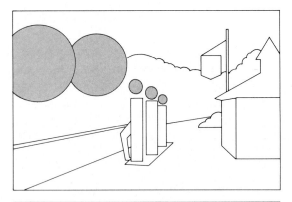

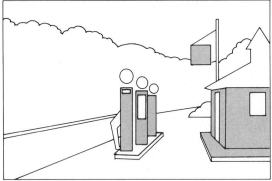

FIGURES 7.2, 7.3 Shown above are two diagrams of *Gas* by Edward Hopper. The repetition of circular shapes (top) and rectangular shapes (bottom) contributes to the harmony of this composition.

Next, you draw the group's attention to the different kinds of lines in the drawing. You make sure that everyone notices how the vertical lines repeated in the gas pumps, tree trunks, sign post, and building add to the picture's harmony. These lines, however, contrast with the diagonal lines of the road and curbs. These vertical and diagonal lines also contrast with the horizontal lines of the treetops, sign, and service station. The contrasting lines add variety and visual interest to the drawing.

Seeing that your audience is now involved in analyzing Hopper's drawing, you explain how the artist created the illusion of depth or space. To do so, you introduce the principle of gradation. Space is suggested by the gradual narrowing of the road's shape. The road gradually narrows as it extends back into the drawing until it disappears from view at the base of the trees. Space was also accented by the gradual change in the sizes of the circular shape at the top of each gas pump. (See the design chart with all of these design relationships in Figure 7.4. Of course, there are more design relationships. Take time to look for them before continuing with your reading.)

Since you have found most of the important design relationships in the Hopper drawing, you prepare to move on. But someone asks if you think the drawing is a successful work of art. Before answering, you

DESIGN CHART		**PRINCIPLES OF ART**							
ELEMENTS OF ART		Balance	Emphasis	Harmony	Variety	Gradation	Movement/ Rhythm	Proportion	Space
Color	Hue								
	Intensity								
	Value								
Value (Non-Color)			✕						
Line			✕		✕				
Texture									
Shape/Form				✕					
Space						✕			

UNITY

FIGURE 7.4 Refer to the text for an explanation of the design relationships in Edward Hopper's drawing *Gas*.

remind yourself that as a formalist you think the visual qualities are the most important. You then ask yourself if the artist used visual qualities effectively in this drawing. Were the elements and principles of art combined to achieve unity? If so, it is a good drawing.

But maybe you believe that the drawing is something more than a collection of parts. You might believe that it will interest you after repeated viewings as much as it did when you first saw it. If so, you may want to classify it as a great drawing. Everyone is waiting. What is your decision? (You can see Hopper's painting *Gas* in Figure 3 in the Color Section.)

Gross Clinic

THOMAS EAKINS

You pass several other drawings before stopping at another that appeals to you (on page 93). Several people urge you to analyze this drawing. Of course you agree to do so. (Don't read further until you have completed a thorough analysis of the drawing *Gross Clinic*. To do this, use the design chart in Figure 7.1.)

During this analysis, you try to answer several questions. Included among these are the following:

- What element seems to stand out in this drawing?
- Which principles were used to organize this element?
- You can see the outline of a large pyramid shape in this drawing. What is at the tip of this pyramid?
- Was the placement of that object at the tip of the pyramid a deliberate attempt to emphasize that object?
- Does the use of this pyramid shape suggest balance? Is this balance symmetrical or asymmetrical?
- Is this drawing a successful work of art?
- What aesthetic qualities would you refer to if you had to defend your judgment?

Self-Portrait at Age Twenty-Two

ALBRECHT DÜRER

Later you stop briefly before a drawing by Dürer (Figure 7.5). You look at how certain elements of art such as line, value, and texture have been used in the face, hand, and pillow. But do these parts fit together to form a unified whole? Is this a finished work of art? Or is this work a series of detailed but unrelated drawings? Did the artist draw only to develop an idea, record certain information, or sharpen drawing skills?

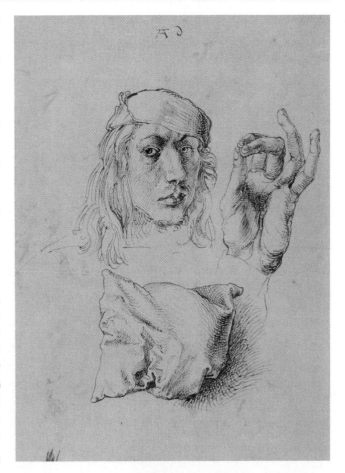

FIGURE 7.5 Albrecht Dürer, *Self-portrait at Age Twenty-Two*, c. 1493. Pen and ink on paper, 10.9 × 8″ (27.6 × 20.2 cm). The Metropolitan Museum of Art, New York, NY. Robert Lehman Collection.

ENRICHMENT

Albrecht Dürer

You might be surprised to learn that Dürer was the first artist to complete a true self-portrait. Your surprise may change to awe when you learn that he created it when he was thirteen years old!

Dürer was born in Nuremberg, Germany, in 1471, the second son in a family of eighteen. He was interested all of his life in reproducing his own sensitive and often troubled features with pencil and paint. Perhaps the worry often seen in his self-portraits was due to the religious conflict between Martin Luther and the Catholic Church. The artist became involved in this controversy. Finally Dürer sided with Luther and became a strong spokesman for change.

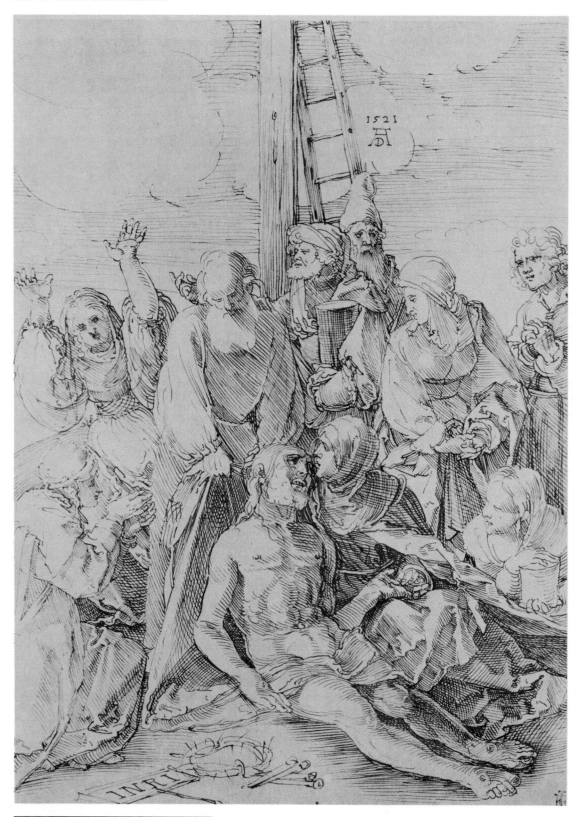

FIGURE 7.6 Albrecht Dürer, *Lamentation*, 16th century. Pen and brown ink on white paper, 11.4 × 8.3″ (29.0 × 21.0 cm). The Harvard University Art Museums, Cambridge, MA. Bequest of Meta and Paul J. Sachs.

Dürer's concern for structure is apparent in his pen and ink drawing *Lamentation* (Figure 7.6), a carefully composed religious scene completed in 1521, seven years before his death. Skillful use of light and dark values draws attention to the figure of the dead Christ, gives roundness to all the figures, and creates the appearance of space.

The mourning figures crowded around Christ form a large triangle. It rises from a wide base to form a point where a ladder rests against the cross. (To the right of this ladder, you can see Dürer's famous signature and the date.) But there is a second triangle in this composition. Can you find it? What important purpose does it serve?

This second, smaller triangle, with its base along the right edge of the drawing, overlaps the larger one. The sides of this triangle are suggested by a series of heads and the legs of the reclining Christ. At the top of this second triangle are the faces of the two main figures in this religious drama—Christ and his mother. Unlike the other sorrowing and gesturing figures around them, they are quiet and still. The mother takes her dead son's hand in her own and seems to be whispering a last farewell. The finality of that farewell is subtly suggested by a woman to the mother's left. She holds a jar of ointment to be used for the burial.

Head of a Girl with Braids
HENRI MATISSE

Your curiosity is aroused by a group of people gathered before a drawing by Henri Matisse of a girl with braids (Figure 7.7). You decide to investigate. A lively discussion about the work is going on. A gentleman quietly informs you that an earlier gallery visitor said this drawing is unsuccessful. (He is, of course, referring to you in your previous role as an imitationalist in Chapter 5.)

This statement is a challenge you can't ignore, so you step forward to inspect the controversial drawing. "What is wrong with this work?" you ask. Someone answers that the other critic said the drawing is unimportant because it doesn't look real. As a formalist, how will you reply to this charge? Will you reply that all works, especially abstract works like this one, should be judged by their visual qualities instead of their literal qualities?

Referring to the drawing, you explain that *what* the artist has drawn is less important than *how* he

decided to draw it. To understand and appreciate this work, a viewer should study how the artist used line in the hair, the curve of the shoulders, and the contour of the face. Instead of looking for details that aren't there, the viewer should notice how only the most essential lines were used to create a sense of rhythm. The repeated curved lines of equal thickness create harmony. Variety was achieved by changing the length and the direction of these lines.

You conclude by saying that this drawing wasn't meant to look exactly like a girl with braids. Instead, it appeals to viewers because of a careful arrangement of lines, which the artist designed after studying a girl with braids. After viewers understand how visual qualities are used, they should decide the work is successful.

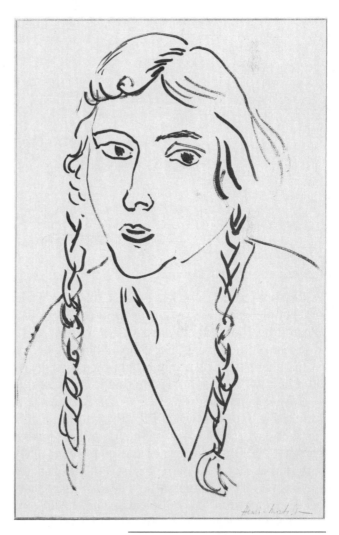

FIGURE 7.7 Henri Matisse, *Head of a Girl with Braids*, c. 1916. Brush with India ink, 22.1 × 14.8″ (56.1 × 37.5 cm). The Art Institute of Chicago, IL. Anonymous gift.

FIGURE 7.8 Vincent van Gogh, *Cypresses*, 1889. Reed pen and ink drawing, 24.6 × 18.3″ (62.5 × 46.5 cm). The Brooklyn Museum, Brooklyn, NY. Frank L. Babbott and A. Augustus Healy Fund.

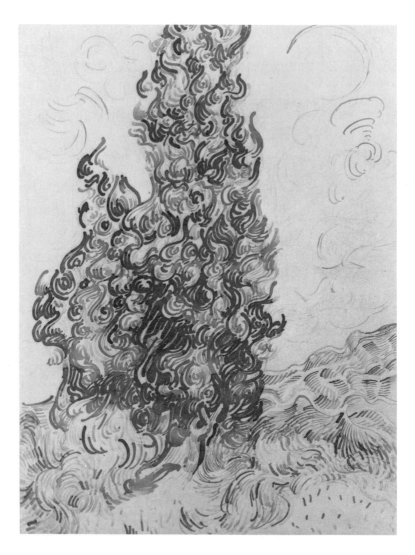

The Last Respects

HENRI DE TOULOUSE-LAUTREC

You are preparing to leave the gallery when several people lead you to a final drawing (on page 175) created by Henri de Toulouse-Lautrec. It shows a workman standing with bared head, holding his hat in his hands, staring at a funeral procession. After studying the work, you decide that it is successful.

Like the Matisse drawing, *The Last Respects* uses only a few lines to suggest the different forms. The distant, dark, solid shapes of the funeral procession contrast with the light values and sparse lines of the foreground figure. This contrast emphasizes the importance of the funeral scene. The man's dark scarf, however, repeats the dark values in the funeral procession and ties these two parts of the picture together into a harmonious whole.

Distance is implied by the contrast in proportions between the man in the foreground and the much smaller figures in the background. The illusion of space is also created by the way the man overlaps the background scene. The artist used the principles of emphasis, harmony, and proportion to effectively arrange the elements of line, shape, and space. The result is a unified and visually exciting composition.

You find another drawing in the gallery exciting because of its effective use of the elements and principles of art (Figure 7.8). Take time to analyze and judge this work. Keep in mind that as a formalist you are mainly concerned with visual qualities. (Don't read further until you have analyzed and judged the drawing in Figure 7.8.)

Noting the time, you are pleased to discover that it is still quite early. If you hurry, you will have enough time to return to your studio to work on drawings of your own—drawings, of course, in which you emphasize visual qualities.

DRAWING AT WORK

Industrial Design: Function into Form

Go into any large department store or mall. Check the new products that weren't on the shelves just a year ago. Then look at all of the items that have been improved or redesigned. Finally, notice the layout of the store or shopping center itself.

All of these areas and more are in the realm of the industrial designer. Industrial designers combine artistic talent with specific knowledge of production techniques and materials to create new products and refine manufacturing procedures. Whatever the project, teamwork is the key word for success.

Joe Sonderman, president of DESIGN/Joe Sonderman, Inc. in Charlotte, North Carolina, has gathered a team of professionals who work in many areas of design, both industrial and graphic. Sonderman's own background is firmly rooted in industrial design. "Coming from a family fathered by a talented artist, my two brothers and I inherited his artistic abilities. My father was an automobile dealer, and because of the close association with the auto industry, the field of industrial design was a natural career choice combining art and industry."

Although he studied no art in high school, Sonderman took private art lessons during his grade school years. After obtaining a bachelor's degree in industrial design from the University of Cincinnati, Sonderman held positions in automotive styling with Chrysler and served as staff industrial designer with Sylvania Lighting, among other jobs. Now, as head of his own consulting firm, Sonderman supervises all areas of the design process.

Teamwork is essential at all stages of an industrial design problem. The first step is to research the client's needs. What will the new product do? What size should it be? Who will buy it? What moving parts may be needed?

Depending on the specific product or piece of machinery, the designers may work with specialists in the fields of physics, electronics, textiles, and other areas. Often a design staff is composed of individuals with knowledge in many of these areas. Other times designers work with specialists from outside the agency. In either case, the purpose of stage one is to develop a clear and accurate picture of the client's needs and expectations.

Step two is generating and refining ideas. Working in teams, the design consultants make and discuss several dozen thumbnail sketches. Both form and function are important considerations. The focus of these drawings is on what the part or product will do, and then the designers consider its components.

It is important to remember that the exterior style will be affected by the interior workings of the product. For example, if a new weed trimmer being designed is too heavy, it probably won't appeal to less muscular customers. Marketable aspects such as color aren't vital considerations at this planning stage and can be determined later.

After many sketches have been discussed, the most promising sketches are shown to the client. These may be prepared with or without color, depending on the client's preference. The next stage is to prepare a two-dimensional rendering, giving specific dimensions of the product. Next, designers prepare three-dimensional drawings that include diagrams of the inner workings. Input from the engineering departments associated with the design firm, or provided by the client, is important at this stage.

Finally, these drawings are translated into models or prototypes. Now color and other graphic considerations such as labels are considered. For example, black may not be the best choice for a new hair dryer because it may make the dryer appear too heavy. On the other hand, yellow is a color that usually appeals to both men and women. If white is used for the hair dryer, red might be a good color for the control buttons. After all of these decisions have been made and the client is satisfied, the project moves on to the next stage of development—weighing production considerations such as cost of materials and methods of manufacture.

Product design requires the creativity of many people with a variety of talents and skills. Industrial designers have the satisfaction of knowing that their work results in functional products used by consumers every day.

Making Formal Drawings

After reading this chapter and doing the activities, you will be able to

■ explain different ways that artists use visual qualities in their drawings;

■ make drawings of objects and people, emphasizing the visual qualities;

■ make abstract drawings;

■ make rubbings for the purpose of discovering ideas for formal drawings;

■ use selective vision to find concepts for formal drawings;

■ use different media to enhance the effect of the visual qualities in drawings;

■ demonstrate the use of different drawing tools and media; and

■ demonstrate the use of different drawing techniques.

A formal drawing may express an idea or a strong emotion. Everything in it may be easily recognizable or may even look real. The chief emphasis of a formal drawing, however, is on the visual experience created by the structure—the elements and principles of art. In other words, a formal drawing's main subject is *itself*. A formal drawing is art about art, although it may also communicate on other levels.

The formal or expressive qualities of a drawing—the ways the artist has used the visual vocabulary—are quite important in *all* works of art. This doesn't mean, however, that the literal and expressive qualities of drawings aren't important. They are. What it does mean is that an artwork that imitates reality or expresses emotion may be judged primarily on its use of the literal or expressive qualities. Still, it is unlikely that the work will be judged successful if it fails to use formal qualities effectively.

In this chapter, you will learn ways to organize visual qualities in drawings. You will also discover ways to get visual ideas for creating formal drawings.

UNDERSTANDING VISUAL QUALITIES IN DRAWINGS

Even emotional drawings require the use of structure to express the artist's idea. The fascinating technical pen work by Frank Cheatham in Figure 8.1 is an example of skillful formal drawing. He has organized elements to create an exciting visual experience. Whatever symbolic meaning this drawing communicates, its main impact is visual.

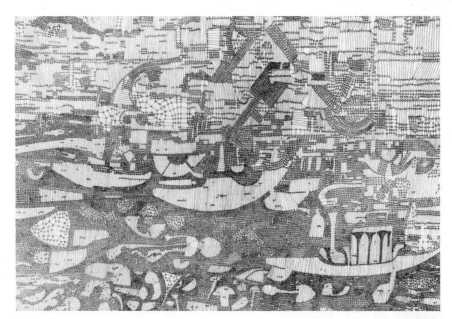

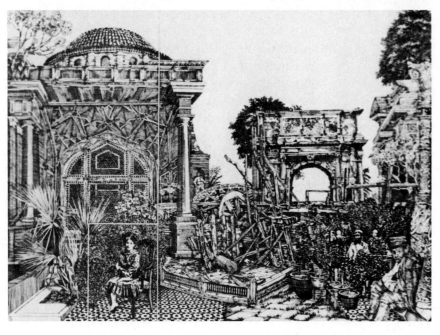

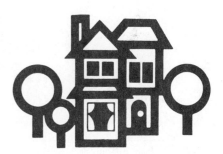

FIGURE 8.1 (left) Frank Cheatham's drawing was done with a Rapidograph technical pen. It reflects his interest in primitive design structures and mysterious artifacts.

Courtesy of the artist.

FIGURE 8.2 (below left) This intricate etching is by artist and museum director Gary Edson. While the images are imitational, they are used in a formal structure.

Courtesy of the artist.

FIGURE 8.3 The little illustration of the house (above) from a newspaper ad becomes symbolic and strongly formal.

Courtesy of *The University Daily*, Texas Tech University.

The work in Figure 8.2 is by Gary Edson. This fine art print is more imitational than Cheatham's work, but it still relies on strong formal qualities for its impact. For instance, note the complex way the shapes are organized, the way repetition creates unity, and how variety adds interest.

The drawing in Figure 8.3 is an **illustration** from a newspaper. An illustration is a drawing used to tell a story, give instructions, or make a product look attractive.

The artist drew this illustration to sell a service. To do this, the artist had to be at least as concerned with creating a visual experience for the viewer as with the need to advertise real estate in a newspaper.

To serve the primary goal of the advertiser, the artist had to create strong formal qualities in the illustration, which this artist did. The illustration intrigues the viewer by the way it uses the element of line. The lines outlining shapes are broad enough to be shapes, also. These narrow black shapes that outline other shapes are so strong that they become part of the image they define. The repetition of the three basic geometric shapes (circle, square, and triangle) creates unity. And the combined effect of these uses of

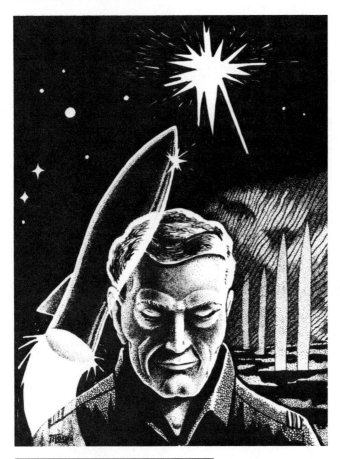

FIGURE 8.4 The formal or structural qualities of this science fiction illustration by Marvin Moon are strengthened by the stippled rendering technique. Courtesy of the artist.

the elements is a harmony and visual economy that creates an effective, quickly recognized symbol for a home.

Even though the main reason for making an illustration is to promote a product or tell a story, the drawing must produce a visual experience for the viewer before it communicates the artist's message. To create this visual experience, the artist must use the principles of design to organize the elements in the drawing. The drawing must have a unified structure. The science fiction illustration in Figure 8.4 accomplishes this with its stippled rendering and overlapping and partly transparent shapes. The man's features suggest emotion.

Visual qualities can also be used effectively to show viewers how subjects really look—but from the point of view of the artist. The drawing done with technical pens in Figure 8.5 imitates reality to the

extent that at first we wonder if it is supposed to portray an actual farm scene from the 1930s. On second look, however, we notice strange things in the drawing. There is a baboon-like creature under the quilting frame with the little boy. Also we see the antique pistol and the floating transparent planes—to say nothing of the pterodactyls outside the window. Could this drawing also illustrate a science fiction story or a fantasy?

Actually, Figure 8.5 isn't an illustration. It is simply a fantastic drawing. Even so, it shows both the real and imagined people and objects in a realistic way. The drawing's imitational qualities—the real people and their everyday activity—are important because they give the fantastic images more impact. How has the artist used proportion, perspective, and shadows to enhance the drawing's imitational qualities?

The drawing's success as a work of art, though, is due to the visual qualities of its structure. It is based on a one-point perspective with a vanishing point at the center of vision on a horizon that is somewhere outside the lower windowpane. Around this central vanishing point are distributed two groups of large figures. They share the darkness of the room and are connected by the quilting frame. The figures in each group overlap each other, unifying the groups into single shapes. These shapes, in turn, frame the window above and the boy and the fantasy creature below. Note also how the artist has used light and dark values and different textures in the composition.

All of the directions established by the axis (vertical dividing line) of each figure, the window, the chair backs, and the legs of the quilting frame are in line with each other and with the vertical sides of the drawing. The quilt, chair rungs, seats, and window crosspieces all align horizontally. The viewer perceives repetition, alignment, and balance in the directions, shapes, lines, and textures. The drawing is unified, even though there is a great variety of figures and objects. The viewer sees the scene from the point of view of a child seated on the floor at the near side of the room. How has the artist used the principle of emphasis to draw attention to him?

As you have seen from these examples, both emotional art and imitational art need structure. For a drawing to convey a complex message or unify a variety of realistic images, the artist must effectively organize its visual qualities, or the viewer will miss what the artist is trying to communicate, and the impact of the work will be lost.

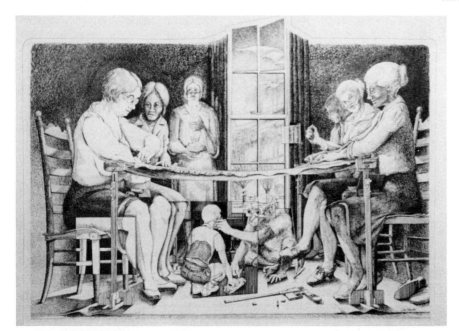

FIGURE 8.5 While the images in this technical pen rendering are imitational, the overall structure is formalized.

STUDIO

Formal Drawing of an Object or Animal

MATERIALS

Pen and ink, drawing paper

For your first formal drawing, make one similar to Figure 8.6. Use a familiar animal with a distinctive outline for your subject. Choose the element you want to emphasize (line, shape, form, value, texture, or space). Then decide which principles of art to use in emphasizing this element (balance, harmony, variety, gradation, movement, rhythm, proportion, or space).

The subject matter will express something to the viewer. The main purpose of the drawing, however, is to create a visual experience using the elements and principles of art. Do a series of thumbnail sketches to help you design your drawing.

Art student Judi Eudy decided to emphasize line in her drawing of a kangaroo in Figure 8.6. Knowing that the kinds of line are limited only by the imagination, she developed cross-contour lines made up of different patterns. These lines gave her drawing variety. Repetition—of the lines themselves, within each line, and of the directions of the lines—creates harmony and makes her drawing unified.

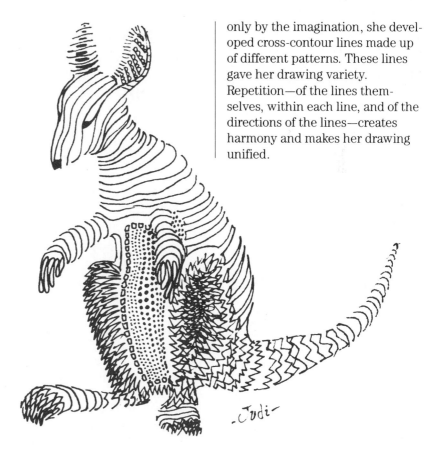

FIGURE 8.6 Student Judi Eudy's kangaroo can be classified as a pen line patterned drawing.

Formal Drawing of a Model

MATERIALS

Graphite or charcoal pencil, layout or tracing paper, drawing media of your choice

In this drawing you will again emphasize a certain element, but this time you will use the element to define the form of a person. Also, you will direct the viewer's attention to places you want to emphasize by using the principle of variety. You can create variety by a sudden change in the size or value of an element. Or you can interrupt the rhythmic repetition of an element by introducing a contrasting element.

Look at Ken Torres's ink line drawing in Figure 8.7. This portrait of a girl is probably a good likeness. But the most striking thing about the portrait is the artist's use of line. Notice how the thin, spidery line draws attention to a carefully controlled point of emphasis at the eyes.

If you choose to emphasize space, you could do this by drawing attention to the planes of the face. Or you could repeat geometric shapes to define features. You could also emphasize line, value, color, or texture. Remember that value and color are a product of light and sometimes shadow.

You will need to do several graphite or charcoal sketches to become familiar with the model's features. Make these sketches larger than thumbnail size. While you are designing your drawing, use overlays of layout or tracing paper. If you decide to emphasize shape, you can use the final overlay as a preliminary drawing and transfer it to the rendering surface.

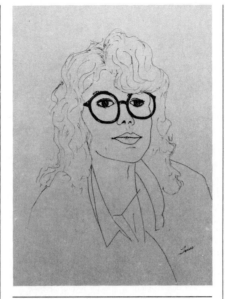

FIGURE 8.7 Note how drawing student Ken Torres made use of dark accents in this fine-line pen portrait.

Using the Wash Medium

MATERIALS

Black watercolor, tempera, acrylic paint, or India ink; #2 and #5 round brushes; shallow dishes or watercolor palette; small sponge; medium-rough watercolor paper or block

In this activity you will become familiar with using wash. Mix two gray washes by adding paint or ink, a little at a time, to water in two bowls or a watercolor palette (a special board for mixing paints). Watercolor is a transparent paint consisting of pigment mixed with water. Test the washes by brushing them onto watercolor paper. Add pigment until the washes dry to the values you want to use.

Now follow these steps:

1. Dampen an area of paper with the sponge, and brush one wash into the damp area as smoothly as possible.

2. Do the same in another area, floating more pigment into one side to create a gradation of value.

3. Dampen another area, and float some of the other wash into it. Dry the brush and use it to pick up pigment from the wet area.

4. Outline an area with a brush, and color it with wash.

5. Draw some simple three-dimensional forms with the small brush, and add wash for shadow.

6. Experiment.

Formal Wash Drawing

MATERIALS

Same as the previous activity

Make a formal wash drawing using placement, repetition, and alignment to emphasize shape. By using several mixtures of the paint or ink and water, you can create several dark-to-light gradations to emphasize value. Use an outdoor scene or a still-life setup for subject matter.

Look at the wash drawing by Holly Stewart in Figure 8.8. It emphasizes all of the formal elements of art and is definitely not imitational. Although it was based on figures and a street scene, viewers notice this subject matter only after they have absorbed the visual impact of the drawing.

This visual impact results from manipulating space, which is represented by shape, line, and pattern. Placement and repetition were used to achieve unity and emphasis. The many variations create interest.

wash
watercolor palette
watercolor

Analyze this drawing by your-self, and then discuss your findings with the class. The following questions will get you started:

■ Why is the ellipse shape of the bottom of the barrel acceptable even though it is thinner than the ellipse at the top of the barrel?

■ What is the big, dominant shape in the drawing? What is it composed of? How does its placement strengthen its dominance?

■ How many parallel alignments can you find? Start with the edges of the picture. Consider the vertical and horizontal axes of individual shapes as well as lines and edges.

■ Where can you find repeated shapes in the drawing?

■ How does the brick pattern contribute to the unity and interest of the composition?

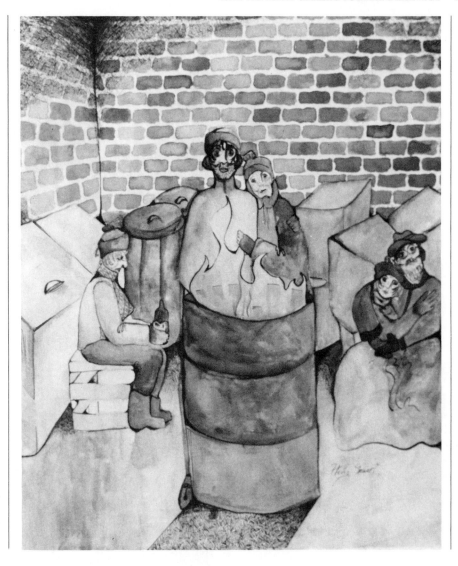

FIGURE 8.8 The people in student Holly Stewart's drawing were rendered with watercolor wash. Note the care-fully structured composition.

SUBJECT MATTER IN FORMAL DRAWINGS

It is difficult to find a purely formal drawing. By definition, a formal drawing could have no literal qualities or subject matter. Most people call that type of drawing *abstract* or *nonobjective* art.

Purely formal art should also have no expressive qualities. Finding a drawing without expressive qualities is almost impossible. It could be argued that even the coldness caused by eliminating any feelings is in itself the expression of an attitude.

The graphite drawing in Figure 8.9 by Grey Rigney is probably about as purely formal as any we could ever find. Rigney's drawing is a product of careful planning and many sketchbook drawings.

Even though this work of art is almost totally abstract, its formal elements were originally derived from nature and from shapes found in industrial scenes. The artist was very successful in putting together hard-edged shapes and an area of expressive lines in a drawing that actually becomes three-dimensional. This work of art is a combination of illusion and real three-dimensional form. Many fine artists are working with the mixing of illusory space and real space as well as mixing various media in the same piece of art.

A piece of fine art that would be considered simply imitational by many people is the drawing by Marvin Moon in Figure 8.10. This is a sketch for a watercolor that was made to record facts. But it was

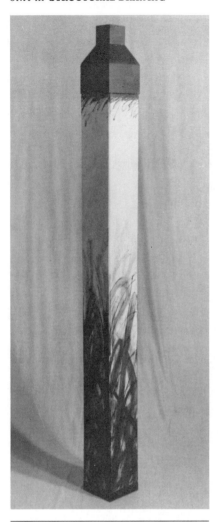

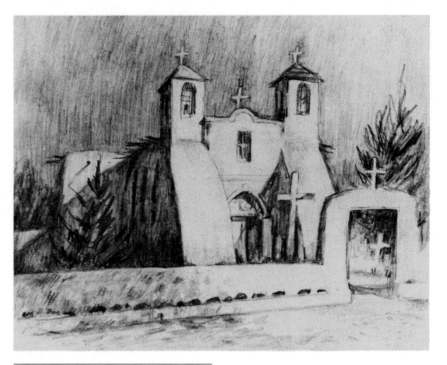

FIGURE 8.10 This graphite sketch for a watercolor of the old St. Francis Church at Ranchos de Taos, New Mexico, was done on the back of a piece of scrap paper. The artist, Marvin Moon, took advantage of the formal qualities already present in the church's structure.
Courtesy of the artist.

FIGURE 8.9 Sometimes drawings become part of three-dimensional works. Grey Rigney has made a strong statement in graphite on a 7′ column of wood and canvas.
Courtesy of the artist.

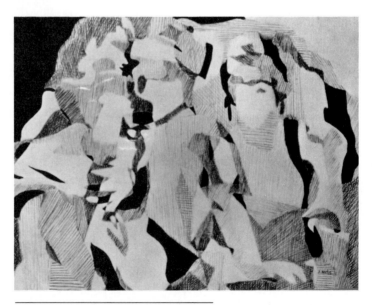

FIGURE 8.11 This student drawing was developed by overlapping three blind contour drawings and controlling values by hatching and cross-hatching. Note the careful placement of black shapes.

also created as a compositional study to preserve strong formal qualities in the finished work. Some of these qualities are the massive shapes and their repetition with variation. The shapes are related to the darkening sky by gradation through the values of the shadows and the dark trees.

Figure 8.11 is another drawing that is almost completely formal because of the way it was made. The approach to this drawing was to make several blind contour drawings from a model (recording contours without looking at the drawing). Then the artist developed shapes by overlapping the contour drawings as if they were transparent. Values were shown by hatching, cross-hatching, and filling in the black areas. The original subject matter—the model—almost disappeared from the drawing.

Composite Drawing of Shapes Using Hatching

MATERIALS

Soft charcoal pencil; ruler (optional); tracing paper, tracing vellum, or layout paper; pen and ink, or dry drawing medium of your choice; drawing paper

For this almost purely formal drawing, you will draw a collection of shapes. Start by doing at least three blind contour drawings on tracing paper, vellum, or layout paper. Use a soft charcoal pencil that makes a strong line.

Now lay the contour drawings on top of each other so that they overlap, creating many new shapes. Adjust the overlapping until you create shapes that form alignments to hold the composition together.

When you have a unified composition that includes some size changes for variety, lay another sheet of tracing paper on top of the first three to make a composite tracing of the shapes in all of them. If the tracing makes the subject matter of your original drawings disappear, don't worry about it.

At this point, you can decide whether you want to finish the drawing in a dry medium or in ink. If you use a dry medium, keep working on the same paper. If you want to work in ink, transfer the drawing to bristol board or a lightweight or medium-weight illustration board.

For the sake of simplicity, and also to provide some interesting patterned areas, use two values of gray plus black and white. Make the values of gray by using lines.

Look again at Figure 8.11. Besides the areas of black and white, the areas of lighter gray in the drawing were made by a pattern of lines going in the same direction. This is called *hatching*. *Cross-hatching* is overlaying these lines with a second pattern of lines going in the other direction. Cross-hatching produced the darker grays.

Of course, you can control the values in your drawing by how thick and how close together you make the lines. You can also relate the direction of the lines to the axis of any shape in the composition so you can enhance the unity of your drawing.

Before you start your pattern of hatching, practice to find out how to space the marks. If you want the drawing to be even more formal and less expressive, you can draw your lines with a ruler.

Perhaps you would like to eliminate outlines altogether and let the values define the shapes. To do this, make the preliminary drawing in light graphite pencil, do the hatching in ink, and then erase the pencil lines.

Decide whether your drawing will be a **bleed** or a **vignette**. In a bleed the shapes in the drawing reach the edges of the working area. You might find it easier to create unity with a bleed because the straight, rectangular edges of the working area become part of the drawing.

In a vignette, the shapes often fade gradually into the empty working area around the edges of the drawing. Other times they end abruptly, floating in their sea of negative space, never actually contacting the edge of the drawing. This negative space can be used to emphasize the overall image of your drawing.

Harmony and Variety

Whatever media you use, you have created a fairly complex design. It should be unified, however, by the careful placement of the horizontals and verticals in the rectangular working area or by the related directions in which you have placed the different shapes.

You need not worry too much about variety at this point. Attaining an interesting amount of variation is rarely a problem. Achieving harmony is much more difficult.

Comparing the drawing process to making a stew might help you understand this delicate relationship between variety and harmony. In cooking the stew, you want all the ingredients to blend together (be unified) into a good stew. Then you sprinkle in just enough spices (variety) to give the stew an interesting—but not *too* interesting—taste.

As an artist you want to do the same thing with your drawings. You want to devote most of your attention to the overall unity. Overall unity is achieved by adding just the right blend of harmony and variety.

Formal Drawing Using Shadow

MATERIALS

Graphite pencil, charcoal pencil, pen and ink, or watercolor; drawing paper

Select an object, put strong light on it, and make a formal drawing based on the object and its shadows. If you can't find a light-colored, clean wall, put up a paper backdrop first. Also experiment with two light sources.

The drawing in Figure 8.12 is a visual idea that was created by taping a vine to the studio wall and flooding it from the side with artificial light. The dark but soft shadows are as important to the overall image as the object casting them. The cast shadows in this case are soft because the light, which is almost as large as the vine, is also close to the vine. The closeness of the light gives the effect of two light sources, or of somewhat diffused (spread out) light.

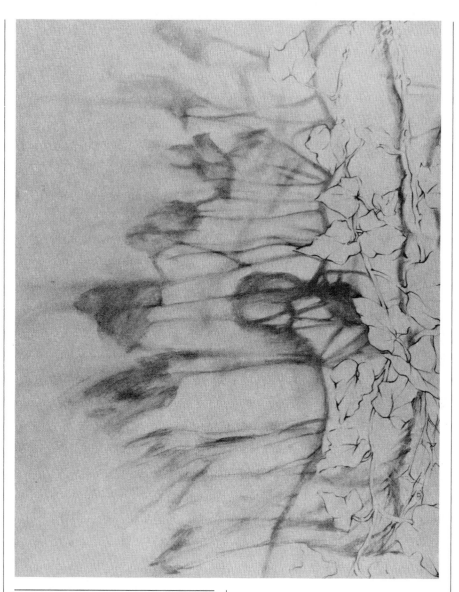

FIGURE 8.12 Control of light and shadow gave this drawing by student Annette Berlin its strong formal character.

The combination of defined shapes and soft cast shadows on the same surface melts into an interesting gestalt pattern. This image is more important than the vine itself. The pattern is what gives the drawing its effective visual qualities. The fact that we can recognize the vine adds imitationalism to the formalism.

Another example of a formal drawing with some literal qualities is Figure 17 in the Color Section. In this drawing by Shelley Settle, you can easily identify some of the real-life sources for the images you see in the drawing. But she has made several structural changes to create a stronger formal statement. (This drawing is also highly emotional. Compare it with Cherie Miner's work in Figure 10.5).

For your drawing, emphasize formal qualities, and minimize imitational qualities.

Formal Drawing of Fragmented Objects

MATERIALS

Drawing media of your choice

The drawing you see in Figure 8.13 is a powerful formal drawing that came about as the result of a powerful expressive act on the part of a teacher.

Picture this, if you will: Students are sitting in a circle around a setup of pottery that they assume they are going to draw. The teacher enters, walks over to the setup, and says, "This is today's still-life setup, but before you start drawing, let me change it a little bit." Then the teacher pulls out a hammer from under his coat and smashes all of the pottery! "*Now* draw it," he says.

Then he explains that the pieces are all individual shapes and forms that the students will have to observe carefully. The selective eye of each artist and the area of shattered pottery chosen by that artist will help determine the formal and expressive qualities of the drawing.

Now do your own formal drawing of something that has been fragmented. You can control the design by choosing the part of the setup you want to draw, enlarging objects for emphasis, and repeating patterns to create unity.

FIGURE 8.13 This student drawing of a broken object is a product of careful composition derived from a seemingly unorganized source.

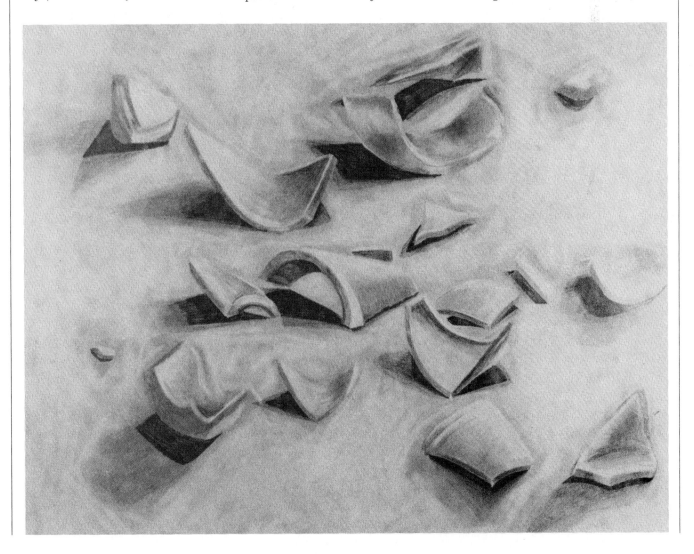

FINDING VISUAL IDEAS FROM RUBBINGS

You may have noticed from the last few activities that formal drawings often have their roots in real objects. Starting your sketch with a real object in front of you can stimulate your thinking and help you arrive at a *visual* idea. Of course, the identity of the original subject often becomes difficult to recognize as the visual statement takes shape. This is fine since the visual qualities, not the imitational qualities, determine the success or failure of a formal drawing.

In addition to sketching an object, another way to find a visual idea is to take a **rubbing** from the surface of a natural or man-made object and to use part of the rubbing in a design. A rubbing (also called a **frottage**) is the image caused by putting a piece of fairly smooth, flexible paper over an object with a raised image or textured surface and rubbing pencil lead or graphite stick over it. You can see examples of rubbings in Figure 8.14.

Selecting a small area of a picture to use as an independent design is called **cropping**. An easy way to visualize this area is to separate it and determine its proportions with a pair of cropping Ls. Again look at Figure 8.14. The two L-shaped pieces of white cardboard lying on the rubbing in the lower right corner are cropping Ls. As you can see, these Ls could be moved to isolate a square or rectangle of any size in the rubbing. After this, the area could be marked with a ruler, cut out, and mounted in a sketchbook.

FIGURE 8.14 Rubbings from wood and stone. The one in the lower right is being condensed to a strong formal structure by the use of cropping Ls.

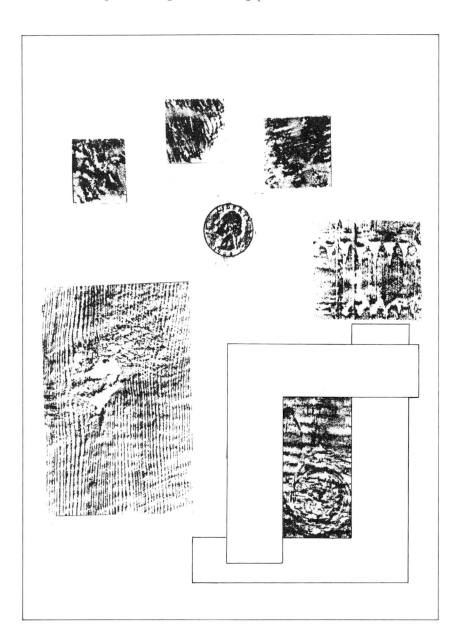

cropping Ls

Rubbings

MATERIALS

Black or dark blue pencil, drawing paper, cropping Ls

Make from ten to twelve rubbings. Then crop interesting designs from them and mount the designs in your sketchbook.

Rub with the side of the pencil, not the tip. Use moderate pressure, and keep the strokes going in the same direction. Don't choose paper that is too thick or stiff. Also, remember that you will have to keep the paper and the object stationary. The design you crop from the rubbing should use effective placement and alignment of shapes, repetition of elements, balance, and variety.

Enlargement of a Rubbing

MATERIALS

Graphite pencil, drawing paper, drawing media of your choice

Choose the rubbing from your sketchbook that you like best. Enlarge it four times its actual size for a finished drawing.

For a fairly accurate representation on a larger scale, draw a grid of $3/16''$ (5 mm) squares on the small rubbing with a sharp pencil. Then, on the sheet for the finished rendering, duplicate this grid exactly using $3/4''$ (20 mm) squares. This grid will be four times as large as the small grid and have exactly the same proportions.

Now copy the lines, values, and shapes from each of the small squares into the corresponding square on the large grid. Use any medium, but try to reproduce the range of values and the gradations that are found in the small squares.

Put the drawing in a hinged mat. Even though the drawing is small, make the sides of the mat at least $2\frac{1}{2}''$ (6 cm) wide.

Drawing into a Rubbing

MATERIALS

Black or dark blue pencil, drawing paper, drawing media of your choice

Make a rubbing of an area of texture large enough for a finished drawing, at least $12 \times 18''$ (30.5 × 46 cm). Tape your paper to the surface on one edge only, since the paper will probably stretch a little in the rubbing process.

Then, instead of cropping to make a good design, draw into the rubbing. Emphasize some shapes and values. You might need to combine some shapes to unify the composition or restructure others for better alignment. Try to draw so that there is no difference between the original rubbing and the added drawing.

FINDING VISUAL IDEAS THROUGH SELECTIVE VISION

Since a camera records only the things at which it is pointed, photographers need good judgment about where to point the camera. There are many technical things that photographers can do to improve their pictures, but the people who practice photography as an art form know what, when, and how to shoot. They use selective vision to find visual qualities—the elements and principles of art—in their subjects.

As you make drawings that are effectively structured and have exciting visual qualities, you can also use selective vision. You can find an interesting scene and emphasize its formal qualities. Or you can make a carefully organized setup and find a formal design within it to draw.

Annette Berlin's colored pencil drawing from a still-life setup in Figure 18 in the Color Section is a good example of the selective vision approach. Not only was her judgment in cropping the drawing important, but also the structure of the setup itself was carefully thought out to emphasize the elements and principles of art. Of course, the unusual combination of a satin dress and a catcher's mask adds considerable interest to the composition, but that choice affects imitational qualities more than visual qualities.

Formal Drawing of a Setup

MATERIALS

Drawing media of your choice

Draw your own setup using visual qualities to create a unified but interesting design. Use one big shape to occupy most of the space in the setup. Having an anchor shape for the composition promotes unity. The smaller shapes can also add to the unity if you align them using harmony to reflect the axis of the large shape and the other smaller shapes.

Repeating some other qualities will also help make the design unified. Most of the objects should be rendered in somewhat analogous colors, but also use a few objects in complementary or near complementary colors for accents.

Decide whether to surround your composition with negative space, creating a vignette, or to crop in closely, as Berlin did in Figure 18 in the Color Section. For the vignette, apply some color and gradation in the negative area to keep that space related to the whole composition. For cropping, try a few thumbnail sketches first, and use cardboard cropping Ls to decide on your design.

Even though you will emphasize the visual qualities in the setup, remember that the objects you choose to put in the setup that look real will contribute to the character of your drawing and people's psychological response to it. The selection, arrangement, and color of the objects and the cropping of your composition all depend on your selective vision.

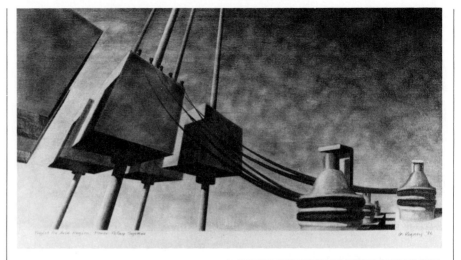

Formal Drawing from an Industrial Scene

MATERIALS

Drawing media of your choice

Use selective vision to create a composition based on an industrial scene. Isolate some part of the scene that interests you. For example, you could use a cable connector floating in space and glinting in the sun, supported only by taut wires. You could choose the joining point of two huge concrete walls with a small drain hole in the bricks between them. Or you could select a section of the inner workings of some machine, isolated from their setting and rendered in detail.

If you are a good photographer, you might do some of your research with a camera. Remember, though, that a camera has its limitations. Shoot to find a design in the scene, using the viewfinder as a frame like the cropping Ls. To record details, use a sketchbook.

Grey Rigney found graphite a good rendering medium for a drawing (Figure 8.15) similar to the one

FIGURE 8.15 This Grey Rigney graphite drawing is an effective structural composition using subject matter that seems real. It is actually a distortion of reality.
Courtesy of the artist.

you will make. Remember, though, that graphite can be rather cold and inflexible for those who aren't expert in its use. It will be easier to render in graphite if you use both soft and hard pencils. Shade dark areas with a soft pencil instead of using more pressure on a hard pencil. The less graphite you have to add to an area, the less likely you are to create a greasy-looking graphite shine on the surface.

SAFETY NOTE

Safety in Industrial Areas

Before you go wandering around an industrial area with your camera and sketchbook, be sure to get permission from someone in authority. Most of these areas have rules for the protection of visitors, such as staying out of dangerous sections and wearing protective goggles or hard hats.

Color Drawing Using Aberrant Scale

MATERIALS

Colored pencils, drawing paper

Another type of selective vision that can be used to create a formal drawing is **aberrant** or abnormal **scale**. To use aberrant scale, you could enlarge something that is normally quite small to become a major element of form in the drawing. Or you could draw something that is normally gigantic to look tiny. Using aberrant scale manipulates the element of shape to create emphasis.

The drawing done by student Nicole Brints (Color Section, Figure 19) uses aberrant scale in enlarging objects. The drawing features a fragment of a basket and a piece of barbed wire that have been enlarged several times. These items have become impressive subjects in a formal drawing.

In your drawing, use abberant scale to enlarge some objects that are even smaller than the ones in Brints's drawing. Use a magnifying glass if necessary to see details of the objects. For example, you could draw carefully placed rows of closed safety pins with a few jacks or marbles and one open safety pin where you want some emphasis. Remember that the formal statement made by the size emphasis must be supported by other principles of design.

USING MEDIA TO ADD VISUAL QUALITIES

Using certain media or tools can themselves produce strong visual qualities in drawings, in addition to those qualities designed by the artist. We can find examples of how media can affect visual qualities in both fine art and illustration.

Scratchboard

The medium chosen by the artist added visual qualities to the drawing in Figure 8.16. Roger Beikmann's drawing is done on a surface called *scratchboard*. Scratchboard is illustration board or bristol board that has been coated with a chalk-like substance. It can be drawn on with ink. Heavy, dark areas are usually filled in with a brush. Since the chalky surface can be easily scratched, white lines can be brought out by scratching into the dark areas with a stylus (a metal pen-shaped instrument), a #11 Exacto knife, or other special tools. Scratchboard is relatively expensive, but it provides an interesting drawing experience. Many illustrators who make black and white line drawings for newspapers and magazines prefer scratchboard.

Beikmann's drawing has formal qualities similar to many wood **engravings**. An engraving is an artwork in which an image is cut into a surface. The formal qualities result from what is often called *value reversal* or *white-on-black* rendering.

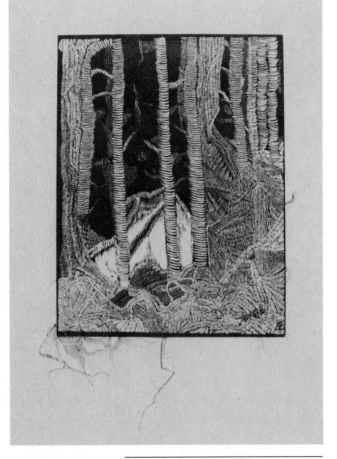

FIGURE 8.16 Scratchboard is a medium usually associated with illustration, but student Roger Beikmann used it for an almost abstract drawing.

scratchboard
stylus

Sensitized Shading Sheets

Another black and white illustration and cartooning medium is sensitized shading sheets like Grafix Duoshade. (See the student drawing in Figure 8.17.) Applying chemical developers to the surface of this paper creates instant hatching and cross-hatching. As you have already discovered, hatching and cross-hatching can add the visual element of a texture to shaded areas.

After the lines are drawn, one developer is brushed on the areas of light gray value to raise the hatching stripes to the surface. In the darker areas, another developer is applied that creates a cross-hatched pattern.

For professional examples of the use of shading sheets, see Figures 12.8 and 12.11 in the chapter on cartooning.

Media That Enhance Visual Qualities

Figures 13 and 20 in the Color Section are two different formal works by the same versatile artist, Paul Hanna. All of his works have effective structure, but in these two the media he chose enhanced the formal qualities.

Acccording to most people, Figure 13 is a glass engraving and Figure 20 is a painting. The first artwork is an image made up of lines that were cut into the surface of a glass bowl. The marks on the second were made with paint. We could, however, refer to both artworks as drawings. The engraving tool was used like a drawing instrument, and the painting consists only of lines.

No matter what we call them, both of these works of art have powerful visual qualities related to the media used to make them. A glass engraving is transparent and reflects light. These qualities cause the piece to take on some of the character of its surroundings. Shapes and colors from the surroundings can be seen through the bowl or are reflected from its surface. These shapes and colors, in turn, blend with the engraved image to produce a complex kind of art object.

Paul Hanna also gave his painting formal qualities through the medium he used. It has no imitational qualities. Instead, the painting is a statement made up of the elements of shape, form, space, color, texture, and value. All of these elements are created by applying the principles of design to the element of line.

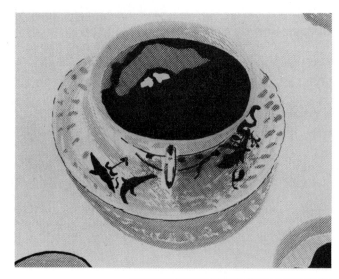

FIGURE 8.17 This rendering of a cup was done by drawing student Cylinda Baker. She used a shading medium called DuoShade. The cross-hatching is developed by painting a clear developer on sensitized paper.

This painting was done on a circular stretched canvas that is large enough to absorb the viewer's visual attention. It uses formal qualities to create spatial illusions with complex color and value overlapping. In other words, it seems to be an absolutely pure *formal* statement. Its compelling use of formal qualities creates a powerful visual experience.

But then, after looking more closely, we find ourselves caught up visually in an agitated mass of energetic lines going in hundreds of directions. Suddenly, we become aware that the piece is also totally *expressive* in quality. It communicates an idea about the action of making art.

ENRICHMENT

Paul Hanna

Traditionally, the Paul Hanna painting would be called a *tondo*. This term was often used to describe a painting that was round instead of the more usual rectangle. Today it would probably be called a round painting.

It is interesting to note that Paul Hanna, in addition to being expert at drawing, painting, and glass engraving, is a nationally published cartoonist. Some of his cartoons appear in Chapter 12.

Formal Drawing on Sensitized Shading Sheets

MATERIALS

Graphite pencil, drawing paper, Grafix Duoshade, brush, chemical developers

Choose as a subject a group of simple objects that can be reduced to white, black, and two gray values. Make a clear pencil drawing of it, and transfer the drawing to a sheet of Duoshade for rendering. Your drawing should have clear form and cast shadows. Fill in any solid black areas first. Then apply the lighter developer to create the form shadows and the darker developer to make the cast shadows. Follow the instructions that come with the Duoshade.

Nonobjective Linear Drawing

MATERIALS

Dry color drawing medium or acrylic paint and drafter's ruling pen, drawing paper

Use a visual idea to create a formal drawing that expresses the action of the drawing process. For example, you could draw a square that has a complex pattern of crisscross lines. You could use gradation from cool to warm colors and make a transition from the square outer shape of the drawing to a circular form on the inside of the square, still using crisscross lines.

If you use a dry medium, be sure to keep your drawing instrument sharp. Acrylic paint should be thinned before you use it in a drafter's ruling pen, which makes consistent lines.

The working area of your drawing should bleed off the edge on all sides of the paper. You will want to wrap the finished drawing in acetate without matting it.

Consistent Line

Paul Hanna achieved an absolutely consistent line in acrylic paint by using an automobile painter's pin-striping pen. This device distributes an even flow of paint onto a metal roller. The width of the roller determines the width of the decorative striping on the car or, in this case, the width of a line drawn on a canvas by an inventive painter.

Silverpoint

Another medium that affects some of the formal elements of design is called *silverpoint*. The lines of a silverpoint drawing are made with a pencil that has a silver point. Silverpoint was a popular medium at the turn of the century, but it isn't used much now since graphite pencils are easy to obtain.

Silverpoint can be used to mark on certain surfaces only. The only surfaces that strip tiny particles from a pencil point of silver are those with a clay or clay-like coating. The two surfaces usually used for silverpoint drawing are a cream-colored, clay-coated paper called *cameo paper* or some stiffer surface (like a wood panel or illustration board) that has been coated with gesso. Gesso is a white, plaster-like surface used for drawing or painting.

You can see a silverpoint drawing done on a gessoed surface in Figure 8.18 on the next page. The value changes in the drawing are subtle. Silverpoint produces a value range of only about 50 percent gray to white. This limitation requires the artist to be disciplined and precise. As a result, silverpoint drawings often are characterized by subtle gradations and delicacy.

Another formal quality affected by using silverpoint as a medium is line. Since the silver wire tends to stay fairly sharp, the artist is limited in the kinds of line used in silverpoint drawings.

Color is another element affected by using silverpoint in a drawing. After exposure to air, silver tarnishes, or takes on a patina, somewhat like some metal sculpture. This means that its surface turns brown from oxidation. If you could see the drawing in Figure 8.18 in color, you would see that the entire surface has changed from gray to a kind of rich sepia (grayish brown). That is, the formal element of color has changed because of the medium used.

silverpoint
cameo paper
gesso

drafter's ruling pen

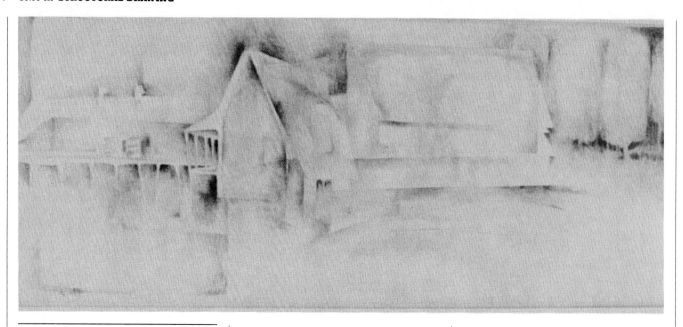

FIGURE 8.18 The value range of silverpoint is somewhat limited. It has an interesting delicacy, however, and it takes on a patina as the silver tarnishes.

Silverpoint Drawing

MATERIALS

Graphite pencil, drawing paper, acrylic gesso, soft brush, heavy illustration board, fine sandpaper, drafter's mechanical pencil (lead holder), silver wire

Create a formal drawing using silverpoint. Make a preliminary pencil drawing of a still-life setup.

Put several light coats of gesso on a sheet of illustration board about 20 × 15″ (51 × 38 cm). Thin the gesso with water before you apply it. Use a brush about 2″ (5 cm) wide. Sand the board thoroughly between coats with fine sandpaper. Gesso dries rapidly, so wash your brush between coats.

After you have prepared the illustration board, transfer your preliminary drawing to it, and render the design in silverpoint. You can get silver wire from a jeweler. You will need about 2″ (5 cm) of wire, about 1 mm thick. Remove the sharp point on your piece of wire with fine emery paper or a nail file, and insert the wire into a drafter's mechanical pencil (or lead holder).

Leave a border of about 2″ (5 cm) around the drawing for a mat, and use a 16 × 11″ (41 × 28 cm) working area.

drafter's mechanical pencil (lead holder)

Fine Artist: Drawing Income with Graphite

All the rewards of making a living from fine art aren't financial. Tom Woodward is able to support himself by selling his finely detailed graphite drawings, but he finds that creating art is a rewarding career.

Woodward always had an interest in art and found outlets for his talents even though his high school offered no art classes. He drew illustrations for his high school annual. After graduation from high school, he attended Auburn University for a year and a half, majoring in commercial art.

Woodward worked for several years as a freelance commercial artist while creating drawings in his spare time. Around his hometown he sold small works such as notecards with his original drawings, drawings of local homes, some caricatures, and watercolors. Then he started showing his larger works at area art shows.

Woodward began to specialize in drawings using graphite pencil, a medium chosen by relatively few artists. He became interested in drawing fabrics and creating different patterns with a variety of textures and later added figures to his drawings.

Woodward took commission work for several years—that is, he made drawings only on special order—until the sale of his drawings provided his primary income. Then he could draw whatever he wanted and sell the works of art. He has been able to achieve the independence that results from being a self-employed artist by gaining contacts from the outdoor fairs and festivals where he first showed his work. Woodward now attends six to eight shows yearly. Choosing the larger and more famous shows, he travels from Texas to south Florida and also sells drawings through art galleries and museums.

Working in a studio in his home in Alabama, Woodward, who is disabled, averages four to six hours a day at the drawing board. A typical drawing may take from one to three weeks to complete. He has no set routine, but a general approach begins with a vague idea for a drawing. Using a model and fabric (for example, a wrinkled sheet), Woodward takes photographs, and may use from three to twelve rolls of film. He poses the model in different positions and varies the lighting.

Woodward uses these photographs to help him focus his original idea. Something in one of the photographs may capture his attention and lead to a drawing. At other times, he may combine details from several pictures for the subject for his work. After he determines the composition he wants, Woodward sketches the basic shapes and their arrangement on either a sheet of high-quality drawing paper or the reverse side of a sheet of four-ply bristol board. This step usually takes no more than thirty minutes. He uses a mechanical pencil with a moderately soft lead.

The next step consists of scribbling in the sketch with cross-hatching strokes. Woodward determines the location of the dark and light areas during this stage. Next, he builds up layers of graphite on the areas. After three or four layers, the loose lines of the cross-hatching disappear, and the drawing begins to look textured. This is a detailed process because the darker areas require twelve to twenty-four layers of graphite.

Using this technique, Woodward creates carefully detailed drawings with strong contrast between dark and light forms. One drawing, *Sleeper*, was chosen as a winner in the *American Artist* magazine's 1986 Golden Anniversary National Art Exhibition. Although he admits that his occupation doesn't provide financial security, Tom Woodward has experienced success as his drawings win prizes and gain recognition across the country.

UNIT III

Evaluation and Review

MEETING YOUR OBJECTIVES

By answering the following questions and doing the exercises, you will demonstrate your ability to meet the learning objectives listed at the beginning of Chapters 7 and 8.

Chapter 7

1. How does a formalist judge drawings?
2. Pick one drawing each from Chapters 1, 3, 4, and 6. Use the design chart on page 24 to analyze each drawing. Place a checkmark (✔) in at least three intersections on the chart, indicating a link between an element and a principle. Then explain why you checked those intersections.
3. Find one drawing that you think a formalist would judge *unsuccessful*. Explain why a formalist would consider this drawing unsuccessful.
4. Find one drawing that you think a formalist would judge *successful*. Explain why a formalist would consider this drawing successful.

Chapter 8

1. Describe at least three ways that artists use visual qualities in their drawings.
2. Pick an object or a person you want to draw. Make several realistic sketches of your subject, looking for an element and principle of art you want to emphasize. Make a final drawing emphasizing the chosen element and principle.
3. Do three gesture drawings from a model emphasizing value gradations. Work transparently in any medium so that your drawings are on top of each other. Work on a large drawing pad. Select areas formed by the transparent overlapping for rendering in two values of gray and black. Fill in the selected black areas first. Then render the two gray values by hatching and cross-hatching. Leave some areas white and leave a 2″ margin around the entire drawing.
4. Take rubbings from several different surfaces. The rubbings should be as dark and large as possible. Use a dark charcoal pencil to make an outline contour drawing of a landscape, cityscape, or still-life setup that includes a number of objects. Transfer the outlined shapes to the back sides of different rubbings. Then cut the shapes out of the rubbing sheets and lay them aside in their original arrangement. On a piece of light illustration board repeat the outline contour drawing with black paint or India ink. Make your lines heavy—about an inch wide. You may draw in pencil first. Now box the entire drawing with a rectangle drawn in the same weight line. The outermost edges of your contour drawing should just touch the rectangular box. Finally, tear about ¼″ off the edges of the rubbings you made earlier and glue them over their corresponding shapes on the illustration board.
5. Use selective vision to identify an unusual space or composition in a rural landscape or an urban setting. Make a black and white photograph that dramatizes your selected composition and enlarge the photo to a minimum size of 5 × 7″. Then make a drawing that exaggerates the content in the photo. *Note:* Take several photos and select the photo to be enlarged from a contact sheet.
6. Do an ink drawing in black, white, and two values in between. Use either Duoshade paper and developers or ''stick-on'' contact sheet patterns for the middle values. Choose your media to enhance the visual qualities being emphasized.
7. List the drawing tools and media you used in doing the studio exercises in Chapter 8.
8. List the drawing techniques you learned and used in doing the studio exercises in Chapter 8.

LEARNING DRAWING TERMS

You encountered several new drawing terms in this unit. The most important terms are those printed in heavy, bold type. Write all the terms on a sheet of paper. Then, without looking in your book, tell what each terms means in your own words. If you are not sure of a meaning, use your book to write a definition.

EXPERIENCING DIFFERENT MEDIA

Each new drawing medium is listed at the bottom of the page on which it is first mentioned. Review your experiences with all the media, comparing strengths, weaknesses, and personal preferences. Then write a report summarizing your experiences with these media.

SEEING YOUR ENVIRONMENT

Learning to see the world around you as it really is is one of the first steps in improving your drawing skills. Doing the following exercises will get you in the habit of seeing your environment more closely.

1. Look for manufactured objects in your environment that you believe were well designed. Identify five such objects and use the design chart on page 24 to note the design relationships.
2. Notice as many different textures in your environment as you can in three days. Try to recreate these textures in your sketchbook.
3. Find a scene in a magazine or television advertisement in which asymmetrical balance can be identified as a principle of design. Use harmony and an element of your choice to create a similar scene.

EVALUATING DRAWINGS

1. Evaluate the drawing you did for number 3, Chapter 8, under "Meeting Your Objectives." Rate yourself from 1 to 10 for the following categories: 1) variety in the sizes of shapes, with some dramatic scale changes, 2) gradation or distribution of sizes, 3) unity through alignments and value distribution, 4) distribution of accents (not random pattern), and 5) craft.
2. Use the art criticism steps you learned in Chapter 2 to evaluate the same drawing you critiqued above.
3. Decide which of your drawings most resembles the work of art shown at the right in terms of subject matter, media, or use of the elements and principles. Write two paragraphs discussing the similarities and differences of the two works. Then use the art criticism process to evaluate both works.

EXPANDING YOUR HISTORICAL KNOWLEDGE

Learning about the history will help you improve your drawing skills. It will also increase your understanding of your own culture and the cultures of others, both past and present. Answering the questions below

indicates that you are learning art history. You will be able to answer most of the questions by referring to the Enrichment sections and to Chapter 3. To answer the last question you will probably need to refer to art history books, such as those listed in the Bibliography at the back of the book.

1. In what way was Albrecht Dürer unique among German artists of the 16th century?
2. Who was the first artist to complete a true self-portrait?
3. What German artist who was Durer's contemporary rejected the new style of art in favor of the older, Gothic style?
4. What French artist is often referred to as the "first modern artist"?
5. In one or two sentences describe how Figure 7.7 is representative of the new style of art in the early 20th century.
6. Research the group of artists known as the *Fauves*. Discuss their influences, the major characteristics of their style, and their impact on the art of the 20th century. Also express your personal opinion of their works.

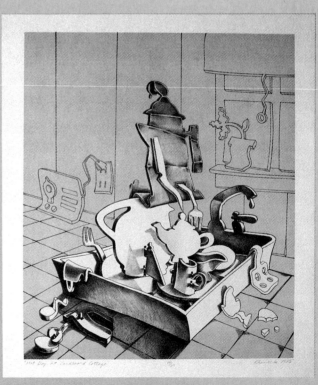

Lynwood Kreneck, *Hot Day at Cardboard Cottage*. Serigraph and air stencil. Courtesy of the artist.

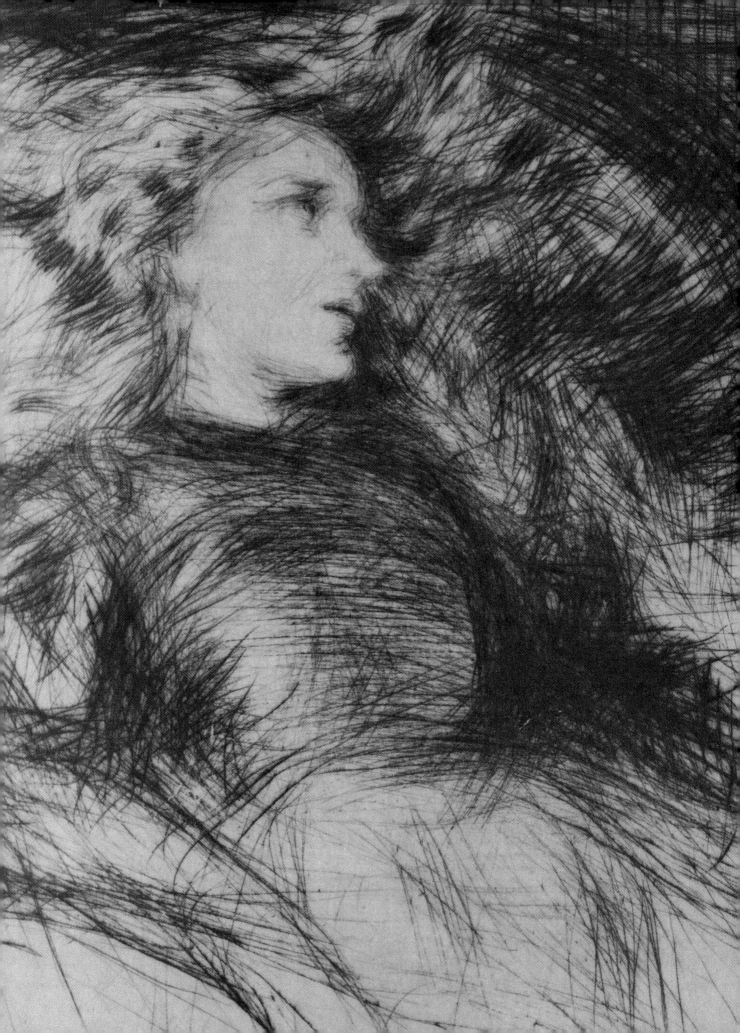

Expressive Drawing

In Unit IV you will focus on a third style of drawing—expressive drawing. In Chapter 9, ''Understanding and Judging Expressive Qualities,'' you will make a final imaginary visit to the art gallery to consider how successfully drawings communicate feelings, moods, and ideas. As an emotionalist critic, you will interpret and judge drawings according to their expressive qualities.

After you have studied expressive qualities in drawings and discovered through art history how other artists have expressed emotion, you will learn techniques for personal expression in Chapter 10, ''Making Emotional Drawings.'' Drawings with expressive qualities are often used to tell stories and to advertise products. By your choice of subject matter, the manner in which you draw it, and the way you organize visual elements, you can communicate a message to viewers in emotional drawings.

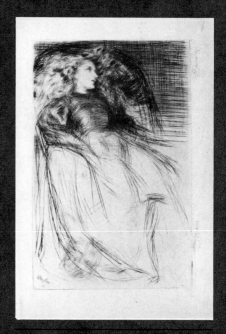

James Abbott McNeill Whistler, *Weary*, 1863. Etching. 7¾ × 5⅛″ (19.7 × 13.2 cm). National Gallery of Art, Washington, DC. Lessing J. Rosenwald Collection (detail at left).

CHAPTER NINE

Understanding and Judging Expressive Qualities

After reading this chapter and doing the activities, you will be able to

■ explain how an emotionalist judges drawings;

■ interpret the feelings, moods, and ideas expressed by artists in drawings; and

■ judge drawings based on their expressive qualities and give reasons for your judgment.

Since you have already played the roles of an imitationalist and a formalist in previous chapters, in this chapter we will ask you to become an emotionalist. When you examine a drawing, you will study its expressive qualities. You will try to decide what feeling, mood, or idea it communicates. As an emotionalist, you will decide that a drawing is unsuccessful if you can't determine what message the artist wanted to convey.

Since you are an emotionalist, you find that works of art with expressive qualities are especially appealing to you. When a friend tells you that a local gallery has scheduled an exhibition that includes emotional drawings, you arrange to attend . . .

Gas

EDWARD HOPPER

The gallery is jammed with people. They are all voicing their opinions about the wide assortment of artworks on display. The room becomes silent when you enter; everyone is eager to see how you will react to the drawings. People edge closer as you pause before a black conte crayon drawing by the American artist Edward Hopper (Figure 5.2 on page 92). They all watch as you study it closely. (Don't read further until you have studied the drawing *Gas* and decided what it means. To do this, you must not only decide what feeling, mood, or idea it communicates, but you must also be prepared to indicate the clues in the drawing that led you to this decision.)

Glancing up from the drawing, you notice that several of the onlookers are waiting for your reactions. What will you mention first? Will you review the clues you found as you tried to discover the meaning of the picture? You point out the narrow, deserted road; the line of dark trees bordering the far side of this road; the three gas pumps manned by a single small figure; and the tidy, compact service station with a sign that, like the tops of the gas pumps, provides no information at all.

You pause for a few moments, allowing your audience to think about these clues. Then you ask if anyone can explain what the work could mean, based on these clues. No one answers. Maybe they are afraid of making the ''wrong'' interpretation.

You explain that there could be several meanings for this drawing. You remind your audience that each one of them is influenced by his or her unique experiences. These experiences may cause them to see and respond differently to the same clues in a drawing. You suggest two meanings for this drawing. The first can be understood easily and may not seem too exciting. The second meaning, however, is less obvious. The viewers will have to think about it carefully.

To introduce your first interpretation, you refer to the tops of the gas pumps, the sign, and the door and window of the tiny service station. All of these objects are illuminated by artificial lights. Light from the door and window can be seen on parts of the concrete drive, too. The dull sky, dark trees, and shadowed roadway suggest the approach of darkness.

It is dusk, and the lonely figure at the gas pumps is going through the boring routine of closing the service station for the night. The air is still. Only the occasional sounds made by the attendant disturb the stillness and remind us that the station isn't entirely deserted. You suggest that the approaching night, the absence of sound, and the single figure create a mood of loneliness.

You make another interpretation of the drawing that suggests a specific reason for the lonely mood. You ask your audience to look again at the road in the picture. Does it look like a busy highway? There are no signs of traffic at the moment. But is there any reason to believe that there ever is much traffic on this road? Is this gas station there only to service the rare car that happens to drive down this remote country road? Why was it built in such an out-of-the-way location?

Maybe conditions have changed since the station was built. Maybe at one time this road was crowded, and business at the little service station was brisk. When automobiles were first manufactured, they could move only at a slow, deliberate pace. Since the passengers had more leisure time than people do today, they were content to enjoy a slow ride in the country. But cars—and people—change. Cars became more powerful, and more people owned them. People became more impatient because they needed to travel from one place to another quickly.

These changes created a need for superhighways, which soon replaced the country roads. Left behind and almost forgotten were the service stations along those country roads. Like the one pictured in Hopper's drawing, they are reminders of a different time and a different way of life.

It is always fascinating to learn how others have interpreted the same work of art. Unfortunately, there is no time for that now. Already someone is asking you to make a judgment about the Hopper drawing. Is it a good work of art? (Before reading further, decide for yourself if it is a successful drawing. Keep in mind, however, that you are an emotionalist. You base your decision on whether or not a drawing uses expressive qualities effectively.)

You might say that Hopper's drawing is an excellent work of art. It communicates an overpowering sense of loneliness. You might also state that it expresses an idea about changes caused by the passing of time and new ways of living. Anyway, you must make a decision. You will also have to defend that decision by pointing to the things you learned while studying the drawing. Already the crowd of people around you is becoming impatient to hear your decision. (You can see Hopper's painting *Gas* in Figure 3 in the Color Section.)

ENRICHMENT

Edward Hopper

Hopper worked for twenty years designing book covers, illustrations, and advertisements for an advertising agency in New York City. He was forty-three years old when a gallery owner agreed to exhibit his watercolors. A few months after his first exhibition, which was highly successful, Hopper resigned from the agency. He spent the rest of his life drawing and painting.

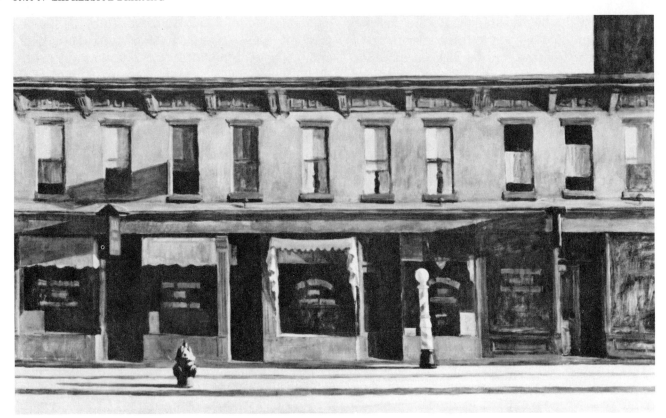

FIGURE 9.1 Edward Hopper, *Early Sunday Morning*, 1930. Oil on canvas, 35 × 60″ (88.9 × 152.4 cm). Whitney Museum of American Art, New York, NY. Photo by Malcolm Varon, NYC.

Edward Hopper can best be described as a portrait painter. His portraits, however, weren't of people; they were of places. Other portrait artists tried to capture the appearance and mood of people. Hopper tried to capture the appearance and mood of places. He especially liked the man-made features that gave the modern landscape its unique character. His plain, carefully composed portraits of the modern city—monotonous, impersonal, and lonely—have rarely been equalled (Figure 9.1).

Edward Hopper started working on his drawing *Gas* in 1940. Modern ways of transportation were rapidly changing America into a nation of commuters. People thought nothing of boarding buses, trains, and planes to travel great distances for business or pleasure.

But the favorite means of transportation was, by far, the automobile. More and more cars crowded onto the highways. Superhighways had to be built to replace the narrow roads that had been adequate in the past. Soon people used highways instead of the narrow country roads. The tiny service stations sprinkled alongside the old roads were doomed. These gas stations would meet the same fate as the hitching posts and watering troughs they had replaced earlier. Hopper observed this change and saw in it the subject for a painting.

The first thing he had to do was find a gas station to paint. He wasn't satisfied, however, with painting just any service station. He was determined to find one that matched the image that had been slowly taking shape in his mind. After a long, fruitless search, he admitted that there was no such gas station.

He then began a series of drawings combining features he had noted in several gas stations. In this way he was able to put his mental image into visual form, first as a drawing and finally as a painting.

Comparing the drawing and painting reveals that the design of the painting differs only slightly from that of the drawing. In the painting, the artificial light from the service station is stronger. The sign has been moved closer to the road. The viewer notices the road as it curves out of sight in the darkness beyond the building. The station in the painting seems to be in danger of being overrun by the high, flame-like, orange grass surrounding it. The trees also seem more threatening, as though they were preparing to march across the deserted highway and surround the defenseless station.

The pose and appearance of the attendant have also changed. In the painting he stands straighter and wears a vest and a tie. Why is he wearing a vest and a tie? Is business at the gas station so slack that it is pointless for the attendant to change into work clothes?

It is impossible to say how many drawings Hopper may have made before completing his final drawing of *Gas*. He often did thirty or more drawings in preparation for a painting. In this case, his patience and determination were rewarded with two memorable works of art. They show a place out of step with its time. The twilight indicates more than the passing of another day. It marks the end of an era—an era symbolized by a gas station on a narrow country road.

Gross Clinic

THOMAS EAKINS

After deciding about the Hopper drawing, you move on to the other works on display. You pass by several before you stop at a large drawing by Thomas Eakins (on page 93). Since you are an emotionalist, the work arouses your interest. You decide to look at it closely. (Don't read further until you have studied the drawing *Gross Clinic* and arrived at an interpretation of it.)

As you try to decide what feeling, mood, or idea the drawing communicates, several important questions arise:

■ What is happening here? What profession is being practiced?

■ Why are the people of this profession wearing street clothes? Are they like modern street clothes?

■ Why has the important gentleman in the center (Figure 9.2) stopped working, even though the event is so serious?

■ This gentleman seems to be speaking. What could he be saying?

■ Who are the people seated in the background? What are they doing?

■ Why is the cowering woman at the left present (Figure 9.3)?

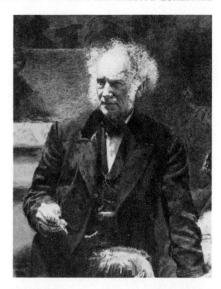

FIGURE 9.2 Thomas Eakins, *Gross Clinic* (detail), 1875. India ink wash on cardboard, 23⅝ x 19⅛" (60 × 48.6 cm). The Metropolitan Museum of Art, New York, NY. Rogers Fund.

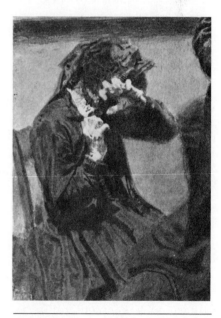

FIGURE 9.3 Thomas Eakins, *Gross Clinic* (detail).

■ At what point in history could this scene have taken place?

Having answered these questions and others like them, you make first an interpretation and then a judgment. What emotions did the artist want to convey? Do you think this drawing is a successful work of art? What are the reasons for your decision?

Self-Portrait at Age Twenty-Two
ALBRECHT DÜRER

As you walk around the gallery, you are fascinated by what you can learn from drawings by studying their expressive qualities. Of course, expression isn't the main goal of every artwork. A drawing by the German artist Albrecht Dürer (on page 143) is an excellent example of this fact. This drawing is interesting because of the artist's skill in making a lifelike self-portrait, but it fails to communicate a mood, feeling, or idea. For this reason, as an emotionalist you give it little more than a quick glance as you walk by.

Head of a Girl with Braids
HENRI MATISSE

The loud whispering of excited voices attracts your attention. Looking about, you see people engaged in a lively debate in front of an ink drawing by the French artist Henri Matisse (on page 145). Joining them, you are told that two earlier gallery visitors had expressed completely different opinions about this drawing.

This news doesn't surprise you since you played the part of the two gallery visitors in previous chapters. In Chapter 5 you were an imitationalist, and in Chapter 7 you were a formalist.

Suddenly you become aware that the people have stopped arguing. Everyone is looking at you. Apparently they are waiting to hear what you have to say about the Matisse drawing. You ask how the earlier visitors reacted to it. The first one said it was unsuccessful because it wasn't a lifelike portrait. The second critic, however, decided the drawing was successful because of its sensitive use of the elements of art, especially line.

As an emotionalist, do you agree with either of these two opinions? No, instead you judge the drawing from a completely different point of view. You ignore both the literal qualities and the visual qualities. Instead, you focus on the expressive qualities in the Matisse drawing.

You see that the simply rendered face of the young girl in the picture shows only a trace of emotion. Her wide-open, dark eyes don't appear to be focused. Although her eyes are directed downward to her left, she doesn't seem to be looking at anything. Perhaps she is lost in her own thoughts or daydreams. If so, are her thoughts pleasant or unpleasant? It is difficult to say for certain. Unfortunately, the slightly curved line of the mouth doesn't give any more clues about her thoughts or feelings. Her mouth isn't completely relaxed, but we can't tell whether the girl has just finished speaking or is about to speak.

Using the expressive qualities to judge, you decide that this drawing is at least partly successful. It does communicate a mood or feeling, but it is hard for viewers to tell exactly what that mood or feeling is. The few clues suggest a quiet moment of thought. Something has triggered the young girl's imagination to drift away from the here and now to a fascinating inner world.

Old Man Figuring
PAUL KLEE

A drawing that is almost as simple in design as the Matisse drawing is on display nearby, and you walk over to it. This work by Paul Klee (Figure 9.4) should be easy to interpret. Like the Matisse work, it is an outline drawing, although it is overlaid with thin, irregularly spaced, horizontal lines. These lines form a screen between the viewer and the portrait of an

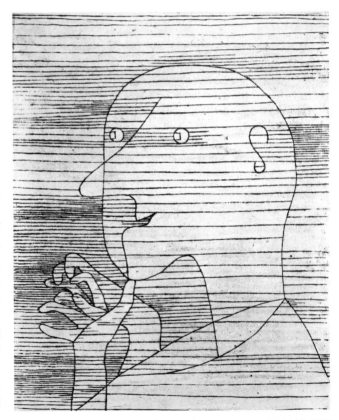

FIGURE 9.4 Paul Klee, *Old Man Figuring*, 1929. Etching, printed in brown-black, plate: 11¾ × 9⅜″ (29.8 × 23.8 cm). Collection, The Museum of Modern Art, New York, NY.

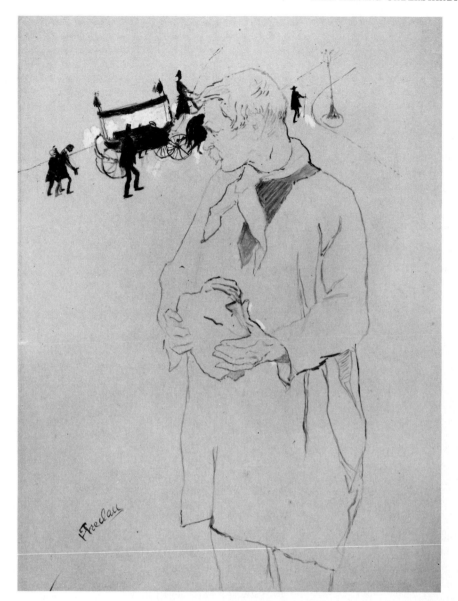

FIGURE 9.5 Henri de Toulouse-Lautrec, *The Last Respects*, 1887. Ink and gouache, 25¾ × 19⅜″ (65.4 × 49.2 cm). The Dallas Museum of Art, Dallas, TX. The Wendy and Emery Reves Collection.

old man. The man scratches his chin. His face expresses wide-eyed surprise. What causes that expression? And what is the reason for the veil of horizontal lines?

Klee may have been trying to answer these questions when he titled his drawing *Old Man Figuring*. The gleeful expression on the man's face suggests that he has finally solved a problem or riddle. He smiles and his eyes open wide as he discovers the answer. He is separated from the viewer by a veil of ignorance, shown by the horizontal lines. He has figured out the problem, although the viewer is still puzzled by it. No one asks your opinion, but if someone did, you would say that the drawing was both clever and amusing. It communicates humor in a sophisticated way.

The Last Respects

HENRI DE TOULOUSE-LAUTREC

Before leaving the gallery, you look at another work in detail. It is a large drawing by Henri de Toulouse-Lautrec entitled *The Last Respects* (Figure 9.5). You are attracted to it because it expresses a touching message in a quiet, respectful way. The bowed and bared head of a workman looking over his shoulder at a funeral procession shows his sense of loss. The artist successfully avoided overdramatizing this scene by adding unnecessary details. The picture's restraint adds dignity to a simple scene of one human being offering a silent farewell to another. What could the workman be thinking? As an emo-

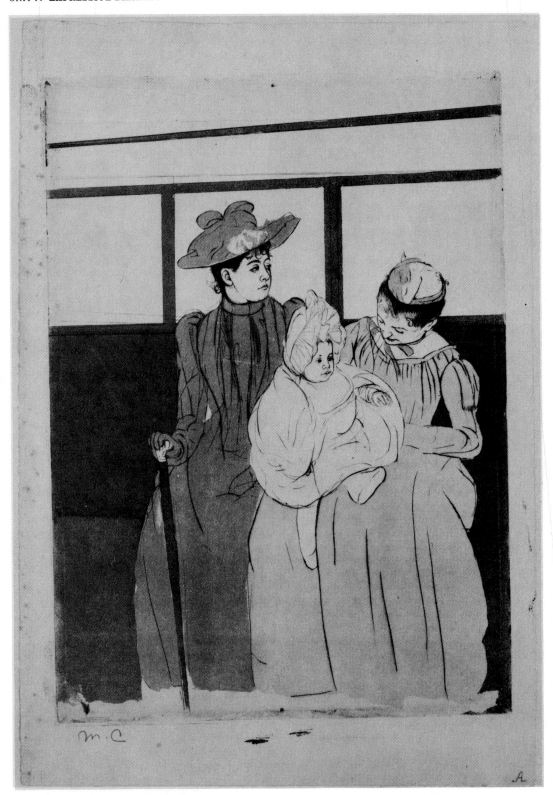

FIGURE 9.6 Mary Cassatt, *In the Omnibus*,
c. 1891. Soft-ground etching, drypoint and
aquatint, printed in blue, brown, tan, light
orange, yellow-green, red, and black, 14⅜
× 10⅜″ (36.5 × 26.4 cm). National Gallery
of Art, Washington, DC. Lessing J. Rosenwald Collection.

tionalist, what judgment would you make about this drawing?

You find another work in the gallery inviting because of its exciting use of expressive qualities (Figure 9.6). Study this drawing, and then make an interpretation (or interpretations) of it. Complete your study of the drawing by making a personal judgment about it. Remember that you are an emotionalist who relies on expressive qualities. (Don't read further until you have interpreted and judged the drawing in Figure 9.6.)

The emotional drawings you have seen in the gallery make you eager to create your own. Glancing at a clock on the gallery wall, you see that there is enough time to return to your studio to work. Of course your drawings will emphasize expressive qualities.

DRAWING AT WORK

Art Director: Meeting Deadlines with Style

Producing a magazine like *Chicago* every month takes the combined talents of many people. As art director, Cynthia Hoffman is responsible for the layout and design of each individual issue. She is also responsible for maintaining a continuity in design from month to month. It is this continuity that gives *Chicago* its unique look and style.

Publication design is a specialized area in the graphic arts. The art director is the specialist who develops the artistic theme of an issue. The art director also supervises the preparation of material by sketch artists, layout artists, mechanical artists, and paste-up artists. The Society of Publication Designers recognizes excellence in all areas of publication design, and *Chicago* and Cynthia Hoffman have won their share of awards.

Surrounded by talented artists (grandmother, father, brother, cousin) in her family, Hoffman became interested in art at a young age. After taking many art courses in high school, she went to the University of Chicago and graduated with a bachelor of arts degree in ideas and methods. Hoffman worked for three years as a painter and printmaker and for six years as a free-lance publications designer before joining the staff of *Chicago* magazine.

Each issue of the magazine presents a new challenge. Hoffman and her staff must interpret the intent of each article to determine the best way to present the material visually. The illustrations or photographs selected must attract the reader's attention. At the same time, each individual article must coordinate with the overall theme of the month's issue.

In addition, the art director must see that the general appearance of the magazine is consistent from issue to issue. Readers expect to find familiar elements each month. Changing the typeface radically or moving the location of a regular column may upset habitual readers. The challenge is to present a fresh and eye-catching magazine each month while maintaining the flow of the design from issue to issue. Doing all of this while meeting deadlines can sometimes cause stress, but Hoffman finds that her enthusiasm for her job carries her through the hectic times.

Hoffman is also enthusiastic about the opportunity her job gives her to work with free-lance talent, both illustrators and photographers. She is constantly searching for new talent. When reviewing portfolios of drawings and photographs, Hoffman looks for personal style. She sees showcasing new talent as part of her job.

The challenge of improving every issue of the magazine provides Hoffman with continued job satisfaction. After each issue is completed, she goes through each page with a red marker—analyzing, criticizing, looking for ways to make next month's issue better. It is this desire for excellence that makes *Chicago* an award-winning magazine.

CHAPTER TEN

Making Emotional Drawings

OBJECTIVES

After reading this chapter and doing the activities, you will be able to

- express emotions in abstract drawings;
- express emotions in realistic drawings;
- express emotions in works of art created with mixed media;
- express humor in drawings;
- create illustrations that express emotion;
- demonstrate the use of different drawing tools and media; and
- demonstrate the use of different drawing techniques.

Emotional drawings are those that make their most obvious impact through expressive qualities. As we explained in Chapter 4, however, very few drawings fit into only one style category. Few drawings are purely emotional, purely imitational, or purely formal.

In this chapter, you will learn that imitational images—literal qualities, or subject matter—are often required in emotional drawings to communicate the artist's feeling or idea. You will learn that the formal qualities—the elements and principles of art—must be present in any drawing for it to function visually. You will also learn to use a mixture of media to create emotional drawings, use drawing to express humor, and create emotional illustrations.

VISUAL QUALITIES IN EMOTIONAL DRAWINGS

A group of artists in the 1940s and 1950s thought they had discovered a way to make purely emotional art. These artists were called *Abstract Expressionists* (see Chapter 3, page 60). Their paintings didn't have recognizable subject matter, except for the elements and principles of art, so the works were *abstract*. The works were *expressive* because the artists tried to communicate emotion by applying paint to canvases freely and spontaneously, without careful design. The act of painting itself—and expressing the emotions the artists felt while painting—was so important to Abstract Expressionists that they called their work

FIGURE 10.1 (top) Though it isn't always evident in her finished pieces, Tina Fuentes derives many of her images from the human figure, as she did in *Moreno.*
Courtesy of the artist.

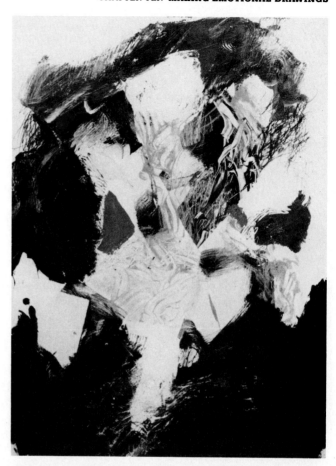

FIGURE 10.2 (bottom) Anita Mills took advantage of the flexibility of a dry medium to use it almost like paint in this drawing. Sometimes what is omitted or removed from a composition is as important as what remains, as you can see in this work.
Courtesy of the artist.

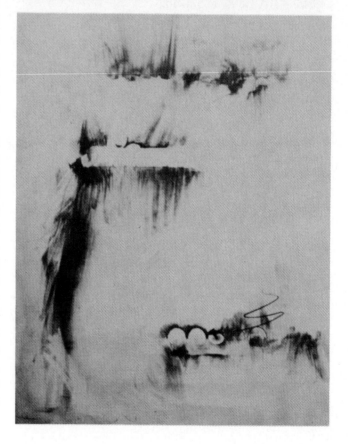

action painting. You can see an example of Abstract Expressionist painting in Figure 21 in the Color Section.

Many expressionist artists today, however, realize the need for effective organization of visual structure, even in very expressive abstract work. Look at Tina Fuentes's drawing in Figure 10.1, for example. In this drawing Fuentes expressed emotion and energy, but she approached her drawing with control and created a unified image.

Although Fuentes's work might barely suggest figures or objects as the origin of her subject matter, the mixed media drawing by Linda Kennedy (Figure 22 in the Color Section) has only one large abstract object filling the working area. The object—if it is an object—is extremely complex, but rhythm in the strokes and repetition of color and value give the drawing unity. This drawing is probably as close as a drawing can come to being purely emotional.

Both Kennedy and Fuentes expressed emotion in the almost athletic act of making the marks, and the marks remain as a record of this emotion. This kind of emotional drawing is probably the most basic kind because it doesn't rely on subject matter to express its meaning. It uses structural or formal qualities to express feelings about the process of drawing itself.

The charcoal drawing by Anita Mills (Figure 10.2) also uses formal qualities to convey emotion. The effective design organizes shapes, uses several alignments, and unifies the entire working area. The drawing also creates interesting ambiguity between positive and negative space. The marks, however, are definitely expressive and indicate strong emotion involved in their making. Many of the marks were made with an eraser, establishing a balance between creation and destruction of form.

Action Drawing

MATERIALS

Compressed charcoal, red conte crayon, pastel chalk, colored pencil, technical pen or fine-line marker, bristol board

Try expressing some emotions by making an action drawing. Make some angry marks with a piece of compressed charcoal, red conte crayon, or pastel chalk. Next, make some fast marks with a colored pencil. These marks will be thinner and straighter than the angry marks and will probably go in only one direction. Choose a color that you think expresses speed.

For the next group of lines, use a technical pen or fine-line marker to make some slow lines—thin, black, spidery, leisurely lines that wander in and out and all around the drawing. Even though you are making an emotional drawing, it needs structure to communicate effectively. Make some of the slow lines overlap other kinds to tie some elements of your drawing together and create unity.

Eraser Drawing Using Stencils

MATERIALS

Layout or typing paper; rubber cement; medium-weight, medium-surface bristol board; charcoal or graphite; sandpad; felt pad, cotton, or tissue; kneadable eraser; charcoal pencil

In this drawing you will manipulate shapes to express an emotion. Start by cutting simple shapes that you can align on a rectangular sheet from layout or typing paper. Use rubber cement to glue these to a sheet of bristol board. Rubber cement will attach the shapes firmly, but after it dries you can peel off the shapes.

Now make some carbon dust from charcoal or graphite with your sandpad, and rub it onto the drawing with a felt pad, cotton, or tissue. Don't worry about applying the dust smoothly. An uneven application will give the drawing more character.

Carefully peel off the paper stencil shapes. Then draw into the gray ground with an eraser to connect some of the shapes and soften some of their edges. Complete your composition by alternating a charcoal pencil with the eraser, applying more carbon dust, or using more stencils for a transparent effect. Restenciling some areas will help relate the shapes to the surface and provide unity.

Do several of these drawings. Practice will improve them rapidly and noticeably. Choose the best ones to spray with fixative and mat.

LITERAL QUALITIES IN EMOTIONAL DRAWINGS

Even though you can make an emotional drawing without recognizable images, as you did in the last two activities, not all emotional drawings are abstract. Long before the Abstract Expressionists were expressing emotion about the act of painting, other artists were expressing emotion about subject matter. An outstanding emotional drawing is shown in Figure 2.13. In this work, the artist communicated feelings about a subject by the way the subject was drawn.

Look at the drawing of an old woman's head by Geila Gueramian in Figure 10.3. The artist expressed her message by the way she made the marks and by the extreme distortion of the facial anatomy. In Chapter 6, you saw the expressive distortion in the Steve Haynes portrait (Figure 6.53). These distortions are moderate. The artist used them only to make the drawing more interesting. In Gueramian's drawing,

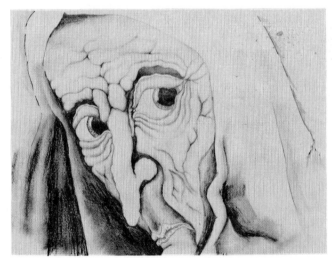

FIGURE 10.3 The expression and distortions are as important in this student work by Geila Gueramian as the kind of marks she used.

rubber cement

however, exaggeration is largely what makes the drawing expressive. Along with the crinkly, spidery lines that cut into the wrinkles and folds of the face, and the harsh charcoal marks in the dark areas, the distortions suggest the resentment that can accompany old age and sadness. In Mike McAfee's drawing of a back fence and vines (Figure 10.4), the combi- nation of pen line and graphite effectively expresses the tangled complexity and linear shadows of the scene.

Emotion expressed in a realistic figure can often be seen in the body attitude or gesture of that figure. How could you use gesture to express fear, anger, or joy when drawing a figure?

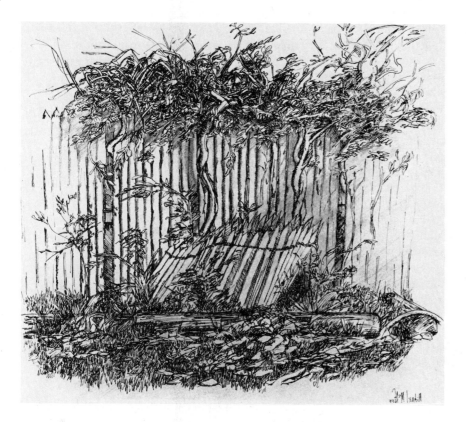

FIGURE 10.4 Student Mike McAfee added expressive qualities to a back fence scene by using pen and ink.

Emotional Drawing of a Person

MATERIALS

Charcoal pencil, drawing paper, tracing vellum or layout paper, drawing media of your choice

Draw a person's head and face using exaggeration to communicate emotion. You can work from either a model or a photograph.

First, use a charcoal pencil to make an imitational drawing. Note the shapes and planes of the face and how they fit together. Then overlay the drawing with a sheet of tracing vellum or layout paper. Trace the areas that will remain imitational in the finished drawing, and greatly exaggerate the areas you want to emphasize.

Using this overlay as a rough sketch, do a finished drawing in the media of your choice and exagger- ate even more. Use the character of the lines to express your meaning.

Color Emotional Drawing of a Person

MATERIALS

Charcoal pencil, drawing paper, tracing vellum or layout paper, color drawing media of your choice

Repeat the steps of the last activity until you are ready to do the finished rendering. Then decide how to use color to express emotion in the portrait.

An analogous color structure in hues and values of reds might express anger. Cool colors suggest tranquility. Purples and violets are often associated with the exotic or mysterious. Remember that a totally analogous color structure can be dull without some complementary accent and some value gradation. Pastel chalks are a good medium for this drawing since you can use brilliant colors and make expressive marks.

STUDIO

Color Emotional Drawing of a Group of Figures

MATERIALS
Drawing media of your choice

Draw a group of figures like the one in Philip Ford's drawing (Figure 23) in the Color Section. This expressive pastel and conte draw-

ing is based on *commedia dell'arte* characters from the Italian theater (see Enrichment) as well as on some of Ford's childhood puppets.

For an idea for this drawing, consider occasions when people gather. A scene from a play or a crowd scene in history or literature would be good subject matter for this emotional drawing. Remember that you are making an expressive statement about the people and the event. Since you aren't drawing an illustration, you shouldn't try to tell a specific story.

Make a preliminary drawing to decide how to arrange the figures and objects to create unity. You can use large, nondetailed shapes for this rough drawing. For the finished drawing, concentrate on making a unified placement of the shapes instead of a perspective drawing with accurate proportions.

Use the marks in your drawing to express the emotion you want to convey. Use colors that you think suggest this emotion.

ENRICHMENT

Commedia Dell'arte

Commedia dell'arte is the name of a style of stage comedy that was performed from the sixteenth to the eighteenth century in Italy. Like many of today's television situation comedies, it was based on a group of standard situations and a company of stock characters. Everyone loved these characters and expected certain attitudes and responses from them.

These characters included Columbine, the saucy sweetheart of Harlequin, who was a masked clown with colorful tights and a wooden sword. Other characters were the old man, Pantalone (or Pantaloon); Punchinello, the buffoon; and Scaramouche, the cowardly braggart.

USING EMOTIONAL DRAWING WITH MIXED MEDIA

Some approaches to expressing emotions are highly individual. Artists invent ways to use both media and the formal elements of art. They might use visual qualities as symbols to represent the subject of their message.

Often these works of art are difficult to classify. They can be called paintings, sculpture, or photographs. Or they might be **collages** (two-dimensional works of art) or **assemblages** (three-dimensional works of art) consisting of many pieces attached to a surface. Since drawing is often involved in creating these works, we are including them in our discussion of emotional drawings.

Look at the work of Cherie Miner in Figure 10.5. Although this work has no immediately recogniza-

ble images, it is full of emotion, which is expressed in the maplike quality of the shapes held by the linear stitches. We suspect that the drawing contains symbolism based on the artist's personal background, but that meaning is hidden from us. Still, the work is interesting because of its expressive qualities, even if we don't know the origin of the symbols.

The work also has interesting formal elements, although Miner hasn't stressed the principles of design. The expressive qualities of the shapes and marks, however, are quite obvious. Making the marks was a fairly slow and calculated process, which means the emotion is expressed not about the action involved but about the drawing's origins and formal elements. The drawing is abstract (it has no recognizable subject matter) and expressionist (it communicates emotion), but it isn't an Abstract Expressionist drawing. It doesn't express emotion about the act of drawing.

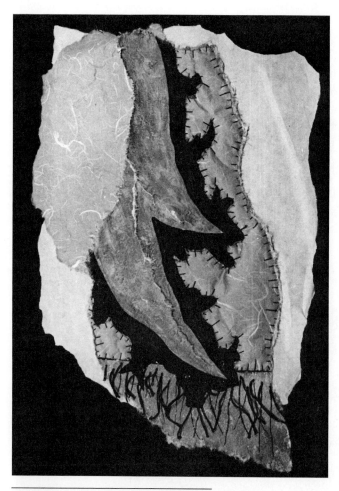

FIGURE 10.5 The emotional qualities in Cherie Miner's work are evident not only in the use of collage and stitchery but also in the symbolism of land forms and patchwork. In what sort of environment do you think the artist grew up?
Courtesy of the artist.

The **bas-relief** construction or assemblage by Fred Hudgeons (Figure 10.6) is another example of how drawing can be combined with other art forms to express a feeling or idea. *Bas relief* means that some areas of the artwork project slightly from the surface. The subject matter of the drawing isn't easy to recognize. It could be a section of some old building, deteriorating because of age and exposure to the weather.

Drawing, painting, and other art forms were used to create a work that calls for certain responses from the viewers. Since some of the work's expressive qualities are created through the careful organization of visual qualities, we could call this work an example of *structural expressionism*.

The work by Nancy Merchant (Figure 10.7, next page) also uses the formal or structural elements of art to produce an emotional response in the viewers. In this work, however, we can recognize human figures, so the artist has also used literal qualities.

Look at Figure 10.8 on the next page. This charcoal and pastel drawing by Sara Waters is another example of using images to express emotion. Symbols are even more evident in her large construction (which involves drawing) in the Color Section in Figure 24. The title of this imposing work is *Crossing. . . .* Analyze it by using your awareness of shape and line, your knowledge of color, your experiences, and maybe some knowledge of symbols. Studying Waters's drawing could also help.

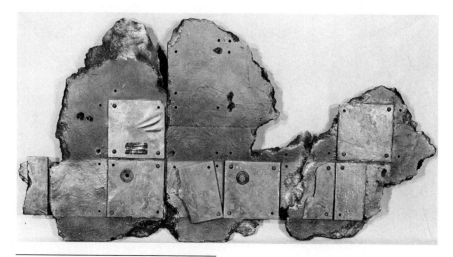

FIGURE 10.6 Fred Hudgeons's massive work would seem out of place in a drawing text except that it depends on illusions that are created with drawing media.
Courtesy of the artist.

FIGURE 10.7 Emotion and symbolism are evident in Nancy Merchant's complex mixed media drawing. What do the symbols mean to you?
Courtesy of the artist.

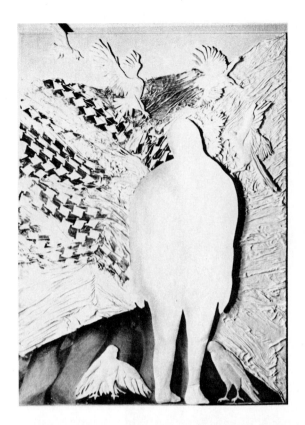

FIGURE 10.8 Sara Waters's pastel and charcoal drawing is called *Having Words Again*. Energetic emotional expression is also evident in her large, three-dimensional pieces. One that uses drawing is shown in Fig. 24 of the Color Section.
Courtesy of the artist.

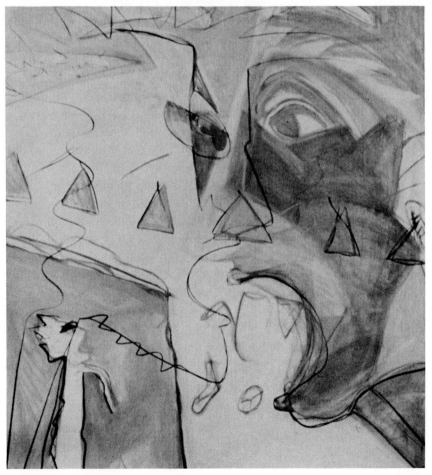

Drawing on Mixed Media Collage

MATERIALS

Graphite pencil, tracing paper, various kinds of paper or fabric, found objects, colored pens or pencils, illustration board, glue or acrylic medium

For this activity you will create a mixed media collage and then use drawing to add line, value, and color to the composition.

First, find some items in your sketchbook that you like or about which you feel strong emotion. Trace these items on overlays, refining their shapes to reflect some of the emotion you feel about them.

Transfer these shapes to different kinds of paper or fabric of your choice. Cut or tear them out. You might re-create some of the shapes by making them out of **found objects**—natural or man-made objects found by chance. For example, you could sew sequins to cloth, glue leaves to paper, or attach net to board.

Draw on these shapes with colored pens or pencils to add line, value, and color. Then glue the shapes to the illustration board in a way that reinforces the expression of emotion. Acrylic matt or glossy medium, the liquid used to mix acrylic paints, makes a good collage glue. Finish the collage by drawing into it to unify or emphasize areas of the design.

Mixed Media Construction Using Symbolism

MATERIALS

Materials of your choice to assemble (examples: roll of wrapping paper, corrugated cardboard boxes painted with gesso); scissors or a mat knife to cut out pieces; felt-tipped markers to draw on the pieces; yarn, heavy string, or masking tape to hold pieces together

Work with your classmates to create a symbolic construction (assemblage). The construction will fill a three-dimensional space and should unite the wall and floor from any viewpoint around it. The size of your construction will be determined by the amount of space you can use.

Start by making rough sketches. Remember that you are going to symbolize some action, event, state of mind, or condition. The marks on the shapes you select or cut out should express how you feel about the subject. Make marks large enough to be easily seen. Photograph the construction before you take it down.

USING HUMOR IN EMOTIONAL DRAWINGS

An emotional work of art doesn't have to express a serious idea to be important. A drawing can have a strong visual significance and still be humorous or playful. For example, look at the Verne Funk drawing in Figure 10.9 on the next page. This work could also be classified as a painting or a sculpture. The artist drew on a life-sized hollow clay column that had been fired like pottery in a kiln.

He used this work to poke fun at some dancers. The work is good-natured enough, however, not to offend the subjects of the joke. As you can see in Figure 10.10, this work was exhibited along with several similar to it in a museum installation depicting a dance hall. It contributed greatly to the good spirits of the usually sober crowd of museum visitors.

As an emotional work of art, this drawing is successful. But Funk's dancers are more than simply entertaining. He emphasized their formal qualities by use of line and value and by alignment of shapes. He established visual unity by drawing on a column of clay.

The drawing of Suzanne Durland (Figure 10.11) also expresses some playful emotions. Although its formal aspects have an impact on us, the childlike quality catches our attention first. Ms. Durland is half of a family team of artists. There is also humor in the art of Don Durland, her husband, but it is often expressed as gentle ridicule. You can see this quality in the almost ornate treatment of the subject in Figure 10.12.

acrylic matt or
gloss medium

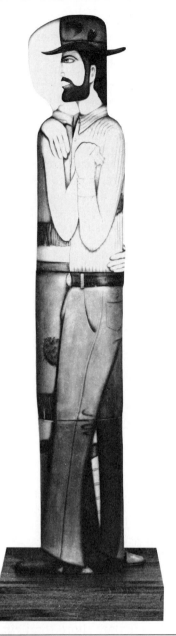

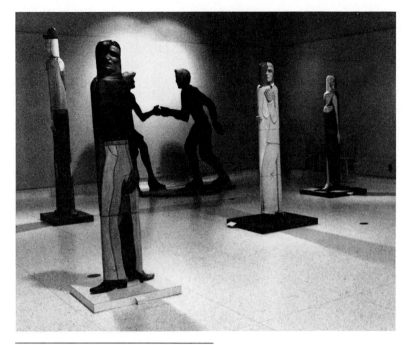

FIGURE 10.10 Verne Funk's work shown as a dance hall scene in a museum gallery. Do you think he is poking fun at anyone?
Courtesy of the artist.

FIGURE 10.9 Life-sized drawings on ceramic columns express Verne Funk's gently satirical sense of humor.
Courtesy of the artist.

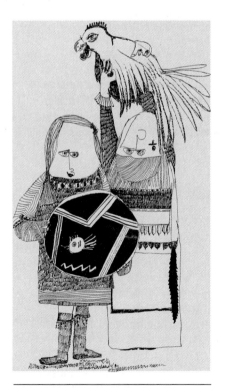

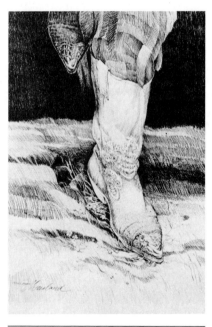

FIGURE 10.12 Don Durland's walking boots are an imposing image. How do they also express satire or humor?
Courtesy of the artist.

FIGURE 10.11 Suzanne Durland's humorous exaggerations and wandering line ask the viewer to respond to the playful emotions of childhood. Can you find other emotions expressed here also?
Courtesy of the artist.

Drawing on a Three-Dimensional Object

MATERIALS

Cardboard box or tube, white acrylic gesso, brush, sandpaper, magazine photographs, acrylic medium, drawing media of your choice

In this artwork you will poke fun at some well-known figure. You will need a long, narrow cardboard box, or a cardboard tube about one foot long. Paint the box or tube with two or three coats of white acrylic gesso, sanding between coats. When you are finished painting, the box or tube should have a uniformly white surface. For extra durability, paint the inside of the box also.

Find a magazine photograph of the face of the public figure you want to use as your subject. You can cut it out and glue it with acrylic medium to one end of the box or tube. Or you can transfer it as described in the Technique Note. Use any drawing media you like to finish the design. You can also add more photographs.

To protect your finished art, apply a coat of acrylic medium. Test the medium first, however, to make sure it won't dissolve any drawing media you have used.

You can see some examples of student drawings on three-dimensional objects in Figure 10.13. Even though you are using drawing to communicate playfulness, remember to control the visual qualities of the artwork to create an effective design.

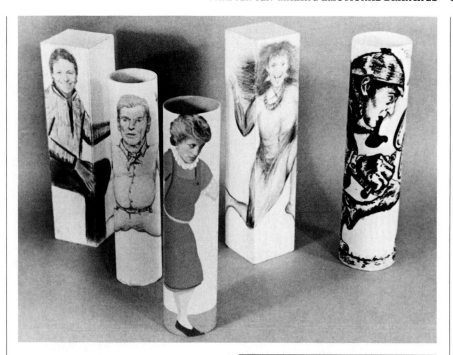

FIGURE 10.13 These student works began from an idea like the one used in Figure 10.9. They were done by (left to right) Susan Nall, Nancy Fagan, Brad Fuoss (two), and Rob Wilson.

TECHNIQUE NOTE

Transferring Printed Photographs

To transfer a magazine or newspaper photograph to another white surface, soak the printed picture briefly in turpentine, lighter fluid, or some other solvent. Then lay the photograph facedown on the surface, and absorb the excess solvent with tissue. Rub the back of the photograph firmly with a smooth stylus or ballpoint pen.

After you remove the printed photograph, you will see its mirror image on the working surface. Turpentine transfers work best when you use freshly printed magazines or newspapers.

You can also use a turpentine transfer for an image made on a photocopying machine by rubbing a light-colored permanent felt-tipped marker or a blending marker on the back. This method produces a darker transfer, but the transfer won't have the texture caused by the stylus.

The decoupage method is another way to transfer magazine photographs. It takes more time than a turpentine transfer, but it produces a smooth and permanent transfer. Put about three coats of clear acrylic medium on the painted surface. When the surface is dry, soak and sponge most of the paper off the back with water. Dry the image, and glue it to the surface with more acrylic medium.

SAFETY NOTE

Using Solvents

Turpentine, lighter fluid, and most other solvents are flammable. Be careful to keep them away from flame. Also, most of them emit poisonous fumes, so work in a ventilated area.

Solvents can also damage your skin, so wear rubber gloves. Some solvents, such as turpentine, can blister your skin painfully if they soak through clothing.

CREATING EMOTIONAL ILLUSTRATIONS

An illustration, you will recall, is simply art that is used to help tell a story, give instructions, or make a product attractive. The pictures in this book are illustrations. Thanks to the invention of printing, illustrations can be used to communicate with many people. In order to communicate, illustrations often need strong emotional qualities.

The simple line drawing is the easiest kind of illustration to reproduce by modern printing methods. A line drawing, referred to as **line art**, is made up of solid blacks and whites. Future Akins's *Bedroom Heroes/Cowboy's Fantasy* in Figure 10.14 is an excellent example of line art that dramatically uses the high contrast of white line on black.

Akins originally made a **linocut print**; that is, she cut her design into a block of linoleum (a kind of floor covering), put ink on the surface, and pressed the

paper onto the linoleum block to make the print. By using this medium, she captured the white-on-black contrast and expressive line quality. This print was later reproduced by modern commercial means as an illustration for an art center calendar. How would you describe the emotion that the artist expressed about the subject by her style of drawing?

Figure 10.15 is another expressive illustration in line. It didn't start out as line art, however. It was done on a somewhat grainy paper with pen and then shaded with a black pencil. After this, it was reproduced on a photocopying machine. All of the gray values of the pencil shading were translated into black dots, which give the shading strokes a crude, almost stippled look. This approach expresses the tough and somewhat unpleasant personality of Mister Suitcase, a character in a story by the artist James Johnson.

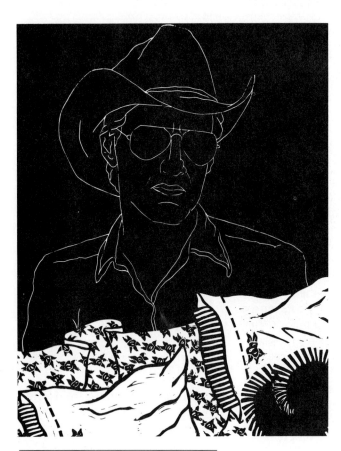

FIGURE 10.14 Future Akins chose linocut for this expressive, high-contrast piece called *Bedroom Heroes/Cowboy's Fantasy*. It has been used on an art gallery poster. Courtesy of the artist and Lubbock Fine Arts Center.

ENRICHMENT

Prints and Reproductions

To an artist, a print is an artwork produced by applying ink to a surface on which the artist has created images and pressing paper against that surface.

Images are made by marking on, carving out of, or etching into a surface. The surface from which images are transferred to paper is referred to as the *printing plate*.

The surface may be

- a linoleum block (for a **linocut**),
- a wood block (for a **woodcut**),
- a metal plate (for an **intaglio**),
- a stone or metal plate (for a **lithograph**), or
- a silk screen (for a **serigraph**).

The surface can be used to make several prints of the same composition. Prints of the same composition are referred to as an *edition* and are usually individually signed, numbered, and titled by the artist.

Some art dealers advertise works as prints that are really only reproductions. Reproductions are created by photographing works of art through screens and color filters. The resulting film is used to make metal plates for a high-speed commercial press. These reproductions are lower in quality than prints and are less valuable because they aren't produced by the artist or made from plates on which the artist has created images.

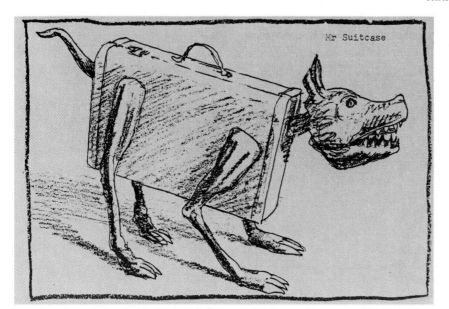

FIGURE 10.15 The character of James Johnson's Mr. Suitcase is clearly expressed by the kind of line and reproduction method.
Courtesy of the artist.

STUDIO

Linocut Greeting Card Illustration

MATERIALS

Drawing medium of your choice, linoleum block, gouge, tray or plate, brayer, block printing ink, wooden spoon, rice paper or other smooth, somewhat absorbent paper

A good way to use line art for an illustration is to print your own greeting cards. You will draw your design on a linoleum block, scoop out the negative areas, ink the block's surface, and use the block to make a print. A **woodcut print** is made the same way as a linocut print, except a block of wood is used instead of the linoleum. You can see a good example of a woodcut print by Paul Hanna in Figure 10.16.

First, make several correctly proportioned rough sketches of the scene or symbols you have chosen for your illustration. You should realize that the image produced on the print will be in reverse, as if you were looking in a mirror. Any

letters will be reversed unless you draw them in reverse on the block. We recommend that you omit lettering on your first linocut; you can leave space on your cards for a handwritten message or make a double-folded card and write on the inside.

When you have finished designing your illustration, draw it on a small linoleum block, 4 × 6″ (10 × 15 cm) in size. Now you are ready to cut out the design. Fasten strips of wood to your workbench or table in the shape of an L, and place the block in the corner of the L so that it won't slip when you push against it. Use a knife called a *gouge*, which is designed for cutting a wood or linoleum block. (See the Safety Note on block cutting for instructions on using this knife.) Cut away the parts of the block that you don't want to print in the design.

The next step is to apply ink to the block. The rubber inking roller used for this process is called a brayer. The block printing ink you will use is a thick kind especially designed for block printing.

Squeeze some ink from the tube onto a smooth, nonabsorbent surface, like an old tray or plate. Roll it

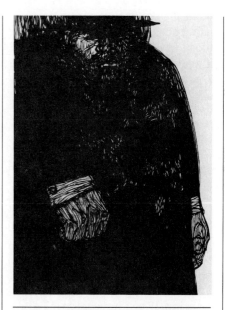

FIGURE 10.16 Paul Hanna's large, brooding woodcut, *Resistant Man*, has been featured in a number of exhibitions.
Courtesy of the artist.

smooth with the brayer. Then roll some ink onto the printing surface of your block, and lay the rice paper (or any other smooth, absorbent paper) over it. Actually, rice paper isn't made from rice, but from fiber of the mulberry plant or an herb called *rice paper tree*.

linoleum block

gouge
brayer
block printing ink

rice paper

To print the design, rub the back of the paper with a wooden spoon or a similar smooth tool. You will have to practice to learn how heavily to ink the block and what tools to use for pressing the design onto the paper.

After you have printed the design, clean the ink off both the brayer and the block.

SAFETY NOTE

Cutting Blocks

When you use the gouge to scoop out the portions of the block that you don't want to be inked (such as the pillow or white lines in Figure 10.14), always push the gouge away from you, using both hands. Never hold the block in your hand to cut it. Put it against the inside corner of an L-shaped block fastened firmly to a table or bench, or put it in a wood vise.

SAFETY NOTE

Cleaning Blocks and Brayers

You should always wipe any remaining ink from a block and brayer after you have finished printing. If you have used a water-based printing ink, you can use water for cleaning. If you have used oil-based ink, however, you should use a solvent such as turpentine. Remember that if you use a solvent, you should be careful not to breathe in the fumes, get the solvent on your skin, or let it come in contact with your eyes.

STUDIO

Two-Color Woodcut Illustration

MATERIALS

Pastels, drawing paper, wood block, gouge, tray or plate, brayer, woodcut or linoleum block ink, wooden spoon, rice paper or other smooth, absorbent paper

Choose a story and illustrate it with a two-color woodcut print. You can see an example of this kind of print in Figure 25 in the Color Section. Make your print at least 11 × 14″ (28 × 36 cm) in size.

Use pastels for your rough sketches. Use only flat areas of color or colored lines since you can't easily reproduce gradation on the wood block.

Basswood, the light wood of a linden tree, is one of the best kinds to use for a woodcut, but you can use any soft wood block. You can even use an old drawing board, but don't cut too deeply if the board is hollow.

To transfer the chalk sketch to the wood block, turn the sketch facedown on the block and rub the back side of the drawing with your hand. You can correct any details by drawing directly on the block. Use the gouge to cut around the design on the block. Don't forget to clean off all remaining chalk before trying to ink the block because the chalk will stick to the inked brayer.

You will need one block for each color you want to use in the print. Often woodcuts are printed in black and one color, but if you have patience and enough blocks, you can print as many colors as you wish—and you don't have to use black. Using more than one printing block requires a method of registration, or positioning the paper and the inked blocks so that the colors print in the correct places.

To produce the correct color registration, make the printing block for each color exactly the same size and shape, and transfer the drawing to exactly the same place on each block. Mark the outline of the block's corners on the drawing the first time you transfer it, and align the other blocks the same way when transferring the drawing to them.

To place the paper on the blocks in the same spot each time you print a color, tape the paper to the block for the first color, and mark the outline of the two sides and corner of the paper on the block. Measure where these lines forming the corner are located on the first block; then measure and draw them in the same place on all other blocks. You will have to tape the paper to the block on one edge so that it won't slip while you are rubbing with the wooden spoon.

On a woodcut, overlap the edges of the colored areas about ⅛″ (3 mm) to avoid leaving a white space between colors. Print the more transparent colors and the colors with a lighter value first. The darker or more opaque colors will cover the edges of the others, making a clean division between colors.

Let the ink dry between each color printing. Water-based inks may dry in minutes, but you may need to wait an entire day for oil-based inks to dry.

wood block

USING FIGURES IN EMOTIONAL ILLUSTRATIONS

It is often the job of an illustration to convey emotions about people to viewers. The subject in a drawing may be real, as in a photograph advertisement of a product. Or the subject may be imaginary, as in a story illustration. In either case, the way the artist draws human figures is important in communicating the message of the illustration. Figure 2.1 (Chapter 2) is an expressive preliminary drawing for a *Saturday Evening Post* cover by Norman Rockwell. How did Rockwell express the sadness of parting in his drawing of the figures? Where do these people live? Which person is leaving, and where is he going?

Figure 10.17 is a fashion advertisement. What does this figure express? Is this elegance the result of any distortion? Why do you think the artist selected ink and wash as a medium? It may be interesting to note that the same artist did the expressive thumbnail sketches in Chapter 4 (Figure 4.33) and the painting in Figure 6 in the Color Section.

The charcoal pencil illustration of the old mountain man (Figure 10.18) uses distortion to express emotion. This same kind of illustration could have been done in ink or watercolor wash like the fashion drawing. Is the old fellow in the drawing a large man or a small one? (Look at the size of his hands in relation to his rifle.) Is he stalking a bear, seeing a ghost, or thinking about his lonely way of life? (Look at his stance, the way he holds his head and shoulders, and his face.)

FIGURE 10.17 (top) Jane Cheatham's elegant illustration was done for a high-quality women's clothing store. What emotions does her drawing elicit from the viewer?
Courtesy of the artist and Margaret's.

FIGURE 10.18 (bottom) What physical exaggerations do you see in the illustration of the old man? What do they tell you about him? Does the drawing's technique reinforce these ideas?

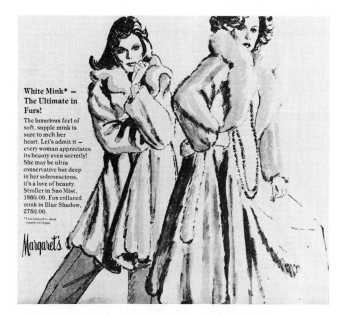

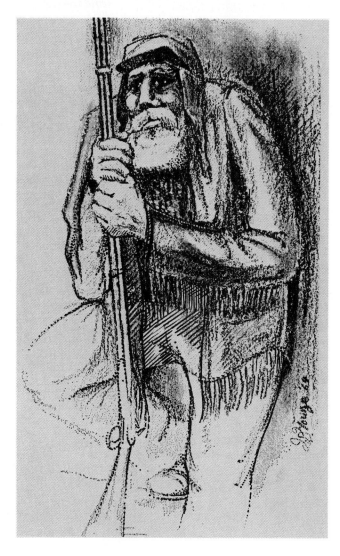

Drawing Single Figures in Wash

MATERIALS

India ink, pen, fiber-tipped pen, transparent watercolors, #2 and #5 round brushes, shallow dishes or watercolor palette, small sponge, medium-rough watercolor paper or block

Study the single figures in Kathy Hicks's drawings (Figures 26 and 27 in the Color Section). Pose a friend—in an interesting costume if possible—and make some similar wash drawings with pens and brushes. Don't make pencil sketches first. Spend about twenty minutes on each drawing, and make the figures about 14″ (36 cm) high. Try to create drawings that are free and expressive.

Make two of these drawings each day for a week. Mat the best three of these drawings for display.

Story Illustration

MATERIALS

Same as the previous activity

Do an illustration from a story of your choice. You will use the same techniques as in the previous activity but show the whole setting in which the character is found.

Find a story you like about a person who expresses some strong emotion or character trait. Select a scene in which this emotion or trait is clearly shown. This scene should feature the character you want to draw.

To decide how to express emotion about the character, ask these questions:

■ How can I show the character's age and position in society?

■ What are the surrounding objects or people I will need in the composition?

■ How can I use the character's size, build, posture, and facial expression to reveal inner qualities?

■ Should I exaggerate or distort the character's size, build, posture, and facial expression to show emotion?

Find an illustrated book or magazine that might publish the story you selected. Use illustrations from the book or magazine to set guidelines for your drawing. If these illustrations use only black and one color, do the same in your illustration.

You can also use the printed illustrations to determine the proportions of your drawing—that is, the length of your drawing in relation to its width. Your finished drawing should be about twice the size of the printed illustration.

After you have determined the proportions of your illustration, do thumbnail sketches to decide on a composition that expresses your message about the character. For your first story illustration, the character should dominate the space. Then the figure will be large enough to allow some expressive drawing, and the design will be more unified.

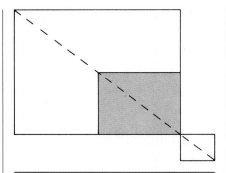

FIGURE 10.19 Rectangles whose corners fall on the same diagonal line will have the same proportion no matter what their size.

TECHNIQUE NOTE

Finding Rectangular Proportions

If you draw a diagonal line through opposite corners of a rectangle, any other rectangle whose corners fall on that diagonal will have the same proportions. If you put tissue paper over a book illustration, you can draw a rectangle around it. You can then draw a corner-to-corner diagonal line on the rectangle and extend it as far past the corners as you like. Any larger rectangle you construct on this diagonal will have the same proportions as the small one. You can make your finished drawing the size of a larger rectangle.

Look at Figure 10.19. The darkened, middle-sized rectangle represents the illustration in the book or magazine. The large rectangle represents the size you select for the finished drawing, and the smallest rectangle shows a suitable size for thumbnail sketches. All of the drawings have the same proportions.

Children's Book Illustrator: Legend into Art

Careers in book illustration provide opportunities for many talented artists. John Steptoe does more than just illustrate books. He preserves culture and interprets experience. *Stevie*, his first book for children, launched his career in 1969, when he was eighteen. He has been producing illustrations for his own books and for those of other authors at the rate of about one book every two years since then.

As a child growing up in Brooklyn, New York, Steptoe drew pictures and told stories about them. Later he attended Manhattan High School of Art and Design. A shy student, Steptoe discovered that the "only way [to] connect with the world is to draw it." He found that the illustration of children's books was an avenue of expression. "I want to tell stories that communicate how I see things," he says, "and I like to tell stories that will be read out loud."

Although *Stevie* was published when the author was eighteen, Steptoe began work on the book when he was only sixteen. His story is about a young boy who resents the little boy his mother babysits. Steptoe used bold, glowing colors and strong lines in the drawings to express feelings.

While his drawing style has changed since his first book, Steptoe's work hasn't lost any of its intensity. *The Story of Jumping Mouse*, published in 1984, is Steptoe's version of a native American legend illustrated with black and white drawings. This book was chosen as a 1985 Caldecott Honor Book. The American Library Association gives those awards every year to recognize excellence in books published for children.

Mufaro's Beautiful Daughters (1987) is Steptoe's retelling of an African tale. He considers it to be an African version of the Cinderella story. His illustrations are full of rich colors and were influenced by the ruins of an ancient city in Zimbabwe.

Steptoe says about these illustrations, "I was challenged by the problems of maintaining the sensitivity of black and white that I was able to achieve in *The Story of Jumping Mouse* while using bright, strong colors. In *Mufaro's Beautiful Daughters* I wanted both of these elements—the sensitivity and the strong colors—to balance in my paintings."

Still a resident of Brooklyn, Steptoe continues to develop as an artist and as a storyteller. Whether retelling ancient legends or interpreting modern life, Steptoe's books have sensitivity and visual appeal. The illustrations play an important role in communicating his message.

UNIT IV

Evaluation and Review

MEETING YOUR OBJECTIVES

By answering the following questions and doing the exercises, you will demonstrate your ability to meet the learning objectives listed at the beginning of Chapters 9 and 10.

Chapter 9

1. How do emotionalists judge drawings?
2. Pick one drawing each from the first four chapters in this book. Describe the expressive qualities in each drawing.
3. From Chapter 3 select one drawing that you think an emotionalist would judge as *unsuccessful*. Write one or two paragraphs telling why you think an emotionalist would judge this work unsuccessful.
4. From Chapter 3 select one drawing that you think an emotionalist would judge as *successful*. Write one or two paragraphs telling why you think an emotionalist would judge this work successful.

Chapter 10

1. Express the emotion of sadness in an abstract, non-objective drawing. Try similar drawings in two or three different media. Write a paragraph explaining why one media used seems more expressive for the emotion of sadness than the other media.
2. Make a realistic drawing that expresses an emotion you feel about the subject of the drawing. Choose colors that express the emotion desired. Use pastels or a combination of pastels and colored pencils.
3. Decide on an emotion you want to express. Use found objects to create an assemblage that expresses that emotion. Do preliminary sketches in your sketchbook to develop ideas for your assemblage. You may want to draw on the parts of the assemblage to enhance your desired effect.
4. Draw a group of five people engaged in some amusing or unusual activity. Use magazine or newspaper photograph transfers for the heads. Use the media of your choice for the bodies. Work on illustration board and allow enough margin for a hinged mat.
5. Create an illustration for a greeting card. Do a direct drawing on watercolor paper using ink or watercolor wash. Work from a model.

6. Make a list of the drawing tools and media you used in doing the studio exercises in Chapter 10.
7. Make a list of the drawing techniques you learned and used in Chapter 10.

LEARNING DRAWING TERMS

You encountered several new drawing terms in this unit. The most important terms are printed in heavy, bold type. Write all the terms on a sheet of paper. Then, without looking in your book, tell what each term means in your own words. If you are not sure of a meaning, use your book to write a definition.

EXPERIENCING DIFFERENT MEDIA

Each new drawing medium is listed at the bottom of the page on which it is first mentioned. Review your experiences with all the media, comparing strengths, weaknesses, and personal preferences. Then write a report summarizing your experiences with these media.

SEEING YOUR ENVIRONMENT

Learning to see the world around you as it really is is one of the first steps in improving your drawing skills. Doing the following exercises and others like them will help you get in the habit of seeing your environment more closely.

1. Look for scenes, objects, and facial expressions that convey emotion. Make sketches that capture that emotion. Then experiment with different techniques and media to more clearly communicate the emotion.
2. Find a landscape or group of objects that convey emotion due to the dominance of one of the elements of art in the scene. Make several sketches of that scene emphasizing the element. Do your sketches convey the same emotion?
3. Make sketches of a sad scene or setting that you've witnessed. Then focus on the use of one principle and one element of art to change the scene to communicate happiness rather than sadness.

EVALUATING DRAWINGS

1. Evaluate the drawing you did for number 4 under "Meeting Your Objectives" for Chapter 10. Rate yourself from 1 to 10 for three categories: 1) craft in making transfers and matting, 2) quality of humor in the idea for the drawing, and 3) structural-compositional quality.
2. Use the art criticism steps you learned in Chapter 2 to evaluate the same drawing you critiqued above.
3. Study closely the work of art shown at right. Is this a successful work? Does it appeal to your personal taste? Give reasons for your answers. Going through the art criticism process will help you make and support your decision.

EXPANDING YOUR HISTORICAL KNOWLEDGE

Learning about the history of art will help you improve your drawing skills. It will also increase your understanding of your own culture and the cultures of others, both past and present. Answering the questions below indicates that you're learning art history. You will be able to answer most of the questions by referring to the Enrichment sections and to Chapter 3. To answer the last question you will probably need to refer to art history books, such as those listed in the Bibliography at the back of the book.

1. How are Edward Hopper's "portraits" different from most portraits?
2. Why did many European artists turn to fantasy and surrealistic subject matter after World War I?
3. Paul Klee is not usually classified as either a Surrealist or a Realist, but suppose you had to classify him as one or the other. To which group would you assign him? Why?
4. Henri de Toulouse-Lautrec was one of a number of artists, including Cezanne and van Gogh, whose art tried to solve the problems they had with an earlier artistic style. Name that style.
5. Lautrec painted many scenes of nightlife in what European city? Locate and study several of Lautrec's works. Then write several paragraphs describing Lautrec's view of his city and its people as shown in his work.

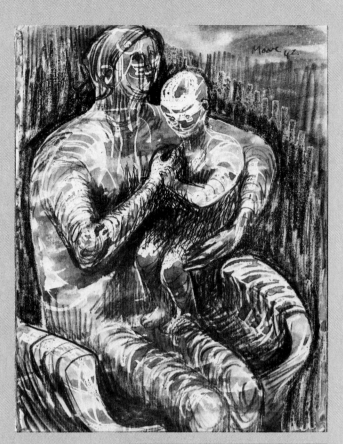

Henry Moore, *Study for Northampton Madonna*, 1943. Black and orange crayon and transparent pen and black ink, gray-black wash over graphite on off-white paper, 8⅞ × 7" (22.5 × 17.6 cm). The Harvard University Art Museums, Cambridge, MA.

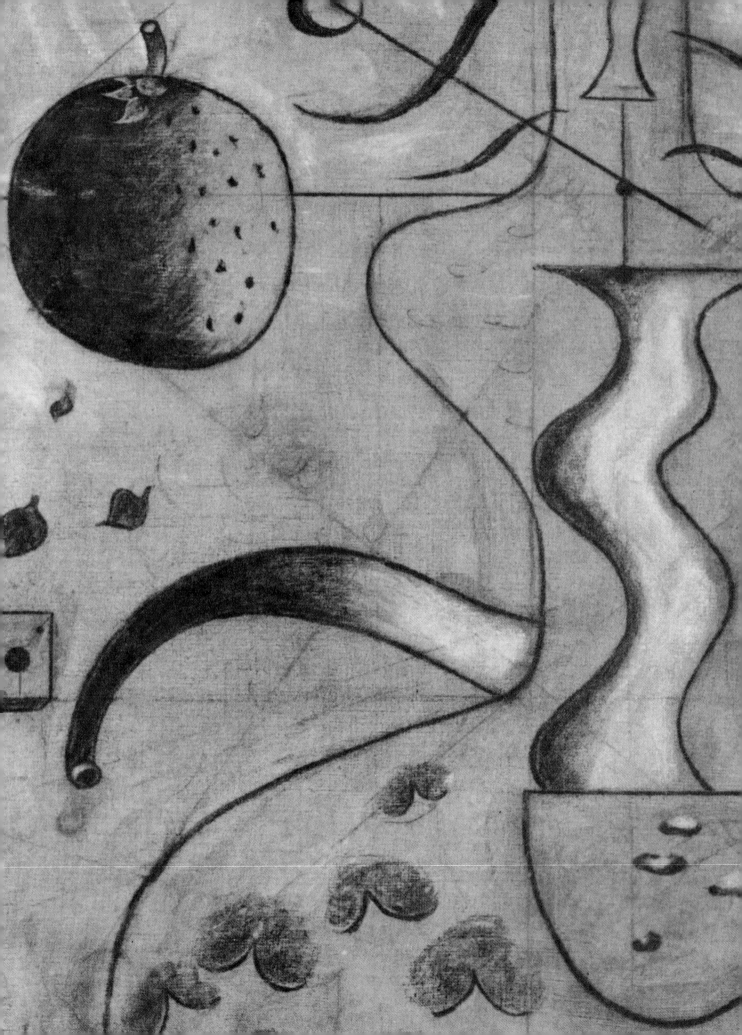

Special Topics in Drawing

Unit V provides information about and techniques for three special kinds of drawing: accurate perspective drawing, cartooning, and computer drawing.

Accurate perspective drawing requires special measuring tools. For the activities in Chapter 11, ''Linear Perspective,'' you will expand on what you learned in Chapter 6 about freehand perspective drawing. Knowledge of linear perspective is essential in the fields of architecture and industrial design as well as in fine art. Using special tools, you will make accurate one- and two-point perspective drawings.

To draw cartoons, you will use tools that you are already familiar with. However, besides drawing skills, creating effective cartoons requires a sense of humor and the writing skills to put humorous ideas into words. In Chapter 12, ''Cartooning,'' you will read about the first steps toward becoming a cartoonist. You will also draw several types of cartoons.

Cartoons are an ancient art form, but images drawn with computers are a modern development. In Chapter 13, ''Computer Drawing,'' you will find information about using the computer as a drawing tool. The computer offers new possibilities for the process of drawing.

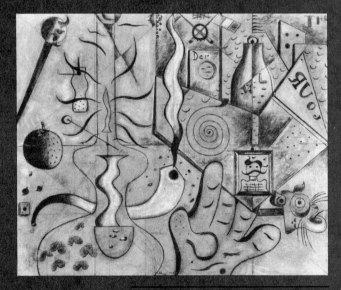

Joan Miró, *The Kerosene Lamp*, 1924. Black and white chalk with touches of pastel and red pencil on canvas, 31.9 ×39.5" (81 × 100.3 cm). The Art Institute of Chicago, IL. Joseph and Helen Regenstein Foundation, Helen L. Kellogg Trust, Blum-Kovler Foundation, Major Acquisitions Fund, and gifts from Mrs. Henry C. Woods, Members of the Committee on Prints & Drawings, and Friends of the Department (detail at left).

Linear Perspective

Knowing how to make accurate perspective drawings in scale is essential in the fields of architecture and industrial design. This skill is also important in illustration and fine art. You can see examples of linear perspective used in drawings in Figures 11.1 through 11.5 on pages 199 and 200.

The architect's rendering in Figure 11.1 is necessary for several reasons. This kind of drawing helps the architect visualize a finished building from the two-dimensional plans he or she has made. The architect can show the drawing to the client. The drawing may also be used as an illustration to promote the sale of houses in a development. If a drawing is used to help sell houses, it must be at least reasonably accurate in scale and arrangement of parts. Any serious distortion of the true size and shape would be unethical because the product would be misrepresented.

The expressive architect's sketch of a neighborhood by Steve Rich (Figure 11.2) was made by a man who is an expert at linear perspective. The drawing is somewhat free and undetailed, but it effectively communicates the character of a large area of housing.

The illustrator who did the rendering of the automobiles pictured in Figure 11.3 is obviously a master of freehand perspective. It is likely, however, that the artist made an accurate-to-scale linear perspective drawing of the cars before attempting this dramatic rendering.

The technical illustration in Figure 11.4 is called an *exploded* view. The object is visually blown apart to show all of its components. The artist had to draw

FIGURE 11.1 (below) This rendering by Dan Engen, a student of architecture, pays particular attention to reflections.

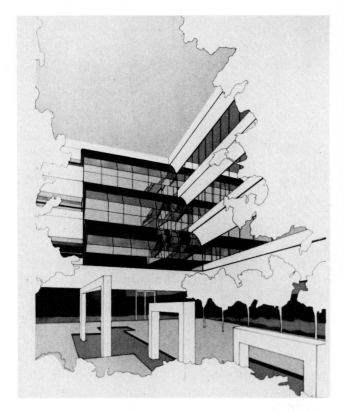

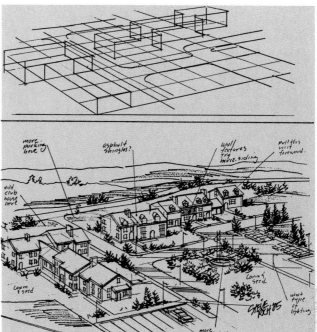

FIGURE 11.2 (above) Steve Rich did this graphic overview of a development to illustrate a rapid perspective technique. Why do you think this technique would be useful to architects? The drawing appeared in *Representation* magazine.

Courtesy of the artist.

FIGURE 11.3 (at right) In the reproduction of this Mark Neeper rendering that appeared in *Automobile* magazine, the car done with an airbrush was shown in brilliant color. The car rendered with a dot pattern remained a black and white ''ghost'' image.

Courtesy of the artist.

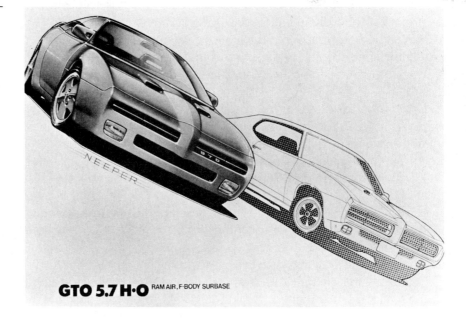

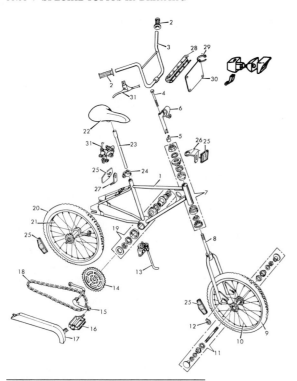

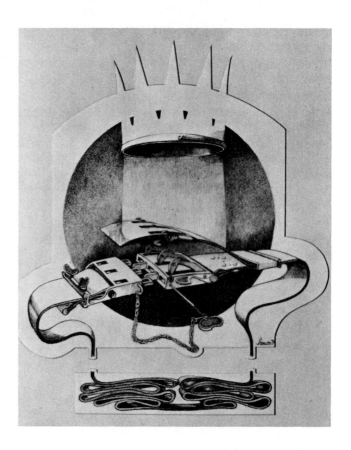

FIGURE 11.4 (above) This illustration of a bicycle shows how useful an exploded view can be in describing how something works.
Courtesy of The Murray Ohio Manufacturing Company.

FIGURE 11.5 (at right) *World Class Buckle* is a fine art drawing in charcoal pencil that makes use of the exploded view idea seen in the technical rendering in Figure 11.4.

the proportion and alignment of the parts accurately, showing where they fit. A technical illustrator must have knowledge of linear perspective even if the artist uses a prepared perspective grid or a computer as an aid.

World Class Buckle is a fine art drawing done in charcoal pencil. It shows how perspective can be applied for close-up objects. This drawing also used the idea of the exploded view, like the one in Figure 11.4. Do you think the exploded view is appropriate? What do you think of the title?

No matter what kind of art you want to create, you need to know something about accurate perspective drawing. There is no better way to learn to make accurate freehand drawings than to learn to make perspective drawings created with the aid of measuring tools. Practicing linear perspective will even help you draw figures more believably.

In this chapter, we will present the basics of accurate perspective drawing. There are many good technical reference books on drafting and linear perspective that you can study to learn more details. The activities we suggest are a sample of the exercises you can find in these books. We will show you how to construct basic box shapes and put them in correct perspective. After you have constructed the boxes, you can draw objects inside them either freehand or by using perspective to accurately project images.

To do an accurate perspective drawing, you must have detailed and accurate measurements and sketches of anything you expect to draw. An extra hour spent in research, sketching, and noting down dimensions, or an extra hour spent in drawing or finding plans, can save you five hours on your finished art. You should return to the studio from your research with every bit of information you will need to do the whole drawing.

For example, if you are drawing a leather chair, you will need not just the dimensions of the chair's back, but also the distance between the buttons on its back, the buttons' diameter, the depth the buttons sink into the leather, and the exact angle at which the back of the chair tilts.

The Basics of Perspective Drawing

Before you study perspective further, review what you learned in Chapter 6 about perspective drawing. You should always

■ put each object in the drawing in a basic box,

■ draw the shape of each basic box and object on the ground or floor first, and

■ draw everything transparently.

THE BASIC BOX

The charming little ivory carving in Figure 11.6 was sawed out of a tusk over fifty years ago in Africa by a local craftsperson. We used the elephant to show you how to draw a basic box. (We enlarged the carving, however, for our drawing. The elephant's actual height is about ¾″ or 2 cm.)

An elephant is symmetrical. *Symmetrical* means that something is the same on both sides of a central plane slicing through it. Many objects are symmetrical, and an easy way to draw them is to construct the central plane in the basic box. In Figure 11.7, this central plane is defined by the thin, black line around

the center of the box. To draw the elephant, the "center slice"—or actually just an extremely flat section—of the elephant was projected onto the central plane and expanded at all points to fill the box.

Figure 11.7 shows the basic box for the elephant carving. Notice the shaded portion on the ground that we drew first. Also note that the box is transparent, just as everything else in the drawing must be transparent.

In the bottom of a box, the lines going away from you into space would meet if they were extended to a shared vanishing point on the horizon. (See 1 in Figure 11.7.) Lines that aren't going away from you, such as Lines A-A and B-B, are parallel to the horizon. They don't meet anywhere. Lines C-C and D-D are also parallel to Lines A-A and B-B as well as to each other.

The next job after building the floor of the box on the ground was to raise the corners to the proper height (Figure 11.7, Lines A-C and B-D). Then we connected the corners to form the top (Lines C-C, C-D, and D-D), and the transparent box was finished.

To find the central slice going through this box toward the vanishing point, we had to find the center of the bottom, top, or one of the ends. To find the center of any square or rectangle in real space or in perspective, draw an X from corner to corner. The center of the X is the center of the square or rectangle.

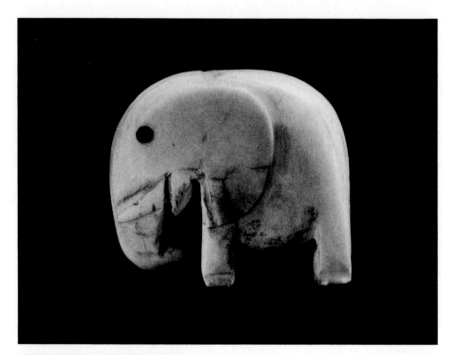

FIGURE 11.6 Some African craftsperson carved this little ivory totem from a tusk over fifty years ago.

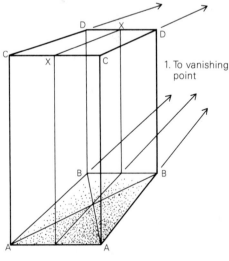

FIGURE 11.7 This is a basic box drawn for the little ivory elephant.

We drew the X on the ground to find the center of the floor of the box. A line drawn through this point to the vanishing point divides the floor into halves in perspective. Where this line crosses the ends of the floor, we raised verticals to cut the ends of the box in half. Where the verticals cross the top lines, we connected them with Line X-X to bisect the top of the box. (This line should also cross the vanishing point if it were extended. Seeing if it would reach the vanishing point is a good way to check the accuracy of the drawing.)

ENRICHMENT

Units of Measure for Perspective Drawing

In the rest of this chapter, we give measurements in feet and inches only. You will be using a standard American architect's scale, which doesn't indicate metric measurements. An engineer's scale would have different measurements, and so would the standard measuring devices of some other countries.

The system of measurement used actually doesn't affect the way accurate perspectives are drawn. In fact, you could invent your own unit of measure as long as you used it consistently throughout a drawing—as you do when you use the human head as a unit of measure in figure drawings.

STUDIO

Drawing a Basic Box in Perspective

MATERIALS

Graphite pencil, ruler (optional), eraser, drawing paper

Draw a box like the one you have been studying. Make the front end a simple vertical rectangle. The top and bottom should be parallel to each other, and the sides should be straight up and down. The sides should be parallel, also.

Pick a point somewhere above and to the right or left of the rectangle for a vanishing point. The vanishing point will be on an imaginary horizon at eye level. Draw lines from each corner of the rectangle to the vanishing point. (Use a ruler if you like.) These are the parallel lines of the four corners of the box moving away from you toward the horizon.

Now decide where to cut off the box at the back, and construct another rectangle just like the one in front. Of course, the back rectangle will be smaller because perspective has caused the sides to come closer together as they move toward the vanishing point.

To make the box easier to see in perspective, draw more heavily the lines that you could actually see if the box weren't transparent. (In Figure 11.7, these lines are A-A, A-C, C-C, A-B, C-D, B-D, and D-D. A cube or box has eight corners, each one formed by the meeting of three planes. From your eye level, you could see at least part of seven corners if the box were opaque.)

Find the center of the floor of the box by drawing an X from corner to corner. Through the center of this X, draw another line that would extend to the vanishing point, starting at the front edge of the floor of the box and stopping at the rear edge. Raise verticals at the points where this line touches the front and rear edges. These verticals will cross on the front and rear edges of the top panel, too. You can connect the points at which they cross to divide the panel in half.

These lines will outline the center section through the length of the box.

Remember that anything in perspective is foreshortened. **Foreshortening** means shortening an object in a drawing to make it look as if it extends backward into space. The length of the side panel of the box that you would actually see can be even shorter than the width of the front panel—unless the box is extremely long. Look again at the box we started to draw in Figure 11.7. If you measure the visible length of the side panel and compare it with the width of the front panel, you will easily see foreshortening.

USING A GRID TO LOCATE POINTS IN SPACE

To draw a two-dimensional, paper-thin elephant on the center slice of the box, we had to locate points on that plane where various lines come together, or where various features of the elephant are located. Where did we locate these points first? On the ground.

Look at Figure 11.8, where we located various points on the ground along the center line of the box (base of the center slice). Since we weren't working with a scale and all the other tools of mechanical perspective, we located these points by estimation. We based our estimates on a grid, as in Figure 11.9.

Figure 11.9 is a sketch of the side **elevation** of our little elephant. An elevation shows no depth or perspective. It is drawn from a station point at a ninety-degree angle to the object and shows the entire image on a vertical plane. Over this elevation, we placed a grid of equal-sized squares. We marked the places where the vertical lines of this grid touch the ground on the base of the center slice in Figure 11.8. Notice that we allowed for foreshortening by decreasing the distance between each of the verticals as they move back toward the vanishing point. (A good way to do this is to start at the center, 5½ squares back, and work in both directions.)

Figure 11.10 shows the completed grid on the center section of the box. Since the vertical measurements for the grid squares on Line B-B are close to us against the picture plane, they don't decrease in size. The squares can be marked on Line B-B at their actual or true height, so Line B-B is called a **true height line**. In fact, any vertical line at the front of a plane that goes back into space—if it is against the picture plane—can be a true height line for things in the receding plane.

Of course, the lines of the grid that go back toward the horizon from the true height line extend to the vanishing point. The distance between them naturally gets smaller as they recede into space.

Look again at Figure 11.9. We said we were going to draw a flat elephant on the perspective plane in the box. The elephant in Figure 11.9 is flat, but it isn't in perspective. The grid in Figure 11.10 is in perspective, but it doesn't have an elephant on it.

We wanted to transfer the flat elephant to the grid. How? We started with just one point—the elephant's eye. In this case, the eye is two squares back from the front (picture plane/true height line) and six squares up from the ground. You can see the eye at that location in Figure 11.11 (on the next page).

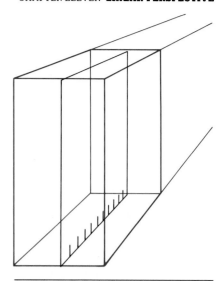

FIGURE 11.8 The marks along the center line of the floor of the box indicate where we estimated the vertical lines of the grid should be drawn.

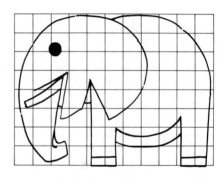

FIGURE 11.9 Elevation or a flat view from one side of the elephant.

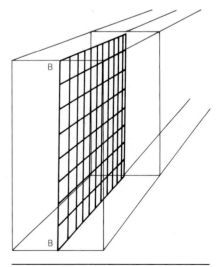

FIGURE 11.10 Completed grid on the center "slice" of the box.

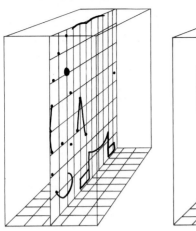
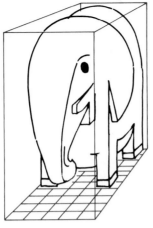
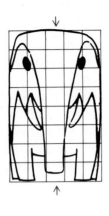
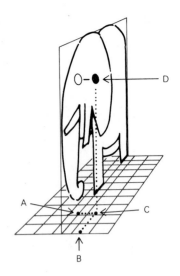

FIGURE 11.11 (at left) The eye and other points are located on the grid.

FIGURE 11.12 (second from left) A perspective showing planes and volumes of the little ivory statue is the result of using a grid.

FIGURE 11.13 (third from left) An elevation can show the front as well as the side. We could even draw one as a "slice" through the object; it would be called a section.

FIGURE 11.14 (far right) The eye must be located by marking three measurements: the distance from the front of the box, the distance from the center, and the height.

Also, we put on the perspective grid the points where its tusks start and stop, the points where its feet are located, and other points where it touches the outside of the grid. We even located many of the points where the curved lines of its body cross lines on the grid. Knowing the location of these points made it easy to draw the elephant.

We have demonstrated an important skill. To locate a point in perspective accurately, you need to know only three measurements:

■ the distance a point is back from the picture plane,

■ the distance a point is from the side of the drawing, and

■ the distance a point is up from the ground.

If you know these three measurements, you can locate any point even if it is floating in the air.

If you can locate enough points on a plane, you can stretch them to the right and left into proper positions. Then you can connect the points and make the complete drawing of a form within the basic box, even if the form is irregular and curving.

Figure 11.12 shows our completed drawing of the elephant. Figures 11.13 and 11.14 show how we did it.

Figure 11.13 is another elevation of the ivory figure, but this time the elephant is viewed from the front instead of the side. After we constructed another grid in the same scale as the first one, we measured from the center to the eye on the right to see how far out from the center to place the eye. In Figure 11.14, Point A marks the distance on the ground from the eye to the front of the box (picture plane). Point B marks the distance (1½ squares) from the eye to the right of the center plane.

We raised a vertical line from the intersection (Point C) and drew a horizontal line to the right from the eye in the central plane. The intersection of these lines (at Point D) was the expanded and real location of the elephant's eye. We could expand every point on the flat elephant that we wanted to in this way. Then we could see how to draw it as a volume instead of a flat plane. Note that the lower front line of the basic box—because it is against the picture plane—becomes a **measuring line** on which full measurements can be used, just as they can be used on the true height line.

STUDIO

Drawing an Object in One-Point Perspective Using a Grid

MATERIALS

Graphite pencil, ruler, eraser, drawing paper

Draw some fairly simple object that is symmetrical but interesting in one-point perspective. You could use a vase or clay pot or an uphol-stered furniture piece. You could also enlarge something small, like an ink bottle or a padlock.

Measure the object you have selected carefully, and draw a pair of elevations of it on a grid of equal-sized squares. For a drawing that is to be about 9 × 12", use ½" squares. (This size is a little coarse for real accuracy, but a good size for practice.)

If you are enlarging an object, use accurate proportions. For example, to enlarge a padlock four times its real size you might decide that ½" on your grid should equal ⅛" on the padlock. This scale would make a 2" padlock 8" high in the drawing.

Next, draw a one-point, or par-allel, perspective of the basic box for the object. To draw the basic box, you need to duplicate your efforts in the previous activity. This time, however, you need to mea-sure the box and center section to fit the proportions of the object you want to draw, at the size you want to draw it. Don't be disturbed by the fact that your vanishing point may be as much as 2' away from the drawing. This distance would be normal for a drawing of this size.

Study Figures 11.8 through 11.14, and follow the same steps to make your drawing.

TECHNIQUE NOTE

Drawing a Curved Object in a Basic Box

To draw the elephant, we expanded points from a center sec-tion outward, using a front eleva-tion as a guide. You can use a different procedure to visualize a solid object with long, smooth curves, such as a boat hull, aircraft fuselage, automobile—or even a human figure—in a basic box. For such an object, use careful estima-tion or measurement, and draw the outlines of transverse (crosswise) sections at several points through the object instead of just the front.

Find the proper spot on the floor of the box, or on the central grid, and project each of these transverse sections into the box; then complete the outline. (See Figure 11.15.)

This kind of drawing will be complex, so use colored pencils: one color for the basic box and cen-ter section, one color for the trans-verse sections, and black for the final outline of the volume.

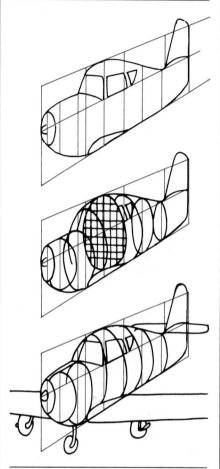

FIGURE 11.15 Irregular, curving shapes are best handled by drawing the shapes of "slices" or sections first by working transparently. Could a care-fully measured basic box be helpful here?

ONE-POINT PERSPECTIVE

You have learned how to fit an object into a basic box in one-point perspective. Now you are ready to do a complete perspective—an interior or scene that you can transfer and render as a complete and accurate drawing in scale.

Remember that it is important to be accurate. Where do the two lines of the X cross in Figure 11.16 (next page)? Not where the vertical line is in the top drawing, nor where it is in the middle drawing. Only the bottom drawing passes the vertical through the true intersection of the X.

In Figure 11.17 is a photograph of tools that are useful in making perspective drawings. They are placed on a drawing board with accurate edges and 90° corners. How to use the mechanical drawing tools is explained in the Technique Note that follows. From left to right, they are:

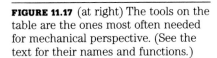

FIGURE 11.16 (above) In mechanical perspective, drawing accuracy is a "must." In which drawing does the vertical line pass through the true intersection?

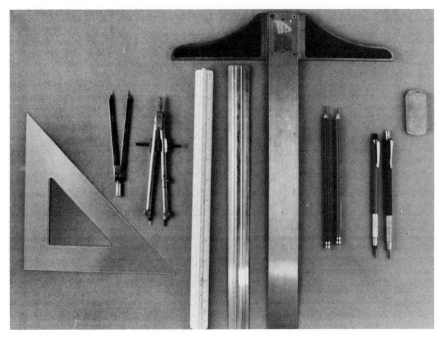

FIGURE 11.17 (at right) The tools on the table are the ones most often needed for mechanical perspective. (See the text for their names and functions.)

- a 45° triangle,
- a pair of dividers,
- a compass,
- an architect's scale (which looks like a triangular ruler),
- an aluminum molding, 4' to 7' long (which can be bought at lumber yards),
- a T square,
- Berol *Verithin* colored pencils,
- two drafting lead holders (you can use pencils), and
- an eraser.

Before you draw, memorize some abbreviations you will need for your first drawings. In these drawings, label points and lines in order to keep track of them. Abbreviations for the items you will need to label on your drawings are listed below. The most important ones are marked with an asterisk. The points and lines are:

- horizon line—HL*
- picture plane—PP
- vanishing point—VP*
- right vanishing point—RVP
- left vanishing point—LVP
- center of vision—CV*
- measuring line—ML
- ground line—GL*
- measuring point—MP*
- true height line—THL*
- station point—SP
- distance line—DIS
- reference line—REF
- reference point—RP

You will need some colored pencils so that you can color-code certain lines to avoid confusion. You might, for instance, use one color for the lines you use to set up the perspective, such as the frame of the picture plane, the horizon line, and the distance line. You can use another color for structural lines, such as basic boxes, grids, and reference lines. You can draw the outlines of the form with a fairly hard pencil at first, transparently, and then go over the lines you would actually see with a blacker pencil. Be sure to keep all of your pencils sharp while you draw.

TECHNIQUE NOTE

Using Mechanical Drawing Tools

Use the *T square* to draw horizontal lines. Hold the T square with its head hanging over the side of the drawing board on the opposite side from your drawing hand. If the head of the T square is against the edge of the board, it will slide up and down this edge so you can draw as many horizontal lines as you like. Don't use it to draw vertical lines.

T square

Use the *triangle* to draw vertical lines. Depending on which edge of the triangle you set on the T square, the triangle will allow you to make vertical lines or lines at 45° angles all across the paper.

Use the *architect's scale* to measure, not to draw straight lines.

Apply the measurements from the scale you choose to the drawing by using the *dividers*. The dividers will also allow you to hold a measurement and repeat it several times.

The *compass* is used to draw circles. Hold the points against the architect's scale to measure a proper radius (length from the center of a circle to its edge).

The light *aluminum molding* is used as a straightedge for lines going to vanishing points. The best kind to buy forms an upside-down T when you look at the end of it (see Figure 11.18). Lines to vanishing points can be 6′ long or longer on a large two-point perspective drawing. Stick a push-pin in the vanishing points to help you locate them with the end of the molding.

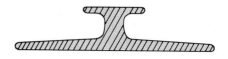

FIGURE 11.18 This is a drawing of a section cut though a long piece of aluminum molding. The molding makes a light, convenient straightedge for reaching distant vanishing points.

STUDIO

Setting Up a One-Point Perspective for a Room

MATERIALS

Tools for perspective drawing (listed above), drawing paper

Draw the room pictured in Figures 11.19 and 11.20 on the next page, using a larger scale and labeling the indicated points and lines. Draw the size and shape of your working area, using a T square and triangle. Label this area as the picture plane (PP).

For this drawing, use a picture plane that is (in scale) 14′ wide and 8′ high, because this is the width and ceiling height of the room. Use a scale in which 1″ equals 1′. (On the architect's scale, this is the scale that has a 1 at the end. The large-sized numerals show measurements for the scale you are

using. The smaller numerals starting at the other end of the scale indicate measurements for the scale of ½″ equals 1′.)

You have removed an end wall of the 14′ wide room and inserted a 14 × 8′ window—the picture plane—in its place. You will need about 8′ (8″ in scale) of empty paper to the right and the same amount below your picture plane for working area. You will need about 3′ to the left side of the picture plane, also. (See Figure 11.19.)

Next, decide where your eye level should be (how high). Draw your horizon line (HL) across the picture plane at that height, and label it. Extend it several inches beyond the right side of the picture plane. In our illustrations, we used an average eye level for a standing person of 5′4″ above the ground (or in scale 5⅓″). Since an ordinary ruler isn't divided into thirds of inches, if you use a ruler instead of an architect's scale, you have to estimate that ⅓″ is just a bit larger than 5/16″.

Label the bottom line of the picture plane as the measuring line or ground line (ML or GL). This line is used for measuring and marks where the picture plane touches the ground or floor. Label the right vertical of the picture plane as the true height line (THL). Actually, any vertical that climbs up the picture plane from the measuring line or ground line can be a true height line, but right now you only have two of these, and you only need to label one.

Now find the center of vision (CV) at the midpoint on the horizon, and label it. Also label it *VP* because in a one-point perspective it is also the one and only vanishing point. From this vanishing point, draw a **distance line** (DIS) vertically (using your T square and triangle) down toward the bottom of the paper, and label it.

Now find your station point. This is the place on the distance line where you could stand in order to see all of the room without distortion. The station point marks your distance from the center of vision.

triangle
architect's scale
dividers

compass
aluminum molding

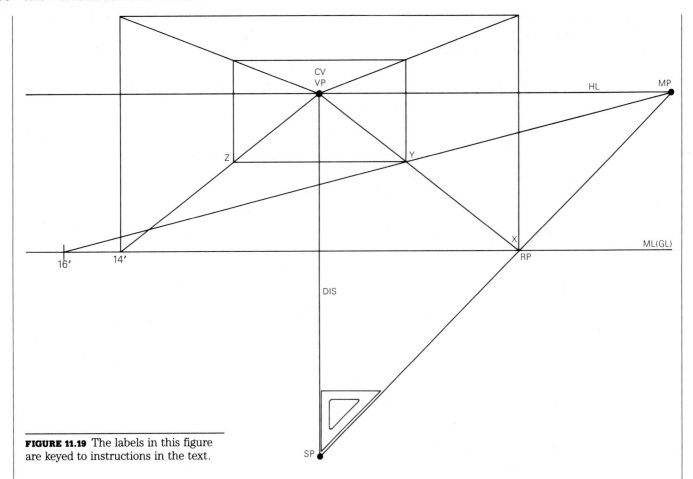

FIGURE 11.19 The labels in this figure are keyed to instructions in the text.

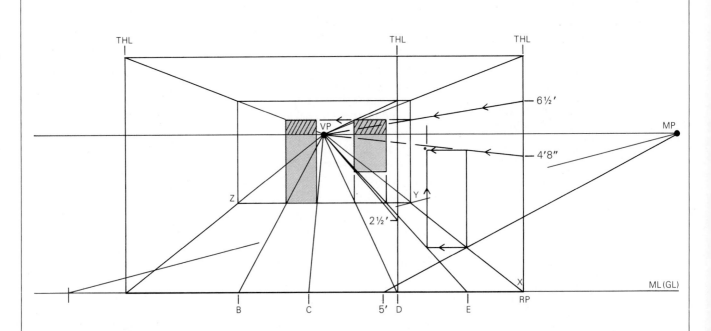

FIGURE 11.20 The labels in this figure are keyed to instructions in the text.

To find the station point, lay one of the short legs of the 45° triangle against the right side of the distance line, with the 45° angle pointing down. (See Figure 11.19.) Slide the triangle up or down until an extension of this angle would just touch the lower right corner of the picture plane.

Extend this forty-five-degree line up until it crosses the horizon line out to the right of the picture plane. The place where this line started on the distance line is where you are standing, or the station point (SP). Where it crosses the horizon line is a **measuring point** (MP). Mark these points and label them.

You now have located all the points and lines necessary for drawing an accurate one-point, or parallel, perspective of the room. You may cut off most of the distance line and the station point now, if they are in the way. You are finished with them.

Extend lines back to the vanishing point from both lower corners of the picture plane. Any lines that originate on the ground line at the picture plane and go to a vanishing point are called **reference lines** (REF). The points on the ground line where they originate—in this case the corners—are called **reference points** (RP). Mark and label these.

These particular reference lines form the right and left edges of the floor of the room. If you eliminated the walls and ceiling, they could form the right and left edges of any piece of ground you chose. But since you are building a room, you must find a place at the back end to cut the room off and build a wall. Right now the floor goes on forever—back to the horizon, like a road. To cut off the room at a depth of 16′ (a good length for a small room), we must measure 16′ *left* from the right reference point on the measuring line.

From that point at 16′ (16″ in scale) on the measuring line, draw a line up to the measuring point on the right end of the horizon. Where this line crosses the right reference line that goes back to the vanishing point (at Y in Figure 11.19) is 16′ back into the picture along that reference line and *only* along that reference line. The right side of the floor, then, is Line X-Y. The line from the measuring line's 16′ mark measures depth *only* on the right reference line.

To find a point 16′ back toward the horizon on any other line besides the reference line, carry that measurement straight across horizontally from the right reference line. This is what you will do to cut off the left reference line and form the back edge of the floor with Line Y-Z.

Now look at Figure 11.20. You will build a ceiling and some walls. Take lines from the top corners of the picture plane back to the vanishing point. These are the edges of the ceiling. Cut them off by raising verticals from the back corners of the floor, 16′ back at Points Y and Z. Next, connect the back upper corners to form the rear of the ceiling to complete the back wall.

How high is the room on the true height line at the right front of the picture plane? How is this height transferred in the picture to the back corner of the room? Is the left vertical edge of the picture plane also a true height line?

Remember that measurements made at the picture plane are true or full measurements from your scale, but measurements aren't true anywhere beyond the picture plane. To get correct proportions farther back into the picture, you must carry a reference line from a true height line or measuring line back toward a vanishing point until the reference line crosses the distant line you want to measure. The

line back in the picture to which you are carrying the measurement must also be in the same plane (in this case the right-hand wall) as the true height line or measuring line you are using.

STUDIO

Adding a Door and Window to the Room

MATERIALS

Tools for perspective drawing, drawing paper

Now that you have drawn a room in the previous activity, you can add a back door and window to it. Remember to find points and lines on the floor first. Refer to Figure 11.20 for locations of points and lines.

Make a door in the back wall that is 6½′ high and 2½′ wide. Set it 4′ from the left-hand wall toward the center. On the measuring line at the front, measure left from the reference point and mark 4′ for the distance from the wall and then 2½′ more for the width of the door (Points B and C in Figure 11.20). Carry these measurements to the back wall by drawing lines to the vanishing point. Where these lines cross the back wall, raise vertical lines for the sides of the door.

Measure up 6½′ on the true height line at the right front corner of the room. By taking a line to the vanishing point and turning left where it crosses the rear corner of the room, take the measurement horizontally (parallel to the horizon) across the back wall to cut off the vertical lines of the door at the right height in perspective.

Now put a window in that back wall, too. Make it 2½′ wide, 4′ high, and 2½′ above the floor. Put it about 24″ from the right wall (24″

equals 2′). Measure 2′, then 2½′ more (the width of the window) from the right-hand wall on the ground at the picture plane (Points D and E). From these points extend lines to the vanishing point. Raise verticals from the points of intersection (where the two reference lines from Points D and E cross the rear line of the floor) on the rear wall.

The process of measuring heights on the right front corner true height line, taking them to the back of the room, turning a corner, and using the T square to take them across horizontally to the back wall is complicated. There is a more direct route.

Raise a new true height line at Point D, which will be in the same plane as the window (Line D-VP). Measure up 2½′ from the floor on this new true height line. Then carry the measurement back to the vanishing point until it crosses the left side of the window, and turn a small corner to the right, taking the line horizontally to the right vertical of the window. Having found the height from the floor to the bottom of the window, find the height of the top on the same true height line. Carry this height back to the same vertical and finish the window. Is there another way to find the top of the window without measuring?

Locating Points Within a Room

MATERIALS

Tools for perspective drawing, drawing paper

By now you may have realized that the room you have drawn is a giant basic box. You can locate any point you want within it.

Let's imagine that a gnat just flew into the room. He is hovering 5′ from the front of the room and 2′ from the right wall at an altitude of 4′ 8″ from the floor. Find the gnat by locating the spot on the floor above which he is hanging.

Measure left on the ground line from the reference point a distance of 5′ (as you did to find the 16′ depth of the whole floor). Carry a line to the measuring point. This line will measure 5′ back along the right edge where it crosses the floor. Mark this measurement on the right edge of the floor (which is also a reference line).

Draw a line horizontally to the left from this measurement on the reference line. It will be 5′ back into the picture. To find out how long this line should be, measure 2′ left (again from the reference point) on the ground line. Note: you have made this measurement once before. Carry that measurement back toward the vanishing point until it crosses the horizontal line on the floor at a point 5′ back into the picture and 2′ from the right-hand wall.

Raise a vertical; you know that the gnat is hanging 4′ 8″ above the floor on that vertical. Measure 4′ 8″ up on the true height line at the front corner. Take that height measurement back along the wall to the vanishing point.

Raise a vertical from the floor up at a point 5′ back on the reference line. The line 4′ 8″ high on the wall will cross it. Where it crosses, turn left to find the gnat's location.

TECHNIQUE NOTE

Making Measurements Behind the Picture Plane

Using true height lines to make correct scale height measurements works only at the picture plane. These measurements must be transferred back into the picture by

extending them toward the vanishing point until they cross a vertical line drawn in the same receding plane as the true height line.

The ground line or measuring line is at the picture plane, but it can be used to make both width measurements and depth measurements. Width measurements can be carried back into the perspective by drawing lines along the floor to the vanishing point. Depth measurements must be made to the left from a reference point and then carried to the right reference line by using a measuring point on the right end of the horizon line.

This system can be reversed, however, if you are left-handed, or if you need to use a left reference point for some other reason. Find a measuring point on the left end of the horizon line the same way you found one on the right end. Measure to the right to find depth measurements from your left reference point.

Drawing Furniture in the Room

MATERIALS

Tools for perspective drawing, tracing vellum, drawing paper

You know about setting up a one-point perspective for building a room or large basic box. You can find any point in space you wish. Now you can furnish the room you have drawn (Figure 11.21). Project the basic boxes for furniture into it. Then carefully project the furniture by measuring it point by point, *or* carefully draw the furniture freehand into the boxes.

Using one or two tracing vellum overlays may help in the process. You can see through an overlay to

KEY

1 Table width and location	8 Plan of hanging lamp
2 Table distance back and length	9 Width of lamp on floor
3 THL for table	10 Plan on floor
4 Height of table	11 THL for lamp
5 Thickness of tabletop	12 Top of lamp
6 Locating legs on floor	13 Bottom of lamp
7 Center of floor (X'ed)	

FIGURE 11.21 Use the instructions below to add a hanging lamp and table to your one-point perspective drawing of a room.

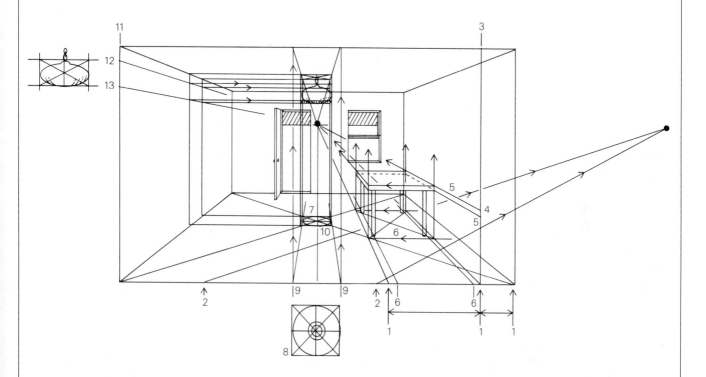

To draw the lamp:

A. Locate distance from left wall.
B. Take line to vanishing point.
C. Locate distance back into room (from reference point).
D. Draw line to measuring point.
E. Draw horizontal line to left, crossing line drawn in step B.
F. Draw vertical line from intersection (length not known).
G. Draw vertical line up right wall and left across ceiling.
H. Locate center of lamp.
 I. Find width of lamp globe on measuring line, 9″ from either side of center, and carry back to vanishing point.
J. Find depth of lamp globe on measuring line (it is circular), and carry back to measuring point crossing reference line (floor).
K. Raise verticals from crossing point at floor up to ceiling.
L. Carry lines across from ceiling intersection.
M. Carry lines across from floor intersection with lines drawn in step J.
N. Draw sides of box for hanging lamp base and globe, and carry up to ceiling.

To draw the table:

(Note that a left measuring point has been added on the horizon.)

A. Place width of table on measuring line at desired distance from wall, and carry lines to vanishing point.
B. Measure distance into drawing of front and rear edges of table (measure from *left* reference point on measuring line).
C. Draw lines from wall to cross width lines of table.
D. Measure height of table on *newly erected* true height line, and carry to vanishing point.
E. Raise verticals for corners of box.
F. Carry lines from intersection to form top of basic box.

find all of your points. You might want to make a composite tracing from your base sheet and overlays on good vellum. Then you could mount and mat this finished drawing.

Figure 11.21 on page 211 shows you how to add a table and a hanging light to the room. There are numbered steps for you to follow to draw these items. If you make the drawing large enough, there is no limit to the details you can accurately project into the room. Whether details are projected accurately or drawn freehand by estimation, add many of them.

Some of the details will require research, but they will also make your drawing much more believable. These details include door facings, moldings in windows and on the edges of tables, thickness of walls seen at the edges of doors and windows, rugs on the floor, pictures on the walls, handles attached to drawers, and any important decorative features.

In addition to these, anything seen through the window should be indicated, even if aerial perspective makes it much dimmer than things close at hand. Another way to add realism is to draw the thickness of very narrow objects such as lamp cords or curtain tiebacks. Never treat these items just as single lines.

TWO-POINT PERSPECTIVE

In Chapter 6 you learned that people hardly ever draw faces or objects at a 90° angle. This means that their picture planes are seldom parallel to the nearest side of every object in the picture. Because this is true, one-point perspective is less useful in showing the ''real world'' than is two-point perspective.

Two-point perspective can show us two sides of any object we choose to represent. If we put our horizon line high enough, two-point perspective can also show us the tops of these objects. Like one-point perspective, it can help us draw each object at the correct size for that object's location in the picture.

Besides being a tool for making accurate imitational drawings, two-point perspective is valuable in other ways. Like one-point perspective, it helps us to see the way things are put together because it forces us to draw transparently. It also helps us see objects as they are placed in relation to other objects because we must learn to locate them on the ground first. Finally, it makes us better judges of size relationships of both close and distant objects seen at an angle to our line of vision.

The method we will use to project a two-point (angular) perspective requires the use of a plan and either an elevation or a good set of notes and sketches on vertical dimensions. This method is sometimes referred to by architects and interior designers as the **office method**. You can draw a **plan** of your own on a piece of paper on which you have drawn a grid with squares of a convenient size. The plan needs only the exterior lines and details of the object you are drawing. In most cases, interiors are unnecessary in a plan; but remember: *the scale of the plan will determine the scale of the perspective.*

Setting Up a Two-Point Perspective Drawing of a Barn

MATERIALS

Tools for perspective drawing, tracing vellum, drawing paper

In this activity you will set up a perspective for the outdoor scene pictured in Figures 11.22 through 11.25 and draw the barn. You will base your drawing on a plan and elevation. This activity may seem complicated, but if you study the illustrations and follow the directions closely, you will find that the drawing can be completed fairly quickly.

First, redraw the plan and elevation in Figure 11.22 (on the next page) on tracing vellum. Use a scale that is twice the size of the scale of the textbook drawing. This larger scale will allow you to draw the details of the barn and shouldn't require vanishing points located off your drawing board.

Don't draw the plan at the slanted angle used in Figure 11.22. Fasten your paper to the drawing board parallel to the sides (use your T square), and draw the plan straight and parallel to the paper. You can fold back a corner and tape the plan at the proper angle on your drawing later.

Use dividers to measure small dimensions in Figure 11.22. Then hold the points against your architect's scale or ruler to translate them into inches. (The lines on most architect's scales are grooved to catch the point of the dividers.) Double each measurement before you draw.

Remember that none of the basic things you have learned about linear perspective have changed just because the drawing has become more complex. The horizon is still at eye level. Parallel lines moving back away from you (and the picture plane) still come together at a common vanishing point. Vanishing points are still on the horizon. Draw everything

- in a basic box,
- on the ground first, and
- transparently.

After you have completed your scaled-up plan of the barn, silo, and hay bale shed, you will need to tape the plan securely to the top of the paper on which you will project your perspective. Attach the plan to the picture plane at an angle that allows you to see what you wish from your station point (8 in Figure 11.22). What you must do is to look down on top of yourself, the picture plane, and the center of vision (2), just as you look down on the plan (1).

In other words, you must see everything first as a plan. The picture plane becomes a straight line, just like the edge of a pane of glass. A line from your station point to the picture plane marks the center of vision on the plan of the picture plane. This is the distance line.

You don't know yet how far away you must stand on the distance line, but looking down on things will help you decide where to put the plan in reference to the center of vision and the angle at which to put it. If the angle is very sharp on one side, the vanishing point for lines on that side will be far out on the horizon in that direction.

Our plan isn't set exactly at a forty-five-degree angle to the picture plane, but the view is fairly evenly balanced. If we had needed to see a great deal more of one side than the other, we would have tilted the plan more and used a distant vanishing point on that side and a closer one on the other.

For most perspective drawings, you will place the center of the plan approximately opposite the center of vision on the picture plane. Usually you will allow one of the basic boxes to touch the picture plane with a front corner. In this case, we have used the basic box for the barn.

Draw a line across the top of your paper for the plan of the picture plane, and locate and mark a center of vision. Then measure the distance between the corner of the basic box for the barn and the center of vision in Figure 11.22. Double this distance (two times the scale of the illustration), and mark the spot for the corner of the barn.

To get the right angle, lay a piece of vellum over the page in the book. Carefully trace the two lines of the corner of the barn and the line of the picture plane. Then duplicate this angle when you tape your plan to the picture plane on your drawing. (You will have to cut off or fold under one corner of your plan.)

The perspective drawing could be projected anywhere directly above or below (or even on) the plan, but artists usually project it below the plan. With this in mind, drop down below the picture plane and draw the horizon line (3) and ground line (4) all the way across your paper. The distance between the plan of the picture plane and the horizon line doesn't matter, but you want to leave plenty of space to make your drawing.

The distance between the horizon line and the ground line, however, is important. This distance is the height of the horizon above the ground that determines eye level—how high or low you are standing while you look at the barn. Measure the distance in Figure 11.22. Don't forget to double it when you put the horizon line and ground line on your drawing.

Now you have changed from seeing things *in plan* to seeing them *in elevation*. The horizon and the ground line (bottom of the picture plane) are in elevation. You are projecting things down from a plan onto a vertical picture plane as a perspective illusion. Look at Figure 11.22 to see the early steps in setting up the projection.

You have indicated your center of vision on the plan of the picture plane a little to the left of the corner of the plan for the barn (2).

Drop a line from this point to the bottom of the page for a distance line (5).

How far away you stand is just as important in two-point perspective as it is in one-point perspective to prevent distortion in the image you draw. If you are too close, the image is distorted, like one photographed using a wide-angle lens. The perspective is greatly exaggerated because the vanishing points are too close together.

FIGURE 11.22 Don't be intimidated by this finished perspective. Read the text, and follow the process one step at a time.

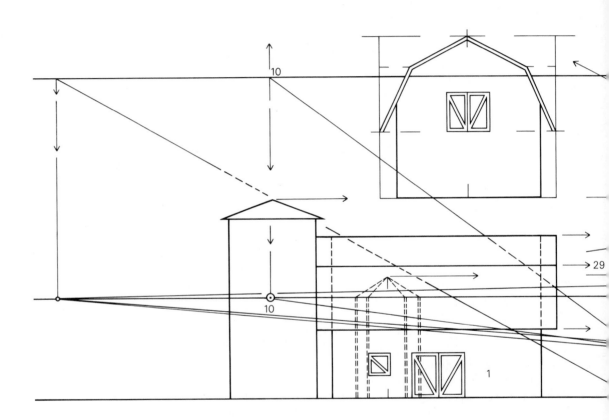

KEY

1	Plan and elevation
2	Center of vision on PP
3	Horizon line
4	Ground or measuring line
5	Distance line
6	Plan of visual cone
7	Base of visual cone in plan
8	Station Point
9	Circular base of visual cone
10	Right and left Vanishing Points (Barn)
11	Legs of 90° angle at SP
12	THL for basic box (barn)
13	Reference Point
14	Line to SP from rear corner
15	Vertical to Reference Line
16	Line from rear corner to SP
17	Vertical from PP to REF
18	Hidden corner, floor of basic box
19	Verticals up from corners
20	True (PP) height of box
21	Top line of box to VP
22	Top rear line to VP
23	Line from hidden corner to SP
24	Line from PP to box corner
25	Line from center of plan to SP
26	From PP vertically to center of box
27	From plan of roof angle to SP
28	From PP down front of box
29	Height of roof angle
30	Connecting front wall to PP
31	Vertical from PP to ground line
32	To LVP along base of wall
33	Locating rear corner

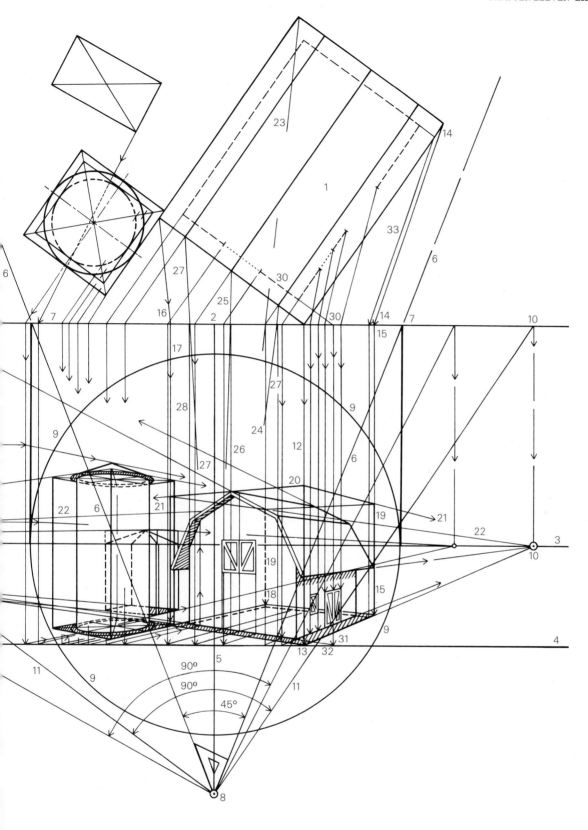

In a two-point perspective, use what is called a **cone of vision** to determine how far down the distance line to locate your station point. The cone of vision, or visual cone, is imaginary. Your eyes are at the point of this cone. The cone's circular base is on the picture plane. In this circle, you can see things clearly without moving your head. The farther you move away, the farther your vision spreads and the larger the circular base of the cone becomes. The farther you move away, the more you can see without distortion.

Though a forty-five-degree angle isn't precisely accurate for human vision, it is close enough to avoid serious distortion. You can use a 45° triangle.

You are looking down from above on the distance line (5), so you see the distance line in plan. To see the cone of vision in plan, lay the triangle on the distance line with the distance line bisecting one of the forty-five-degree angles (cutting the angle in half). Lines marked 6 indicate the sides of the visual cone in the plan view.

It will be helpful to mark on your triangle a line that bisects one of the forty-five-degree angles all the way across the opposite leg. This is the line you will lay on the distance line while using the triangle as a cone of vision in the plan view. Draw the forty-five-degree angle on paper first, and bisect it. Then lay the plastic triangle over it carefully, tape it down, and scratch the bisecting line in the plastic using a straightedge and something with a sharp point, like the point of a compass.

Slide the forty-five-degree angle down the distance line, extending the sides of the angle and letting the sides cross the plan of the picture plane. Make sure the sides are far enough apart to clear the outer edges of the plan of the objects you will draw (6). Don't forget that the objects have height as well as width.

The place where the legs of the angle cross the plan of the picture plane indicates the diameter of the base of your visual cone (Line 7-7). The place where the point of your triangle is resting on the distance line is your station point (8).

The heavy lines dropped from each side of the base of the visual cone (7) will cross the horizon. These lines indicate the diameter of the circular base of the visual cone in elevation (9). The center of vision, in elevation, is the spot where the distance line crosses the horizon line. If you put the point of the compass on this center of vision and expand it until you have the radius correct, you can draw the circular base of the visual cone on the picture plane in elevation. Nothing projected into this circle will have any noticeable distortion.

You only need two more things to start your projection. These are the right and left vanishing points marked 10 in Figure 11.22 on page 215. The two upper vanishing points are the ones in the plan view on the picture plane. The two lower vanishing points are the *working* vanishing points you will

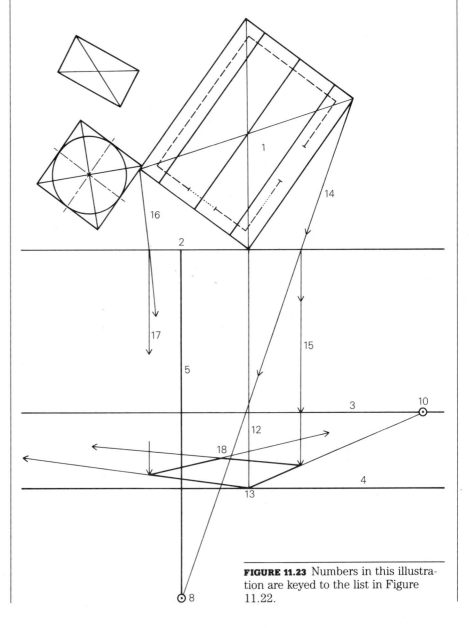

FIGURE 11.23 Numbers in this illustration are keyed to the list in Figure 11.22.

use for the barn and silo, so they are on the horizon. To find them, proceed as follows.

The lines marked 11 are the legs of a ninety-degree angle with its apex, or point, on the station point. The right leg is parallel to the right side of the *plan* of the basic box for the barn. To find it, extend the line for the side of the plan of the basic box until its end is even with your station point. You can tell when they are even by using the ninety-degree angle of your triangle. Measure the distance between them; then draw Line 11 so it remains parallel to the plan. The left leg is parallel to the left side of the plan. The points at which these legs cross the picture plane (at 10) are the vanishing points in the plan. Directly below these on the horizon line (at 10) are the working vanishing points seen in elevation.

Now you are ready to draw the floor of the barn, so look at Figure 11.23 on the opposite page. (Figure 11.24 will help you draw the walls.) You will start by locating the true height line (12) and the reference point (13).

You can find the true height line and reference point for the basic box for the barn easily because the corner of the basic box is touching the picture plane in the plan. To transfer this reference point to the perspective, drop the true height line straight down from it (with a ninety-degree angle) until the line touches the ground line. The true height line, 12 (also the corner of the basic box), and the reference point, 13, are ready to use.

To locate the front edges of the floor of the basic box, draw reference lines (marked 14) from the reference point to each vanishing point—right and left. Now you must find the rear corners of the floor to know where to cut off these front edges and draw the back edges.

The place marked 14 indicates a line that is drawn from the plan of

the rear corner of the basic box to the station point. It crosses the picture plane. This point where it crosses the picture plane then should be dropped vertically to the reference line at the floor of the basic box to find the rear corner (15).

Any point along a line in the plan (like the rear corner) can be projected to the proper spot on its corresponding reference line in the perspective. Just transfer it to the picture plane with a line aimed at the station point. Where it crosses the picture plane, drop it vertically to the reference line in the perspective (15).

You will follow this same process to find the rear corner of the floor on the left side. Look at 16 and follow the line to the picture plane. Then turn (17) and follow the line to the floor of the box (reference line, left). There is the other rear corner of the floor. You can find the hidden corner of the basic box—the one farthest back in space—by drawing lines from the corners you just located (15 and 17) to the opposite vanishing points. These lines will cross at the hidden corner (18).

If a reference line, like the side of our basic box, didn't exist for the

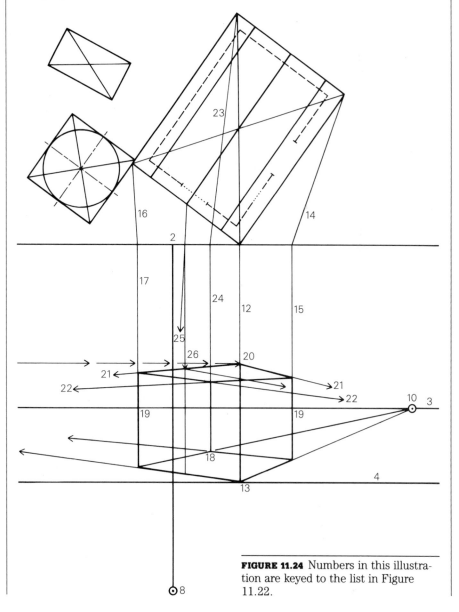

FIGURE 11.24 Numbers in this illustration are keyed to the list in Figure 11.22.

point you wanted to project, you could draw one through this desired point in the plan. You would draw it parallel to one side of a basic box and connect it to the picture plane. From there, a vertical could be dropped to the ground line and carried to a vanishing point. This process would create a new reference point, a new reference line, and a true height line for heights in the same plane as that reference line.

Now it is time to raise verticals from all four corners of the floor of the box (19 in Figure 11.24 on page 217). If you knew where to cut these verticals off, you could put a roof on the box and put the barn in it.

Fortunately, one corner of the box (the closest one) is up against the picture plane because that corner of the plan touches the picture plane. Any vertical line that rises from the ground line against the picture plane is a true height line. It can be used to measure any other vertical rising from its reference lines. These reference lines extend from the base of a true height line along the ground to the vanishing points. Since the right and left edges of the floor of the box are such reference lines, you can measure the true height up from the ground (in scale, of course), just as we have indicated at 20.

We determined this height by transferring it straight across with a T square from the elevation at the left (1). We placed this elevation on the ground line to make this procedure convenient. It isn't necessary, however, for the elevation to be located there. You don't even need an elevation if you have good sketches with notes about the various heights. If you had these, you could just use an architect's scale and dividers to determine height.

The lines marked 21 are the top front edges of the box extended to the vanishing points. The lines marked 22 are the top rear edges of the box that start from where the front edges cross the verticals 15 and 17 and go back to the opposite vanishing points.

If you would like to check your accuracy, draw a line (23) from the rear corner of the box in the plan to the station point. Where it crosses the picture plane, drop down a line at a ninety-degree angle (24). This line should go right down the rear corner of your basic box in the perspective projection.

Next, find the peak and angles of the roof. This is fairly easy because the roof fills the basic box completely to its walls. (The walls of the barn don't reach the walls of the basic box because the roof has a large overhang. See the dotted line in the plan for the barn walls.) The roof fills the basic box horizontally, and its peak touches the top of the box. Find the top center of the basic box, and carry a line to the vanishing point on the right. Line 25 extends toward the station

FIGURE 11.25 Numbers in this illustration are keyed to the list in Figure 11.22.

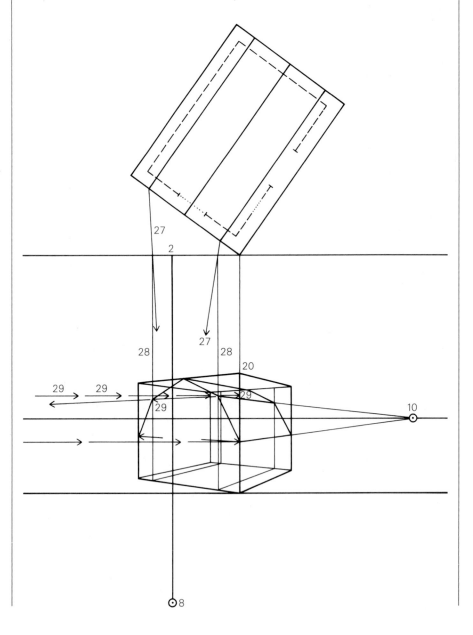

point until it reaches the picture plane. Then the line turns to become line 26, which touches the center of the basic box.

The secondary breaks in the roof slope are a little more difficult to draw than the roof's top line. Although these angles touch the front of the box, you don't know how far they are from the ground. First, find these secondary breaks on the ground. Look at Figure 11.25 on the opposite page. The two lines marked 27 take the secondary roof angles to the picture plane toward the station point. The lines marked 28 take them to the ground, where they cross the reference line that is the front of the basic box's floor. These secondary roof angles are at points somewhere on the lines, but how high are they? The height of these secondary peaks in the elevation is marked 29. You can carry that height from the elevation over to the true height line.

Take the height of the eaves from the true height line to Lines 28. When all points are connected, you will have drawn the shape of the roof against the front of the basic box. Extend lines to the proper vanishing points, raise verticals at the rear wall, and the roof is done.

In Figure 11.22, you may have noticed a line going up and to the left as a continuation of the top front slope of the roof. The point where this line crosses a vertical raised from the left vanishing point locates a vanishing point for that particular slope of the roof.

This extra vanishing point can help when you need to draw chimneys, shingles, or skylights. The lower slope also has a vanishing point, but it would be much higher up on the vertical from the left vanishing point.

If you can find the base of the barn walls on the ground, you can draw the rest of the barn freehand. In the plan, the foundation is

shown by a broken line with openings for the doors and windows. As you can see, this line is set back a bit from the edge of the basic box.

First, extend a side of the foundation until it reaches the picture plane. In Figure 11.26 below, 30 shows the side we used. In the illustration, 31 is the point at the ground line where a vertical dropped from its intersection with the picture plane ended. A line from there to the left vanishing point (32) will extend along the front lower edge of the barn wall. The edge going to the right vanish-

ing point can be found in the same way. You can see how the rear corner is cut off in the usual way by looking at 33. Line 33 is correct both in Figure 11.26 and in Figure 11.22. What is the difference? Windows and doors can also be projected down from the plan this way.

At this point most artists would probably raise some verticals at the corners and draw the roof overhang, windows, and doors by careful estimation.

FIGURE 11.26 Numbers in this illustration are keyed to the list in Figure 11.22.

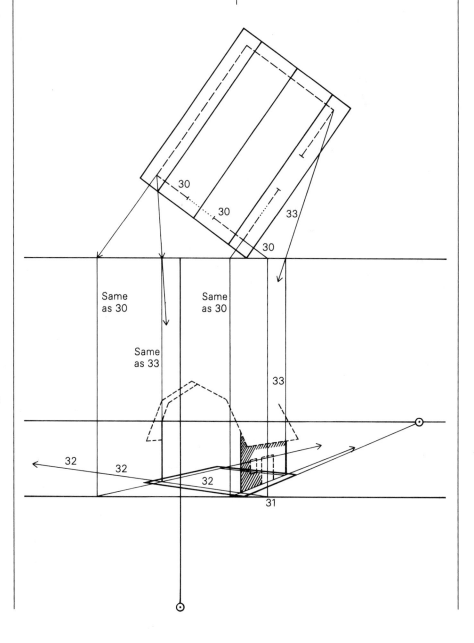

STUDIO

Adding a Silo and Hay Bale Shed to the Scene

MATERIALS

Tools for perspective drawing, drawing paper

There are two other items that you should draw in the barn scene with some accuracy. They are the silo, which is a cylinder, and the shed, which is set at a different angle from the barn. Draw the points and lines labeled in Figures 11.27 and 11.28 in their numbered order.

FIGURE 11.27 Follow the instructions in the text to draw circles in perspective.

The silo is a cylinder, a circle with walls raised around it. It is really an infinite number of circles stacked on top of each other. Imagine that you are standing on the ground and can see all of the circles, like a series of slices across a vertical sausage. None of the shapes would look like circles, and no two of them would be exactly the same.

The ones above our eye level (horizon line) would get fatter and fatter as they went higher and higher. The ones below our eye level would get fatter and fatter as they went farther down. What would happen to the one right at our eye level on the horizon?

To start the silo drawing, look at Figure 11.27. (The horizon is higher in this drawing than in Figures 11.22 through 11.26 to make it easier to see the ellipse on the ground.)

We will call these circles in perspective *ellipses*, although using this name isn't precisely correct. An ellipse is a regular geometric shape in plans or elevations. These are irregular shapes because they are in perspective.

To construct a cylinder, you must start at the ground and put the cylinder in a basic box. On the floor of the basic box, draw the ellipse, which will touch the basic box at four points. These points are at the center of each side of the basic box. Look at the circle in the square, which is the plan of the silo.

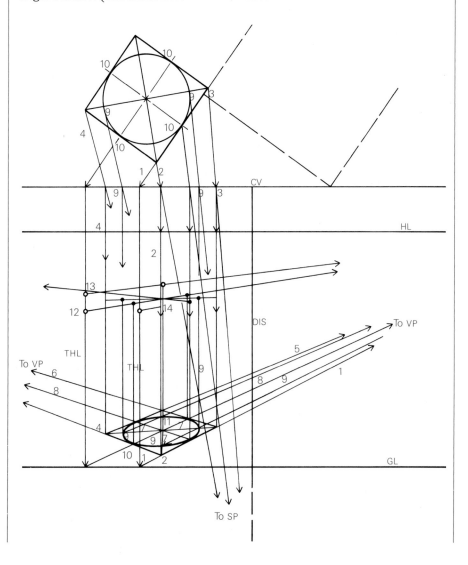

KEY

1–6	Project square to ground
7	X the square corner to corner
8	Line to VPs through center
9	Project points where circle crosses X
10	Points where circle touches sides of box
11	Freehand ellipse through 8 points (This is the silo roof projected onto the ground)
12	True height of roof eaves
13	True height of peak
14	Raise spokes to height of eaves

To find the center of a square in perspective, draw an X through it. The cross of the X is the center, and if you draw lines to the opposite vanishing points through the center, the lines will cross the edges of the floor at the center of each side. These center marks are where the curve of the ellipse touches the four sides of the box. They are also where the long arcs and the short arcs of the ellipse start and stop. The arcs cross the diagonals of the X. To find those locations, use your plan and project the points down onto the diagonals in the basic box.

You have marked the eight points at which the ellipse crosses the spokes of a wheel-like structure. You can slide the hub of this ''wheel'' and the attached spokes up and down a central pole or axis of the cylinder to draw all of the other ellipses you need without building basic boxes for them. Use the true height line for the central plane to find their height. Then carry the points where the ellipse crosses the spokes straight up or down with the triangle.

To draw the ellipses freehand, you can draw through the eight points. Remember that no matter how narrow they get, ellipses never have pointed ends. As ellipses move higher or lower, above or below eye level (the horizon), they get fatter. At exactly eye level, they become a straight, horizontal line.

Draw the box, draw the ellipses at bottom and top, connect the ellipses with lines, and you have drawn the silo. The roof is an upside-down cone. Extend the central axis up. Then connect it on the ground with a reference line from a vanishing point through its base to the picture plane. Use a true height line, and find its peak. Mark this height on the central axis by taking a line toward the vanishing point. Connect the peak to the sides of the silo.

A two-point perspective can include objects turned at different angles to the picture plane, as in Figure 11.28. The hay bale shed in the plan in Figure 11.22 is at a different angle from the barn. It needs a different pair of vanishing points. Each object that is sitting at a different angle in the plan must have new vanishing points. (The silo, being a cylinder, has no angles, so any accurate set of vanishing points could be used to draw it.)

To find vanishing points for the shed, use Figure 11.28. You will have a new set of vanishing points, a new true height line, and a new reference line for the front of the basic box for the shed. Look back at Figure 11.22 to review how to find these items.

FIGURE 11.28 Study this drawing as you reread directions for locating vanishing points.

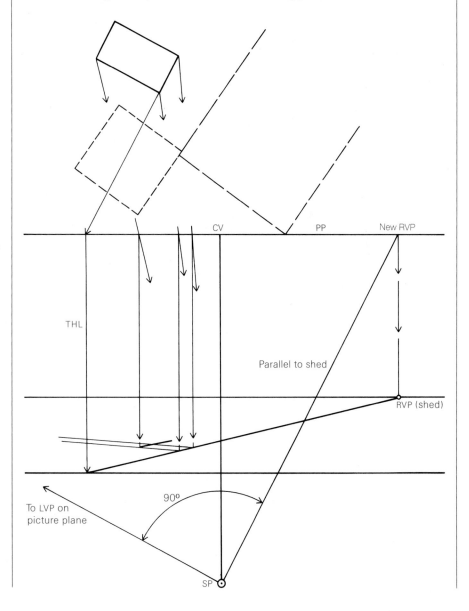

DRAWING AT WORK

Civil Engineer: Drawings to Build On

Civil engineering is a branch of engineering that deals mainly with land surveying, highway building, and construction of waterways and pipelines. Civil engineers use drawing skills in a variety of situations. According to Mike Pearson of Mingus Associates Consulting Engineers and Land Surveyors, Cottonwood, Arizona, about sixty percent of their work involves drawing.

Pearson came to civil engineering with a solid drawing background. He graduated from a trade school as an architectural drafter. He then became a civil engineer trainee in Phoenix, Arizona, and fifteen years later became part owner of Mingus Associates. The company has clients in both the public and private sectors. Pearson's responsibilities include supervision of the field work and design of water and sewer lines.

In general, two types of drawings are needed to complete a civil engineering job. First, surveys and calculations are made in the field. A surveyor's report should include the measurements of the site and all natural and man-made features that will affect the new construction. The ability to draw accurately is essential.

Sometimes the information in the field is too complicated to express in words. In that event, a *plane table survey* is taken in which the surveyor sketches the landscape. To do this, a surveyor uses a *plane table*, which is a special drawing board mounted on a tripod (a three-legged stand). The plane table is equipped with an *alidade* that indicates degrees and angles. This tool helps the surveyor accurately plot maps.

Later, drafters use the surveyor's sketches and calculations to prepare clear working plans and detailed drawings. These drawings document the calculations and must be precise. Drafters use large, tilted tables, protractors, compasses, triangles, T squares, India ink, and sheets of Mylar (thin, strong sheets made from polyester). The drawings must contain specific details since they will be used to guide construction. The ability to draw accurately is essential.

Pearson notes that many people employed as civil engineers started as trainees and then learned on the job. He believes that working in a rather small firm can sometimes offer a person more opportunities for growth than working a large company can because assignments in a small firm are varied. Pearson thinks that hardworking, dedicated people can succeed in civil engineering occupations. He says ''the sky's the limit'' if a person is willing to work.

CHAPTER TWELVE

Cartooning

OBJECTIVES

After reading this chapter and doing the activities, you will be able to

■ discuss the relative importance of the verbal and visual aspects of a cartoon;

■ name three types of cartoons;

■ develop a system for creating, organizing, and publishing gag cartoons;

■ make caricatures; and

■ draw a comic strip.

Cartoonists often say, "Cartooning is a serious business." In fact, it is a serious multimillion-dollar business. Cartooning can be compared to the fields of show business and professional sports. It is glamorous, those at the top of the field are highly paid, and only a very few who would like to be cartoonists can actually earn their living that way.

You may be among those very few who become professional cartoonists. Even if you don't, you can have fun with cartooning and contribute your cartoons to everything from your school newspaper to your favorite candidate's election campaign.

No one knows where or when cartooning actually started, but it is a very old form of drawing. The drawing in Figure 12.1 (next page) is a copy of one of the rock paintings at Tassili-n-ajjer ("Plateau of Rivers") in the North African desert. These paintings were made perhaps as long as six thousand years ago. Experts believe that this drawing was meant to be humorous. There is little doubt that one ancient Egyptian drawing is an unflattering caricature of the father of Tutankhamen, an Egyptian king.

The name *cartoon* is sometimes given to drawings other than the kinds of cartoons you are familiar with. Artists who create murals (pictures on walls) refer to preliminary drawings on paper as *cartoons*. The detail of the drawing for Peter Rogers's mural in Figure 12.2 is this kind of cartoon. (The word *cartoon* came from the Italian *cartone*, which referred to a cheap paper. Our word *carton* came from the same source.)

Today, we use the word *cartoon* to refer to animated cartoons, comic strips, caricatures, and

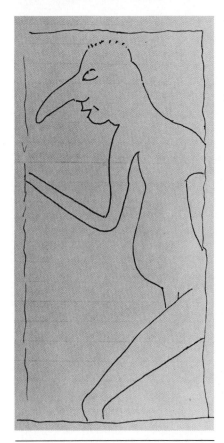

FIGURE 12.1 Perhaps one of the oldest cartoons in existence. It was painted on a rock in the North African desert.

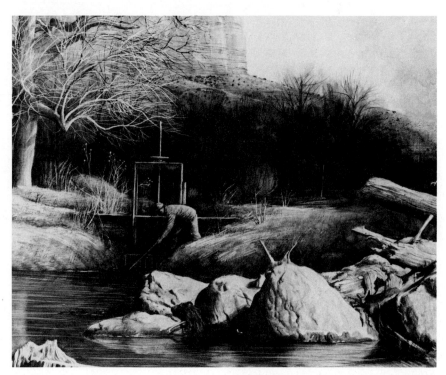

FIGURE 12.2 Many people don't know that the word *cartoon* can be used as the name of a preliminary drawing for a mural. This one was done by Peter Rogers in preparation for a mural (see detail of mural in Chapter 6).
Courtesy of the Museum of Texas Tech University, Lubbock, TX.

humorous drawings. The animated cartoons at the movies or on Saturday morning television are examples of cartoons produced by a team effort. These cartoons require the work of writers, senior creative drawing personnel, animators, and inkers.

Traditionally, a beginning animation cartoonist works as an animation cell inker. (You can see an animation cell in Figure 12.3.) Each tiny movement of an animated character must be drawn on a separate clear acetate cell and colored with inks that stick to the plastic. The cells are then photographed one at a time on frames of movie film. When the film is run rapidly through a projector or video machine and projected on the screen, the motion is re-created. (Computer animation is discussed in Chapter 13.)

Certain artists referred to as *cartoonists* may belong to the same professional societies and subscribe to the same magazines as other cartoonists. These artists, however, are really skilled story illustrators. Some of them draw characters for comic

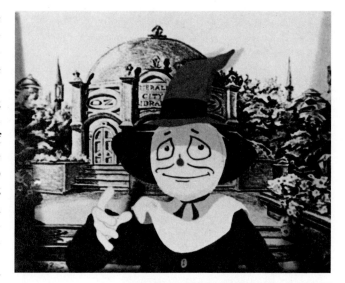

FIGURE 12.3 This animation cell from a movie about the Wizard of Oz has the background on the bottom sheet and the figure to be animated on an acetate overlay.
© Rob Roy Productions, Seattle, WA.

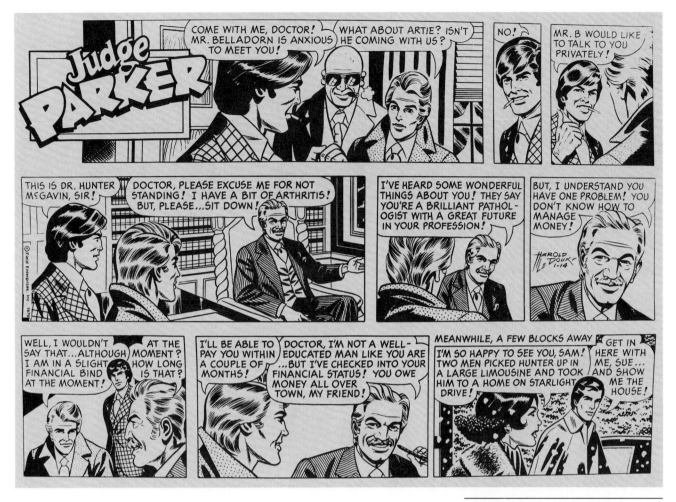

FIGURE 12.4 (above) Harold LeDoux, the cartoonist who illustrates the comic strip *Judge Parker*, is also a skilled painter.

©Field Enterprises/King Features.

books. They also illustrate continued adventure and human interest stories in newspapers, like Milton Caniff's *Steve Canyon* or Harold LeDoux's *Judge Parker* (Figure 12.4), which are followed by many faithful readers.

These people are primarily artists with a knowledge of composition, anatomy, and perspective. They illustrate strips but often don't write the stories. The *Judge Parker* strip, for example, is actually written by a man who prefers to remain in the background. He writes two other strips in addition to *Judge Parker*. The stories for *Judge Parker* are sent to LeDoux, who applies his considerable drawing skills to illustrating them.

Comic strips, caricatures, and humorous drawings appear in magazines to illustrate articles, as decorative filler material in various publications, and as advertisements on television or in newspapers. Figure 12.5 is one example of a cartoon used as an advertisement.

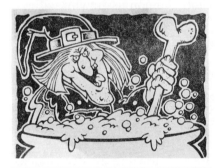

FIGURE 12.5 This cartoon witch obviously comes from an advertisement printed around Halloween.

Courtesy of *The University Daily*, Texas Tech University.

ENRICHMENT

Preparing a Sunday Newspaper Comic Strip

The *Judge Parker* strip (Figure 12.4) is a Sunday newspaper strip. Like most Sunday strips, the artist draws it in black and white. Color plates are made through a syndicate contract with another agency—usually the Greater Buffalo Press. The artist uses numbers keyed to a color chart that is published by the Greater Buffalo Press. These numbers tell the press what colors to print in which areas.

Even though they use the numbers, some artists also prefer to paint the strips with watercolor for their own reference. Among these artists is Hank Ketcham, whose *Dennis the Menace* has captured hearts all over the world.

THE CARTOON AS A VERBAL IDEA

If you are interested in becoming a cartoonist, the first thing you must understand is this: cartooning isn't primarily a visual art form. Yes, cartoons require drawing. Yes, good drawing and design can greatly increase the impact of cartoons. Cartooning, however, is not so much a *visual* art form as it is a *verbal* art form.

A cartoon is first a verbal idea. A cartoon may not have a **caption** (an accompanying comment or title) or a **balloon** (outlined dialogue or thoughts of a character in a comic strip panel). But the cartoon still must express a situation or tell a brief story. A brilliantly humorous drawing without a specific situation for provoking laughter doesn't fit our definition of a cartoon.

Since cartooning is a verbal art form, you must develop your imagination and polish your writing skills just as much as your drawing skills if you want to be a cartoonist. If you don't want to do your own writing, you will have to form a team with someone who can write. Most cartoonists start out both writing and drawing their own ideas. Later, when they are established in the business, they might choose only to write or only to draw.

THE GAG CARTOON

The three types of cartoons you will draw in this chapter are

- the single-panel magazine gag cartoon,
- the editorial or political cartoon, and
- the humorous comic strip.

Traditionally, many cartoonists begin their careers by doing single-panel gag cartoons for magazines. Many major magazines went out of business when television became popular. Even so, there are still national magazines for the general public and many specialized magazines that use cartoons.

Gag cartoonists for magazines enter a highly competitive field. Cartooning for magazines is still a good place to start, however, because it requires discipline and practice. Also, these cartoons can be drawn at home and mailed to magazine publishers.

Gag cartoonists must be able to see the humorous possibilities in everyday situations. They must turn everyday situations around so that the humor emerges. After this, they must be able to convey an idea with an immediately understandable humorous drawing, usually along with a brief, well-edited caption (the sentence or phrase that makes the joke's point). Cartooning is really a show business kind of humor for the print media (magazines and newspapers). A good gag cartoonist could write for Johnny Carson or Bill Cosby.

Besides drawing aptitude and writing skills, there are a few other characteristics you need for professional success as a magazine cartoonist. First, you must have perseverance. You must want the recognition and satisfaction that cartooning can provide badly enough to stay at it for years. Very few gag cartoonists have become instant successes. Beginning cartoonists usually receive enough polite rejection slips from editors to paper the walls of their studios before someone finally buys one of their cartoons and publishes it.

Besides being persistent, you must be efficient. Gag cartoonists must produce a volume of work in an organized fashion. Artists need to send cartoons to several magazines on the average of once a month in batches of six to twelve drawings. That is a minimum of thirty good gags a month needed to approach just five magazines. To meet this requirement, a cartoonist would have to produce one good drawing a day—and an artist must usually draw several to produce one good cartoon.

A System for Gag Cartooning

How can you get started as a gag cartoonist? And how can you organize your work?

Carry a small notebook with you at all times. Many times a day you will see situations that could be very funny with a little twist of the imagination. If you try to remember the situations, you won't. Write them down. You could use a paper napkin if you have nothing else, but a professional would carry a notebook (or maybe even a small tape recorder).

You won't need to write down very much of your idea to trigger your memory. Suppose you are leaving for school, and you see a neighborhood dog chasing your cat. The cat climbs the sycamore tree in the backyard and smugly washes his whiskers to taunt the dog. The dog bounces around at the trunk of the tree, yapping in frustration until you finally send him home. In the process, some funny thoughts about dogs cross your mind. You take out your notebook and write, ''Dog trees cat/dog's viewpoint.'' Then you go on to school.

That night at your regular time you get out a card file and $3 \times 5''$ cards. You open your notebook to the five or six situations you have recorded during the day, and you start editing. On one card you write:

Scene: Cat in tree looking scared. Dog climbing tree with lineman's spurs or mountain climber's rope and spikes; dog nailing boards on tree.

Caption: None

This note records specifics for the idea. Later during your editing process you might add, ''Dog dragging ladder toward tree with teeth,'' or ''Dog floating in air attached by long hose to helium tank.''

Now that you have a well-developed idea, you must choose the best place to market it. The dog and cat gag is probably not suitable for a pet owners' magazine, which might not wish to emphasize conflict between pets. The idea obviously wouldn't fit an automotive or yachting magazine. Since it looks like a good gag for a wide range of the reading public, you decide that it is a general gag. You put a file number in the upper part of the card that indicates this category. After this number, you put a period or a dash and put another set of digits to indicate the number of the gag; for example, ''1.247.'' This idea is the 247th in the group of general gags (1).

You may have been told by the cartoon editor of a certain general publication that he or she doesn't use animal cartoons. Remind yourself by a note on the card not to send this cartoon to that editor. You will save yourself a sure rejection. (Remember, though, that the magazine will probably be in existence for a long time, but the editor may move to a different magazine.)

Now you can file your gag and go on to the next card. You can develop a big idea file by this process in a short time. Meanwhile, you must be drawing these ideas, so start a file of roughs, too.

Do your roughs on sheets of ordinary but high quality typing paper. Then revise your drawings in ink on the same kind of paper. Although some more expensively produced magazines may send drawings back for revision or more finished work, most magazines will photograph those inked roughs for reproduction. Therefore, make your inked drawings as finished as you can. Neatly type the caption below the drawing or print it in black ink. Figures 12.6 and 12.7 on the next page are examples of finished cartoons with captions.

On the back of the inked roughs, up in a corner, put your name and address. You can use a rubber stamp to save time. Also write the file number that corresponds to the idea on the $3 \times 5''$ file card. File all of your inked roughs that aren't being mailed to an editor. File the first pencil roughs with the inked drawings. If a finished drawing gets lost in the mail, you will have the original on file.

Always note in the file when and where each drawing was sent. If you do this, you can avoid sending the same idea to two different magazines at once. A few editors don't mind this, but assume that an editor wants to be the only one considering your idea unless he or she tells you otherwise.

If you write down when and where you send a drawing, you can also avoid resubmitting an idea too soon to a magazine that has already rejected it once. Also record in your file when a cartoon has been sold, and to whom.

To help you sell cartoons more quickly, here are some tips:

■ List subjects (like hobbies or professions) that you know something about.

■ Find as many publications—magazines and newspapers—as you can that publish cartoons on the subject.

■ Send cartoons about the subject from the viewpoint of an insider who would recognize technical or

FIGURES 12.6, 12.7 Two cartoons based on a visual pun by Paul Hanna. You can see that Hanna experimented with two different techniques. The top cartoon was stippled, while the bottom cartoon was done first in pencil and then photocopied. You can find examples of both techniques and other examples of Hanna's work in earlier chapters.
Courtesy of the artist.

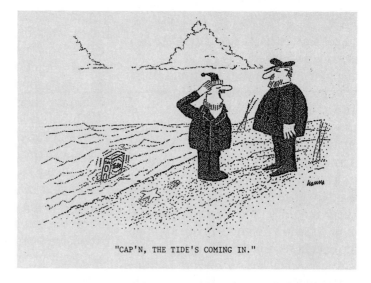

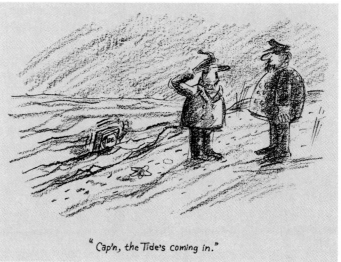

biographical references. (Make sure the gags aren't harshly critical of the hobby or profession.)

■ Know the magazine's and editor's needs.

Many specialized magazines welcome submissions by people who know and sympathize with their particular audience. If your father or mother is a doctor or autoworker, if you build models or hunt, or if you work part-time in a common occupation, you probably have sources of good gags for magazines concerned with these fields.

Publications for Cartoonists

Two publications that should be helpful to any aspiring cartoonist are *The Artists' Market*, which lists many outlets for cartoons and illustrations, and *Cartoonist PROfiles*, which is a magazine with the latest news from the world of professional cartooning. *Cartoonist PROfiles* will also keep you in touch with the latest happenings at the Museum of Cartoon Art.

The Artists' Market can be bought or ordered at your local bookstore. Obtaining *Cartoonist PROfiles* requires a subscription. Write to P.O. Box 325, Fairfield, CT 06430. The price will be over twenty dollars, and it is only published quarterly, but it is worth the money.

Gag Cartoon Notebook, Idea File, and Drawing File

MATERIALS

Notebook, 3 × 5" cards, card file, pencil, typing paper, drawing file, pen and ink

Set up your own gag cartooning system. Keep a notebook and idea file as described above. Make entries in the notebook and transfer ideas to file cards every day for a week. Then start doing pencil roughs of your best ideas, and file these drawings.

Discuss your ideas with your friends and, if possible, with a journalism or English teacher. You will find differences of opinion about which ideas are funny. If nobody you ask thinks an idea is funny, it probably isn't. But if someone looks at an idea, smiles, or chuckles, and says, ''Hey, that's really funny,'' you should be encouraged.

You have to make the final decision about which ideas are best. Develop the roughs for these ideas into a more finished form. Then start looking for places to get them published.

At first, you might have to give your cartoons away instead of selling them. You can get valuable training, however, by cartooning for the school newspaper, community bulletin boards, school election and program posters, club announcements, and newsletters. Sometimes a parent-teacher group needs a cartoon on a printed handout, or the back page of a program for a school play might use a little humor. If your humor would be appreciated by a general audience, ask the editor of a shopper (a small newspaper composed of advertisements and local news) for a little space.

Don't worry too much about developing a cartooning style. If you keep on drawing, your style will develop. You can study the styles of famous gag cartoonists. Their influence will be good for you as long as you don't try to directly copy their styles. Your own personality will assert itself eventually if you continue to try to improve on the styles you see published.

THE EDITORIAL CARTOON

Cartoons that humorously express opinions on politics or social issues are called *editorial* cartoons. Many editorial cartoons use political figures for subject matter. Bill DeOre of *The Dallas Morning News* drew the cartoon in Figure 12.8 that effectively portrays American presidents as insects. In some countries an editorial cartoon like this would endanger the cartoonist's life. In the United States, however, editorial cartoonists can criticize government officials.

Some people call these cartoons *political* cartoons, but the drawings often use other subjects besides politics. Figure 12.9 is a nonpolitical editorial cartoon by the witty and talented Etta Hulme (pronounced like *home*). Figure 12.10 is another nonpolitical editorial cartoon. It was drawn by Dirk West, who is a sports cartoonist for the *Lubbock Avalanche-Journal*. West is quite popular with readers who follow Southwest Conference college football.

On page 237 you will find a brief biography of an editorial cartoonist and a description of the job. The job requires good reading and writing skills and much speed and stamina. Editorial cartoonists have to come up with an idea each day. This idea must usually be based on a news event that occurred that same day—and the idea has to be funny.

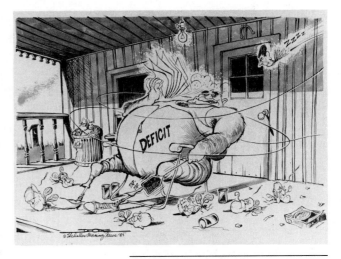

FIGURE 12.8 An editorial cartoonist like Bill DeOre must be quick in both wit and drawing. He must analyze important issues in the day's news and meet very short deadlines.

Courtesy of the artist and *The Dallas Morning News*.

FIGURE 12.9 Etta Hulme has a keen eye for the absurd side of our society. There are few women in the field of cartooning right now, but they are among the best cartoonists in the field.

Courtesy of the artist and *The Fort Worth Star-Telegram*.

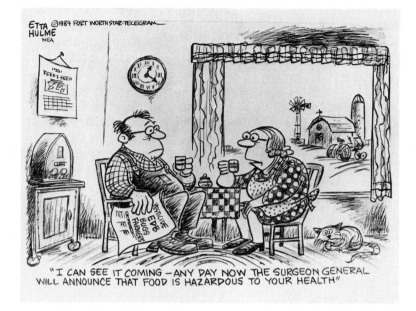

FIGURE 12.10 Dirk West uses a Pentel Sign Pen for much of his editorial cartooning.

Courtesy of the artist and *The Lubbock Avalanche-Journal*.

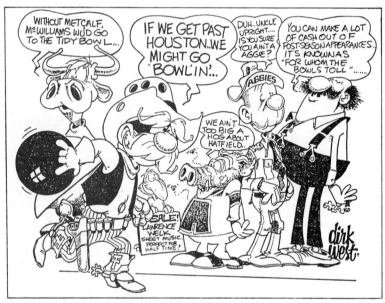

It is also essential that an editorial cartoonist be an expert at the art of caricature. A caricature is a humorous drawing of a person who is easily recognizable because of the exaggeration of the person's features.

To develop your talent as a caricaturist, study the work of both historical caricaturists (like Honoré Daumier, Figures 2.13 and 2.14, and William Hogarth, Chapter 3, page 50) and contemporary newspaper artists. Try doing some caricatures of well-known people from photographs. Carry your sketchbook at all times, and practice drawing caricatures of people you see. As you practice, your ability to convey a point about a person will improve.

You may not become another Dick Locher (see one of his editorial cartoons in Figure 12.11). Who knows, though? And you might choose Locher's other career. He is now the principal artist for the comic strip originally drawn by Chester Gould about the ageless crime fighter, *Dick Tracy* (Figure 12.12).

One word of caution about drawing caricatures: it isn't fair to make fun of anyone's physical disability. (This rule might be waived for an older person who is extremely famous or for a popular actor. The confidence of these people would probably not be shaken, and they would probably thrive on the attention. It would still be in bad taste, however, to make the disability a point of criticism.)

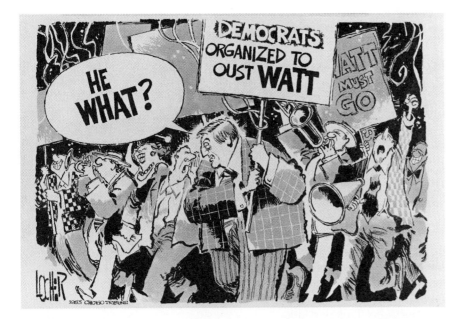

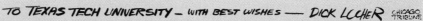

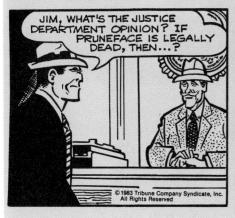
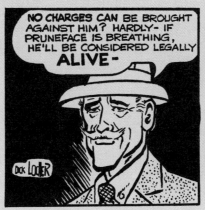
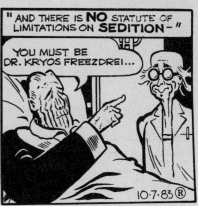

TECHNIQUE NOTE

Shading Media

Both Bill DeOre (Figure 12.8) and Dick Locher (Figure 12.11) drew their cartoons on the same type of shading medium used by the student artist for the drawing in Figure 8.17. Duoshade and press-on types of shading sheets are favored by some editorial cartoonists for speed and ease of printed reproduction.

Caricature Sketching

MATERIALS

Pencil, sketchbook

Study well-known figures around your school or town. List the most prominent features about five of these people (for example, long nose, full lower lip, or large Adam's apple). You will find that older people are usually easier to caricature than teenagers, and pretty girls and children are particularly difficult. Sketch all of your five subjects every day for a week to practice exaggerating their prominent features.

Applying for a School Editorial Cartooning Job

If you have developed your caricaturing skills, you can apply for the job of sports or political cartoonist for the school newspaper. If you want the job on a regular basis, be professional about applying, even though the editor you are dealing with may be a friend your own age. Make an appointment to show the editor your portfolio. This portfolio should contain at least four or five drawings of school personalities or events that the editor might be able to use.

Ask the editor to allow space for your cartoons in each edition. Also, you must agree on whether or not the editor can select an idea from several roughs. You should find out what weekly deadlines you must meet and what drawing medium you should use.

Be prepared for the fact that you might be competing with other people for a job. The editor may decide to alternate the drawings of three or four artists. If that is the case, you would have more time between deadlines to make sketches and revisions.

THE HUMOROUS COMIC STRIP

Many people consider comic strip artists to be the kings and queens of cartooning. Artists like Cathy Guisewite, creator of *Cathy*; Dik Browne and Mort Walker, who draw *Hagar the Horrible*, *Beetle Bailey*, and *Hi and Lois*; and Jeff MacNelly, who does *Shoe* and is also an accomplished political cartoonist, are admired by many young imitators.

The earnings of the top comic strip cartoonists rival those of sports heroes and television personalities. The artists often earn more from "spin-off" licensed products, however, than from drawing the comic strips. These products are manufactured under a license from the newspaper syndicates that distribute the comic strip.

For example, Charles Schulz shares the profits from the sale of Snoopy dolls, stationery, and mugs with United Features Syndicate. Opus dolls, based on Berke Breathed's *Bloom County*, are becoming popular. Even Mr. Peanut dolls are on the market; they are a spin-off not from a strip but from the corporate trademark of Planters' Peanuts. See Figure 12.13 for *Bloom County* and Figure 12.14 for examples of licensed products.

Remember, though, that most cartoonists must work hard for a long time to get their strip accepted by a syndicate. Literally hundreds of comic strips are submitted to cartoon editors of major syndicates each month. Although editors receive thousands of submissions a year, each editor can probably afford to buy only two or three new strips each year. The owners of the syndicates invest thousands of dollars in launching each new comic strip. This investment results from the cost of advertising the strips to newspaper editors and paying salespeople to contact all the newspapers.

For the most part, the newspaper editors who buy strips say they can't afford additional space for comics, so buying a new strip means eliminating an old one. This kind of substitution is sure to make some faithful readers of the old strip angry. Therefore, both syndicate editors, who buy the strip from the cartoonist, and newspaper editors, who buy it from the syndicate, have to be sure that a new strip will appeal to many different kinds of people. Also, busy readers should be able to grasp the gag quickly. Most important, the new strip has to be funnier than most of the other comics already in the newspapers.

BLOOM COUNTY

by Berke Breathed

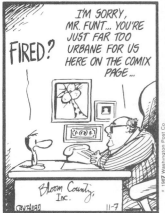
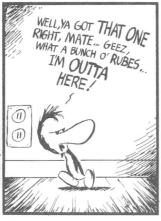
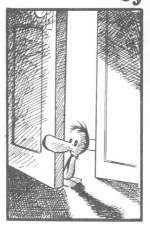
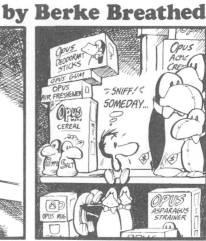

FIGURE 12.13 *Bloom County* by Berke Breathed is a strip that is popular with young adults. Breathed did a comic strip in college called *Academia Waltz*. Do you get the joke in the cartoon above? If not, the photograph below might provide some clues.

© 1987, Washington Post Writers Group, reprinted with permission.

FIGURE 12.14 Millions of dollars yearly are spent on licensed products that originate with cartoons. They helped make Charles Schulz, creator of *Peanuts*, the third-highest-paid entertainer in the United States in 1987.

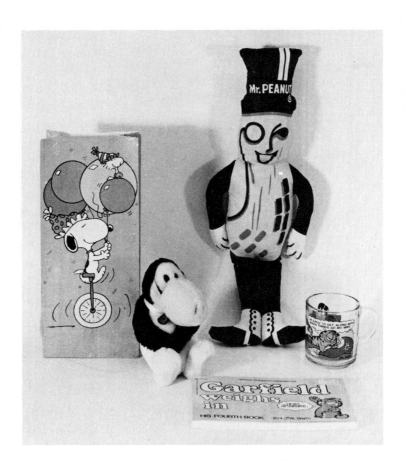

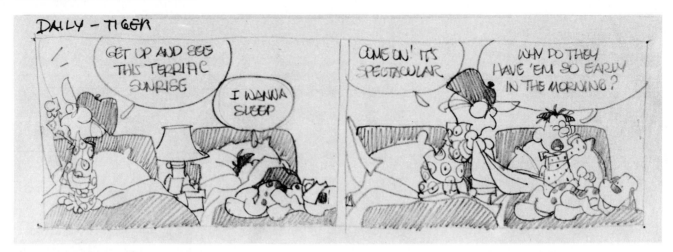

FIGURE 12.15 These preliminary drawings by Bud Blake were done for his *Tiger* strip. Blake is much admired for his excellent drawing and fluid, expressive line.
©King Features.

The comic strip cartoonist must have the same skills as the single-panel gag cartoonist. The comic strip artist, however, can use three or four panels to develop the gag situation. This space allows the artist to prepare his or her audience as a television comedian does. In Figure 12.15, Bud Blake has given you an insider's peek at some of the rough sketches done on tissue for his comic strip *Tiger*. Many comic strip artists use sketches like these to plan their strips.

Most contemporary successes in the comic strip field rely on a gag-a-day format for their humor. This pace requires a huge gag writing output. Comic strip artists (as well as single-panel gag cartoonists) often use the services of professional gag writers. If you start a successful comic strip, don't worry—gag writers won't be hard to find. In fact, they will come looking for you. But selecting some that can cooperate in producing your kind of humor may be difficult. Writers and artists who work together as a team from the beginning of their careers are fortunate.

Some successful comic strip artists start cartooning while they are still in school. Berke Breathed, for instance, drew *Academia Waltz* at the University of Texas long before *Bloom County* was created. For some recent comic strips by college student artists, look at Figures 12.16 and 12.17. These strips usually make jokes about campus life, but occasionally take aim at national politics. The editor who accepts these strips for the Texas Tech *University Daily* tries to encourage campus cartoonists, but she also buys *Bloom County*, *The Far Side*, and political cartoons by Ben Sargent and Jeff MacNelly from syndicates. Langston Brown, of the Lubbock High *Westerner*, is a talented high school cartoonist. His work appears in Figure 12.18 and 12.19 (page 236).

Before you try to start a comic strip for your school newspaper or for syndication, count the words that are used in each of several comic strips. Use strips from the national syndicates for daily (not Sunday) newspaper publication. The word totals for strips in a newspaper we looked at are in the chart below.

Comic Strip	Number of Words
Hi and Lois	29
Marvin	24
Steve Canyon (story strip)	52
Dick Tracy (story strip)	35
Barney Google and *Snuffy Smith*	32
Garfield	39
Hagar the Horrible	19
Archie	26
Blondie	30

We found an average of less than thirty words per strip for the ten strips. Remember that these are the strips that editors have found people will read. You

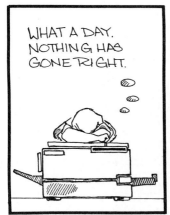
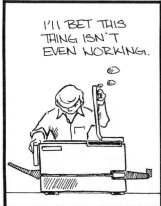
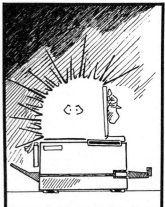
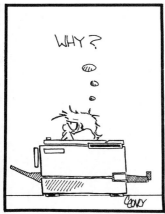

ON THE RUN   by Kenny Duggan

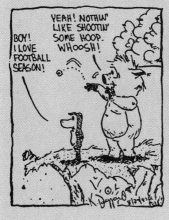
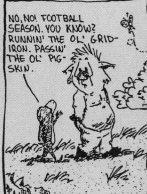
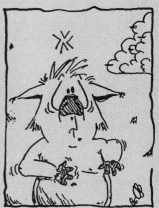
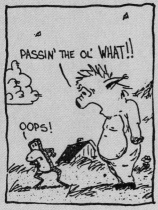

FIGURE 12.16 (top) Chris Conley expressed the feelings of the average student facing a library photocopying machine on a bad day. The artist was a mass communications major in college.

Courtesy of the artist and *The University Daily*, Texas Tech University.

FIGURE 12.17 (center) Kenny Duggan, an art major, drew *On the Run* for his college newspaper. It is about a frog and a pig who escaped from a biology laboratory.

Courtesy of the artist and *The University Daily*, Texas Tech University.

FIGURE 12.18 (at right) Student Langston Brown's cartoons often appeared in the *Lubbock Westerner*, his high school newspaper. With his ironing board surfer, he demonstrates the zany imagination required to succeed as a cartoonist.

Courtesy of the artist.

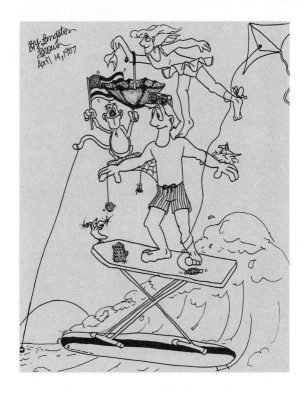

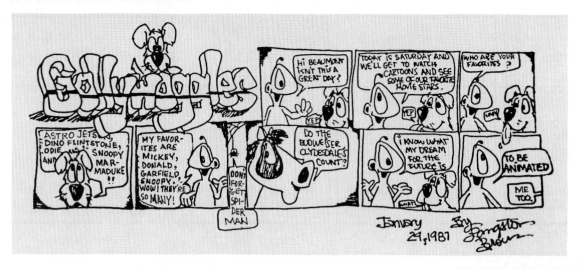

FIGURE 12.19 A comic strip by student
Langston Brown.

must edit and edit until your gags are economical in word use and are immediately understandable by most people (or at least by most people in your selected audience).

Besides counting the words in each strip, count the number of panels in the strips. What is the average number? What is the maximum? Did you find any with five panels? Probably not, because there isn't room. Many papers reduce their strips to around 6½ × 2″, or in printers' measure, 39 picas long and 12 picas high. (Review the Enrichment feature on page 74.)

You will probably want to make cartoons twice this size, but keep the drawings in correct proportion. If you've forgotten how to enlarge or reduce proportionally, check the Technique Note on page 192.

ENRICHMENT

Syndicate Directory

If you want to try selling your strip to a syndicate, a publication called the *Syndicate Directory* is essential. It is published once a year as a supplement by *Editor and Publisher* magazine and contains addresses and other information about syndicates to which you can submit your strip. You can order it by writing to *Editor and Publisher*, 575 Lexington Avenue, New York, NY 10022.

STUDIO

School Newspaper Comic Strip

MATERIALS

Pencil, drawing paper, black ink, pens, brushes, light bristol board

For a final cartooning project, prepare about eight weeks of a comic strip for the school newspaper. If the editor decides to publish it, you will be eight weeks ahead of schedule and can do the rest of the strips as you have time. If you are better at drawing than writing, get a partner to help you with ideas.

Write an outline first if you are creating a continued story strip; then break it down into strips and panels. If your strip fits the gag-a-day format, write descriptions of the characters in the strip and how they are supposed to react. The gag-a-day format would probably be more popular in a school newspaper; like it is in national syndicates.

Don't forget to do proportional roughs. Revise the drawings, and transfer the roughs to light bristol board. Try to use no more than thirty words, and letter them legibly in the panels *first*. Then complete the drawings with black ink.

DRAWING AT WORK

Editorial Cartoonist: Opinions into Images

Drawing as a form of communication is evident in the field of cartooning. Whether the purpose is to entertain, to criticize, or to convince, a picture often succeeds where words alone fail. The editorial cartoonist can affect public opinion in a dramatic and immediate way.

Michael Keefe of the *Denver Post* is a nationally syndicated editorial cartoonist and winner of two major journalism awards. He follows in the tradition of hard-hitting political cartoonists who have been poking good-natured and not-so-good-natured fun at public figures for generations.

Keefe didn't plan to fill one of the approximately 250 full-time positions for editorial cartoonists in the United States. Instead, he earned a bachelor's degree and a master's degree in math. He was taking courses for a doctorate and teaching in a community college when he changed careers.

Even though he had no formal art training, Keefe had been doodling in the margins of his math papers for years. In addition, he had contributed cartoons to his college paper on a weekly basis. Frustrated with looking for teaching jobs, Keefe submitted samples of his cartoons to a well-known editorial cartoonist. These same cartoons sent on a whim led to his position with the *Denver Post*.

Instead of the weekly drawings he produced in graduate school, Keefe must now produce cartoons daily. Five days a week he arrives at work at 8 a.m. and begins by reading newspapers and magazines. When an issue attracts his attention, Keefe thinks about the problem carefully and decides his personal stance. This is an essential step since an editorial cartoonist is trying to communicate a specific point of view. The next step is to creatively illustrate his opinions. Keefe must find a way to express his ideas visually.

Many tools are available to the cartoonist. Keefe may exaggerate a problem in one cartoon. Another time he may use irony or reversal by having the characters in the drawing say the opposite of what Keefe thinks. A favorite technique of a cartoonist is to develop a visual metaphor—an image that implies a comparison.

After the rough sketch is shown to the editor, Keefe draws the approved idea on vellum finish bristol board using brush, pen, and India ink. The finished cartoon is photographed and reduced. The cartoon appears the next morning in newspapers across the country.

Since an editorial cartoonist must respond to current issues and events, Keefe can't stockpile ideas and still be timely. He faces the pressure of producing creative cartoons on a daily basis, no matter how he feels. Yet Keefe enjoys the challenge of generating and expressing ideas in his award-winning cartoons.

Computer Drawing

OBJECTIVES

After reading this chapter and doing the activities, you will be able to

■ list tools for creating images with computers;

■ explain how a computer can be used to make two-dimensional images;

■ name types of programs for drawing three-dimensional images on a computer;

■ explain how a computer can be used for animation; and

■ explain how a computer enhances the creative process.

Imagine that you are about to make a drawing. You can choose one of many different drawing tools—for example, charcoal, conte crayon, colored pencil, or pen and ink.

Today you could also use a computer to make a drawing. Drawing with a computer is much like drawing with any other medium. Computer equipment, called **hardware**, can provide you with many tools for drawing. Drawings created with a computer are known as **computer graphics**.

After you have chosen your drawing tool, you must decide on the technique to use to create the visual effect you want. You might use contours, gestures, gradation, linear perspective, or atmospheric perspective. Can you use all of these techniques on a computer? Yes, you can. You can create a visual image with a computer using many familiar drawing techniques. Instructions, called **software**, tell the computer what to do to create images.

Today artists are using the computer as a drawing tool to show the world around them, to solve problems in design, and to express ideas and emotions (Figure 13.1). They are finding that the computer is a valuable tool for both studio and commercial art. Animators for television and movies use the computer to speed up the time-consuming process of making changes on frames of film.

A computer is a machine that allows people to store, manipulate, and rearrange information. This information can take the form of numbers, letters, or images. As an artist, you are concerned with how you can use a computer to create images.

Instead of making marks on paper with a drawing instrument, computer artists draw with light on a computer screen. They create images in real time and real motion. That is, artists can draw images, move them about, and change them instantly while the images are displayed on the screen. Artists can also freeze one image they select from an entire group of images.

After an image has been completed, it can be stored by the computer for future use. An image can also be printed on paper or some type of film (slide, video, or photographic). This printed image is referred to as **hard copy**.

HARDWARE FOR COMPUTER DRAWING

The basic parts of computer hardware are the central processing unit, the keyboard, and the monitor (Figure 13.2). The central processing unit is the ''brain'' of the computer. It is the part inside the computer that processes information and performs the commands that artists give it. The keyboard is like a typewriter keyboard. Artists use this keyboard to send commands and information to the computer.

The computer's viewing screen, called a *monitor*, is like a television screen. Artists create and manipulate the images displayed on this screen. Most monitors display images only in one color, but artists can also purchase color monitor screens for their computers.

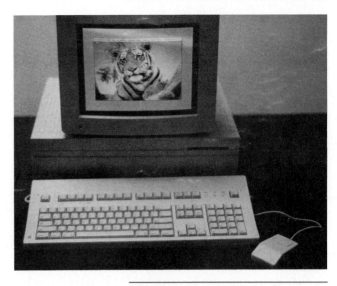

FIGURE 13.1 This image of a tiger is displayed on an Apple Macintosh II computer.

Courtesy of Advanced Technology Learning Center, Texas Tech University, and Apple Computer, Inc. Photo by Tai Kreidler.

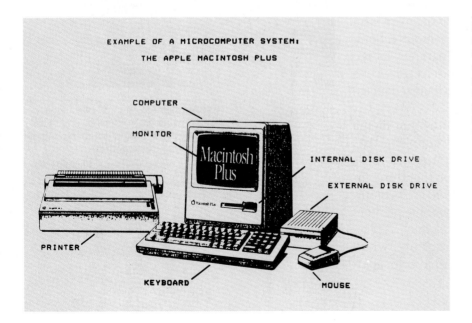

FIGURE 13.2 A simple microcomputer system that can be used to create drawings. Can you identify the piece of equipment that can be held in the artist's hand and used to draw lines that appear on the monitor?

Macintosh is a trademark licensed to Apple Computer, Inc. Line art courtesy of Apple Computer, Inc. Photo by Holle Humphries.

The monitor screen is mapped out electronically like a piece of graph paper. Each square on the electronic graph of the screen is called a **picture element**, or **pixel**. Artists move a **cursor** to make an image on the screen, pixel by pixel. The cursor is a point of bright light on the monitor screen that marks a position.

Input-Output Devices

Different tools can be attached to the computer for use by artists. These are called *peripheral* or *input-output* devices.

Input devices allow artists to give commands or information to the computer to create images. One of these, the light pen, is an electronic pen connected to the computer. Artists use it to ''draw'' directly onto the computer's monitor screen (Figure 13.3). The graphics tablet is like an artist's sketchpad. Artists draw images on this flat piece of equipment with a type of electronic pencil called a *stylus*. The resulting image appears on the computer's display screen.

A ''mouse,'' another input device, is a bulky drawing tool shaped like a box on wheels, small enough to fit in the palm of a hand. Artists can roll the mouse on a tabletop as though drawing on the table's surface. Inside the mouse is electronic circuitry that translates movements into pixel locations to make lines on the monitor screen. Artists can also use the mouse to manipulate images by rolling it in certain directions and pushing control buttons (Figure 13.4).

An optical scanner is another tool for creating images. It can electronically scan (look at) a piece of copy or an image and convert information into a form that can be ''read'' and stored by the computer. Similarly, a digitizer scans images or photographs. It digitizes, or converts, colors or values into electronic bits of information. Artists can call up this digitized image and change it (Figure 13.5).

Output devices print an image onto other media so artists can have a copy of it. For example, artists might want to use a printer. A computer printer is like a small printing press. Information that the computer has read, manipulated, displayed on its monitor, or stored can be printed on paper. Some printers can also print on other kinds of surfaces, such as plastic. Most printers reproduce only black and white images but images can be reproduced in color with more expensive color printers.

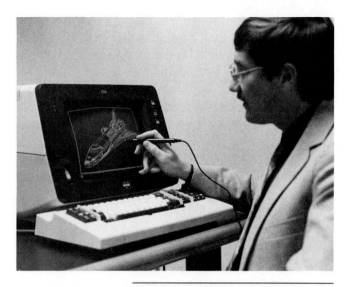

FIGURE 13.3 Light pens have been used to create technical drawings for computer-aided design (CAD).

Courtesy of David McGaughey, programmer analyst, Advanced Technology Learning Center, Texas Tech University. Image of Columbia is from the program AutoCAD from Autodesk, Inc. Photo by Holle Humphries.

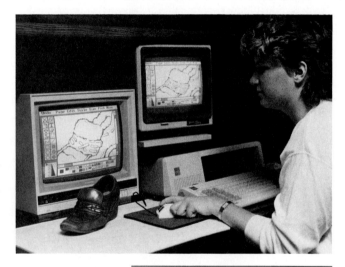

FIGURE 13.4 Movements of a mouse are translated into lines to create an image. Notice the contour drawing of the shoe on the monitor.

Courtesy of Denise Hanna. Photo by Tai Kreidler.

light pen	optical scanner
graphics tablet	digitizer
stylus	printer
mouse	

THERE'S MORE THAN ONE WAY TO SCAN A CAT

When you want to create graphics with your Macintosh, there's no need to pussyfoot around with anything less than Thunder-Scan. Because ThunderScan® turns any printed image into a detailed, high resolution Macintosh graphic. Then lets you change and enhance the image any way you wish. With a powerful set of software tools, written by Mac developer, Andy Hertzfeld.

CAT *(AKA Kitty)*
Start with any original image, black & white or color, up to 14" wide (with a wide-carriage ImageWriter).

FEED THE KITTY
Feed it into any ImageWriter (I, II, or wide-carriage). ThunderScan simply replaces ImageWriter's ribbon cartridge, so you don't need a video camera.

CAT SCAN
Now ThunderScan is zipping back and forth, digitizing the image at up to 288 dots per inch, in 32 shades of gray

CAT & MOUSE
With mouse in hand you have micro-control of the contrast, brightness and half-toning. Over all or selected parts of the image. You can scroll, erase, cut, paste, draw...

CAT'S EYE
...enlarge or reduce...

CAT PRINTS
...then print out your finished work on your ImageWriter or LaserWriter. ThunderScan taps the full resolution of LaserWriter, producing exquisite graphics with up to 300 dots per inch.

CATALOG
Cut and paste scanned images into catalogs, newsletters, reports, correspondence, personalized cards and more. Thunder-Scan works great with page layout software, adding high-quality graphics to your publications.

CAT CALL
You can even send images from Mac to Mac by modem.

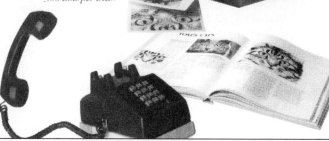

FIGURE 13.5 This advertisement shows the process of entering a photographic image into an Apple Macintosh computer system with a Thunderscan digitizer. At what point in the process can the artist manipulate the design?

Used with permission. © 1986, 1987, Thunderware, Inc. All rights reserved.

Artists can also have an image transferred to paper by using a digital plotter. A digital plotter draws the image on the monitor screen on paper. Two or more armatures, each holding a pen, move vertically, horizontally, and diagonally to plot a contour line image that was created on the screen. A digital plotter gives architects and interior designers a quick method to make blueprint and layout drawings.

Some equipment can be used for both input and output. Artists use these devices first to enter information into the computer and then to retrieve information from the computer. Using optical scanners and digitizers along with other equipment, photographic and filmed material can be entered directly into a computer system. Artists can view and change these images on the computer monitor. Then the computer can replace the images on film.

For example, with a television video camera, a film frame grabber, and a digitizer connected to the computer, artists can freeze images from video film and transfer them to the computer. Images selected from frames of film can be changed. With specialized equipment attached to the computer, the final images can be transferred back to video film. This type of process is being used today to computer "colorize" copies of black and white movie film (see Figure 28 in the Color Section).

SOFTWARE FOR COMPUTER DRAWING

Computer software designed for artists can be used to create a variety of two-dimensional or three-dimensional images and to create the illusion of motion. How does this software work?

Computers must process information as a series of *on* and *off* electronic switches. Instructions (software) for a computer must be written in a special format so the computer can read the instructions and process them electronically. Software that tells a computer how to perform commands is called a **computer program**.

The program instructions are usually recorded on a magnetic medium, such as a disk or tape. This disk or tape is placed in the computer's disk drive or tape player, which spins the disk or tape while the computer is being used. The computer reads the instructions by translating the presence (*on*) or absence (*off*) of magnetic spots on the disk or tape.

Artists activate the computer program by inserting the disk or tape into the computer and typing a command telling the computer to read the instructions. These instructions tell the computer how to carry out the commands it receives.

Some artists can write instructions themselves for the specific jobs they want the computer to perform. If this is the case, they can begin the drawing process by typing instructions on the keyboard.

Most artists, however, use **application programs** for specific drawing techniques. Application programs are already written by a computer programmer, a person who writes computer programs for others. An application program's instructions are recorded on a disk that is inserted into the computer and read.

Artists use an application program to draw new images or change images already stored. The computer's electronic memory, part of the central processing unit, stores these new or changed images temporarily while the computer is being used. When artists finish a work session, the images can be stored permanently. They are transferred onto magnetic floppy or hard disks, video or laser disks, or videotape. When artists want to use the images again, the storage disk or tape is inserted into the computer.

Many application programs have been written specifically for artists. These programs save artists time because the artists don't have to write the instructions themselves. Let's look at some application programs used by artists to create

- two-dimensional images,
- three-dimensional images, and
- animation.

Two-Dimensional Programs

Artists interested in creating graphic designs can use a two-dimensional computer program. The image they create on the computer monitor consists of a set of pixels. Artists use various *draw* or *paint* commands to create a line or a colored area of pixels.

Artists can manipulate sizes and types of lines, colors, shapes, forms, simulated textures, and even electronic brush strokes. For example, artists can create line drawings similar to contour drawings. Or artists can draw shapes and fill them with different values or colors (Figure 13.6). The computer can instantly change a value or color scheme for any image displayed on the computer monitor. With a graphics tab-

---

digital plotter

CHAPTER THIRTEEN **COMPUTER DRAWING** *243*

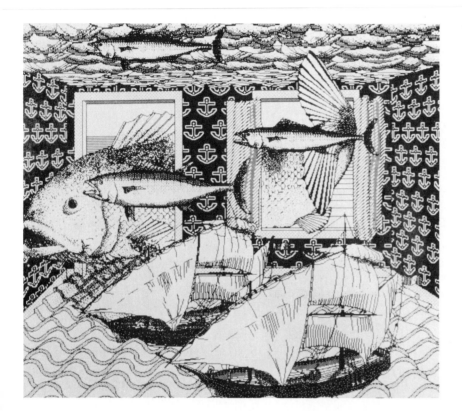

FIGURE 13.6 The illusion of deep space in this image was created by the use of linear perspective.

David Herrold, *Nautical Interior*, 1984. Courtesy of the artist.

let and the right kind of software, artists can use the computer for gesture drawing. Artists can create images that show motion or action (Figure 13.7).

The computer can also be useful to artists who draw from photographs. With some two-dimensional computer programs, artists can use picture processing. Artists digitize an image or photograph to enter it into the computer for display on the monitor screen. Then the image on the screen can be changed.

With some types of two-dimensional image software, artists can create the illusion of three-dimensional space. Programs limited to black and white require artists to use black and white values to create this illusion. With color programs, artists can use color gradation to give their images a three-dimensional appearance. Some programs also allow artists to use value gradation to create atmospheric perspective. With other programs, artists can use linear perspective to create the illusion of deep space.

Most of these two-dimensional computer programs give artists the freedom they need to make changes easily and to manipulate images. Because of this freedom, artists can easily experiment with gradation and atmospheric and linear perspective to create images that look three-dimensional.

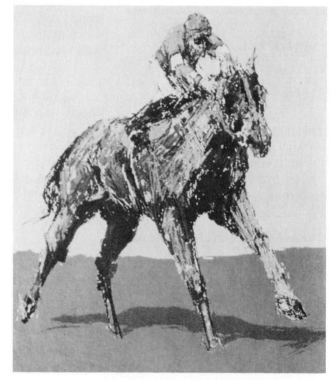

FIGURE 13.7 Artists can use a graphics tablet and stylus to draw lines with freedom and spontaneity.

Tom Christopher, *Running Horse*, 1984. Courtesy of the artist.

STUDIO

Contour Computer Drawing

To become familiar with the drawing tools you are using with your computer, make simple contour line drawings of objects like shoes, a hand, or the contents of your wallet or purse. Practice looking only at the subject you are drawing without watching the lines as they appear on the computer monitor. If you are using a mouse, it may be difficult to draw accurate diagonal lines and circular shapes. Next, draw a contour line portrait.

STUDIO

Gesture Computer Drawing

As you have learned, gesture drawings convey a feeling of movement. Try to capture the dynamic lines of the human figure by using your computer drawing tools for a gesture drawing.

Ask a member of the class to pose for you. The model should assume an action pose, such as the motions of playing tennis or baseball.

It may be easier to create a gesture drawing if you use a graphics tablet and stylus rather than a mouse. If your program allows you to vary line thickness, use thicker lines to draw the major areas of emphasis in the movement of the figure.

STUDIO

Drawing Pattern and Texture with a Computer

The software program you are using may allow you to "fill" different areas of your drawing with textures and patterns. You can create visual patterns pixel by pixel.

Make a still-life setup using objects with different textures (examples: a burlap-covered milk can, garden tools, a wheelbarrow, fish netting, an old hat, sports equipment, or glass containers). Create a computer drawing using software program options to create texture and pattern. Be sure to include a center of emphasis, repetition of some patterns and textures, and contrast.

STUDIO

Linear Perspective Computer Drawing

Some software programs include options for connecting points to make lines. Other programs allow the artist to create rectangles, squares, and circles on the monitor screen and to "erase" lines from the monitor screen. Use these program options to make a linear perspective drawing of a corner of your art room.

When you are finished, find another linear perspective drawing in Chapter 6 and compare it with your computer drawing. What are some of the difficulties you encountered when using a computer to produce a linear perspective drawing? What are some of the advantages?

Three-Dimensional Programs

Software is available to create models for three-dimensional objects and their environments, thus producing convincing illusions of objects in space. Some programs tell the computer to "remember" the dimensions of an object drawn on a screen. Then artists can rotate the object, determine its proportions, and duplicate it. The computer also can remember where the object was positioned. Other objects can be placed in front of the object or behind it.

There are other, more complex three-dimensional programs, but they are hard to write, and their use requires a great deal of technical knowledge. The computer must be given a set of instructions that tell it how to display a three-dimensional image from any angle.

These three-dimensional images are amazingly accurate and realistic. Some of the more sophisticated software techniques used to convey this visual accuracy are described below.

Polygonal Modeling. In polygonal modeling, a model of a three-dimensional form is created out of lines using a technique similar to linear perspective. The final contours of the form are expressed as a mesh of polygon-shaped facets or surfaces. The computer assigns surface characteristics to each facet of the

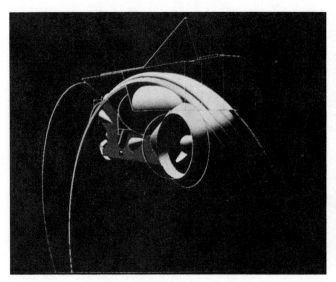
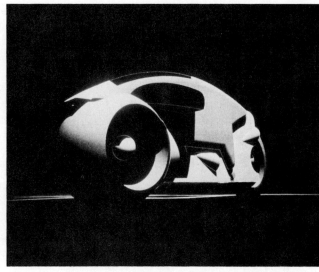

FIGURE 13.8 Synthavision (Mathematical Applications Group, Inc.) is a three-dimensional modeling software based on the principles of combinational geometry. It was used to create and animate the light cycles in the Walt Disney movie *Tron*. The diagram at left shows how simple forms are made from geometric shapes on the computer monitor. The shapes can be joined more smoothly to create the finished form.
Diagram © Peter Angelo Simon, 1988. *Tron* image of a light cycle © 1982, The Walt Disney Company.

polygonal mesh and blends the boundaries between the facets. The final view of the object has the appearance of a smooth, finished solid form.

Texture Mapping. A photograph of an actual textured object, such as a piece of wood or a sponge, can be scanned by the computer and then stored in its memory. With a texture mapping program, the computer can be directed to wrap that texture around a form that has been modeled and stored in the computer's memory. In this way different textured surfaces can be applied to the same form.

Combinational Geometry. In combinational geometry, models of three-dimensional forms, such as boxes, spheres, and cones, are programmed into the computer's memory. The computer is instructed to add and subtract forms to create images (Figure 13.8).

Ray Tracing. Ray tracing describes objects according to paths of light rays moving around those objects and reflected from one object to another. Ray tracing can reproduce highly complex lighting effects, such as reflected illumination, mirror reflections, refraction (bending of light) through transparent objects, and shadows (Figure 13.9 next page).

Fractal-Surface Imagery. Fractal-surface imagery is used to model uneven ground. A form is created from a mesh made of triangular shapes. The computer calculates changes in distances between the triangles of the mesh. This calculation randomly fractures (divides) the triangles into a large number of irregular facets. This process is repeated until the individual triangles are so small that their edges can no longer be distinguished.

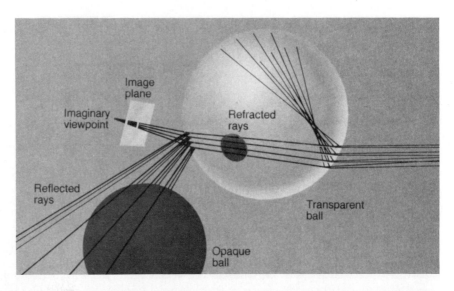

FIGURE 13.9 The diagram (at right) shows how an image is determined by calculating the light ray paths reflecting off or absorbed by the surface of an object. Can you find the shape of each sphere reflected in the surface of its neighboring sphere in the finished image (below)?

Michael Collery and Shaun Ho, *Algorithmic Dream*, Christmas, 1983. Diagram by Mark E. Alsop, 1984, based on material provided by Pat Hanrahan and Paul Heckbart, New York Institute of Technology. Image courtesy of Cranston/Csuri Productions, Inc.

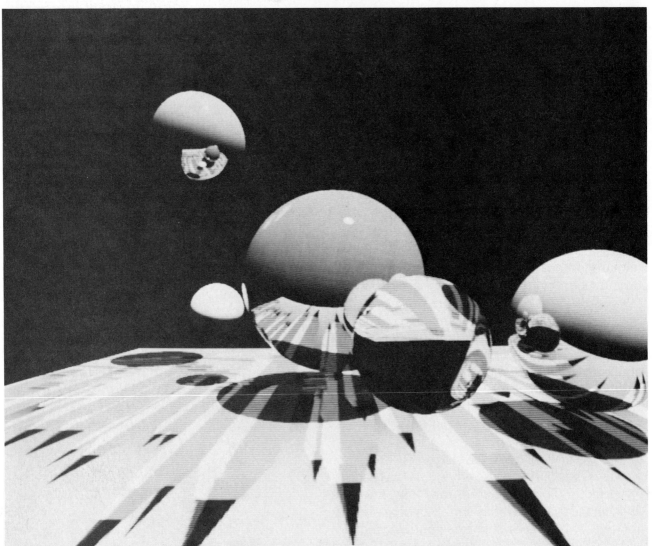

Particle System Software. This software can recreate the appearance of clouds or fire. Each particle or piece created by the computer is randomly spaced and circulated. As the particle moves, the computer alters its color, degree of transparency, and size. Particle systems can also be used to create the illusion of haze or distance, which produces an effect like atmospheric perspective.

Animation Programs

The third type of computer graphics application program is animation. Animation programs use the computer's capability for displaying real motion in real time. The computer can create an object and then move, or animate, that object. Artists can tell the computer to move the object in a certain direction through a certain space. Each view displayed on the monitor screen can be recorded on film, frame by frame.

To move a modeled object and display that movement on the monitor, a set of commands to specify motion must be given to the computer. The computer also must be given instructions for the projected path of the object through space, along with calculations to define any motion of the object itself while it is being projected along that path.

Every sequence of movement through time and space can be frozen through stop-action timing. The sequence of images is flashed on the computer screen at the rate of twenty-four frames a second. These images are recorded on film to create the illusion of motion (Figure 13.10).

The computer can also be programmed for a process known as *in-betweening*. Animators give the computer one frame of action and a frame of action that would occur a number of steps later. The computer then fills in the in-between steps. The computer does this by calculating the predicted action in the missing frames. Once the programming for these calculations is established, in-betweening saves animators hours of work (Figure 13.11, next page).

Today computer artists and scientists working in the area of animation are trying to create a special kind of computer animation called *motion blur*. This effect is like the illusion of vibrating movement. Artists suggest this effect in a picture when they repeat the shapes of an object and vary its tone and color. When an object is subjected to motion blur on a computer, it appears on a frame of film as if surrounded by ghostly blurs of its repeated shape. Motion blur is created through the principles of ray tracing.

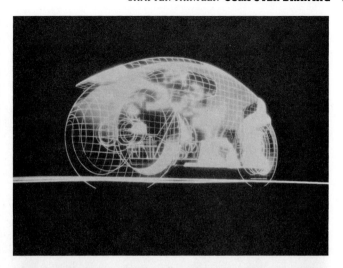

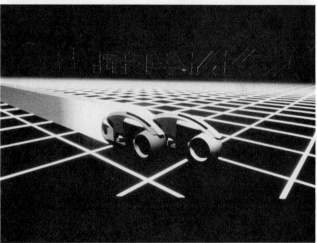

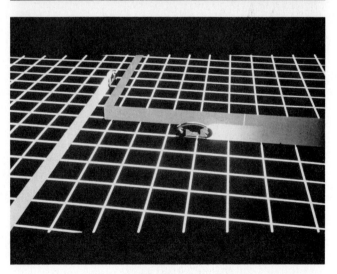

FIGURE 13.10 These images show different film frames from the race of the light cycles in the Walt Disney film *Tron.* The light cycles first are energized (lattice grid) and then speed across a videogame grid.

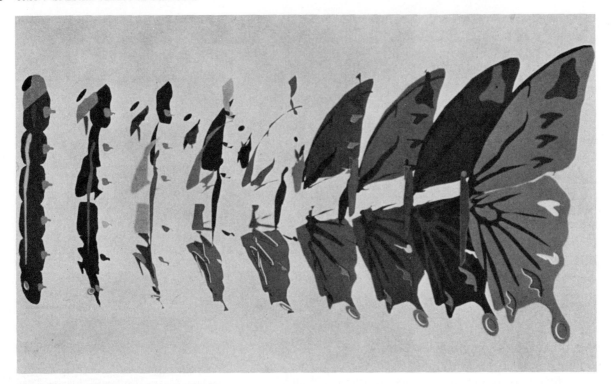

FIGURE 13.11 In-betweening software can be used in animation. How much time do you think this function can save an artist at the drawing table?

Mike Newman, *Metamorphosis* (interpolation between two groups of unlike shapes), 1981. Produced at a Dicomed D38 design station using D148 film recorder. Courtesy of Dicomed Corporation.

TECHNIQUE NOTE

Purchasing Computer Hardware and Software

Before you purchase any computer hardware or software, you may wish to consider the following:

1. What functions do I want the computer system to perform?

   ■ Black and white versus color. Will you work in color, or only with black and white graphic designs? Some computers don't have color capabilities. Also, some color computer printers are quite limited in their printing capabilities. You may wish to consider adding equipment to allow you to photograph full-color images from the computer screen.

   ■ Drawing equipment. Do you wish to draw with a mouse or on a graphics tablet? If possible, experiment with each one before you purchase.

   ■ Visual screen scale. Should you purchase a computer with an unusually large screen? If you have any vision impairment, this kind of screen might be beneficial.

   ■ Video capabilities. Will you need a computer system with the capability of storing images on videotape?

   ■ Graphic design. Will you wish to combine graphics with images?

   ■ Print quality. How will you use hard copy prints? What quality of prints will you need?

   ■ Cost. Do you wish to slowly build a studio of computers that can be interconnected to one printer? Or will a single computer meet your present and long-term needs? If so, you may wish to invest more in the single computer.

   ■ Portability. Do you want a computer system that is easy to transport from one location to another?

2. Make a list of all of the equipment your computer system will need to run your computer programs.

3. Collect information. Read all of the available information on computer equipment and meet with your local computer dealer. If your neighborhood has more than one dealer, visit each one. Ask questions. Although the dealer will be pleased to assist you, the choice of your equipment or software should be determined by you.

4. Consider the range of computer programs available for the equipment you select. Some software programs run only on specific computer hardware. Arrange for a demonstration of various computer

programs from your computer dealer, an educator in your neighborhood, or a local computer user group.

5. Compare prices. Investigate each manufacturer's product line and prices before making a decision. Ask local school district personnel if they can purchase the computer equipment and software for you at a reduced price.

6. Compare warranties and service. If you are buying a computer for the first time, you may wish to consider purchasing an installation contract from the dealer, as well as an extended warranty or service plan.

7. Allot yourself ample time to learn how to use the software. Most computer programs require time and practice to master.

8. Be sure to read thoroughly the manufacturer's operating manuals that are provided with the equipment.

THE COMPUTER AND THE CREATIVE PROCESS

As you have seen, the computer can be used in many ways to make drawings. The computer is also useful to artists as a design tool. It gives them new ways of seeing and new solutions to design problems.

The computer can act as an additional eye for artists. In this respect, it is like a camera, enhancing our view of the world. The computer can sensitize us to certain features of this world, including color and space.

With a camera, artists can alter color through the use of different colored lens filters or types of film. A computer also allows artists to experiment with the effects that different color choices have on a visual image (see Figure 29 in the Color Section).

Artists can use a camera to capture different angles of a subject or to zoom in for a closer view. In the same way, a computer can display several views of an object or scene. It can also zoom in for a closer look. The computer can change an object's position or relationship to other objects appearing on the monitor. Besides showing a variety of exterior views of an object, the computer can display a cutaway view of an object's interior.

The computer can also help artists increase their creative output. It helps artists find more solutions to artistic problems, and it enhances the quality and originality of those solutions.

The computer can quickly create many solutions to the same artistic problem. For instance, assume that an artist wants to use a particular design and color combination for a drawing. However, the artist can't decide whether to include a background or which color combinations would be most effective. The artist could use a computer to create quickly and easily several different versions of the design (see Figure 30 in the Color Section). Then he or she could choose the best version and make that drawing on paper. The artist wouldn't need to redraw the same image several times to decide on the best design (Figure 13.12).

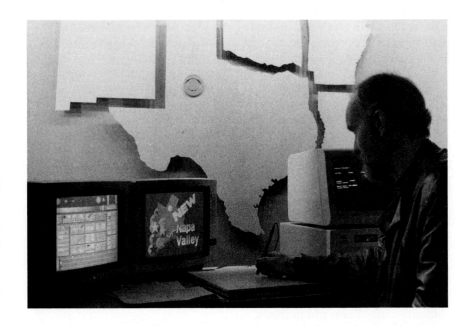

FIGURE 13.12 Dr. Kim Smith creates computer graphics for television news broadcasts. Note the graphics tablet and stylus that he uses to draw images.
Courtesy of KBLK Channel 13, CBS affiliate, of Lubbock, Texas. Photo by Tai Kreidler.

Artists can also experiment with design in more specific ways using the computer. They can use software to

■ select and manipulate art elements and principles,

■ enlarge or reduce images,

■ add animation,

■ enter other images to be combined with those they have created by scanning or digitizing,

■ distort images to create unusual effects, and

■ reproduce images by printing them on different kinds of surfaces.

Using computers encourages artists to take more risks during the creative process. When experimenting with an image on the computer screen, artists can erase it, change it, or save it for later use in a fraction of the time they could do these things without the computer. Artists can store images and make more changes at any time. Because the computer offers so many opportunities to change images, it increases artists' chances for finding highly original solutions to visual problems. Since artists can manipulate images in unusual ways with a computer, they can visualize solutions that would be impossible otherwise.

It is certain that more and more artists will recognize the computer's great potential. They will use it to create works of art unlike any produced in the past—unique drawings that reflect the unique environment in which they are created.

ENRICHMENT

Computer Art on Exhibit

Exhibitions featuring drawings made with a computer have been held since 1965. At that time, only a few American and European artists were experimenting with the artistic possibilities of the earliest computer equipment. Sometimes just one or two artists sponsored a show of their work in small studio galleries or featured an exhibit at a computer conference.

Now exhibits by computer artists are quite frequent and attract large audiences as well as corporate sponsors. "Computers and Art" is an example of an exhibit that toured the United States. This exhibit was jointly sponsored by the IBM Corporation, the Everson Museum of Art of Syracuse, New York, the Edgewater Trust, and the National Endowment for the Arts and Humanities.

The exhibit featured selected works by computer artists from all over the world. Response to the exhibit was so positive that the book published in conjunction with the exhibit, *Digital Visions: Computers and Art* by Cynthia Goodman, was sold out before the exhibit completed its tour.

STUDIO

Computer Visual Autobiography

Use the computer to experiment with making changes in the way you look as you age. Collect several photographs of yourself as a baby and child. Starting with your baby picture, draw a series of four images, each showing yourself at a different stage of growth. Pay attention to the changes in proportion at each stage in the size of your head as compared with the size of your body. Use different options in your computer program to fill in areas of tone and texture to create contrast in your facial features, hair, and clothing. Print each of these images.

Next, draw from a more recent photograph of yourself. Print that image as well. Now imagine how you might look in old age. Starting with the more recent image you just drew, redraw some of the details of your facial features.

What features might change as you grow older? Will your nose appear to be larger or wider on your face? Will you put on weight? If so, add width to the proportions of your cheeks and chin. Do you think you will lead a hard life or a contented life? Then add perhaps a few wrinkles or lines of expression to convey those changes. Position your eyebrows differently to reflect the effects of age. Will your hair become gray? Will you need glasses?

Print this final image.

DRAWING AT WORK

Aerospace Engineer: Designing with Computers

Aerospace engineers work on the design, development, testing, and production of aircraft, missiles, and space vehicles. As a project engineer, Laura Waters specializes in designing the space station under development by NASA (National Aeronautics and Space Administration). To do this, Waters uses sophisticated computer graphics programs that prepare designs and models. Computer-aided design (CAD) has been used in the aerospace industry since the 1960s, but the modern supercomputers are invaluable tools for today's engineers.

Before this job, Waters had little experience with graphics or computers. With a solid background in math and science from high school, she chose engineering as a career because it was a challenging field that would provide financial security. After graduating from high school, Waters entered the engineering department at Virginia Polytechnic Institute and State University at Blacksburg, Virginia, where she earned her bachelor of science degree in mechanical engineering. As part of her summer training while in college, she worked as a student engineer in the Aircraft Carriers Structures Division of the Newport News Shipyard.

After graduation, Waters was employed by Analytical Mechanics Associates, Inc. They were looking for an engineer with a desire to learn more about computers and computer graphics. One of their contracts is to define and model the space station assembly sequence for NASA at Langley Research Center in Hampton, Virginia.

On a typical day Waters works at the computer terminal assembling the space station model or running programs that analyze features of the current design. Engineers in other areas may use T squares and protractors to create designs. The tools for this office include computerized work stations, graphics terminals, Tektronics plotters, and laser printers. Waters can produce drawings, charts, graphs, and three-dimensional forms using CAD programs.

Part of Waters's job is to update the model of the space station as new information is provided. A change in the design of one part affects the entire space station. These changes can be monitored by using the computers to create a sequence of graphic designs that simulate actual processes. Waters explains the importance of this simulation: ''From the model we obtain pictures which help other engineers understand the physical properties of the spacecraft and analyze the structure for control requirements, orbit lifetime, and steady-state microgravity volumes.''

Changes to the model then must be analyzed, the results documented, and reports presented to managers at Langley and other NASA centers. One part of Waters's job is to answer questions about the model at meetings. ''It's very satisfying to see a picture you created on the computer shown to an audience and hear their compliments, followed by requests for copies.''

Aeronautical engineering has provided Laura Waters with the challenge she was looking for as well as personal satisfaction.

UNIT V

Evaluation and Review

MEETING YOUR OBJECTIVES

By answering the following questions and doing the exercises, you will demonstrate your ability to meet the learning objectives listed at the beginning of Chapters 11, 12, and 13.

Chapter 11

1. Select an object or a piece of furniture to draw. Measure it and decide on a scale at which you wish to draw it. Using this scale, draw a plan and an elevation for a basic box that would just fit around the object. Using a separate color, draw a grid of small, equal-sized squares.
2. Draw a one-point perspective of the basic box created in number 1 above. Determine the distance two times the height of the box. Place the vanishing point at this distance above the ground line and about the same distance to one side.
3. Continue the problem above by drawing a plan and an elevation of the object on the plan and elevation of the basic box. Project a perspective of the grid onto the floor and end (or a section) of the basic box. Use colored pencil for this. By counting grid squares and marking intersections, find a series of points through which the lines of the plan and elevation of the object pass. Locate these on the perspective and connect them with freehand drawing. Make a freehand drawing of the outline contours of the object.
4. Draw the plan and elevation below at two times the size it is shown in the book. Draw a two-point perspective setup, including a plan view of the picture plane.
5. Make a list of the mechanical drawing tools you used in doing the studio exercises in Chapter 11.

Chapter 12

1. Is cartooning primarily a verbal or a visual art form? Explain your answer.
2. List three types of cartoons.
3. Carry a notebook for a week. Note situations with cartoon possibilities. At the end of the week, pick the best three ideas and do rough pencil drawings of each one. Then do finished drawings in ink. Write your captions before you do the drawings. Set up a filing system for your cartoons.
4. Do a self-portrait in pencil while looking in a mirror. Then decide on your three most obvious facial characteristics. Do a humorous caricature in pencil

---

Plan and elevation of boxes and cylinders.

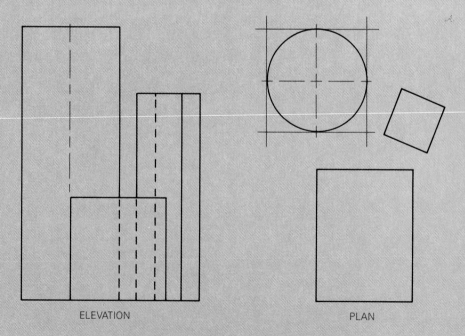

ELEVATION

PLAN

emphasizing these characteristics by exaggerating them.

5. Imagine what you would do if you were a powerful political figure. Write an editorial cartoon featuring the caricature of yourself that you did for number 4 above and the actions you imagine you would take.

6. Write a description of five characters for a comic strip. Describe the way they look, what kind of people they are, and how they feel about things. Now do pencil sketches of each character. When you are satisfied with the five characters, make an ink drawing of all of them together.

Chapter 13

1. Make a list of all the tools mentioned in Chapter 13 that are used to make computer drawings.

2. Write one or two paragraphs explaining how a computer can be used to make two-dimensional images.

3. List six types of software used to make three-dimensional images on a computer.

4. Write one or two paragraphs explaining how a computer can be used to create animation.

5. Explain how a computer enhances creativity.

LEARNING DRAWING TERMS

You encountered several new drawing terms in this unit. The most important terms are printed in heavy, bold type. Write all the terms on a sheet of paper. Then, without looking in your book, tell what each term means in your own words. If you are not sure of a meaning, use your book to write a definition.

EXPERIENCING DIFFERENT MEDIA

Each new drawing medium is listed at the bottom of the page on which it is first mentioned. Review your experiences with all the media, comparing strengths, weaknesses, and personal preferences. Then write a report summarizing your experiences with these media.

SEEING YOUR ENVIRONMENT

Learning to see the world around you as it really is is one of the first steps in improving your drawing skills. Doing the following exercises and others like them will help get you in the habit of seeing your environment more closely.

1. Visit an architect's office and look at blueprints, renderings, and other drawings. Make your own sketches of different styles of buildings in your area.

2. Examine the styles of cartoonists in your local newspaper. Do any of the cartoonists make consistent use of certain elements of art? Explain.

3. Study several computer images. Do you see any differences in the ways that the principles of art have been used compared to the way artists use them to design non-computer art?

EVALUATING DRAWINGS

1. Evaluate the cartoons you did for number 3, Chapter 12, under "Meeting Your Objectives." Rate yourself from 1 to 10 for three categories: 1) selection of a potentially humorous idea, 2) development of a humorous caption, and 3) craft.

2. Use the art criticism process you learned in Chapter 2 to evaluate the same drawing you critiqued above.

EXPANDING YOUR HISTORICAL KNOWLEDGE

Learning about the history of art will help you improve your drawing skills. It will also increase your understanding of your own culture and the cultures of others, both past and present. Answering the questions below indicates that you are learning art history. You will be able to answer most of the questions by referring to the Enrichment sections and to Chapter 3. To answer the last question you will probably need to refer to art history books, such as those listed in the Bibliography.

1. The work of what artist is considered a bridge between Realism and Impressionism?

2. Why was one group of 20th century American artists referred to as the *Ashcan School*? Name one artist who belonged to this group.

3. Compare Figure 3.20 to Figure 3.26. What style is associated with each work? Describe in your own words the differences between the two.

4. What sorts of things did the Pop Artists like to portray in their art? Why? Which illustration in Chapter 3 is an example of this artistic style?

5. Choose one work done prior to the use of perspective and one work created by one of the earliest artists to use the technique. Write a paper comparing the similarities and differences between the two.

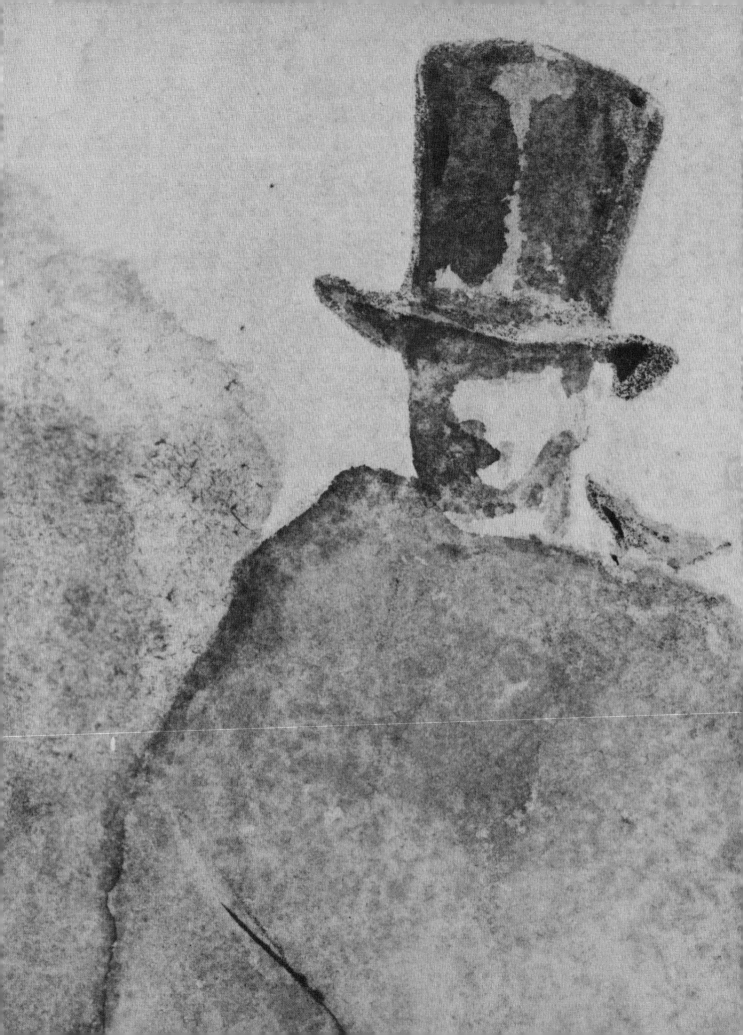

Media Handbook

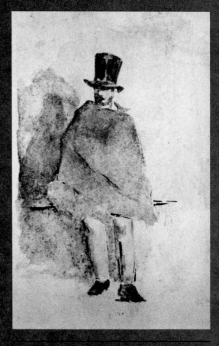

In this handbook you will find information about the various media mentioned in the textbook. Each item is briefly described when it is first mentioned. Here you will find more detailed information that will help you select, purchase, and effectively use the materials. In addition to explanations for the media listed in the text, you will also find information on broader categories of materials, such as *paper* and *ink*.

Acetate is a type of thin, filmy paper used to protect drawings and other artworks. Acetate is moisture-proof and waterproof. It doesn't shrink, stretch, or become brittle. It is available in clear and matte (frosted) styles and can be purchased in sheets, pads, or rolls of various dimensions and thicknesses. Some acetates have an adhesive backing; others are specially prepared for taking paints and inks.

Acrylic is the most commonly used name for synthetic pigments and media. All paints consist of two basic parts: pigment and medium. The pigment provides the color, and the medium provides the liquid in which the pigment is mixed. There are both natural and synthetic pigments and media. Compared with the natural paints, the acrylics are more versatile. They can be cleaned from brushes with soap and water and thinned with water, although they resist water after drying. They shouldn't be mixed with oil paints. The acrylic paints are available in a wide range of colors. The types of acrylic media available are gloss, matt, gesso, modeling paste, and gel. You can buy most of the acrylic products in quantities up to one gallon.

A long piece of **aluminum molding**, four to seven feet long, makes a lightweight, convenient straightedge for reaching distant vanishing points when making accurate perspective drawings. Aluminum molding can be purchased at lumber yards.

Architect's scales are one of several kinds of scales used to prepare drawings to correct scale. Architect's scales are manufactured both in the flat and the triangular form. All of the scales (such as $1/8$, $3/32$, $3/16$) represent one foot and are used primarily to make drawings for buildings and machine parts.

Art gum erasers are free of grit and grease. They are especially good for cleaning artworks. They may be used on all papers and fabrics. They are often referred to by the brand name *Artgum*.

Ballpoint pens are the kind of ink pens that you are probably most familiar with. While they don't offer the quality, variety, or control provided by other drawing pens, they are inexpensive and easy to use.

Block printing inks are fine-quality printing inks. They are manufactured for the purpose of making prints from woodcuts and linocuts. Fine-quality printing inks produce the best results. Both oil-based and water-soluble inks are available. These inks are available in a variety of colors.

Brayers are rollers used to apply ink to a wood or linoleum block. The rollers are available in either soft or hard rubber and in widths ranging from four to eight inches.

Bristol board is a frequently used drawing surface. It is available with smooth, medium, and rough finishes. Manufacturers and people working in art use different terms to describe these finishes and surfaces. The smoothest surfaces are often described as having *high surfaces* or *plate finishes*. These bristols take the most delicate line techniques in pen and pencil. Don't use the plate finish bristol for brush drawings. The plate finish is made for pens and is too slick for a brush. The medium bristols, which are most frequently used, are often said to have *vellum* or *kid* finishes. These boards have a ''toothy''— slightly textured—finish; almost any technique can be used on these surfaces. The kid and vellum finishes withstand both repeated erasures and reworking without feathering. Bristol boards are available in one-, two-, or three-ply, and in various sizes.

Brushes of several different types work well for drawings. Sable, sabline, and synthetic brushes are some examples. The best kind to use for gesture drawing is the sable brush, made from animal fur. It is the most expensive of the three kinds, but if you take good care of it, it will last for many years. Sabline and synthetic brushes are much less expensive than sable brushes. A sabline brush has dyed ox hair instead of sable fur, and a synthetic brush is made from man-made fibers. Don't use a badger hair mop or a so-called camel's hair brush. These are soft, but they won't spring back to their original shape after they are wet.

Cameo paper is a clay-coated paper that is often used as a surface for silverpoint drawing.

Chamois skins are pieces of very soft leather. Artists frequently use them to blend pastels and charcoals. You can buy a chamois at your art supply store and at many department stores.

Charcoal is one of the basic dry media. It is a black or very dark-colored, brittle substance that consists mainly of carbon. Charcoal is made by heating plant or animal material, such as wood or bones, in ovens containing little or no air. The charcoal used by artists is made from plant materials.

Charcoal is a flexible, easy-to-work-with drawing medium. You can erase it easily, and you can smooth and smudge it to create desired effects. These qualities make charcoal an especially good medium for beginning artists, who are often reluctant to make big, bold marks that will be permanent.

Two basic types of charcoal—**vine charcoal** and **compressed charcoal**—are used by artists. Vine charcoal is available in sticks only, while compressed charcoal is available in pencil and powdered forms as well as in sticks.

Vine charcoal is charcoal in its most natural state. It is made by heating vines until only the charred, black sticks of carbon remain. These thin carbon sticks are soft, lightweight, and extremely brittle. You can buy the sticks in thicknesses ranging from that of a rose stem up to nearly one-half inch. The advantage of vine charcoal is that you can erase it and smudge it for effect more easily than compressed charcoal. The disadvantages are that it is less permanent, dirtier, and not as conducive to making fine lines.

Compressed charcoal is made by binding together tiny particles of vine charcoal. This process produces a less brittle, finer medium than vine charcoal. You can buy compressed charcoal in sticks or pencils. The pencils, which are available in different hardnesses, have the advantages of being cleaner and capable of producing fine lines. The disadvantage of the pencils is that the sides can't be used, thus limiting the types of marks that you can make.

The *powdered charcoal* has the same material makeup as compressed charcoal. You can use the powdered form for shading and other special effects by rubbing and erasing the sprinkled powder.

If you wish to preserve a charcoal work, you must apply a fixative. The fixative is sprayed on after the work is completed.

Charcoal pencils are available in both black and white in four degrees of hardness: HB, 2B, 4B, and 6B. They are used primarily for drawing and photographic spotting. It is not our purpose to sell particular brands of art supplies. But charcoal pencils of a consistent, smooth quality are sometimes hard to find. We have had our best experiences with Grumbacher charcoal pencils. The Ritmo pencil (a Grumbacher Italian import) is also good. If you can't find either of

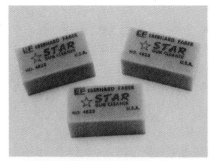
Art gum erasers

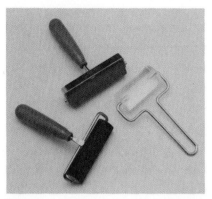
Brayers

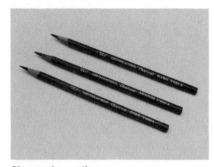
Charcoal pencils

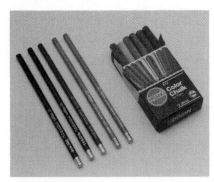

Colored chalks

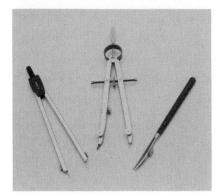

Dividers, compass, ruling pen

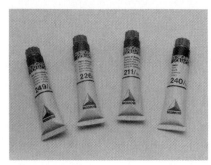

Designer's gouache

these kinds, try the General Pencil Company's product. (See *charcoal* and *pencils*.)

China markers are often called *grease pencils* or *china pencils*. Probably their most common use is to make crop marks on photographs. They are also used for drawing and writing on glass, plastic, metal, and polished surfaces. China markers are available in several different colors.

Colored chalks are dry, powdery sticks of pigments that have been used to create drawings and paintings for centuries. The chalks range from soft, fine chalks that produce brilliant, lasting color to the hard chalks that produce weaker, less durable color. *Layout chalks* are small, hard, square sticks. They are also made in pencil form and are sometimes used by graphic designers, art directors, or illustrators for making rough sketches. *Pastels* are the most widely used chalks. (See *pastels*.)

Colored pencils provide strong, durable colors. The pencils are sharpen easily, and don't crumble. A complete set of colored pencils can include as many as sixty assorted colors. The best-known colored pencils are the Berol Prismacolors. The English Derwent brand is similar and also popular. Conte de Paris pastel pencils are really chalks. They are more suitable for jobs in which you blend colors by rubbing. Colored pencils are waxier, hold a point longer, don't smear so easily, and are harder to break.

Compasses are used to draw circles and arcs. There are many different kinds of compasses, *combination*, *swivel*, *drop*, *bow*, and *beam* being a few of the more common. Many come in sets that include interchangeable pen, pencil, and divider parts.

Conte crayons is the brand name for the best-known brand of drawing crayons. Conte crayons are

available in various assortments of colors and hardnesses, such as HB, B, and 2B. (See *crayons*.)

Crayons, along with chalks, are among the oldest of all art media. They are available in both pencils and square sticks. Various degrees of hardness are also available. Crayons provide a wide range of colors, and they can be applied to many different surfaces. Crayon marks are almost permanent and hard to erase.

Cropping Ls are L-shaped tools used by artists and art production workers to eliminate unwanted areas from drawings and photographs.

Designer's gouache. See *gouache*.

Digital plotters route images from a computer screen to paper. Points and contour lines forming an image are plotted by two marking pens, one making horizontal lines and the other making vertical lines. Digital plotters are often used to produce blueprints, charts, and graphs.

Digitizers convert visual information from printed images or photographs into electronic bits of information for display and storage by a computer. After images are digitized, artists can modify them.

Dividers are used most commonly to mark off equal spaces, divide a line into equal parts, and transfer measurements from one place to another. Special dividers include *proportional dividers* and equal *spacing dividers*. You can purchase replacement needles for dividers.

Drafter's mechanical pencils are actually lead holders that allow the person using the pencil to advance more lead as the point wears away. Some mechanical pencils advance the lead automatically to preset lengths from .3 to .9 mm. Various leads can be purchased separately.

Drafter's ruling pens are used primarily to draw straight and curved lines in ink for technical drawings. An adjusting screw makes it possible to open and close the nibs to allow more or less ink to pass through, thus adjusting the width of the lines being drawn.

Drafting tape is tape used by drafters to attach drawings to a drawing board. This tape is very similar to masking tape. It is available in plastic dispensers and comes in various widths and colors.

Drawing boards provide support and stability for the drawing surface. Drawing boards are available in a wide range of sizes, from $16 \times 21''$ up to $31 \times 42''$, and materials, such as wood and Formica. Various features, such as aluminum edges, attached straightedges, and trays, are also available.

Easels are wooden or metal stands used to support a drawing or painting in process. The easels are adjustable to allow for different-sized media and different heights of artists. In most cases your drawing paper will be attached to a drawing board that will sit on the easel. The drawing board should be almost perpendicular to the floor, but slanted slightly, just enough to keep the board from falling off the easel.

Felt pads are used to rub and smooth materials such as carbon and chalk pigments.

Fiber-tipped pens, also called fine-line markers, are available in a wide variety of point sizes and types. You will find these pens listed under *pens* or *markers* in various catalogs. Most of these pens are sold in a variety of colors as well.

Fixatives protect artworks. Pastels, for example, must have a fixative applied to prevent smearing or deterioration of the pigments. Certain fixatives work especially well with certain media, so select the correct fixative for the work you want to preserve. The most commonly used fixatives are the aerosol type, which are easy to use and dry quickly. Glossy and matte fixatives are available.

Gesso is a coating material that is applied to surfaces to give them the desired properties for receiving paints. It is made by mixing a white pigment, such as chalk, with a binder, such as glue. In addition to being used to coat surfaces prior to painting, gesso is also built up, molded, or carved to make designs and used to decorate picture frames and furniture. Don't confuse this traditional, real gesso with the synthetic, ready-to-use ''gessoes'' manufactured today. These acrylic gessoes are also used to prepare surfaces for painting or other artistic work, and they also have a brilliant white finish. They aren't absorbent, however, which makes them radically different from the real gessoes. The synthetic gessoes are easy to apply, and they adhere to almost any surface.

Gouache is opaque watercolor. It is often referred to as *designer's gouache* and listed in catalogs under watercolor paints. Gouache paints are similar in makeup to watercolor paints—the difference being that the gouaches have more pigment and added materials such as chalk to give them their opaque quality. Designer's gouache (or designer's color) is also similar to tempera, but of a higher quality than school tempera. It is sold in tubes as a paste. When properly mixed and applied, it covers areas opaquely with no streaks. It is usually applied to watercolor paper or medium-surface boards.

Gouges are cutting tools used to carve wood or linoleum to make woodcuts and linocuts. Gouges are much like chisels, but with curved edges. The cutting edges may be on the inside or the outside of the blade. Manufacturers of art supplies also make sets of small, gouge-like linoleum and wood cut-

ting tools of various shapes and sizes, which can be inserted and removed from a handle with an adjustable chuck (attachment) for holding the cutters.

Graphics tablets are like electronic sketchpads. Artists use **styluses** (also called *electronic pens*) to mark positions on the flat tablets attached to computers. Like graph paper, the tablets are electronically divided into squares. Electronic signals from styluses are translated into images displayed on the computer screen.

Graphite pencils are the pencils that people are most familiar with. They are commonly referred to as *lead* pencils, which is an improper description of the pencils since they are made of graphite, not lead. Graphite is a black mineral variety of carbon. Graphite pencils come in a variety of hardnesses. (See *pencils*.)

Illustration board is a surface used for drawings and other types of illustrations. An extremely wide variety of illustration boards are available. You can buy high-quality illustration boards made of 100-percent cotton fiber or with high rag content (see *paper*). You can also buy the boards with different degrees of tooth, different thicknesses, and different finishes.

India ink is black drawing ink. It is available in two types: waterproof and soluble. The waterproof ink will withstand washes after the ink has dried. The soluble is usually better for making fine lines. Both types can be diluted. These inks usually come in dropper bottles. (See *ink*.)

Ink is a versatile medium used for many purposes, such as drawing and writing. You can buy both translucent and opaque inks. Many colors are available. Special inks are made for use on water-repellent surfaces such as acetate and Mylar film.

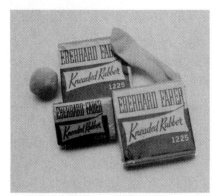

Kneadable erasers

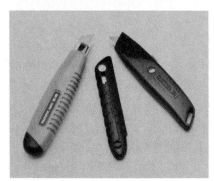

Mat knives

Kneadable erasers, or *kneaded* erasers, are excellent for removing pencil, charcoal, and pastels. Made of rubber, they can be squeezed into any shape.

Layout paper is a high-quality translucent paper used chiefly by graphic designers and artists. Many layout papers are especially suitable for heavy use with markers. Finishes on layout paper are usually rougher than those on tracing paper. You can buy layout paper in 13-, 16-, and 20-pound weights. (See *paper*.)

Light pens are computer drawing tools that resemble electronic pencils. Instead of lead, they use a beam of light to form images on computer screens. This light acts like a cursor to mark the points at which a pen touches a screen.

Linoleum blocks are used to make linocuts. They consist of wooden blocks with a layer of linoleum on top. The most commonly used linoleum is called *battleship* linoleum, which is brown or grayish. You can buy the linoleum separately and mount it on the blocks yourself if you so desire. Linoleum doesn't lend itself to the delicate, subtle cutting that wood does, but it can be worked more easily and quickly. The readymade blocks are type high (the same height as metal type used for printing letters, symbols, and numerals), which makes them adaptable to standard printing processes.

Lithographic pencils, often listed as *litho* pencils in art supply catalogs, are actually crayons. These pencils or crayons are available in seven hardnesses, from extra, extra soft to *copal*, which is very hard. Lithograph pencils are usually paper-covered round sticks of square crayons. They apply a grease-receptive material that resists water.

Mat backing is any material used to provide the support for a drawing, painting, or other artwork being matted. Box board, Fomecor, and mat board are three materials commonly used as backing. You can buy the boards under different brand names, in different thicknesses, and in various sizes. *Museum board* is a specially formulated backing board that doesn't contain chemicals that can stain art over a period of time. It is used by many professionals and others concerned with preserving their art.

Mat board is used to mount all kinds of artworks. You can buy boards in a variety of sizes and colors, either uncut or precut to standard sizes. They are also available in different thicknesses.

Mat knives are box or utility knives frequently used to cut mat boards for framing and mounting artworks. Special mat cutters will cut straight or beveled edges and are adjustable for the desired angle and depth.

A **Mouse** is a computer drawing tool that fits into an artist's hand. Artists roll a mouse on a tabletop as though drawing on the table's surface. Electronic circuitry in a mouse translates these movements into lines on the computer screen. Artists can also modify images by rolling a mouse in certain directions and pushing control buttons.

Newsprint is a good drawing surface for sketching and practice drawings because it is inexpensive. Don't use it for anything you want to keep permanently. Because it is made of wood pulp, and because of the chemicals used in its manufacture, newsprint turns yellow after a few hours in the sun. Even if it isn't exposed to the sun, it becomes brittle and crumbles within a few years.

Optical scanners use a beam of light to scan or "read" information on a printed page or photograph. This information is converted into electronic signals that can be "read" by the computer and used to display and store images, which artists can change to suit their purposes.

Paper in its many forms is the primary surface used for drawing. Have you ever looked at paper under a microscope or watched a film that showed paper being manufactured? If so, you already know that all those sheets of smooth, shiny paper that you buy in the store are quite different from how they appear. Even the smoothest-appearing paper actually consists of many separate fibers joined together in a tangled, weblike mass. This means that rather than having a smooth, uninterrupted surface, paper actually has an uneven, bumpy, rough surface.

It is this rough, uneven quality of paper that makes it possible for the paper to serve as a surface for writing, drawing, painting, and other similar processes. The fibers in the paper act like cutting edges as the medium (graphite, ink, charcoal, etc.) moves across the surface. Tiny particles from the medium are sheared off and come to rest in the small spaces between the paper's fibers, thus forming the marks that you see on the paper.

Understanding the process explained above should help you see that you will obtain different results with surfaces of different textures, even if your other media and techniques remain the same. A paper with more texture will shave off and hold more of the medium. The finest, smoothest papers will take the least amount of medium. With each paper, from roughest to smoothest, you will achieve a slightly different effect.

Texture isn't the only characteristic of paper that affects the final outcome of the drawing process. Certain materials added to paper during the manufacturing process change the way a paper reacts to a medium. Sizing, for example, makes paper less absor-

bent. The thickness of the paper and the coating that is applied also affect the paper's reaction to the medium.

Another characteristic of paper is its rag content. Moderately good drawing paper lasts a long time because of high rag content. This means that it is made from cotton rag pulp mixed with wood pulp. Expensive, high-quality drawing paper made only from rag pulp is referred to as *100-percent rag*. It isn't as brilliantly white as some less expensive papers, but it will last indefinitely without discoloration.

The weight of paper is stated as the weight per ream of a standard sheet size. A retail ream is 500 sheets (like typing paper), but a printer's ream is 516 sheets. For example, 516 sheets of 24-pound paper (of the manufacturer's standard length and width) weighs 24 pounds.

Paper stumps (sometimes spelled *stomps*) consist of soft gray paper that is rolled and pointed. They are used to blend charcoal and pastels. They are available in as many as eight different sizes and usually come packed by the dozen.

Pastels are the chalk or crayon sticks used to create pure, brilliant colors in a dry medium. Depending on the kind and amount of binder, they can be powdery, waxy, or oily. They are applied to high-quality surfaces, usually special pastel papers, by hand or with rubbing techniques. Both round and square sticks are available in sets that can include up to almost fifty hues.

There are many different papers designed just for use with pastels. Among these are papers with a very fine sandpaper surface, velour papers with a surface like velvet cloth in various colors, and charcoal paper in white and other colors.

Many students find that white bristol board or heavy layout paper

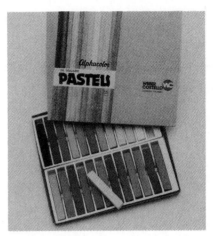

Pastels

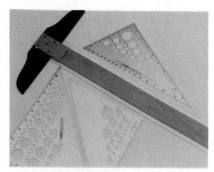

T square and triangles

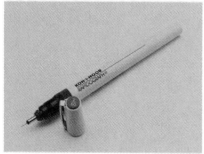

Technical pen

is the best choice for their needs. The surface of layout paper works especially well with pastels. It must be mounted on a white backing, of course, to properly show off the drawing.

Pencils are drawing and writing tools that consist of slender, cylindrical casings around a marking substance. You are probably most familiar with ''lead'' pencils, which actually consist of a graphite marking substance, most commonly encased in wood. Artists use these graphite pencils, as well as many other kinds of pencils, including charcoal, pastel, and various other colored pencils.

You can buy pencils such as charcoal and graphite pencils in various degrees of hardness. Usually hardness is labeled in one of two ways. Some brands use the labels *hard*, *medium*, or *soft*. Others use numbers together with the letters *H* or *B*. A pencil with an *H* is hard and makes light marks. The higher the number, the harder the pencil. A pencil with a *B* is soft and makes dark marks. Pencils range from 9H (extremely hard) to 6B (extremely soft). For freehand drawing, done without measuring tools, a collection of 2H to 6B pencils is helpful. Harder pencils (3H to 9H) are used mainly for mechanical drawing or drafting.

Pink Pearl erasers are soft and pliable erasers. They are smudge-free and come in medium and large sizes.

Printers provide copies of computer images on paper or film. Both color and black and white printers are available. Dot matrix printers function somewhat like sophisticated typewriters, while laser printers resemble photocopiers in the way they reproduce computer images.

Rice paper, also called *oriental* rice paper, is a traditional surface for receiving woodcut or linoleum prints. Most rice papers are actu-

ally made from mulberry pulp or the pulp of a ginseng herb that is called *rice paper tree*. The fibers of the true rice plant aren't suitable for making paper. Rice paper is available in different weights and colors.

Rubber cement is a latex glue that attaches surfaces firmly while still allowing the surfaces to be peeled apart after it dries. Rubber cement is the most commonly used form of adhesive for mounting drawings, photographs, and other artworks, and for assembling art pieces. Some jobs require two coats; others require only one coat. Rubber cement can be purchased in containers up to one gallon in size. Thinners and dispensers are available from the rubber cement manufacturers.

Sand pads, or *sandpaper blocks* as they are often called, are used to shape materials such as pastels, charcoal, crayons, and pencils. The sand pad consists of the fine-grade, medium-toothed sandpaper mounted on a wooden block.

Scratchboard is a good grade of cardboard coated with clay or whiting bound with sizing. You can buy scratchboard in either white or black. It is also available in single sheets or in packages. Some packs include cutting tools and instructions for scratching. Stippled finishes on scratchboard are also available. Scratchboard is relatively expensive, but it provides an interesting drawing experience. Many illustrators who create black and white line drawings for newspapers and magazines prefer scratchboard.

Sensitized shading sheets are specially treated papers used extensively by cartoonists. Applying chemicals to these sheets produces a hatching and cross-hatching effect instantly.

Silverpoint involves making marks on a surface with a silver-pointed pencil or other instrument.

Styluses are instruments used for engraving. They have a sharp point that scratches into the drawing surface, usually to remove a coating that was previously applied.

T squares are used to draw horizontal lines. They also provide a true base for triangles used to draw vertical lines. The two parts of a T square are the head and the blade. T squares are available with blades of different lengths.

Technical pens are most frequently used for fine line work and for lettering. You can buy points (nibs) for these pens that make lines from less than .002 to over .08″ (.5 to over 2 mm) thick. The numerical designations for these different thicknesses range from 000 to 7. Technical pens are often purchased in sets that include the pens, nibs, and ink.

Tempera paint (as it is usually called in school studios) is a water-soluble gouache paint that may come either in liquid form or as a powder to be mixed with water. If properly mixed it becomes opaque after it is applied. Paintings done with tempera are usually brilliant. The effects an artist can create with tempera are more limited than with oil paint or with the true egg (made with egg yolk) tempera, traditionally used by many master painters. Tempera is unsuitable for canvas.

Tracing paper is a lightweight parchment paper. Because it is transparent, it has many uses in the graphic arts and architectural fields. Different sizes and thicknesses are available. Most tracing papers take fine ink lines very well.

Tracing vellum is one of the more commonly used papers with a medium finish. Vellum finishes provide more tooth than smooth, Hot Press finishes, but less tooth than the rough, coarse finishes. (See *paper*.)

Triangles are used primarily to draw vertical lines. You can buy both 30/60° triangles and 45/90° triangles, and you can buy them in different sizes, from 4 to 24″. Various features such as beveled edges and fluorescent colors (that provide better visibility of materials underneath) are available.

Wash is a medium made by thinning ink or paint with water. It is applied with a brush. Sometimes dry media are used in combination with wash.

Watercolor paints consist of transparent pigments in a medium of water or gum. The pigments are ground extremely fine, thus creating the transparent effect that differs so much from the effect created by opaque paints. Watercolor paints are available in tubes or sectioned pans.

Watercolor blocks are pads of watercolor paper. These watercolor papers are specially manufactured to prevent warping and buckling. The blocks are available in various sizes and provide watercolor papers of various colors.

Watercolor palettes are trays or boards upon which an artist mixes paints and other media. Palettes are manufactured in various shapes and sizes and are made of several different materials, such as wood, metal, and plastic.

Wood blocks are blocks of wood used to make woodcuts. Traditionally, hardwoods such as apple, pear, cherry, beech, and sycamore were used to make wood blocks because they were smooth and textureless and because the carving properties of these woods made it possible for the carver to maintain precise control of the knife or gouge. Today, however, softer woods, such as pine, are used more frequently. Soft woods are preferred because larger, broader, less intricate designs, which don't require such precise carving, are popular today. The softwood grains are thought to enhance rather than detract from the design.

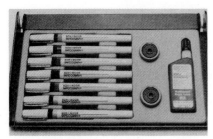

Technical pen set

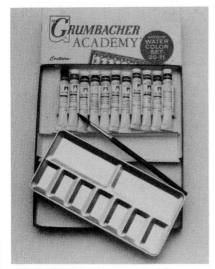

Watercolor set

Glossary

This section contains important words and phrases used in *Creating and Understanding Drawings*. You may wish to refer to this list of terms as you read the chapters and complete the activities.

aberrant scale Type of proportion achieved by making an object or figure in a drawing appear abnormally small or large.

abstract (nonobjective) Work of art that stresses the elements and principles of art and has no recognizable objects.

actual texture Kind of texture that the viewer of an artwork can touch.

aerial perspective Decreasing the value and value contrasts for objects that appear farther back in a composition. This technique is used to create the illusion of space.

aesthetics Ideas about what makes a work of art beautiful or satisfying.

application program Software (instructions) that tells a computer to perform specific tasks.

art criticism Process of examining, understanding, and judging a work of art. It involves four steps: description, analysis, interpretation, and judgment.

art history Information about the artist who created a work of art and when, where, how, and why it was made.

assemblage Three-dimensional work of art made by attaching many pieces to a surface.

asymmetrical (informal) balance Balance created in a work of art by giving unlike objects in the composition equal visual weight.

atmospheric perspective Decreasing the intensity of hues for objects that appear farther back in a composition. This technique is used to create the illusion of space and to suggest the effects of light, air, and distance.

background Area of a picture that appears farthest from the viewer.

balance Principle of art that arranges elements in a work of art to create a sense of stability.

balloon Outlined dialogue or thoughts of a character in a comic strip panel.

bas-relief Work of art in which some areas stand out from the surface.

binocular vision Seeing from two angles with both eyes at the same time and combining the two images into one so that a three-dimensional image is created.

bleed Drawing in which the shapes reach the edges of the working area.

caption Comment or title accompanying a cartoon.

caricature Drawing of a person that exaggerates the person's features to be humorous or to suggest an idea about the subject.

cast shadows Shadows cast by shapes onto other surfaces.

center of vision In one-point perspective, the vanishing point. In two-point perspective, the place opposite the eye of the observer.

collage Two-dimensional work of art made by attaching many pieces to a surface.

color Element of art derived from reflected light. The sensation of color is aroused in the brain by response of the eyes to different wavelengths of light. A color has hue (color name), intensity (strength), and value (lightness or darkness).

computer graphics Drawings created with a computer.

computer program Software (instructions) that tells a computer to perform commands.

cone of vision Imaginary cone with a circular base on the picture plane in which the artist views an object to be drawn in two-point perspective.

contour drawing Drawing the edges, or contours, of figures or objects. Contour drawing records details of shape and structure.

cropping Decreasing the area of a picture to use in an independent design.

cross contour Line that describes the volume of a form, rather than the outline.

cross-hatching Overlapping parallel lines used to create value.

cursor Point of bright light on a computer screen that marks a position.

distance line Line on which the station point is located, dropped vertically from the center of vision. It measures the distance of the viewer from the picture plane.

elements of art Basic components artists use to create works of visual art. The elements of art are line, shape, form, value, texture, space, and color.

elevation Drawing that shows the entire image on a vertical plane, with no depth or perspective.

emotionalism Theory of art that is used to judge a work of art by its expressive qualities (how well it communicates a feeling, mood, or idea to the viewer).

emphasis Principle of art that combines elements in a work of art to point out their differences.

engraving Work of art which is made by cutting into a surface, inking the surface, and pressing paper against it to make a print.

exaggeration Enlargement of figures or objects or their parts in a work of art to communicate an idea or feeling.

expressive qualities Feelings, moods, or ideas communicated to a viewer through a work of art. These qualities are emphasized by the theory of emotionalism.

figure Human form in a work of art. Also any positive shape.

foreground Area of a picture that appears closest to the viewer.

foreshortening Shortening an object in a drawing to make it look as if it extends backward into space. This method reproduces proportions a viewer sees.

form Element of art that is three-dimensional and encloses space. Like a shape, a form has length and width, but it also has depth.

formalism Theory of art that is used to judge a work of art by its visual qualities (by its organization of the elements of art through the principles of art).

form shadows Shadows on the side of forms away from the light source.

found objects Natural or man-made objects found by chance and used in a work of art.

freehand drawing Drawing done without measuring tools or tracing.

gesture drawing Drawing gestures or movements of the body. Gesture drawing quickly records an entire image.

gradation Principle of art that combines elements in a work of art by using a series of gradual changes.

hard copy Computer image printed on paper or film.

hardware Physical parts that make up a computer system.

harmony Principle of art that combines elements in a work of art to stress similarities of separate but related parts.

heroic figure Ancient Greek artists' representation of a human figure. It is eight heads tall, a bit taller than life-sized (7½ heads tall).

highlights Areas on a surface that reflect the most light. In a drawing, these areas are shown by light values to create the illusion of depth.

horizon line (eye level line) Line at which earth and sky seem to meet.

illustration Drawing used to tell a story, give instructions, or make a product look attractive.

imitationalism Theory of art that is used to judge a work of art by its literal qualities (by how well it imitates the real world).

intaglio Print made from ink trapped in the grooves in an engraved metal plate.

landscape Work of art that uses natural scenery as subject matter.

line Element of art that is a continuous mark made on a surface by a pointed instrument.

line art Illustration made up of solid blacks and whites for commercial printing purposes.

linear perspective Technique for creating the illusion of depth for three-dimensional objects on a two-dimensional plane. Parallel lines meet on distant vanishing points on the horizon.

linocut Print made from an inked linoleum block.

literal qualities Realistic representation of subject matter in a work of art. These qualities are emphasized by the theory of imitationalism.

lithograph Print made from an inked stone or metal plate. A drawing is made on the plate with a greasy crayon or ink (tusche).

matting Surrounding an artwork with a cardboard border. Drawings for an exhibition or an artist's portfolilo are often matted, as are framed drawings.

measuring line (ground line) Horizontal line defining the bottom of the picture plane (indicating where the picture plane meets the ground).

measuring point Any point on the horizon used to project a depth measurement into a perspective drawing.

mechanical drawing Drawing done with the help of measuring tools.

media Materials used by an artist to create a work of art. (Singular is *medium*.)

model Person who poses for a work of art.

movement Principle of art that combines elements in a work of art to create the illusion of action.

negative shape (ground) Empty space surrounding a shape or form.

office method Method of projecting two-point perspective using a plan and an elevation or sketch showing vertical dimensions.

one-point (parallel) perspective Perspective in which all receding lines meet at a single vanishing point that corresponds to the center of vision.

opaque Quality of a material that doesn't let any light pass through.

outline contour Line that shows the overall shape around the outer edge of a form.

overlapping Placing one object in an artwork in front of another, partially concealing the object behind. This technique is used to suggest depth.

picture element—pixel Square on the electronic graph of a computer screen. An artist fills pixels on the screen to create an image.

picture plane Surface of a drawing or plane on which images are projected.

plagiarism Unlawful and unethical copying of another artist's idea to present the idea as original.

plan Drawing showing lines of an object from directly above on a flat plane without perspective.

portfolio Collection of samples of an artist's work.

portrait Picture or image that is an attempt to achieve a likeness or representation of a particular person.

positive shape (figure) Shape or form in two- or three-dimensional art.

principles of art Ways artists organize the elements of art in works of visual art. The principles of art are balance, emphasis, harmony, variety, gradation, movement, rhythm, proportion, and space.

proportion Principle of art that combines elements in a work of art to create size relationships of elements to the whole artwork and to each other.

reference line Line extending from a point on the picture plane and receding along the ground to a vanishing point.

reference point Point on the measuring line (ground line) where a reference line begins.

rendering Use of media to create a finished artwork.

rough Practice drawing done in preparation for a finished drawing.

rhythm Principle of art that repeats elements in a work of art to create a visual tempo.

rubbing (frottage) Method of reproducing textures by rubbing a drawing instrument on paper placed over a textured surface.

serigraph Print made through a silk screen using stencils.

setup Group of objects arranged as a subject for drawing.

shape Element of art that is an enclosed area determined by line, value, texture, space, or any combination of these elements. A shape has two dimensions, length and width.

simulated (visual) texture Kind of texture suggested or implied in an artwork.

sketch Drawing done quickly in preparation for a finished work of art.

sketchbook Pad of drawing paper used by artists to record ideas and information for works of art and to practice drawings.

software Instructions that tell the computer how to manipulate information.

space Element of art that is the distance around, between, above, below, and within an object. Also a principle of art that creates the illusion of three dimensions in a work.

station point Point of view from which a drawing and measurements for a drawing are made.

still life Nonmoving objects that are subject matter for a work of art.

stippling Technique of using patterns of dots to create values and value gradation.

studio Room where artists work.

symmetrical (formal) balance Balance created in a work of art by duplicating elements on either side of a line dividing the composition in half.

texture Element of art that appeals to the sense of touch.

thumbnail sketches Small sketches drawn quickly to record ideas and information for finished drawings.

translucent Quality of a material that allows some light to pass through.

true height line Vertical line raised from the point where a reference line from a vanishing point touches the measuring line (ground line). This line can be used for actual measurements for any objects or lines along the reference line.

two-point (angular) perspective Perspective in which different sets of receding lines meet at different vanishing points.

unity   Total visual effect achieved by carefully blending the elements and principles of art in a composition.

value   Element of art that refers to light and dark areas. Value depends on how much light a surface reflects. Value is also one of the three properties of color.

value gradation   Gradual change from dark to light areas used to create the illusion of three dimensions on a two-dimensional surface.

vanishing point   Point on the horizon or eye level line at which receding parallel lines meet in a perspective drawing.

variety   Principle of art that combines contrasting elements in a work of art to create visual interest.

vertical axis   Imaginary line dividing an object, figure, or composition in half vertically.

vignette   Drawing in which the shapes float in the empty working area without touching the edges of the drawing.

visual qualities   Uses of the elements and principles of art to create a unified, interesting artwork. These qualities are emphasized by the theory of formalism.

wash drawing   Drawing made with a brush and mixtures of ink or paint thinned with water.

woodcut   Print made from an inked wood block.

Bibliography

Cheatham, F. R., J. H. Cheatham, and S. A. Haler. *Design Concepts and Applications*. Englewood Cliffs, NJ: Prentice-Hall, 1983. A thorough introduction to the visual language that is especially informative for the beginning student.

Deken, Joseph. *Computer Images: State of the Art*. New York: Stewart Tabori & Chang, 1983. A gallery of color computer images created for the fields of science and art. Available in paperback.

Feldman, Edmund Burke. *The Artist*. Englewood Cliffs, NJ: Prentice-Hall, 1982. Discusses many different kinds of creative artists and their reasons for making art.

Feldman, Edmund Burke. *Varieties of Visual Experience*. 2nd ed. Englewood Cliffs, NJ: Prentice-Hall, 1981. An excellent introduction to the major art styles and several theories of art. Also provides a fine explanation of the steps involved in art criticism.

Gatto, J. A., A. W. Porter, and J. Selleck. *Exploring Visual Design*. Worcester, MA: Davis, 1978. Introduces the elements and principles of design in a way that beginning students find easy to comprehend.

Gombrich, Ernst H. *The Story of Art*. 4th ed. Englewood Cliffs, NJ: Prentice-Hall, 1982. A fine introduction to the entire history of art written in a manner that is especially well suited to newcomers to the subject.

Janson, H. W., and A. F. Janson. *A Basic History of Art*. 3rd ed. Englewood Cliffs, NJ: Prentice-Hall, 1987. A comprehensive survey of the major periods of art history presented in a straightforward style.

Malraux, Andre. *The Voices of Silence*. Princeton, NJ: Princeton Univ. Press, 1978. An absorbing presentation of art history which ignores the typical classifications in favor of a new and exciting set of categories.

Mayer, Ralph. *The Artist's Handbook of Materials and Techniques*. New York: Viking, 1982. Includes specific, practical information and advice on the materials and techniques most commonly used by artists.

Mittler, Gene A. *Art in Focus*. Mission Hills, CA: Glencoe, 1986. Involves students in a sequence of aesthetics, criticism, and history experiences applied to artworks from prehistoric times to the present. Also contains studio activities.

Peck, Stephen Rogers. *Atlas of Human Anatomy for the Artist*. New York: Oxford University Press, 1951. Structures of the body are analyzed and studied in detail.

Prueitt, Melvin L. *Art and the Computer*. New York: McGraw-Hill, 1984. Discussion by a pioneering computer artist of a large selection of computer-generated art. Available in paperback.

Ragans, Rosalind. *ArtTalk*. Mission Hills, CA: Glencoe, 1988. An approach to art history, criticism, aesthetics, and studio experiences applied to visual arts and crafts.

Simmon, Seymour, and Marc Winer. *Drawing: The Creative Process*. Englewood Cliffs, NJ: Prentice-Hall, 1977. A concise, easy-to-read overview of the basic materials and tools used by artists to create and preserve drawings.

Stolnitz, Jerome. *Aesthetics and Philosophy of Art Criticism: A Critical Introduction*. Boston: Houghton Mifflin, 1960. A readable introduction to the theories of art and an approach to the evaluation of art.

Taylor, Joshua C. *Learning to Look: A Handbook for the Visual Arts*. 2nd ed. Chicago: Univ. of Chicago Press, 1981. Begins with a study of specific works of art and extends to a consideration of broad visual arts principles and techniques.

Timmons, Virginia G. *Painting: Ideas, Materials, Processes*. Worcester, MA: Davis, 1978. Interesting and informative background about crayons, chalks, watercolors, and synthetic media.

Index